LANGUAGE DEVELOPMENT
IN EARLY CHILDHOOD

Beverly Otto

Northeastern Illinois University

Merrill
Prentice Hall

Upper Saddle River, New Jersey
Columbus, Ohio

Library of Congress Cataloging-in-Publication Data
Otto, Beverly.
    Language development in early childhood / Beverly Otto.
      p. cm.
    Includes bibliograhical references and index.
    ISBN 0-02-389544-6
      1. Language arts (Early childhood) 2. Children—Language. 3. Child development. I.
Title.

LB1139.5.L35 O83 2002
372.6—dc21   2001034242

Vice President and Publisher: Jeffery W. Johnston
Executive Editor: Ann Castel Davis
Editorial Assistant: Keli Gemrich
Production Editor: Sheryl Glicker Langner
Production Management: Lea Baranowski, Carlisle Publishers Services
Design Coordinator: Diane C. Lorenzo
Cover Designer: Melissa J. Cullen
Cover Photo: Corbis/The Stock Market
Production Manager: Laura Messerly
Director of Marketing: Kevin Flanagan
Marketing Manager: Amy June
Marketing Coordinator: Barbara Koontz

This book was set in Melior by Carlisle Communications, Ltd. It was printed and bound by R. R.
Donnelley & Sons Company. The cover was printed by The Lehigh Press, Inc.

Photo Credits: Yi Hao, p. 68; Amy Levine, p. 276; Kathleen Lyons, pp. 237, 239; Katherine McKnight,
p. 353; Beverly Otto, p. 44; Gayle Perrin, p. 285; Margaret Schmidt, pp. 97, 108, 126, 137; Julia Teich,
pp. 3, 10, 134, 140, 153, 352; Lyle White, pp. 124, 170, 194, 278, 354.

Pearson Education Ltd., *London*
Pearson Education Australia Pty. Limited, *Sydney*
Pearson Education Singapore Pte. Ltd.
Pearson Education North Asia Ltd., *Hong Kong*
Pearson Education Canada, Ltd., *Toronto*
Pearson Educación de Mexico, S.A. de C.V.
Pearson Education—Japan, *Tokyo*
Pearson Education Malaysia Pte. Ltd.
Pearson Education, *Upper Saddle River, New Jersey*

10 9 8 7 6 5 4 3 2 1
ISBN 0-02-389544-6

❊ ❊ ❊

PREFACE

Language Development in Early Childhood is a book about language development from birth through age 8. It is a foundational text that incorporates theory and research as well as guidelines for enhancing language development in early childhood settings. This book provides a comprehensive view of language development, focusing on the acquisition of phonetic, semantic, syntactic, morphemic, and pragmatic language knowledge. Acquisition of knowledge of written language is also included as part of children's language development. This text is designed for use as the main text in an undergraduate language development course for majors in Early Childhood Education or Child Development. It could also be used as a supplementary text in early childhood language arts or reading methods courses.

The text begins with three chapters that address general language issues: Chapter 1, Language in Our Lives; Chapter 2, Learning and Language; and Chapter 3, Language Development Among Children of Linguistic Diversity. Each of these chapters introduces foundational concepts and perspectives that are built upon in subsequent chapters. Chapters 4–11 focus on the different ages of children and guidelines for enhancing language development at that age in early childhood settings. At each age, from infancy through primary years, language development is detailed along with guidelines for enhancing children's language development. Professors and students will find this feature beneficial as it strengthens students' understanding of the ways in which children's language develops in early childhood settings. Chapter 12 addresses issues in both formal and informal assessment and provides a sample of a detailed observation assignment. Chapter 13 focuses on language disorders and includes guidelines for teachers working with these children with special needs. Chapter 14 emphasizes the role of school-home connections in enhancing children's language development and learning.

ACKNOWLEDGMENTS

First of all, I would like to thank my family for encouraging me in this endeavor, especially when adjustments on the home front were necessary. The support and encouragement from my colleagues and students at Northeastern Illinois University are deeply appreciated. A special thanks is extended to Joaquin Villegas for sharing his expertise in the chapter on linguistic diversity. Amyra Smerecky, who served as my research assistant, provided a spirit of energy, intellectual curiosity, and discovery to the development of this text. Students who helped to "field-test" this text provided valuable insights as to the areas that needed strengthening. I am deeply indebted to the many children whose anecdotes and language examples appear in this text, and to their teachers and parents who graciously shared their children with me.

I also thank the following reviewers for their comments and insights: Alice D. Beyrent, Hesser College; Pamela O. Fleege, University of South Florida; Alice Sterling Honig, Syracuse University; Leanna Manna, Villa Maria College; and Edythe H. Schwartz, California State University, Sacramento.

Finally, I would like to acknowledge the support and encouragement from my editor, Ann Davis. Her unwavering support during the extended development phase of this text is deeply appreciated.

DISCOVER THE COMPANION WEBSITE ACCOMPANYING THIS BOOK

The Prentice Hall Companion Website: A Virtual Learning Environment

Technology is a constantly growing and changing aspect of our field that is creating a need for content and resources. To address this emerging need, Prentice Hall has developed an online learning environment for students and professors alike—Companion Websites—to support our textbooks.

In creating a Companion Website, our goal is to build on and enhance what the textbook already offers. For this reason, the content for each user-friendly website is organized by topic and provides the professor and student with a variety of meaningful resources. Common features of a Companion Website include:

For the Professor—

Every Companion Website integrates **Syllabus Manager**™, an online syllabus creation and management utility.

- **Syllabus Manager**™ provides you, the instructor, with an easy, step-by-step process to create and revise syllabi, with direct links into the Companion Website and other online content without having to learn HTML.
- Students may log on to your syllabus during any study session. All they need to know is the web address for the Companion Website and the password you've assigned to your syllabus.
- After you have created a syllabus using **Syllabus Manager**™, students may enter the syllabus for their course section from any point in the Companion Website.
- Clicking on a date, the student is shown the list of activities for the assignment. The activities for each assignment are linked directly to actual content, saving time for students.
- Adding assignments consists of clicking on the desired due date, then filling in the details of the assignment—name of the assignment,

instructions, and whether or not it is a one-time or repeating assignment.

- In addition, links to other activities can be created easily. If the activity is online, a URL can be entered in the space provided, and it will be linked automatically in the final syllabus.
- Your completed syllabus is hosted on our servers, allowing convenient updates from any computer on the Internet. Changes you make to your syllabus are immediately available to your students at their next logon.

For the Student—

Topic Overviews—outline key concepts in topic areas

Web Links—general websites related to topic areas as well as associations and professional organizations

Read About It—timely articles that enable you to become more aware of important issues in early childhood education

Learn by Doing—put concepts into action, participate in activities, complete lesson plans, examine strategies, and more

For Teachers—access information that you will need to know as an in-service teacher, including information on materials, activities, lessons, curriculum, and state standards

Visit a School—visit a school's website to see concepts, theories, and strategies in action

Electronic Bluebook—send homework or essays directly to your instructor's email with this paperless form

Message Board—serves as a virtual bulletin board to post—or respond to—questions or comments to/from a national audience

Chat—real-time chat with anyone who is using the text anywhere in the country—ideal for discussion and study groups, class projects, etc.

To take advantage of these and other resources, please visit the *Language Development in Early Childhood* Companion Website at

www.prenhall.com/otto

CONTENTS

3

Language Development Among Children of Linguistic Diversity   52

4   Language Development of Infants and Toddlers   87

7　Enhancing Language Development in Preschoolers　178

10 Language Development in the Primary Years

11 Enhancing Language Development in the Primary Years

13　Enhancing Language Development Among Children with Communicative Disorders

14 Fostering Language Development Through School-Home Connections   339

1

LANGUAGE IN OUR LIVES

Eric and Scott were pretending to be police officers. They were sitting on a bench in the preschool classroom. Eric said excitedly, "I got a great idea! Let's go to a filling station and ask for some steering wheels!" They crossed the room, grabbed imaginary steering wheels, went back to the bench, sat down, and began to steer their pretend vehicles.

At the beginning of class, Teddy and Tommy were seated at a table playing with manipulatives. Their teacher came over and asked, "How are you today?" Teddy replied, "I am fine." Then, he said, speaking to the teacher, "And how are you?"

John was looking at books in the library corner. When several other children came into the area, John took a book and said, "See my new book?" He then opened the book and told the story to those around him.

When Julie finished her paste-paper art project, she handed it to the new student aide saying, "Write my name on it." When the aide asked what her name was, she replied, "J-U-L-I-E."

In each of these instances observed in a preschool classroom, children used language effectively in communication with others. Eric and Scott used language to direct their dramatic enactment of driving police cars. Teddy's use of language indicated his awareness of the social routine of greeting. John used his oral language and awareness of story content to entertain his friends in the library corner. Julie showed her knowledge of written language symbols that composed her name as well as an awareness that her name needed to go on her artwork in order to claim it.

BECOMING SPEAKERS, READERS, AND WRITERS

How did these children learn to communicate using language? Did it occur automatically without any direct influence by the environment? Is learning to read different from learning to speak? These questions have sparked intense research and debate for many years. Gradually we are coming to better understand the ways in which children become effective speakers, listeners, readers, and writers. Throughout this text, we will explore the ways in which children become effective communicators and the ways in which we as teachers can enhance their acquisition of language. This text differs from other language development texts in its attention to language as communication rather than a focus on speech production and the development of articulation. This approach recognizes that language is a medium of communication with others and within ourselves. The focus here will be on the years from birth through age 8, an age span commonly referred to as the early childhood years. While this text will include descriptions of activities to enhance language development, it is not intended to be a language arts methods text. The language development approach of this text examines the acquisition of both oral and written language within settings in the preschool and primary years. Oral language and written language acquisition are interrelated processes that culminate in children's communicative competencies.

Language is essential to society. It forms the foundation for our perceptions, communications, and daily interactions. It is a system of symbols by which we categorize, organize, and clarify our thinking (Stice, Bertrand, & Bertrand, 1995). Through language we represent the world and learn about the world. Without language a society and its culture will not exist.

To be able to function successfully in a society and its culture (and subcultures), children need to develop a wide range of language competencies. Not only do children need to acquire an oral language, they need to be able to use that language effectively in a variety of settings. Further, in literate cultures, children need to develop competencies in using written language as well. Throughout life people communicate in a variety of settings: talking on the

Language forms the foundation for our perceptions, communications, and daily interactions.

phone with friends, interacting with a store clerk as they purchase groceries, listening to a radio talk show, and using language in professional or educational settings, such as an attorney in a court of law or a college professor and his students in a university classroom. Our language competencies allow us to participate effectively in a variety of social events and occupational settings and in our daily routines.

There is no one standard of communicative competency that teachers should encourage children to attain. Instead, it is important for teachers to recognize that children need a wide range of communication competencies to ensure their effectiveness in a variety of settings throughout their lives.

Children's communicative competencies involve both receptive and expressive language. **Receptive language** refers to a child's comprehension of words (verbal symbols): when a specific word is used, the child knows what it refers to or represents. As a child's speech mechanisms mature and the child begins to gain control over producing specific speech sounds, **expressive/productive language** develops.

Receptive and expressive language development are closely related. While linguists and child development educators agree that receptive language begins to develop prior to expressive language, there is little agreement regarding how long expressive language lags behind receptive language development (Owens, 1988). The relationship between the development of receptive and expressive language appears to be a dynamic one, influenced by a child's specific developmental level and each aspect of language knowledge.

ASPECTS OF LANGUAGE KNOWLEDGE

When children are acquiring language, they are developing different aspects, or components, of language knowledge: phonetic, semantic, syntactic, morphemic, and pragmatic. Each of these aspects refers to a specific domain of language knowledge; however, the aspects do not develop in isolation from each other. These aspects of language knowledge are present in any interaction in which language is used. Initially, a child's knowledge of the aspects or components of language will only be receptive. This means the child will be perceiving the specific characteristics of language but will not be able to produce language that demonstrates this knowledge. In the sections that follow, each of the five aspects of language knowledge are described.

Phonetic Knowledge

As children hear and perceive oral language, they learn that language is embedded in a sound-symbol system. **Phonetic knowledge** refers to knowledge about sound-symbol relationships in a language. A phoneme is the smallest linguistic unit of sound, which is combined with other phonemes to form words. Phonemes consist of sounds that are considered to be a single perceptual unit by a listener (Goodman, 1993; Hayes, Ornstein, & Gage, 1993). Statements of the number of phonemes in American English vary with the specific dialect analyzed and the classification system used (Owens, 1988; Reich, 1986; Sachs, 1989). The number of phonemes in Standard American English exceeds our alphabetic system of 26 letters, so that a specific written symbol system is often used to describe specific aspects of sound/speech production. The **International Phonetic Alphabet** (IPA) was first developed in 1888 (Crystal, 1987). The International Phonetic Alphabet provides a way of encoding or representing an utterance more accurately in writing. Since it is an international alphabet, it provides a way of examining the same or highly similar phonemes in different languages. Figure 1.1 illustrates the difference between using standard English spelling and the phonetic alphabet to encode a word.

The International Phonetic Alphabet has a separate letter/symbol for each distinctive sound. This specialized alphabet uses many Roman letters and in-

FIGURE 1.1
Representing a Word Using the International Phonetic Alphabet

mother = m ə θ r

corporates new letters and diacritical markings as necessary to represent phonemes in a specific language. Diacritical markings are marks, such as accents, added to printed symbols to further indicate how the symbol/letter is to be pronounced. Over the years the IPA has been further developed and modified (Fromkin & Rodman, 1998). It is now used worldwide in dictionaries to indicate pronunciation and in linguistically-related materials where exact phonetic transcriptions are needed. Researchers who are focusing on the acquisition and use of languages use the International Phonetic Alphabet to assure preciseness in their representations of speech.

Children's development of phonetic knowledge is fostered by their perceptual ability to distinguish sounds and also by the ways in which language is used around them. Children's discrimination of sounds precedes their ability to produce those same sounds due to the complex coordination of the speech mechanism required for speaking.

In every language and culture some speech sounds are more important than others. Gradually, young children learn to discriminate and produce the speech sounds that are found in their home language. For example, in English /l/ and /r/ are perceived as significantly different phonemes. In contrast, the Japanese language does not distinguish between the /l/ and /r/. Consequently when Japanese native speakers learn English, they have difficulty articulating English words like *rate* and *late*. Another example of the perception of significant differences in similar sounds is found in situations where native English speakers are learning Spanish. In Spanish, words with *r* or *rr* represent different phonemes, as in *pero* (*but*) and *perro* (*dog*). For English speakers learning Spanish, this is confusing because the two phonemes represented by *r* and *rr* seem indistinguishable (Goodman, 1993).

Phonetic knowledge does not develop in isolation from other aspects of language knowledge. Learning to distinguish between similar sounding words, such as *can* and *car*, is facilitated by the different ways in which those two words are used in meaningful contexts. The phonetic differences between the two words become meaningful because the two words are used to refer to different objects and actions.

Prosodic Features

In addition to the perception of phonemes, a young language learner begins to notice differences in the way in which sounds are used in a language to add meaning to what is said. **Prosodic features** in a language refer to the way in which something is said. These features have both acoustic or sound properties as well as psychological or emotional properties. For example, "they're coming" can be said in different ways to indicate a statement or a question. It can also be said in a way that conveys a sense of boredom, excitement, or dread. The specific prosodic features are intonation, loudness, tempo, and rhythm (Crystal, 1987; deVilliers & deVilliers, 1978; Goodman, 1993). Children's auditory perception of these prosodic features contributes to both their phonetic knowledge and to their subsequent semantic knowledge.

Young children acquire knowledge of the prosodic features and specific sounds used in a language through interactions with people in their environment. Through these interactions children learn how to distinguish sound-symbol relationships and implied meanings.

Semantic Knowledge

In learning that oral symbols, or spoken words, have meaning, **semantic knowledge** is acquired. The development of semantic knowledge is closely tied to the acquisition of conceptual knowledge (Vygotsky, 1962). Semantic knowledge involves the word labels that refer to specific concepts and also to the semantic network, or schema, that represents the interrelationships between concepts. Semantic networks—schemata—are thought to be cognitive structures in our memory that organize our conceptual knowledge. These semantic networks facilitate new learning and recall, and contribute to the reorganization and elaboration of prior conceptual learning.

For example, the English word *ball* references the idea of a round object that has certain properties of rolling and bouncing, which is often used in a game or physical activity. In acquiring concepts, children learn that objects and actions with similar features or functions can be grouped into the same category or into related categories. For example, when a child learns that a small, round, red, plastic object is called a "ball," he may see similarities when he sees a white soccer ball and also call it a "ball" or attempt to roll the soccer ball on the floor. A conceptual schema develops when a child begins to see the relationships between two concepts. Over time, as a child experiences different types of balls that are used for different purposes, a schema develops for *balls*. See Figure 1.2 for an example of what people might have in their ball schema. A young child's schema for *ball* will initially be much more limited in complexity and may only include "roundness," "throwing," and "bouncing."

Vocabulary development is closely related to general linguistic competence and to reading comprehension. Children with larger and more developed vocabularies have more options for expressing what they want to say and, thus, have greater linguistic flexibility. A larger vocabulary also increases children's ability to comprehend written text since reading comprehension is directly related to listening comprehension and oral vocabulary. When a specific word (and concept) is part of a child's oral vocabulary, it is more easily comprehended and decoded when the child encounters the word in written text.

FIGURE 1.2
Example of a Schema for the
Concept *Ball*

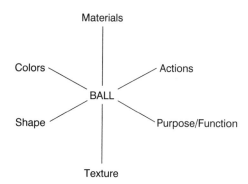

Children's acquisition of semantic knowledge is also influenced by their awareness of the grammatical structure in which language is used. This syntactic knowledge is crucial because the grammatical or syntactic structures carry implied meaning. Word order affects the meaning of what is said.

Syntactic Knowledge

In order to use language effectively, it is necessary to know how to combine words to create meaningful expressions. Each language system has rules or a **grammar** that prescribes how words are combined to create sentences or meaningful phrases or utterances. This aspect of language knowledge is called **syntax.**

Children learn that word order is important in creating meaning and in comprehending another's message. The question "Did you hit Jack?" asks for different information than "Did Jack hit you?" Knowledge of the importance of word order is known linguistically at an unconscious level before children can verbalize their understanding of that language concept. For example, in English, adjectives precede the noun they modify: "The beautiful flower was on the table," not "The flower beautiful was on the table." When children are learning to speak English, their awareness of the position of adjectives relative to the nouns they modify is evident even in their two-word utterances: "big ball," "blue car." This occurs long before children can consciously identify adjectives and the words they modify.

Differences between languages may be problematic for bilingual children/ second language learners since syntax varies from language to language. For example, in Spanish, some adjectives follow the nouns they modify. A young Spanish bilingual child will have the task of learning two sets of syntactic rules, one for Spanish and one for English. (See further discussion of second language learners in Chapter 3.)

Children also learn that words cannot be haphazardly combined, such as in "flower table the beautiful was the on." The fact that such random combinations of words have not been documented among young children indicates that word order knowledge develops early. Research has documented few instances of children violating syntactic rules simply because utterances that do not observe the specific language's syntax are not comprehendible, useful, or meaningful. To speak in a way that violates syntactic rules dooms the speaker to be misunderstood or ignored.

Morphemic Knowledge

This aspect of language knowledge involves word structure. In acquiring syntactic knowledge, children also learn that some words have related meanings but they are used in different ways in speech and in written language and have different word structure. For example, *happy*, *happiness*, and *happily* have related meanings; however, each word is used in a different way grammatically. *Happy* is an adjective, *happiness* is a noun, *happily* is an adverb. Thus, each has a different grammatical function. *Walk*, *walking*, and *walked* are related in meaning; however, the location in time or tense is different. In learning how to use words in an appropriate syntactic manner, children also learn that word endings and prefixes and suffixes change the meaning of the word and its grammatical use.

Words are composed of one or more meaningful linguistic units. The smallest unit of meaning in language is the **morpheme.** There are two types of morphemes: (1) **free morphemes** are used alone as words (e.g., house, turtle, book) and (2) **bound morphemes** must be attached to a free morpheme (e.g., house*s*, slow*ly*, go*ing*.)

Bound morphemes are of two types: derivational and inflectional (Lindfors, 1987; Owens, 1988). **Derivational morphemes** include prefixes (e.g., *un*happy) and suffixes (e.g., happi*ness*). **Inflectional morphemes** are word endings added to change verb tense (e.g., walk, walk*ing*, walk*ed*) or possession (Jack, Jack'*s*), or plurality (cat, cat*s*).

The ability to use morphemes appropriately is one of the characteristics of an effective language user. Knowledge of morphology allows children to comprehend others' speech better, such as understanding plural nouns and verb tense. Knowledge that *cat* means one in number and *cats* refers to more than one cat allows more precise receptive and expressive language.

As children's speech progresses beyond the one-word and two-word stages, their understanding of how words are formed is used as they attempt to communicate. Many utterances of young children are novel, not simply a repetition of prior adult speech. In the production of an utterance, children use their morphemic knowledge of how words are formed to create their message. As children acquire more knowledge of morphemes, their language becomes more precise and meaningful.

Young children acquire morphemic knowledge that is present in their linguistic environments. In settings where a particular dialect is spoken, children will first acquire the morphemic knowledge represented in that dialect. In figuring out how language is used and words are structured, children appear to be looking for patterns and hypothesizing. Children's over-generalizations of morphological patterns are an example of this.

Children's **overgeneralizations** occur when they assume a particular word is "regular" when, in fact, it follows an irregular pattern. For example, the past tense of regular verbs is created by adding -*ed* to the present tense, as in *walk, walked.* Children who assume that *go* is also a regular verb will create the past tense form by adding -*ed* to go, resulting in "goed."

Similarly, when children begin to learn comparative forms of adjectives, they may see the pattern of regular comparative forms, which are made with -*er* (happier) and -*est* (happiest) endings. However, some children apply this rule to all adjectives, as in *fun, funner, funnest,* or even *bestest.* Overgeneralization decreases as language development proceeds and as children have opportunities to interact with adults and older siblings who have acquired more complete morphemic knowledge.

Overgeneralization can also occur in the use of prefixes. For example, children learn that the prefix *un* means "not." They understand that *unhappy* means not happy. Children may create their own words based on their understanding of how prefixes (or suffixes or plural endings) work. To illustrate, a 5-year-old girl was being chided by her mother because a doting aunt had given her another doll during a recent visit to the aunt's home. When her mother asked her why she accepted another doll she really did not need, the girl replied, "Mommy, Aunt Shirley insisted, and I couldn't un-sist!"

Pragmatic Knowledge

Language use is embedded in social-cultural contexts. Different contexts are characterized by differences in the way language is used. Through social-cultural interactions we learn when to speak, when not to speak, what to talk about with whom, and when, where, and in what manner to speak (Gleason, 1993). We also learn the specific style of speaking for certain contexts with respect to the expected phonetic, semantic, syntactic, and morphemic features.

Pragmatic knowledge refers to the knowledge or awareness of the overall intent of the communication. Pragmatic knowledge encompasses the intent of the speaker, the specific form of the utterance, and the anticipated effect the utterance will have on the listener. It contributes to appropriate and effective communication (Ninio & Snow, 1999). In addition to communicative intent, three other components of pragmatic knowledge have been identified: learning conversational rules, learning to be polite, and learning to produce connected discourse, such as narratives (Ninio & Snow, 1999).

Pragmatic knowledge is involved in the development of **social registers,** which are specific ways of using language differently in different social settings/contexts. Children learn that language can serve many purposes or intents. The selection of intent or purpose in communication and the way in which language is used contribute to a child's level of communicative competence in early childhood and beyond. Early on in the development of communicative competence children's efforts appear to have purpose or intent. The 8-month-old child who looks at her mother with outstretched arms and produces strained vocalizations (/uh/ /uh/) is assumed to be communicating she wants to be picked up. If not initially successful, the child may repeat her request, whine louder, or gesture more emphatically (Gleason, 1993).

Children learn to distinguish different times when quiet voices and loud voices are used and they pick up social conventions such as saying "please" and "thank you." Children learn how to talk most effectively to adults and to each other. To illustrate, the mother of a 5-year-old boy was surprised to discover that the verbal whining she often heard at home from her son never occurred at school. Apparently her son had learned that whining was an effective language interaction style at home but would not be effective at school.

Conversational skills are a critical part of pragmatic knowledge since they impact a child's ability to engage in classroom and social interactions (Ninio & Snow, 1999). Genres of conversation include social conversations, classroom discourse, telephone conversations, ritual insults, service encounters, jokes, and doctor-patient talk. Through their direct experiences, children become aware of the rules or expected ways in which conversations are initiated, maintained, and discontinued. In a conversation, both people take on the alternating roles of speaker and listener (Clay, 1998). Conversational competence depends on the development of specific skills of taking turns, keeping similar or related topics as the focus of the conversation, encouraging participation from the other person(s), and clarifying/repairing areas of confusion.

Conversational skills influence a child's ability to interact with others.

FIGURE 1.3
Aspects of Language
Knowledge

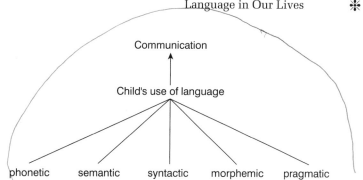

Children also acquire knowledge of how language is used in relation to one's gender, or *genderlect* (Owens, 2001). For example, research has indicated that preschool and kindergarten boys and girls tend to talk about different topics (Haas, 1979, cited in Owens, 2001), with boys talking more about sports and girls talking about school.

Relationship of Aspects of Language Knowledge to Communication

The relationship of these five aspects of language knowledge to a child's use of language and communication is illustrated in Figure 1.3.

Acquisition of each aspect of language knowledge is critical to effective communication. Each aspect does not develop in isolation from the other aspects; instead, the aspects are interrelated. For example, phonetic knowledge can influence the acquisition of semantic knowledge, since perception of sound differences is needed to distinguish between similar words. Syntactic knowledge also influences semantic knowledge since word order implies meaning through grammatical structure. For example, "The XXX went on a train ride." Then, XXX must be a person or thing capable of being on a train. Morphemic knowledge also influences semantic knowledge since some bound morphemes accompany changes in word meaning (e.g., happy vs. unhappy). Morphemic knowledge is also related to syntactic knowledge since some bound morphemes change the grammatical function of a word (e.g., happy vs. happiness).

LEVELS OF LANGUAGE KNOWLEDGE

Knowledge of aspects of language can be categorized into three levels: linguistic, metalinguistic, and metalinguistic verbalization (Otto, 1982). Children first develop knowledge of language at a **linguistic level,** or usage level. This is the "know-how": being able to use language in communicative contexts. This linguistic level of language knowledge can be documented in children's acquisition of each of the five aspects of language knowledge. Children's ability to articulate and discriminate different sounds and words when using language to communicate represents their linguistic level of phonetic knowledge. Similarly, children's ability to comprehend the semantic meanings of other's speech and to create their own meaningful speech represents their linguistic level of semantic knowledge. The linguistic level of syntactic knowledge is evident as children are able to express their ideas in a form that is grammatically appropriate to their dialect or language. Morphemic knowledge at the linguistic level is evident when a child can use appropriate plural forms of nouns or use prefixes and suffixes. The linguistic level of pragmatic knowledge is demonstrated by a child's use of "please" and "thank you" in social situations.

Gradually, children become more aware of the five aspects of language knowledge and can consciously manipulate and reflect on features of language. This conscious awareness of specific features within the aspects of language knowledge is at a level higher than linguistic knowledge, the **metalinguistic level.**

At the metalinguistic level, a child consciously manipulates phonemic, semantic, syntactic, morphemic, and pragmatic knowledge to form the desired message. Metalinguistic knowledge is indicated when a child can respond to questions about words and other linguistic concepts, such as sounds, consonants, and vowels. Children's word play in rhyming games is an indicator of their early metalinguistic phonetic knowledge. Other evidence of early metalinguistic knowledge has been described by emergent literacy research (Ehri, 1975; Schickedanz, 1981; Sulzby, 1986; Voss, 1988), which documented children's spontaneous comments about language, such as "My name starts with a T—Tommy!"

Metalinguistic knowledge acquired through informal interactions with oral and written language develops further when children enter formal schooling since many of the learning activities from kindergarten on focus on the conscious manipulation of both oral and written language. For example, when a child is asked to give the first sound in the word *bat,* she must not only know how to say the word (linguistic knowledge), she must be able to use her concepts of "sound" and "first" in reflecting upon the word and then separating out the sounds.

When children begin to verbalize their metalinguistic knowledge, they are at the most conscious and complex level of language knowledge, **metalinguistic verbalization.** For example, when children are asked to explain how the words *cup* and *pup* are alike, they must be able to verbalize their awareness of the rhyming that is present, thus requiring verbalization of their knowledge about a specific feature of language.

The relationship of these three levels of language knowledge can be represented in a pyramid-like hierarchy (see Figure 1.4). Linguistic knowledge provides the foundation for higher levels of language knowledge. Likewise, the middle level, use of metalinguistic knowledge, provides the basis for the development of the highest level, the ability to verbalize metalinguistic knowledge.

Children acquire linguistic knowledge and metalinguistic knowledge as they use language and through interaction with others. Only after oral language is well established can children begin to verbalize their metalinguistic knowledge. Teachers of young children need to structure their learning activities to

FIGURE 1.4
Levels of Language
Knowledge

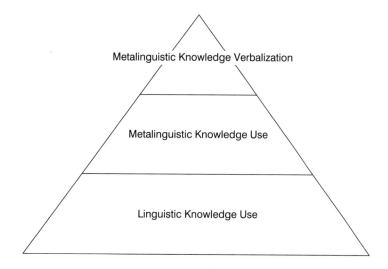

Metalinguistic Knowledge Verbalization

Metalinguistic Knowledge Use

Linguistic Knowledge Use

involve both linguistic and metalinguistic knowledge; however, it is not appropriate to expect that young children will be able to verbalize their metalinguistic knowledge. For example, during a research observation (Otto, 1985), a first-grade teacher became upset with her young students when they were unsuccessful in explaining to her the difference between a *digraph* (two letters representing one sound, such as *ph* in *phone*) and a *blend* (two letters representing sounds that are blended, such as *cl* in *clear*). Yet when asked to read specific words containing either a digraph or a blend, the children were successful. They were able to do this because the *reading* of the specific words drew on their linguistic knowledge. They did not have to be able to metalinguistically verbalize the language concepts in order to respond appropriately to the words when reading. Yet, the instructor appeared to interpret their inability to define the two concepts as evidence that they had not learned the concepts. Instead of focusing only on the verbalization of metalinguistic knowledge to assess acquired concepts, teachers can use observation and recording of language use for evidence of language knowledge acquisition or language competency.

ORAL AND WRITTEN LANGUAGE MODES

Oral and written language each have receptive and expressive **modes.** Listening and reading are receptive in nature—receiving and comprehending a message created by another orally (i.e., listening) or in written language (i.e., reading). On the other hand, speaking and writing are expressive in nature (see Figure 1.5).

As children interact in environments where written language is used to communicate, they acquire knowledge and awareness of how written language is

FIGURE 1.5
Modes of Language

Mode	Oral	Written
Receptive	Listening	Reading
Expressive	Speaking	Writing

similar to and different from oral language. Written language is not just oral language written down (Purcell-Gates, 1989). Written language uses different vocabulary and a more complex word order or syntax (Chafe, 1982; Purcell-Gates, 1989; Tannen, 1982). In addition, written language must convey meaning through the printed message since it carries the meaning without gesture, facial expression, or immediate contextual situations. Awareness and knowledge of the specific ways in which written language works is acquired in each of the five aspects of language: phonetic, semantic, syntactic, morphemic, and pragmatic. Figure 1.6 compares oral and written language with respect to the five aspects of language.

Oral language provides the basis upon which knowledge of written language is acquired. Due to the decontextualized nature of written language, effectively using written language requires, for most situations, more precision and more elaboration. A story told orally can be accompanied by various prosodic features, facial expressions, posture, other gestures, nonverbal behavior, and even the

FIGURE 1.6
Comparison of Aspects of Oral and Written Language Knowledge

Aspect of Language	Oral Language	Written Language
Phonetic	Sound-symbol system; phoneme-based	Combined oral symbol-graphic system; alphabetic encoding
Semantic	Oral word use accompanied by gesture, facial expression, and intonation	Visual/graphic words; more precise vocabulary since written words are spoken and received without gestures, facial expression, or intonation
Syntactic	Phrase and sentence structure/grammar	Sentence and text structure grammar; more complex than oral language
Morphemic	Inflections and word structure tied to oral pronunciation	Word structure; also adds meaning to words; more critical in written language since meaning of message is carried by the print
Pragmatic	Language used differently in various face-to-face interactions; involves all of language knowledge aspects	Language used differently in various text-based settings; influences writer's assumptions about audience and reader's expectations about text

speaker's costume, in order to fully communicate the meaning of the language used in the story. In contrast, a written story relies only on the printed word to communicate the meaning—by the words used, their meaning, the grammatical and morphemic structures, and the pragmatic expectations for a particular genre of story—all of which are communicated through written language.

To be effective communicators, children need to acquire linguistic knowledge in each of the five aspects of language in both oral and written forms of language. Oral language is acquired prior to written language knowledge; however, as written language knowledge is acquired, oral language continues to develop further, refined and elaborated with experiences that involve written language.

CRITICAL ROLE OF CHILDREN'S ORAL LANGUAGE COMPETENCIES

In our classrooms, children who are fluent in oral language are more successful learners (Fey, Catts, & Larrivee, 1995). During the process of learning to read and write, children use their oral language knowledge as a basis for this new knowledge of the written language system along with a focus on the details of written language. Children who are fluent in oral language can communicate their ideas and ask questions during learning activities. In addition, children's oral language competencies influence their acquisition of literacy, since reading and writing both involve processing and manipulating language. Basic oral language abilities related to subsequent literacy acquisition include vocabulary, syntactic production and comprehension, phonemic awareness, and narrative production and awareness.

Children's oral language competencies develop in both receptive and productive/expressive modes. Listening is a critical receptive language skill since it is necessary to "receive language." Listening is not a passive activity. Instead, to be effective, listening must be active and purposeful. At school, children spend much of their time listening to their teacher or to their classmates. Their ability to listen and understand their teacher's directions and instruction and the contributions by their classmates influences what and how much is learned; however, explicit attention to developing listening competencies may be absent in many classrooms (Wolvin & Coakley, 1985).

The expressive mode of oral language is speaking. This involves using oral language for a variety of purposes: for conversation, to direct other's behavior, to express wants or needs, to question, and to solve problems. In a longitudinal study, Wells (1986) identified two oral language characteristics that were effective in predicting children's subsequent overall achievement. For 2-year-olds, use of a range of functions for speech was identified as a predictor of later achievement. For 3 1/2-year-olds, the effective predictor of subsequent achievement was the children's competent use of a range of different sentence types.

Another aspect of school success is a child's social-interactional skills. Children's oral language competencies can influence the development of their social-interaction skills (Windsor, 1995). Children who have oral language competencies will be more successful in communicating with both teachers and peers. Their success in carrying on conversations and in responding in learning activities will contribute to further success at school. Children who have difficulty communicating may be ignored by peers or excluded from informal social or collaborative interactions. The inability to participate successfully in a conversation or the inability to articulate sounds/words clearly may decrease the likelihood that other children will attempt to speak or play with them.

In the section that follows, several research studies will be highlighted to illustrate the importance of oral language development to written language development and the complex ways in which the two forms of language are interrelated.

Insights from Research on Oral and Written Language

In an extensive, descriptive study of language development, Loban (1976) followed 211 children from kindergarten through 12th grade. Each year every child was studied with respect to reading, writing, listening, and other language-related behaviors. After the initial data collection, three subgroups were formed: a high language-ability group, a low language-ability group, and a random group representing the total group. Due to the prohibitive constraints on time and money in analyzing this large data collection, for the detailed analysis Loban selected a random subsample of each of the ability groups along with the initial random (representative) subgroup. Loban's analysis of this random subsample concluded that the children who were identified as having high language ability in kindergarten were those who consistently exhibited these specific language behaviors throughout the 13 years: greater ability and flexibility in the ways in which they expressed their ideas and engaged in conversation, higher reading and writing competencies, more extensive vocabularies, more complex sentences/paragraphs, and higher listening competencies.

Loban's study is significant for the depth of data collected and for the length of time studied. His research documented the importance of oral language ability in kindergarten as a precursor to subsequent competencies in areas of oral and written language with respect to semantics, syntax, and pragmatics.

Loban's landmark study provided the impetus for other researchers to continue exploration of the role of oral language development in children's acquisition of written language and general school performance (Bowey & Patel, 1988; Clay, 1991; Crane-Thoreson & Dale, 1992; Dyson, 1981; Egan, 1996; Fey, Catts, & Larrivee, 1995; Scarborough, 1990; Snow & Ninio, 1986; Sulzby, 1986).

Additional evidence of the significant role of oral language in the acquisition of literacy comes from the field of emergent literacy research. Since the early 1980s researchers have focused on the gradual emergence of literacy-related behaviors and competencies. This emergent literacy perspective examines how children acquire knowledge of reading and writing in their daily, informal encounters with written language.

Dyson (1981) closely observed kindergarten children as they interacted in a classroom writing center she had introduced to the classroom. Dyson documented numerous ways in which oral language played a significant role in children's early writing.

Children were observed using talk as they started to write, while they were in the process of writing, and then as a way of explaining or expanding upon what they had written. Oral language was also used to solicit help from a nearby adult. During the process of creating their written messages, children also reread frequently as a way of monitoring what they had written and what part of their message they had yet to put on paper.

In Dyson's study children used oral language (talk) to guide and facilitate the creation of their written stories. They used oral language as a tool in conjunction with written language to create stories. In addition to using oral language in the process of producing written language, young children are also developing in their ability to use language differently in different settings. Sulzby's research (1986) explored children's use of language in interview settings, story dictation, storytelling, and rereading of their own handwritten compositions. Her research documented the ways in which children use language differently in those varied settings. She also reported that children appear to be exploring the ways in which oral language and written language differ. Sulzby noted that some children put written features into their speech and/or inserted oral language (syntax, semantics) into their written language. Sulzby (1991) concluded that young children acquire written language alongside oral language and further stated that oral and written language are interrelated and intertwined in dynamic roles during the acquisition process.

Research by Purcell-Gates (1989) has documented children's use of different registers. She concluded that children use language differently in oral narrative than they do in written narrative. Children demonstrated that they "implicitly understood that written narrative is more integrative, involving, literary (stylistically) and decontextualized than oral narrative" (p. 291). Purcell-Gates concluded that children know that the vocabulary and sentence structure of books have a different quality than oral speech. She also noted that children continue to use this knowledge as they become involved in reading and writing.

In addition to documenting the importance of oral language development in children, these research studies have further contributed to our understanding that young children are actively acquiring written language knowledge as their oral language knowledge continues to develop in their early childhood years.

SUMMARY

The child's acquisition of language has been a source of fascination for centuries. Gradually, and without formal instruction, children learn how to communicate.

They learn how to express meaning through the use of spoken symbols and through using these symbols (words) in a systematic or structured way.

Language is acquired through knowledge and awareness of the phonetic, semantic, syntactic, morphemic, and pragmatic aspects of both oral and written language. Children who are in environments where oral and written language are used in meaningful ways will gradually acquire competencies in using language to communicate and to solve problems. Knowledge and awareness of each aspect of language knowledge contributes to a child's effectiveness in communicating in both home and school settings and forms the basis for continued language development. The developmental acquisition of each of these five aspects of language awareness and knowledge will be explored in future chapters in this text.

✳ ✳ ✳   CHAPTER REVIEW

1. Key terms to review:
   receptive language
   expressive/productive language
   phonetic language
   International Phonetic Alphabet
   prosodic features
   semantic knowledge
   grammar
   syntax
   morpheme (bound and free)
   derivational morpheme
   inflectional morpheme
   overgeneralizations
   pragmatic knowledge
   social registers
   conversational skills
   linguistic level
   metalinguistic level
   metalinguistic verbalization
   modes of language
2. Explain this statement: Language is essential to society.
3. Identify and define the five aspects of language knowledge. Give an example of each.

4. Identify and explain the three levels of language knowledge.

5. Are oral language competencies related to the acquisition of literacy? Give examples to support your answer.

✷ ✷ ✷ CHAPTER EXTENSION ACTIVITIES

1. Observe a group story time in a preschool or kindergarten classroom. Identify examples from the interaction that involve one or more of the five aspects of language knowledge.

2. Observe a kindergarten classroom and describe the modes of language that are encouraged by the curricular activities and by the learning resources in the classroom.

3. Observe a first-grade reading lesson. Identify the level(s) of language knowledge encouraged by the reading lesson. Give examples to support your conclusions.

✷ ✷ ✷ REFERENCES

Bowey, J., & Patel, R. (1988). Metalinguistic ability and early reading achievement. *Applied Psycholinguistics, 9,* 367–383.

Chafe, W. (1982). Integration and involvement in speaking, writing, and oral literature. In D. Tannen (Ed.), *Spoken and written language: Exploring orality and literacy* (pp. 35–54). Norwood, NJ: Ablex.

Clay, M. (1991). *Becoming literate: The construction of inner control.* Portsmouth, NH: Heinemann.

Clay, M. (1998). *By different paths to common outcomes.* York, ME: Stenhouse Publishers.

Crane-Thoreson, C., & Dale, P. (1992). Do early talkers become early readers? Linguistic precocity, preschool language, and emergent literacy. *Developmental Psychology, 28,* 421–429.

Crystal, D. (1987). *The Cambridge encyclopedia of language.* Cambridge, England: Cambridge University Press.

deVilliers, J., & deVilliers, P. (1978). *Language acquisition.* Cambridge, MA: Harvard University Press.

Dyson, A. (1981). Oral language: The rooting system for learning to write. *Language Arts, 58*(7), 776–784.

Egan, K. (1996). Literacy and the oral foundations of education. In B. Power & R. Hubbard (Eds.), *Language development: A reader for teachers* (pp. 189–208). Upper Saddle River, NJ: Prentice Hall.

Ehri, L. (1975). Word consciousness in readers and prereaders. *Journal of Educational Psychology, 67*(2), 204–212.

Fey, M., Catts, H., & Larrivee, L. (1995). Preparing preschoolers for the academic and social challenges of school. In M. Fey, J. Windsor, & S. Warren (Eds.), *Language intervention: Preschool through the elementary years* (Vol. 5, pp. 5–37). Baltimore, MD: Paul H. Brookes.

Fromkin, V., & Rodman, R. (1998). *An introduction to language* (6th ed.). Fort Worth, TX: Harcourt Brace College Publishers.

Gleason, J. (1993). *The development of language* (3rd ed.). Upper Saddle River, NJ: Merrill.

Goodman, K. (1993). *Phonics phacts.* Portsmouth, NH: Heinemann.

Hayes, C., Ornstein, J., & Gage, W. (1993). *The ABCs of languages and linguistics.* Lincolnwood, IL: National Textbook Co.

Lindfors, J. (1987). *Children's language and learning* (2nd ed.). Upper Saddle River, NJ: Prentice Hall.

Loban, W. (1976). *Language development: Kindergarten through grade twelve.* Urbana, IL: National Council of Teachers of English.

Ninio, A., & Snow, C. (1999). The development of pragmatics: Learning to use language appropriately. In W. Ritchie & T. Bhatia (Eds.), *Handbook of child language acquisition* (pp. 347–386). San Diego, CA: Academic Press.

Otto, B. (1982). A Vygotskiian perspective on word concept development. *Northwestern University Psycholinguistic Newsletter, 7*(3), 15–33.

Otto, B. (1985). Unpublished research notes. Chicago: Northeastern Illinois University.

Owens, R. (1988). *Language development.* Upper Saddle River, NJ: Merrill.

Owens, R. (2001). *Language development: An introduction* (5th ed.). Boston: Allyn & Bacon.

Purcell-Gates, V. (1989). What oral/written language differences can tell us about beginning instruction. *The Reading Teacher, 42*(4), 290–294.

Reich, P. (1986). *Language development.* Upper Saddle River, NJ: Prentice Hall.

Sachs, J. (1989). Communication development in infancy. In J.B. Gleason (Ed.), *The development of language* (2nd ed., pp. 35–58). Upper Saddle River, NJ: Merrill.

Scarborough, H. (1990). Very early language deficits in dyslexic children. *Annals of Dyslexia, 41,* 207–220.

Schickedanz, J. (1981, November). "Hey! This book's not working right." *Young Children,* 18–27.

Snow, C., & Ninio, A. (1986). The contracts of literacy: What children learn from learning to read books. In W. Teale & E. Sulzby (Eds.), *Emergent literacy: Writing and reading* (pp. 116–138). Norwood, NJ: Ablex.

Stice, C., Bertrand, J., & Bertrand, N. (1995). *Integrating reading and the other language arts.* Belmont, CA: Wadsworth.

Sulzby, E. (1986). Writing and reading: Signs of oral and written language organization in the young child. In W. Teale & E. Sulzby (Eds.), *Emergent literacy: Writing and reading* (pp. 50–87). Norwood, NJ: Ablex Publishing.

Sulzby, E. (1991). Roles of oral and written language as children approach conventional literacy. In M. Orsolini & C. Pontecorvo (Eds.), *Early text construction in children* (pp. 56–75). Rome: La Nuova Italia.

Tannen, D. (1982). The oral/literate continuum in discourse. In D. Tannen (Ed.), *Spoken and written language: Exploring orality and literacy* (pp. 1–16). Norwood, NJ: Ablex.

Voss, M. (1988). "Make way for applesauce": The literate world of a three-year-old. *Language Arts, 65*(3), 272–278.

Vygotsky, L. (1962). *Thought and language* (E. Hanfmann & G. Vakar, Eds. & Trans.). Cambridge, MA: M.I.T. Press.

Wells, G. (1986). *The meaning makers: Children learning language and using language to learn.* Portsmouth, NH: Heinemann.

Windsor, J. (1995). Language impairment and social competence. In M. Fey, J. Windsor, & S. Warren (Eds.), *Language intervention: Preschool through the elementary years* (Vol. 5, pp. 213–238). Baltimore, MD: Paul H. Brookes.

Wolvin, A., & Coakley, C. (1985). *Listening.* Dubuque, IA: Wm. C. Brown.

2

LEARNING AND LANGUAGE

LEARNING TO COMMUNICATE: THEORETICAL PERSPECTIVES

During the past 50 years, many linguists and developmental psychologists have studied language acquisition with respect to what is learned, when it is learned, and what variables or factors seem to explain the process of acquisition. Several different perspectives have been proposed as theoretical bases for more fully understanding language acquisition. As scholars and researchers have studied language, they have documented the amazing complexity of language and the remarkable ability of young children to learn languages, regardless of the culture in which they live and the language used at home.

In the first part of this chapter, four predominant theoretical perspectives will be described. While no one theory provides a complete and irrefutable explanation of language acquisition, each theory contributes significant ideas and concepts, which over time have clarified our awareness of the ways in which language is acquired. A comprehensive theory of language acquisition would consider linguistic complexities and address acquisition of each of the five aspects of language knowledge. The study of languages has occurred concurrently with the development of theories of language acquisition; thus, earlier theories of acquisition do not address all the knowledge of language of which we are aware today.

In the sections that follow, four theoretical perspectives of language acquisition will be presented. While each of the perspectives focuses on the acquisition of language knowledge, some of them focus more generally while others focus on one or more specific aspects of language knowledge. By understanding the contributions of each theory, teachers will better understand the process of language acquisition and will be better able to facilitate language acquisition in their classrooms.

Following the discussion of theoretical perspectives is a section on conceptual development that incorporates the contributions of researchers and theorists from the dominant theoretical perspectives. The final section of this chapter focuses more specifically on the contexts of home and school in language acquisition and describes patterns of interaction involved in language acquisition.

Behaviorist Perspective

This perspective describes learning or changes in behavior as arising from associations established between stimuli, responses, and events that occur after the response behavior. While the behaviorist perspective focused on learning in general, it has also been applied to the understanding of how language is learned; however, specific aspects of language knowledge are not addressed.

An example of learning language within the behaviorist perspective is pairing the word *cracker* with the piece of food so that the child gradually begins to associate the word with the item. Repeated pairings result in the child responding when the word *cracker* is heard with no visible snack present. Initially, a parent asks a child, "Do you want a cracker?" as the parent holds a cracker for the child to see. Gradually, the child will respond when the parent asks the question while the cracker is still in a box in the cupboard.

Another aspect of behaviorism explains the way in which voluntary behavior may be shaped or changed. This type of conditioning (or learning) is called *operant conditioning* (Skinner, 1957). The use of the word *operant* acknowledges the child's active role in the learning process. This type of learning occurs when environmental consequences occur contingent upon the specific behavior. When a certain behavior is followed by a particular result, that consequence influences whether or not the behavior will be repeated. This perspective has been used to explain productive speech (Bohannon III & Bonvillian, 1997).

For example, when an infant is making sounds while in the presence of a parent and says "mama," the parent may rush to the infant, show signs of delight, and say, "Oh, you said 'ma-ma'!" This positive response from the parent increases the chances the infant will repeat those sounds. Likewise, speech that elicits no response or is ignored is less likely to be repeated.

Operant conditioning also explains the process of imitation, since children's attempts at imitating adult speech are often followed by reinforcement from the communicative environment in which the child is interacting. *Imitative speech* involves the production of speech that approximates the speech of another person. Imitation may occur as a result of direct modeling, such as when an adult tells a child, "Now say 'bye-bye'," and the child responds with an immediate attempt to repeat the specific word(s). Or it may occur as a result of delayed modeling, when the child approximates previously modeled speech in a similar setting without being prompted. In other instances, imitative speech may occur without the models' awareness that their speech was being learned. A child who hears his dad utter an expletive upon accidentally hitting his thumb with a hammer may surprise his father by using the same word (and intonation) in a similar situation in the child's dramatic play.

Many types of environmental responses serve as reinforcers. Positive reinforcement may come from the excited response of parents to their child's verbal attempts. It may also come from the success of the communication to express a want or need. A child who is thirsty and can say "drink" in a way that results in being given a drink is positively reinforced for that attempt. When adults are teaching a child to say "bye-bye," the child's attempts are often followed by positive reinforcement such as a hug, embrace, or verbal praise.

Recent research that has explored the context of young children's language acquisition has identified specific ways in which different contexts and the people in those contexts interact with children who are acquiring language and learning to communicate. Using the contributions of behaviorism as a basis, researchers are no longer simply focusing on identifying the stimuli, responses, and reinforcing contingencies, but are exploring the dynamic processes that occur in various contexts that support language acquisition where children are actively involved in constructing their knowledge of language.

Nativist Perspective

The nativist perspective emphasizes inborn or innate human capabilities as being responsible for language acquisition. Linguist Noam Chomsky is the major theorist associated with the nativist perspective. Chomsky's contributions to our understanding of the acquisition and structure of language have been significant (1965, 1975; Pinker, 1994). Chomsky contends that all people inherently have the capacity to acquire language due to cognitive structures that process language differently than other stimuli.

A major focus of the nativist perspective is on the development of syntactic knowledge. Semantic knowledge is also studied with respect to its relationship to syntax. Much of Chomsky's work involved identifying grammatical aspects of language and describing the rule systems for using language. Chomsky defined this rule system, or **universal grammar,** as "the system of principles, conditions, and rules that are elements or properties of all human languages not merely by accident but by necessity—of course, I mean biological, not logical necessity" (Chomsky, 1975, p. 29).

Chomsky proposes that this universal grammar is an innate property of the human mind. This component explains the ability of all humans to learn their culture's specific language. The ability to learn language is a property of the human species since humans obviously are not designed to acquire one language over another. Chomsky's description of the high level of grammatical complexity acquired by young children has contributed to our understanding of the significance of universal language acquisition among people of diverse language environments.

Building on Chomsky's work, Steven Pinker (1994) contends that language is an instinct, not simply a cultural invention: "Language is a biological adaptation to communicate information . . . language is the product of a well-engineered biological instinct" (p. 19). As evidence of the universality and instinctive nature of language, Pinker notes that throughout history no mute civilizations have ever been discovered, even among primitive societies. In the 1960s, when Stone Age people were discovered in New Guinea, some 800 different (new) languages were documented. Each language was a complex linguistic system. While languages may differ dramatically with respect to linguistic features, the development and use of language in all cultures is universal. Since language exists in every culture, Pinker concludes that it must come from human biological instinct rather than from the existence of the culture.

In the nativist perspective, children learn language by discovering the structure of their language. This discovery process is thought to be aided by an inborn mechanism specific for language learning. This mechanism is called a *language acquisition device*, or LAD (Chomsky, 1982), which enables children to process and acquire language through innate knowledge of grammatical classes, underlying deep structure, and transformations. While the exact nature of the LAD has been challenged, there remains agreement that children are active participants in their learning of language. In a sense, children teach themselves language. Through the acquisition process children construct their knowledge of the ways in which language is used and manipulated. This process is sometimes referred to as **hypothesis testing.** Children test hypotheses of how language is spoken, articulated, used, and manipulated.

Cognitive Developmental Perspective

The cognitive developmental perspective is based in the work of Jean Piaget. The emphasis of this perspective is that language is acquired as cognitive competencies develop. There is also an emphasis on the close relationship between cognitive development and language. This perspective focuses on the semantic and morphemic aspects of language knowledge.

Jean Piaget's theory of cognitive development proposes that language development is based in cognitive growth (Piaget, 1955). In the first stage of cognitive development, the sensorimotor stage, children are prelinguistic. According to Piaget, children's understanding of the environment comes only through their immediate direct (sensory) experiences and their motor (movement) activities. Through sensorimotor experiences in infancy, children develop the cognitive ability to understand object permanence and begin to use symbols, such as words, to refer to objects and actions (Sinclair-deZwart, 1969). Object permanence involves an awareness that an object continues to exist even when it is out of sight. Further, when the object reappears, it is the same object with the same properties.

According to Piaget, language appears when children's cognitive growth reaches a point that they use and manipulate symbols (Piaget, 1961, in Paciorek & Munro, 1999). Piaget's definition of language is narrower than that of other psychologists or linguists. For "language" to exist, Piaget contends that the "capacity for mental representation must be present" (Brainerd, 1978, p. 110). Thus, vocalizations and babbling that occur during infancy are not language according to Piaget. The development of symbolic representation changes a child's thinking because it is now possible to "invoke objects which are not present perceptually . . . reconstruct the past . . . or make plans for the future" (Piaget, 1961, in Paciorek & Munro, 1999).

Symbolic representation is evident when a child uses signs and symbols in response to a new situation, whereas earlier the child would have used trial and error to deal with the situation (Atkinson, 1983). For example, if a child is presented with a new box to open that differs slightly from previous boxes with which the child has played, symbolic representation is evident when instead of simply using trial and error to find a way to open the box, the child appears to use her prior experiences in a symbolic way in "thinking out" a solution to the task before manipulating the box.

Around the age of one year, some children are beginning to represent actions and objects mentally and symbolically. During this time, relationships between actions and objects develop and are organized into abstract cognitive structures called **schemata** (Brainerd, 1978). One of the distinguishing features of concepts and schema is that they reflect experience broader than that of the individual person. This means that concepts and schemata develop from inter-personal interaction and communication. This communication relies on "signs" (Piaget, 1962). Piaget contends that the development of verbal signs or words facilitates cognitive development because it makes possible "the trans-formation of sensory motor schemas into concepts" (1962, p. 99).

Piaget (1955) considers children's initial speech to be egocentric, focused on their own perceptions which may reflect distorted perceptions or relation-ships. Gradually, as children develop cognitively, their speech becomes social-ized or reflective of more logical thinking. In the next section, the interaction-ist perspective will be described. It differs significantly from Piaget's definitions of language and functions of speech.

Interactionist Perspective

The primary role of environmental interaction in children's acquisition of lan-guage knowledge is a central focus of the interactionist approach (John-Steiner, Panofsky, & Smith, 1994). Children acquire language through their attempts to communicate with the world around them. This perspective provides insight to the ways in which children acquire pragmatic language knowledge. The ways in which an environment supports children's language explorations has been termed the *language acquisition support system,* or LASS (Bruner, 1983).

Another aspect of this approach is its focus on the language acquisition *process* rather than on language as a *product* of acquisition. The interactionist approach draws on behaviorism's recognition of the environment's responses to young children's communicative attempts, nativism's recognition of the human capacity for processing linguistic information, and the cognitive developmen-talist's contention that language acquisition is influenced by the nature and se-quence of cognitive development. In the interactionist perspective the interac-tion between the language acquisition device, or LAD (Chomsky, 1975), and the language acquisition support system, or LASS (Bruner, 1983), is responsible for children's language acquisition.

Vygotsky

The work of Vygotsky (1896–1934) has also been associated with this interac-tionist approach (1962, 1978; John-Steiner et al., 1994). Vygotsky's basic premise was that language development is influenced by the society in which the indi-vidual lives: ". . . higher mental functions are socially formed and culturally trans-mitted" (Vygotsky, 1978, p. 126). Speech has social origins. It develops in situa-tions where people are interacting with each other in a communicative context.

The development of language involves higher mental functions and is re-lated to the development of cognition. Vygotsky (1962) described the close rela-tionship between young children's thought and language to involve concurrent and independent, but not parallel, development. Vygotsky did not consider chil-dren's crying, cooing, and babbling during infancy to involve thinking; instead, he considered them "affective-conative," or emotional, behavior. According to Vygotsky, the development of thought and speech join during the second year so that speech begins to serve the intellect, and thoughts are spoken. A major event here is the child's realization that everything has a name. This discovery appears to motivate children to explore the use of language actively to learn more about the world around them.

Vygotsky (1962) described the functions of children's speech distinctly different from Piaget. Vygotsky contended that the main function of speech is social, involving both egocentric and communicative speech. Egocentric speech is thought to represent a child's use of directive speech (for example, from parent-child collaborative situations) to his own behavior—that is, self-directing speech. In time, a child's egocentric speech becomes inner speech, which is internalized self-directing speech. Thus, one of the main differences between Vygotsky and Piaget is in their conceptions of speech development. Piaget sees egocentric speech as a precursor to socialized speech and logical thinking while Vygotsky sees egocentric speech and communicative (socialized) speech as existing concurrently, with egocentric speech gradually becoming internalized into inner speech. Vygotsky also contends that egocentric/inner speech has a significant role in cognitive development as it is incorporated into the child's thought processes. The differences between Piaget and Vygotsky with respect to egocentric and socialized speech are represented in Figure 2.1.

Vygotsky (1978) describes the role of adults in the communication process to be crucial in supporting children's language acquisition. Since the child is a novice communicator, an adult in the conversational dyad serves as the expert who often creates conditions that make for effective communication. The difference between what a child can accomplish alone and what she can accomplish with an adult's (or more capable peer's) mediation or assistance is termed the **zone of proximal development.** What a child accomplishes independently is her **developmental level.**

With respect to language development, the zone of proximal development can been seen in situations where an adult interprets or mediates a child's attempts at communicating. In this setting the adult is providing a supportive *scaffolding* that gives a child opportunities to participate in a conversation,

FIGURE 2.1
A Comparison of Piaget's and Vygotsky's Conceptions of the Developmental Sequence of Egocentric and Socialized Speech

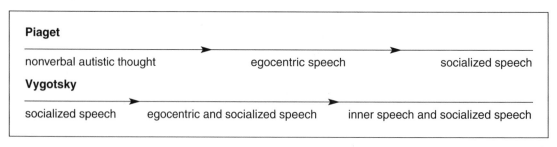

with the child's communicative attempts supported by additions or clarifications by the adult. Harris (1990) points out that the success of these scaffolded conversations depends on the adult's interpretation of the child's communicative attempt. The most effective scaffolding promotes the highest level of functioning with the lowest level of support.

In the example that follows, a mother and her daughter are in a homemade tent in their backyard, which has been constructed of blankets draped over lawn chairs and a rope strung between a tree and a swing set. The daughter, Allison (age 2), has been playing in the tent without her shoes on. Since it is April in the Midwest and a bit cool to be going barefoot, her mother decides it is time for Allison to put her shoes and socks back on. Her mother uses scaffolding to engage Allison in a rhyming song as she puts on Allison's shoes and socks. Not only does this distract Allison from protesting putting on her shoes and socks, it provides a way for Allison to learn more about a song which she had heard previously, and enabling her to participate in recreating the rhyming song.

Mother: Allison, come here and get your socks and shoes on (draws Allison onto her lap, and begins to put her socks and shoes on).

Allison: (squirms, resisting) Don't.

Mother: Allison, want to sing? How about (begins to sing) Four little ducks went out to play (continues with shoes and socks throughout this singing) over the fields and far away. Mama Duck said, 'Quack, quack, quack, quack' and only three little ducks came back. (pause) Three little ducks went out one day over the fields and far away. Mama Duck said (pause)

Allison: Quack, quack, quack.

Mother: How many ducks came back, Allison?

Allison: One (singing tone) (holds up one finger)

Mother: One. (pause) You sing it. (long pause) One little duck (pause) went out to play . . .

Allison: (joins in, softly) Went out to play . . .

Mother and Allison: Over the fields and far away . . .

Allison: *One little duck, quack, quack, quack . . .*

Mother: (nods head)

Allison: One little duck (indecipherable) quack, quack, (sings alone, with fingers up on one hand, looking at fingers) four little ducks, four little ducks, (indecipherable) three little ducks, quack, quack, four little ducks, (pause) four little ducks . . .

Allison's shoes and socks were now on, and Allison became distracted by her 4-year-old sister who was also playing in the backyard. Allison left her mom's lap, and the singing ended. Two minutes later, Allison was observed singing the duck song to herself as she walked in the backyard.

In this segment, the mother's scaffolding took the form of beginning the song, and then pausing at predictable points in the song for Allison to participate. The mother verbally faded away when Allison began to sing and accepted Allison's version of the song. This type of linguistic support was effective in initially engaging and sustaining Allison in this routine. The observation of Allison repeating a version of the song to herself only moments later indicated that Allison was then able to sing the song on her own.

Not only does the concept of the zone of proximal development provide us with an idea of development to come, it emphasizes the crucial role of adults in children's acquisition of language. Adults serve as mediators who introduce children to higher levels of functioning within a supportive scaffolded setting. Psychologists have concluded that it is not possible for children to imitate something that is beyond their respective developmental levels. Thus, when a child, such as Allison, successfully incorporates some of the new behaviors (i.e., linguistic structures or vocabulary), it is not simply imitated behavior but a reflection of the developmental readiness of the child for acquiring more advanced language knowledge.

ACQUIRING CONCEPTS AND CONCEPT LABELS

Before children can use concept labels, symbolic thinking and symbol formation must occur. In Werner & Kaplan's (1963) description of symbol formation, the process of **distancing** the presence of the actual object or action (referent) from the use of the concept label (word/symbol) is a significant step in **symbol formation** (see also Sigel & Cocking, 1977). Four components are present in any symbol situation: the addressor (adult or older child), the addressee (young child), the object or referent (e.g., rattle, ball, bottle), and the symbolizer's means for representing the referent (word or gesture) (see Figure 2.2).

When adults share objects with young children, they verbally label the object, establishing a verbal symbol for that object ("rattle," "ball"). Through repeated experiences during infancy, children acquire receptive knowledge of language symbols and their referents that are important in their environment.

FIGURE 2.2
Components of Symbol
Formation

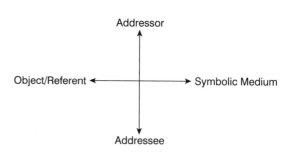

FIGURE 2.3
Distancing of the Concept
of Ball

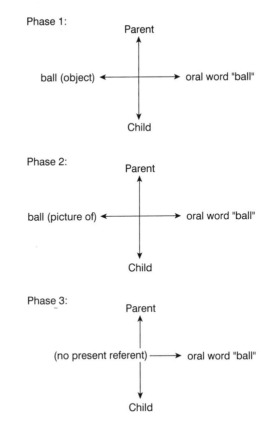

Phase 1:

Parent

ball (object) ←————————→ oral word "ball"

Child

Phase 2:

Parent

ball (picture of) ←————————→ oral word "ball"

Child

Phase 3:

Parent

(no present referent) ————→ oral word "ball"

Child

These early symbols usually represent objects or actions important in a child's environment.

At first the actual object or action must be in the immediate environment in order for the child to comprehend or produce the concept label. After repeated experiences that pair the object/referent with the symbolic medium (oral word), the word alone will elicit the concept for the child. When this occurs, symbolic representation has developed, since the presence of the symbol alone elicits the concept. Figure 2.3 illustrates the distancing principle as the actual referent (a ball) is first replaced by a pictured ball and then distanced further when the word "ball" is used without either a pictured ball or a real ball present. Symbol formation is evident when a parent says, "Go get your ball," and the child responds by going to another room, retrieving the ball, and bringing it back.

Role of Experiences in the Development of Semantic Knowledge

Children develop semantic knowledge through their experiences in varied environmental contexts that foster conceptual development. Harris (1990) describes children's actions on the material world as providing stimuli for conceptual

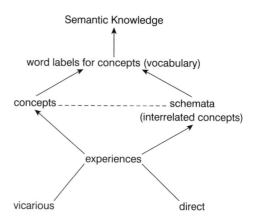

FIGURE 2.4
Developmental Relationship
Between Experiences and
Semantic Knowledge

development. The first concepts children learn represent important objects, people, or actions in a culture (Menyuk, 1988). From those experiences we develop
ideas or notions of the ways in which stimuli (objects, actions, and other phenomena) are similar, different, or interrelated. As children process this information cognitively, they develop ways of categorizing this stimuli into abstract conceptual groupings, or schemata.

Conceptual knowledge may develop before language labels (words) are attached to the concept. However, when children begin to attach conventional
words to those concepts, they are on their way to understanding the speech of others and to communicating their thoughts and ideas (Vygotsky, 1962). Figure 2.4
represents the relationship between experiences and semantic development.

Interactions in the environment that facilitate conceptual and semantic development are of two types: direct and vicarious. Direct experiences occur from
birth on and vicarious experiences occur with the beginning of a child's symbolic thinking.

Direct Experiences

During infancy, children's experiences are essentially all "firsthand." Infants
experience objects and events in their world as a direct participant—touching,
tasting, smelling, seeing, and hearing. During this time, interaction with adults
or older children serves to assist a child in safely exploring the environment
through the senses and provides the child with object or action labels.

Vicarious Experiences

When a child acquires symbolic representation and begins to use and comprehend language in late infancy, **vicarious experiences** begin to contribute to further concept development. Children experience or communicate the concept or
action through visual representations (pictures, print) or through verbal description alone without the actual referent being present. For example, listen-

ing to a book read about trucks is a vicarious experience, while riding in a truck or watching a big garbage truck rumble down the street is a firsthand experience. Both direct and vicarious experiences make valuable contributions to conceptual development; however, direct experiences have a greater impact on concept development.

Concept labels (i.e., words) and schemata are culture- and language-specific. Children's home language is the language they learn first. Thus, a child whose home language is different from English might have a similar concept of ball with respect to what a ball looks like and what it does; however, the word referring to that concept might be quite different. The ball schema would be different for people living in other cultures since each culture may use balls differently in different activities. Children's use of words to indicate culturally common concepts is evidence they are acquiring semantic knowledge.

Detailed descriptions of children's semantic development provide evidence of the complexities of semantic development and the complex ways in which semantic development has been studied (deVilliers & deVilliers, 1978; Pease, Gleason, & Pan, 1989; Owens, 1988; Reich, 1986). Exploration of children's semantic development is difficult because children cannot tell the researcher or linguist what a specific word or phrase means to them due to their limited language abilities. Thus, researchers must make their conclusions and hypotheses based upon children's responses to linguistic and nonlinguistic contexts (Owens, 1988). Nor can children explain how their concepts evolve and are organized cognitively. Again, conclusions and hypotheses are based upon inferences from children's responses to specific linguistic and nonlinguistic contexts. Hypotheses proposed to explain concept formation and word learning include: (1) semantic-feature hypothesis (Clark, 1973a, 1973b), (2) functional-core hypothesis (Nelson, 1974, 1977), (3) associative complex hypothesis (Vygotsky, 1962), and (4) prototypic complex hypothesis (Bowerman, 1978). Each of these hypotheses increases our understanding of ways in which children may be developing and organizing their semantic knowledge. Inhelder, Sinclair, & Bovet (1974) also caution that "concepts do not develop in closed systems but are in constant interaction with each other" (p. 15).

Semantic knowledge is refined through the processes of assimilation and accommodation. During conceptual development, overextension and underextension occur when children increase or decrease the number of examples of a specific concept when compared to a conventional understanding of the concept. When perceiving new information related (or not related) to an existing concept, assimilation and accommodation occur.

For example, calling all four-legged animals "doggie" would be an **overextension.** Using "kitty" to refer only to the family's pet cat and not the neighbor's kitten would be an example of **underextension.** Children's overextensions and underextensions diminish as children receive implicit and explicit feedback from others around them (Owens, 1988).

Another part of semantic development is the expansion of vocabulary to refer to more specific exemplars, or shades of meaning. For example, a cat may also be referred to as a kitten, feline, tabby, mouser, or a member of the larger cat family, such as a leopard, tiger, or lion. The process by which children acquire these elaborated conceptual networks and complex semantic knowledge is based in their direct and vicarious experiences.

Vocabulary Counts

The volume of distinct words in a child's vocabulary has been considered a way of measuring a child's vocabulary knowledge. These vocabulary counts are lists of words representing the quantity of words children are likely to know at a particular age. Lindfors (1987) recommends cautions in using children's vocabulary counts as an index of vocabulary knowledge by pointing out complexities of receptive and expressive vocabularies that are often overlooked by word count reports. Whether the vocabulary counts take into consideration a variety of contexts is important. Varying settings and contexts influence whether or not a child will comprehend or use a particular word. Another important consideration is if the vocabulary count is based on receptive or productive language. A specific word may be part of a child's receptive knowledge but not his/her productive language. In addition, while vocabulary counts provide early childhood educators with general ideas of semantic growth, it is important to recognize the role of various contexts and situations in a child's receptive and expressive semantic knowledge. With consideration of Lindfor's cautions, vocabulary counts are referred to as a way of estimating vocabulary growth.

In the next section, the various contexts in which concept and language development occur will be presented. Patterns of interaction and specific types of settings will be discussed.

HOME, COMMUNITY, AND SCHOOL

Home, community, and school are the environments in which children's language develops. The important role of social and cultural contexts for language acquisition is the focus of the interactionist perspective discussed earlier in this chapter. Language is acquired in a social setting; it cannot be acquired in a solitary setting. The language learner must have interaction with another person who is a language user. By understanding the types of contexts and interaction patterns in which children experience language, teachers are better able to establish settings within their classrooms that foster language development.

First we will consider specific patterns of adult-child interaction. Then we will examine two main types of social contexts or settings: formal and informal. The principle of developmental appropriateness will be introduced as a way of evaluating the potential effectiveness of specific contexts on language acquisition. Then differences between home and school as language contexts will be described. The final section of the chapter focuses on the role of the teacher in establishing and maintaining contexts that foster language development.

Patterns of Interaction: Overview

In this section, several specific patterns of linguistic interaction will be described. Each of these patterns plays a role in enhancing language acquisition. Each pattern is present in some manner throughout early childhood. The pattern may be modified in some way reflecting the developmental level of each child, but the characteristic nature of each pattern of interaction is maintained.

Eye Contact and Shared Reference

We begin communicating with children through establishing eye contact and **shared reference.** This is a basic interaction pattern (Tronick, Als, & Adamson, 1979). Eye contact is established between an adult and a child and involves jointly focusing on an object or event. Through eye contact and shared reference, objects and events are "contemplated" and become subjects of conversation. When eye contact and shared reference are not established, communication often breaks down or is not even initiated since there is no clear common focus.

Eye contact is usually established by an adult first looking directly at a child and gesturing (pointing) or speaking a short, attention-getting phrase such as "look." Sometimes the adult touches the child briefly on the shoulder or arm to get his attention. If eye contact and shared reference are not established, the attention-getting phrase and gesture may be repeated. If repeated attempts are not successful, then the interaction may be discontinued as the child may not be interested or sufficiently alert to engage in the shared activity. When this routine has been repeated successfully with infants (6–12 months of age) over time, they begin to respond to the verbal phrase or word by looking at the speaker and then to the location signaled by the adult's gesture. After shared reference is established, communication about the object or event occurs.

Early interactions with children are more individualized so that eye contact and shared reference with infants and toddlers occur with one child at a time. When classroom activities involve more than one child at a time (such as in preschool, kindergarten, or primary rooms), teachers then establish eye contact and shared reference with several children for that one activity. As teachers interact with more than one child at a time, they spend more time establishing eye contact and shared reference. Though the technique is similar to the one described for infants, the attention-getting language used with toddlers and older children will gradually become more complex and elaborated. Children who do not participate in these contexts of shared reference often lose out on the communication and thus the instruction.

Maintaining shared reference may require constant monitoring and verbal interaction to keep a child focused on the desired object or event. Animated speech

FIGURE 2.5
Communication Loop

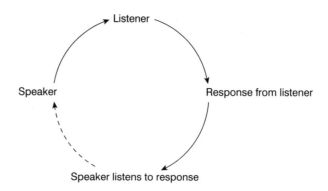

or speech with varied intonations and gestures is often effective in maintaining a child's attention. For example, when sharing a storybook with an infant or toddler, the parent may use animated speech and gestures to maintain the child's attention.

Communication Loop

All patterns of interaction are characterized by a *communication loop,* a circular or cycle-like sharing and exchanging of the roles of speaker and listener. The loop begins with a speaker initiating the conversation and continues to a listener, who then becomes a speaker while the first speaker listens. Thus, a conversation may continue through many turns, during which time topics of conversation may be introduced, elaborated, or changed. The communication loop is severed whenever one of the participants fails to continue participating either by not listening to the speaker or not responding as a speaker. With infants, a communication loop is first initiated through eye contact and shared reference. Rather than a verbal response from the child, the child's eye contact and focus of shared reference serve as active responses in this communication loop. A diagram of a communication loop is presented in Figure 2.5.

This communication loop can also be thought of as a continuously spiraling loop that changes or develops as the conversation develops since the participation by both speaker and listener influences the subsequent interaction. The evolving nature of communication loops is represented in Figure 2.6.

The notion of a communication loop is also described in Bruner's (1978, 1983) language acquisition support system. The language acquisition support system (LASS) is a routinized, repeated interaction between a child and an adult. In this interaction a series of turns defines the context and creates a structure for further negotiation or clarification of the meaning of actions or objects in the environment. Initially the adult does most of the work in sustaining the interaction. As a child's ability to participate develops, the child assumes more control over the interaction.

FIGURE 2.6
Evolving Communication Loop

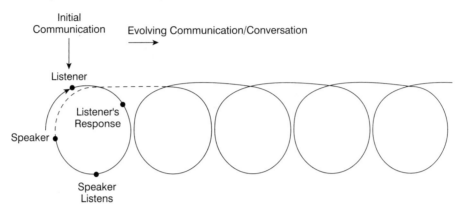

Adult-to-Child Speech

The specific language adults use with young children is also distinctive and serves to enhance language acquisition. This specific language has been termed "baby talk," "motherese," or "child-directed speech" (CDS).

In a review of research, Pine (1994) identified the following characteristics of child-directed speech:

1. Child-directed speech utterances are short and well formed.
2. Utterances have fewer false starts than adult-to-adult speech.
3. Child-directed speech has fewer complex sentences and subordinate clauses.
4. The pitch used in CDS is higher, and intonation is more exaggerated.
5. In CDS, utterances are redundant or repetitive in part or in whole.
6. The rate of speech or tempo is slower than adult-to-adult speech.
7. In CDS the utterances are more closely tied to the immediate context.
8. CDS uses discourse features that encourage children to participate and to clarify the child's responses.

Researchers have debated whether the existence and use of CDS indicates it is a conscious vehicle for "teaching" language or whether it is an intuitive response by adults (or other fluent, though younger, language users) when they are attempting to communicate with children who are just beginning to communicate (Newport, Gleitman, & Gleitman, 1977). This latter position is supported by the observation that speech resembling CDS is often used by English speakers when they attempt to communicate with non-English speakers or even their pets (Pine, 1994). Child-directed speech has also been observed in settings where older siblings/children are attempting to communicate with younger children.

The role of child-directed speech in language acquisition may be a combination of both informal teaching and communicative necessity. Because these specific characteristics are successful in enhancing communication between fluent and novice/beginning speakers, it creates an environment in which the novice is exposed to aspects of the language and the act of communication that enhance the child's language acquisition. When utterances are short and well formed, the child can process the utterances more efficiently, and a more accurate model utterance is provided to the young language learner. Utterances that have fewer false starts also provide the young child with better language models to facilitate comprehension; utterances with many false starts would be confusing and impair communication. Utterances that are syntactically simple (few complex sentences and subordinate clauses) would also facilitate young children's linguistic processing. Speech directed to children that has a higher pitch and more exaggerated intonation would hold children's attention more and enhance perception of speech sounds due to the wide variety of intonation. Utterances that are redundant, either in part or in whole, facilitate comprehension of meaning and context through the repetition of key aspects of the utterance. When speech directed to young children is at a slower pace/tempo, it allows for linguistic processing: it takes time to process speech cognitively. If you have ever been in a setting where you were a nonnative speaker, you may have wished that the native speakers would just speak more slowly!

Utterances that are more closely tied to the immediate context foster language acquisition. Referents of utterances found in the immediate context give the young child a visible connection between the oral symbol and its actual referent.

Discourse features that encourage children's participation include questioning (see subsequent section) and conversational "rules," such as turn-taking, active listening, and maintaining eye contact. The presence of these features in child-directed speech increases participation by children, and engaging in communication furthers their language acquisition.

Adults actively monitor the success of their speech to young children and change their expectations for children's responses as their children's levels of language acquisition increase. Some differences between the interaction styles of mothers and fathers have been noted (Barton & Tomasello, 1994). Mothers typically adjust their speech to young children to a greater extent and in more different ways than do fathers or older siblings. While initially this might seem to indicate that communication is less beneficial when fathers and older siblings are involved, young children's communicative competence might be enhanced in this type of setting where they must respond or adapt to the communicative demands of others, rather than having the style of communication always adapted to them.

Verbal Mapping

This interaction pattern occurs when an adult verbally describes (not just names) the object or action in a level of detail appropriate to the developmental level of the child with whom the interaction is occurring. Verbal mapping employs language that fits the situation, providing the symbols for a child's subsequent representation of that event. In most cases, the verbal mapping serves to orally identify the concepts being experienced. Shared reference and eye contact are essential for the effectiveness of verbal mapping. Verbal mapping is monologic in nature. The adult provides a verbal description of what is occurring or what is being experienced or seen. The mapping episode may be short or it may be extended, depending on the situation and the child's attention to the adult's mapping.

This pattern of interaction occurs with all ages of children and can enhance development of all five aspects of language knowledge: semantics, syntax, phonology, morphology, and pragmatics. During infancy, verbal mapping provides a narrative to daily routines of dressing, eating, and exploring. At later developmental stages, verbal mapping is crucial during new experiences, since verbal mapping involves modeling or showing how language is applied to those experiences.

For example, when helping a toddler put on shoes, an adult engages in verbal mapping as she describes what she and the child are doing: "Where are your shoes? (Child gestures.) Yes, those are your shoes. Bring me your shoes. (Child gives shoes to adult.) Let's put this shoe on first. (Holds shoe to child's foot.) Slip your foot into the shoe. (Child responds.) There you go. Now let's buckle it up. (Buckles shoe.) Now let's put on your other shoe . . . "

Another example is when a teacher stops by the block corner and finds that children are engaged in building a city. Her verbal mapping focuses on describing the types of buildings the children have made. The teacher's mapping continues briefly and is contingent on children's responses to her. She focuses on providing descriptions of the children's actions and accomplishments.

Verbal mapping also occurs as children share discoveries with their teachers, parents, or other adults. While outside on the playground, a child might run up to a teacher with a caterpillar on a leaf in her hand. The teacher's responses might include the following instances of verbal mapping: "What do you have here? Oh, yes, it is a caterpillar. It has yellow and black stripes. Can you see how it moves? Slowly, slowly, little by little. It can even climb up a hanging leaf. See where its eyes are? It looks furry. See the tiny hairs that cover its body? Look at all of its feet."

Verbal mapping is not just idle chatter on the part of an adult. Instead, it involves a conscious focus by the adult on the concepts and vocabulary relevant to the ongoing learning activity. To be effective, the verbal mapping needs to take into account the developmental level of children's receptive language skills. Since verbal mapping occurs as action is ongoing, it occurs when the referents for the objects and actions are present. This provides children with important opportunities for conceptual development. As the specific concepts are used in the verbal mapping, children are exposed to syntactic, pragmatic, morphemic, and phonemic knowledge related to those concepts. In this way, verbal mapping extends and expands children's receptive language and serves as a basis for their productive/expressive language as well.

Questioning

Adults ask children questions from infancy on. This interaction pattern occurs frequently. Questions asked of very young children are often answered by the same adult who takes both parts in the conversation, since the infant is not yet verbally responding. Infants' nonverbal responses—their gestures and facial expressions—may be interpreted by many adults as responses to their questions, even if the child's responses are unintentional or random. The way in which adults respond to children's unintentional responses, by assuming the verbal or nonverbal behavior as an intended response, sets up an interactive pattern in which the child begins to participate in a dialogic interaction. The rising intonation that ends a question, the anticipatory facial expression, and gestures of the adult encourage children to respond. Questions are a way of "passing the conversational turn" to the child (Pine, 1994, p. 19).

Questioning takes several different roles in communicating with young children. Questioning can focus on clarifying something the child said previously. Sometimes questions are used to ask the child to repeat what was said earlier or to rephrase the utterance. At other times questions are used to determine the child's knowledge or awareness of a concept or action. This "recitational questioning" is also found in classrooms, where a teacher asks a student a question to which she, the teacher, knows the answer, but is checking to see if the child knows the answer. Informational questioning occurs when an adult seeks information from a child that the adult does not know (e.g., "Where are your shoes?").

Children experience responding to these three types of questions—clarifying, recitational, and informational—from early childhood on and gradually begin to incorporate the use of questioning in their productive/expressive speech. Around the age of 8 to 9 months, children show intonation patterns accompanied by gestures (pointing) as if they were asking questions. As children acquire more complex language and reach the early preschool years, questioning others becomes one way they find out information.

Linguistic Scaffolding

Using language to provide a scaffold for children's attempts to communicate is an interaction pattern used frequently with infants and older children. Scaffolding refers to a supportive manner in which adults or older children interact with young children in a dialogue (Bruner, 1978; Wells, 1986). This scaffolding assists children in participating at a higher level than they could perform independently. By exploring children's participation in scaffolded interactions, it is possible to see their future learning and development (Dixon-Krauss, 1996; Vygotsky, 1978).

Linguistic scaffolding involves supporting children's speech by recognizing their linguistic capabilities and assisting them in building a conversation. Linguistic scaffolding may include the use of questioning, expansion, and/or repetition. The questioning used during linguistic scaffolding serves to lead the child ahead in the dialogue or discourse and maintains the verbal interaction. For example, in the following dialogue, a teacher uses questioning to maintain the conversation. Without the use of questioning, the dialogue would have stopped.

Child:	I ate at McDonald's with grandma and grandpa.
Teacher:	Oh, you did?
Child:	Uh-huh.
Teacher:	What did you eat?
Child:	Cheeseburger, Coke, fries.
Teacher:	Did you go on the playground?
Child:	Yes.
Teacher:	What did you play on?
Child:	The slide and the horses.

Through the use of questioning the teacher was able to engage the child in sharing more complete information about lunch with his grandparents.

Expansion, or *recasting* (Camarata, 1995), is another aspect of linguistic scaffolding. It is used to "fill out" what a child says (Reich, 1986; Wells, 1986). Expansion is also a way to model more complex syntax, morphology, semantics, and correct pronunciation (phonology). In the following dialogue, expansion (indicated by italics) enhances syntax and morphology by creating complete sentences and adding inflectional endings and correct past tense forms.

Child:	New shoe (looking down at his feet)
Adult:	Oh, Tim. You have new shoes.
Child:	(Nods and grins.)
Adult:	What color are your shoes?
Child:	Blue.
Adult:	Yes. Your shoes are blue. Where did you get them?
Child:	Mommy buyed at K-Mart.
Adult:	Oh, your mother bought them at K-Mart.

Repetition is also an aspect of linguistic scaffolding. In the previous example the adult's repetition of specific key words used by the child served to reinforce pronunciation and to confirm the meaning of what the child said.

Scaffolding often occurs as a result of an adult's intuitive sense that young children need assistance and support in developing and carrying on a conversation. In such instances, adults may not be aware they are engaged in linguistic scaffolding. At other times, they may be aware they are scaffolding the interaction for a child. **Strategic scaffolding** involves a conscious awareness by an adult that he is teaching or modeling to the child how to carry on a conversation or how to describe an event or object (Beed, Hawkins, & Roller, 1991). Strategic scaffolding provides a stronger support for a young child's verbal interactions since it is employed with a greater level of metacognitive awareness on the part of the teacher or adult and may reflect specific educational or developmental goals for the child. It is important that adults remain sensitive to communicative cues from children with respect to topic interest and intended meaning. This involves confirming children's intentions and extending their topic or inviting the children to extend the topic (Wells, 1986). In addition, adults should form and phrase their responses at the level of the child's communication or just beyond that level with respect to syntax, semantics, or phonology to create a zone of proximal development.

Mediation

This type of interaction focuses on simplifying the learning stimulus or task to facilitate the language interaction with, and comprehension by, the child. The nature of mediation appears to be influenced by an adult's awareness of a child's level of comprehension (receptive language) and ability to respond (expressive language). The adult serves as a mediator, a go-between for the child and the learning stimuli.

At the preschool level mediation may be seen in spontaneously altered texts as storybooks are shared. When teachers encounter text they feel is too difficult for children to understand, they spontaneously change the text to fit their understanding of their children's semantic and syntactic development. Sometimes teachers may mediate the text by pausing after a new concept/label is introduced in the text and explaining the concept. Mediation may also occur in home settings where the parent simplifies the explanation of a complex event such as their response to a child's question about why it rains.

Through these patterns of interaction children's language acquisition is enhanced. Communication loops, shared reference, child-directed speech, verbal mapping, questioning, linguistic scaffolding, and mediation all facilitate language development. These interaction patterns are present in home, community, and school settings, although there may be some modifications due to the child's level of development and the interaction style of the adults or older children in the environment.

CONTEXTS OF LANGUAGE ACQUISITION

Communicative contexts experienced by children vary depending upon the patterns of linguistic interaction that occur in those contexts. Cultural diversity also increases the variations in communicative contexts. Cultures develop their own distinctive language, which reflects the knowledge, belief systems, and phenomena within each culture. Languages also differ in terms of the five aspects of language knowledge: phonetic, semantic, syntactic, morphemic, and pragmatic. Issues related to cultural diversity are presented in Chapter 3.

Even without considering social-cultural differences between distinct groups, home and school environments still vary in the ways in which communication occurs in those settings. At home, verbal interactions may have more of a focus on the immediate context of events, actions, and objects present in the home (Wells, 1986; Wilkinson, 1984). In home settings, children interact with a limited number of people with whom they have daily experiences. Their conversations with adults are more frequent and involve more "turns," or a wider range of topics, and more questions from the child (Tizard, 1981). At school, children interact with a much larger number of people, and their interactions are often governed by school rules or protocol (Geekie & Raban, 1994; Mehan, 1979).

Verbal interactions with children at home are more tailored for each child or, at most, shared with one or two other children. In contrast, at school, a child must share the teacher in conversation with fellow students. The result is that children at school have less opportunity for conversations with adults. In addition, their relationship to the teacher is less personal, and the dialogue that occurs is often teacher-directed to focus on specific instructional objectives and activities (Geekie & Raban, 1994). Verbal interactions at school often focus on events and objects not physically present in the classroom. This decontextualized speech is a contrast to the type of speech experienced by children at home. Further, in school settings, the wait time between adult questions and expected children's responses is also much shorter than that experienced in home settings.

Informal Settings, Formal Settings, and Routines

Another way of examining the different language contexts in which children acquire language is to look at the specific types of settings that are present in home and school environments. Within these contexts, some settings are informal and others are more formal.

Informal and formal settings differ along several aspects: (1) the way in which concepts are presented; (2) the expectation of a response by the learner; (3) the way in which skills are presented; and (4) the sequence and outcome of the activity.

Informal settings are those in which aspects of language knowledge are embedded within purposeful language use. A mother speaks to her child as she dresses the child, carries her child while on an errand, or looks out the window. In contrast, aspects of language knowledge are isolated and directly taught in formal settings. For example, in a third-grade classroom, the teacher may announce, "Today our lesson will be on new vocabulary words." Formal settings may occur in the home environment when a parent focuses directly on a language concept. For example, a parent may use a letter-sound-picture matching game with a preschool child to enhance the child's awareness of speech-print-meaning matches (see photo on the following page).

Skills or competencies in using language are also embedded in informal settings. Children learn to use words, form sentences, and engage in conversations within actual communicative contexts. In formal settings, skills or competencies are isolated for the purposes of instruction and practice. This is evident when a particular aspect of language knowledge such as vocabulary is singled out for a specific instructional lesson.

A letter-sound-picture matching game enhances a child's awareness of speech-print-meaning relationships.

In informal settings, a child's participation is invited, not required. While in formal settings, the child's participation is not only expected but in many cases mandatory. For example, a toddler who is restless at story time may be allowed to wander off and engage in another quiet activity, whereas a first grader who is restless during reading class may be admonished to sit still and be ready to take his turn reading orally.

In a formal setting, children are expected to participate in the same activity, specifically directed by the teacher. The expectation is that all students will learn what the teacher presents. Often a worksheet, project, or other product results from the language activity. The presence of a visual product is often taken to indicate the children learned what was desired. Conversely, in informal settings the language activities are more process oriented. Children participate in informal language activities by exploring the materials or processes, such as verbally interacting while working at a sand table, using finger paint, manipulating play dough, or paging through a storybook with a classmate.

The sequence of the learning also differs between formal and informal settings. In informal settings, the child often initiates the language-related activity.

The direction of this activity is influenced by the child's responses. In a formal setting a teacher or adult decides to start the specific activity and also decides the direction the activity will take.

In informal settings the activities are open-ended, allowing participants' responses to influence the direction of the activity. Storybook time in a preschool may provide children an opportunity to look at books individually and determine for themselves when they are ready for another book. In a formal reading class in a second-grade room, children may be instructed not to look in their books beyond the page their small group is currently reading aloud.

Language acquisition is also influenced by social routines. Routines may be linguistically patterned or more informal. They are usually culturally based, influenced by family and/or community. In linguistically patterned routines, children are introduced into the routine through adult/teacher direction. Specific responses are expected (no open-endedness), and specific concepts and skills are taught directly. Children participate in a variety of formal or fixed linguistic routines from infancy on. Pat-a-cake or peek-a-boo are two common routines to which infants are often introduced. For older children, formal school-based linguistic routines may include saying the Pledge of Allegiance, taking attendance, greeting someone in the morning, and saying good-bye in the afternoon.

Informal, home-based routines may involve daily or weekly events in which the child may be a "tag along" on a trip to the grocery store or a participant in routines centered on being dressed, bathed, or fed. Informal linguistic routines also involve turn taking within communication loops. Recitational routines that occur in instructional settings are also informal linguistic routines. While the exact speech for these routines is not fixed (as it is in the Pledge of Allegiance), the turn-taking, question-answer interaction pattern is routinized.

Within routines, children experience each of the five aspects of language knowledge: phonemic, semantic, syntactic, morphemic, and pragmatic. However, social routines emphasize pragmatic knowledge: knowledge of knowing how to use language in different settings. Knowing when and how to say "please," "thank you," and "excuse me" is just one type of language-related knowledge learned through social routines. Home social routines that are also part of the larger society allow young children to learn how to interact successfully in community settings.

Sometimes vocabulary is also learned during routines. When her preschool teacher was taking attendance at the beginning of the school year, a little girl, Nicole, arrived late and went to the group circle and sat down. Nicole heard the other children saying "present" when their names were called. When her name was called, Nicole replied, "Well, I'm here, but I don't have a present." Her teacher then explained that "present" also meant she was "here."

Informal settings typically occur at home or in early childhood classrooms for children under the age of 6 years. Formal settings occur predominately in classrooms for children 6 and older. While both informal and formal contexts can enhance language acquisition, the need for both types within early childhood settings has often been overlooked. Both types are important because children will interact in both types of settings throughout their lives. In addition, language is enhanced differently in each setting.

DEVELOPMENTAL APPROPRIATENESS

The concept of developmental appropriateness can be applied as a principle criteria in evaluating the potential effectiveness of various contexts upon children's language acquisition. This concept is based on the recognition that learning activities within specific contexts (home and school) should reflect consideration of children's developmental needs: physical, emotional-social, and cognitive-linguistic.

Role of Teacher

The classroom teacher has a critical role in establishing a learning environment in which the language contexts are developmentally appropriate. Through a teacher's understanding of the importance of verbal interaction and the ways in which it can be enhanced through curriculum planning and implementation, children's language acquisition can be encouraged. A teacher needs to communicate to parents, colleagues, and administrators the specific aspects of the classroom curriculum and environment that will enhance children's language acquisition. When this is done, parents, colleagues, and administrators will have a better appreciation of the ways in which children's educational and developmental needs are being met.

Because they are child-directed and open-ended, informal learning activities may appear to be "just playing" to observers (parents, upper-grade teachers, and administrators) who may not be aware of the value of process-oriented, exploratory activities in providing a basis for conceptual learning and language development.

At the preschool and primary levels, the debate between using informal settings and formal settings has been influenced by national educational concerns about the achievement of elementary and secondary students. The lack of desired levels of educational achievement among elementary and secondary students has resulted in many educators pointing to the preschool and primary years as a time for greater emphasis on learning certain skills or accomplishing specific academic objectives. This attitude appears to be based on the rationale that since students are having difficulty in achieving goals found in elementary and secondary curricula, they must be introduced earlier to academic tasks. As a result, in some preschools and kindergartens, curricula reflect learning objectives and academic activities formerly present in first grade, such as reading subskill worksheets or penmanship practice. Formal, skills-focused instruction is often considered "real learning," while informal, process-focused instruction has been considered to have little value. When formal academic activities become part of the preschool/kindergarten curricula, there is less time for the informal, exploratory type of activities.

Concerns such as these were publicized in the 1980s and resulted in national early childhood organizations developing position papers defining and describing developmentally appropriate practice for infant programs through primary classrooms (Bredekamp, 1987; Bredekamp & Copple, 1997). Language development activities that are developmentally appropriate should be integrated throughout the curriculum and should be exploratory and interactive in nature. Children's individual developmental needs and their individual interests should also be reflected in the curriculum. Hands-on activities that stimulate conceptual development and vocabulary acquisition are important. Opportunities for frequent conversation, both in small groups and one-on-one, should be present throughout the day. Adults in the classroom need to respond promptly and directly to children's efforts to communicate.

SUMMARY

Each theoretical perspective has added to knowledge of the complexity of language acquisition and to an awareness of the wide variety of language stimuli and contexts experienced by young children. The different theoretical perspectives vary in their focus on one or more of the five aspects of language knowledge.

Children acquire language in a variety of settings and contexts. The ways in which language is used in each setting and the linguistic features of the language/dialect used influence children's acquisition of language. Through an understanding of the various interaction patterns and the characteristics of the different settings, teachers will be able to develop and implement language-related, developmentally appropriate activities to enhance children's language acquisition.

✳ ✳ ✳ CHAPTER REVIEW

1. Terms to review:

   universal grammar

   hypothesis testing

   schemata

   language acquisition support system

   zone of proximal development

   developmental level

distancing

symbol formation

vicarious experiences

overextension

underextension

shared reference

strategic scaffolding

2. Distinguish between these theoretical perspectives: behaviorist, nativist, cognitive developmentalist, and interactionist. Name the theorist/researcher associated with each perspective.

3. Describe the zone of proximal development. How does this concept relate to language acquisition?

4. Describe each of the following interaction patterns: adult-to-child speech, verbal mapping, questioning, linguistic scaffolding, and mediation.

5. Give an example of a *communication loop.*

6. Identify five distinguishing characteristics of a formal learning setting.

7. Identify five distinguishing characteristics of an informal learning setting.

8. In what ways might a school setting and a home setting differ with respect to interaction patterns?

❋ ❋ ❋ CHAPTER EXTENSION ACTIVITIES

1. Observe a parent and a child engaged in reading a storybook. Describe their interaction in terms of Vygotsky's zone of proximal development.

2. Observe several activities in a preschool setting. Analyze the ways in which the activities were conducted for the types of language competencies enhanced in the activities.

3. Observe an adult and child involved in an activity. Analyze your observation as to the type of interaction pattern present. Explain whether or not you consider the interaction to be a positive one with respect to language acquisition.

4. Visit a preschool/kindergarten classroom for 40 to 60 minutes. Categorize the activities that occur as representing formal or informal settings. Provide detailed examples to support your conclusions.

5. Audiotape a conversation between a child and an adult. Describe the way in which a communication loop was formed, elaborated, or changed. Include a transcript of the conversation in your written report.

❋ ❋ ❋ REFERENCES

Atkinson, C. (1983). *Making sense of Piaget: The philosophical roots.* London: Routledge & Kegan Paul.

Barton, M., & Tomasello, M. (1994). The rest of the family: the role of fathers and siblings in early language development. In C. Gallaway & B. Richards (Eds.), *Input and interaction in language acquisition* (pp. 109–134). Cambridge, London: Cambridge University Press.

Beed, P., Hawkins, E. M., & Roller, C. (1991). Moving learners toward independence: The power of scaffolded instruction. *The Reading Teacher, 44*(9), 648–662.

Bohannon III, J., & Bonvillian, J. (1997). Theoretical approaches to language acquisition. In J. Gleason (Ed.), *The development of language* (4th ed.). Boston: Allyn and Bacon.

Bowerman, M. (1978). Systematizing semantic knowledge: Changes of time in the child's organization of word meaning. *Child Development, 49,* 977–987.

Brainerd, C. (1978). *Piaget's theory of intelligence.* Upper Saddle River, NJ: Prentice Hall.

Bredekamp, S. (Ed.). (1987). *Developmentally appropriate practice in early childhood programs serving children from birth through age 8.* Washington, DC: National Association for the Education of Young Children.

Bredekamp, S., & Copple, C. (Eds.). (1997). *Developmentally appropriate practice in early childhood programs* (rev. ed.). Washington, DC: National Association for the Education of Young Children.

Bruner, J. (1978). The role of dialogue in language acquisition. In A. Sinclair, R. Jarvella, & W. Levelt (Eds.), *The child's conception of language* (pp. 241–256). New York: Springer-Verlag.

Bruner, J. (1983). *Child's talk: Learning to use language.* Oxford, England: Oxford University Press.

Bruner, J., & Haste, H. (Eds.). (1987). *Making sense: The child's construction of the world.* London: Methuen.

Camarata, S. (1995). A rationale for naturalistic speech intelligibility intervention. In M. Fey, J. Windsor, & S. Warren (Eds.), *Language intervention: Preschool through the elementary years* (pp. 63–84). Baltimore, MD: Paul H. Brookes.

Chomsky, N. (1965). *Aspects of a theory of syntax.* Cambridge, MA: MIT Press.

Chomsky, N. (1975). *Reflections on language.* New York: Pantheon.

Chomsky, N. (1982). *Lectures on government and binding.* New York: Foris.

Clark, E. (1973a). What's in a word? On the child's acquisition of semantics in his first language. In T. More (Ed.), *Cognitive development and the acquisition of language.* New York: Academic Press.

Clark, E. (1973b). Non-linguistic strategies and the acquisition of word meanings. *Cognition, 2*(2), 161–182.

deVilliers, J., & deVilliers, P. (1978). *Language acquisition.* Cambridge, MA: Harvard University Press.

Dixon-Krauss, L. (1996). *Vygotsky in the classroom: Mediated literacy instruction and assessment.* White Plains, NY: Longman.

Elkind, D. (1986). Formal education and early childhood education: An essential difference. *Phi Delta Kappan, 67,* 631–636.

Geekie, P., & Raban, B. (1994). Language learning at home and school. In C. Gallaway & B. Richards (Eds.), *Input and interaction in language acquisition* (pp. 153–189). Cambridge, London: Cambridge University Press.

Harris, J. (1990). *Early language development.* London: Routledge.

Hayes, C., Ornstein, J., & Gage, W. (1987). *The ABCs of languages and linguistics: A basic introduction to language science.* Lincolnwood, IL: National Textbook Company.

Inhelder, B., Sinclair, H., & Bovet, M. (1974). *Learning and the development of cognition* (S. Wedgwood, trans.). Cambridge, MA: Harvard University Press.

John-Steiner, V., Panofsky, C., & Smith, L. (1994). *Sociocultural approaches to language and literacy: An interactionist perspective.* New York: Cambridge University Press.

Lindfors, J. (1987). *Children's language and learning.* (2nd ed.) Upper Saddle River, NJ: Prentice-Hall, Inc.

Mehan, H. (1979). *Learning lessons.* Cambridge, MA: Harvard University Press.

Menyuk, P. (1988). Language development: Knowledge and use. Glenview, IL: Scott Foresman/Little, Brown College Division.

Nelson, K. (1974). Variations in children's concepts by age and category. *Child Development, 45,* 577–584.

Nelson, K. (1977). The syntagmatic-paradigmatic shift revisited: A review of research and theory. *Psychological Bulletin, 84,* 93–116.

Newport, E., Gleitman, H., & Gleitman, L. (1977). Mother, I'd rather do it myself: Some effects and non-effects of maternal speech style. In C. Snow & C. Ferguson (Eds.), *Talking to children: Language input and acquisition* (pp. 109–149). Cambridge, London: Cambridge University Press.

Otto, B. (1991). Developmentally appropriate literacy goals for preschool and kindergarten classrooms. *Early Child Development and Care, 70,* pp. 53–61.

Owens, R. (1988). *Language development* (2nd ed.). Upper Saddle River, NJ: Merrill.

Pease, D., Gleason, J., & Pan, B. (1989). Gaining meaning: Semantic development. In J. Gleason (Ed.), *The development of language* (pp. 101–134). Upper Saddle River, NJ: Merrill.

Piaget, J. (1955). *The language and thought of the child.* New York: World Publishing.

Piaget, J. (1961). The stages of the intellectual development of the child. In K. Paciorek & J. Munro (Eds.), *Notable selections in early childhood education* (pp. 3–10). Guilford, CN: Dushkin/McGraw-Hill.

Piaget, J. (1962). *Play, dreams, and imitation in childhood.* New York: W. W. Norton.

Pine, J. (1994). The language of primary caregivers. In C. Gallaway & B. Richards (Eds.), *Input and interaction in language acquisition* (pp. 15–37). Cambridge, London: Cambridge University Press.

Pinker, S. (1994). *The language instinct: How the mind creates language.* New York: Morrow.

Reich, P. (1986). *Language development.* Upper Saddle River, NJ: Prentice Hall.

Sigel, I., & Cocking, R. (1977). *Cognitive development from childhood to adolescence: A constructivist perspective.* New York: Holt, Rinehart & Winston.

Sinclair-deZwart, H. (1969). Developmental psycholinguistics. In D. Elkind & J. Flavell (Eds.), *Studies in cognitive development: Essays in honor of Jean Piaget.* New York: Oxford University Press.

Skinner, B. (1957). *Verbal behavior.* Upper Saddle River, NJ: Prentice Hall.

Tizard, B. (1981). Language at home and at school. In C. Cazden (Ed.), *Language in early childhood education* (pp. 17–27). Washington, DC: National Association for the Education of Young Children.

Tronick, E., Als, H., & Adamson, L. (1979). Structure of early face-to-face communicative interactions. In M. Bullowa (Ed.), *Before speech: The beginning of interpersonal communication* (pp. 349–372). Cambridge, London: Cambridge University Press.

Vygotsky, L. (1962). *Thought and language* (E. Hanfmann & G. Vakar, Eds. And Trans.). Cambridge, MA: M.I.T. Press.

Vygotsky, L. (1978). *Mind in society: The development of higher mental psychological processes* (M. Cole, V. John-Steiner, S. Scribner, and E. Souberman, Eds.). Cambridge, MA: Harvard University Press.

Wells, G. (1986). *The meaning makers: Children learning language and using language to learn.* Portsmouth, NH: Heinemann.

Werner, H., & Kaplan, B. (1963). *Symbol formation: An organismic-developmental approach to language and the expression of thought.* New York: John Wiley.

Wilkinson, C. (1984). Classroom status from a sociolinguistic perspective. In A. Pellegrini & T. Yawkey (Eds.), *The development of oral and written language in social contexts* (pp. 145–153). Norwood, NJ: Ablex.

3

LANGUAGE DEVELOPMENT AMONG CHILDREN OF LINGUISTIC DIVERSITY

LANGUAGE DIFFERENCES

This chapter focuses on two distinct types of linguistic diversity: differences in dialect and differences in language. Both types of differences impact learning in the classroom and require specific strategies on the part of the teacher. In addressing the needs of children with each type of linguistic diversity, it is important to remember that there is one common goal—success at school and preparation for successful living. An initial step in understanding how to meet the needs of language diverse students is to better understand the concepts and issues involved in both dialect usage and second language acquisition.

The power of language to reflect culture and influence thinking was first proposed by an American linguist and anthropologist Edward Sapir (1884–1939), and his student, Benjamin Whorf (1897–1941). The *Sapir-Whorf hypothesis* stated that the way we think and view the world is determined by our language (Crystal, 1987; Hayes, Ornstein, & Gage, 1987). Instances of cultural language differences can be seen in some languages having specific words for concepts, while other languages use several words to represent a specific concept. For example, the Arabic language includes many specific words for designating a certain type of horse or camel (Crystal, 1987). To make such distinctions in English, where specific words do not exist, adjectives would be used preceding the concept label, such as *work horse* or *race horse.*

Cultural differences have also been noted in the ways in which language is used pragmatically. In our American culture, new skills are typically taught and learned through verbal instruction (Slobin, 1979). In some cultures, new skills are learned through nonverbal observation.

Differences in the social roles of adults and children also influence the use of language. Home and school contexts may represent different cultures and/or subcultures and may influence language acquisition in noticeable ways. In some cultures, prelinguistic children (who are not yet verbalizing) are *spoken about* rather than *spoken to* (Heath, 1983). Children may be expected, and thus taught, to speak only when an adult addresses them. They are not encouraged to initiate conversations with adults or to join spontaneously in ongoing adult conversations. Additionally, in some cultures, children who enthusiastically volunteer answers at school are considered show-offs (Peregoy & Boyle, 1993). In some cultural settings, children are not asked recitational questions. Instead they are only asked questions of clarification or for new information. Thus, when these children experience recitational questions in a school setting, they may be confused as to the purpose of the questioning and the expected response.

During the 1970s and 1980s, educators and linguists researched and debated the "verbal-deficit" perspective. This perspective contended that anyone who did not speak standard English did not have a valid language and thus was verbally deficient. Although the verbal deficit perspective has been proven invalid, it is important to understand the research that was conducted with that perspective in mind. Bernstein (1971), Bereiter & Englemann (1966), and Labov

(1979) were among the researchers who studied language differences between different social groups, including middle- and lower-income groups and ethnic groups. This body of research identified specific differences in the way children from different socioeconomic and ethnic backgrounds used language in school and out-of-school settings.

Basil Bernstein (1971) documented the different linguistic codes used by children from lower- and middle-income families in England. Lower-income children were described as using a "restricted code" or highly contextualized language, while children from middle-income families used an "elaborated code", or decontextualized language. His research also documented differences in school achievement for these two groups of children. Bernstein's work was interpreted to support a "verbal deficit" theory that proposed that the working class environment created a verbal deficiency responsible for subsequent low educational achievement (Winch, 1990).

Here in the United States, Bereiter and Englemann (1966) conducted further research from the verbal-deficit perspective. They focused on the language of preschool African American children in Urbana, Illinois. Bereiter and Engle-man concluded that the language used by African American children was not a valid language and thus recommended that these children needed to be taught English in the school setting (Winch, 1990). Academically oriented preschool curricula were developed (e.g., Blank, Rose, & Berlin, 1978) to provide the needed English language training for verbally deficient children.

William Labov (1979; Winch, 1990) explored social dialects of lower-income, African American children in urban settings. He studied the differences in children's in-school and out-of-school (e.g., playground) language competencies. His data directly challenged the verbal-deficit theory, documenting the elaborated and systematic linguistic properties of nonstandard English, such as Black English. His research supported the idea that Black English was a separate system with its own grammar and rules. He described dialects as having "slightly different versions of the same rules, extending and modifying the grammatical processes which are common to all dialects of English" (Labov, 1995, p. 54). Labov's research supported the idea that verbal differences are not verbal deficits. Because Labov's research focused on language used in academic and nonschool settings, he also created a greater awareness of the role of context and dialect in communication.

Tough (1977) conducted a longitudinal study of children from advantaged (college-educated, professional parents) and disadvantaged (parents who were in unskilled or semiskilled occupations) homes. The study began when the children were 3 years old, with follow-up at 51/2 and 71/2 years. At age 3, the disadvantaged children and the advantaged children showed significant differences in the ways they used language. Specifically, the disadvantaged children did not use language to recall and give details of prior experiences, anticipate upcoming events and possible outcomes, reason about current and remembered events, problem solve using language for planning and considering alternatives, reaching solutions, creating and sustaining dramatic play events, and understanding other's experiences and feelings. When these children were studied again at 5 1/2 and 7 1/2 years, the disadvantaged children produced shorter, less complex responses. This research contributed to our understanding that children from different cultural environments may be learning to use language differently and may experience difficulty in participating in the language environment in classrooms.

Further awareness of the role of cultural environments in the acquisition of language was influenced in the 1980s by ethnographic research techniques that were used by language researchers. Ethnography uses participant observation in real-life settings and focuses on individuals within their social and cultural contexts. Ethnographic studies, such as Heath's (1983), have contributed significantly to our understanding of linguistic diversity. Heath studied children's acquisition of language at home and school in two communities in the southeastern United States and found differences in communication in working-class black and white families as well as among middle-class townspeople of both ethnic groups.

Heath found the story structures, language, and sense of "truth" (fiction v. non-fiction) that children learned at home were different from those expected at school. To be successful at school, these children had to be able "to recognize when a story is expected to be true, when to stick to the facts, and when to use their imaginations" (Heath, 1983, p. 294).

Heath's research also documented valid and authentic differences in the ways language is used and in the ways in which children in those respective communities become competent language users. Heath concluded that the contrasts she found in language were not based on race, but on complex cultural influences in each community.

The importance of family context in language acquisition was more recently described by Hart & Risley (1995, 1999). Findings from their longitudinal study document the significance of "talkativeness" in families in influencing language acquisition rather than the family's socioeconomic status or ethnic group identity. Thus, differences in language use developed as a result of the family culture—and not simply due to socioeconomic status or ethnic group identity.

A more current hypothesis on why second language learners experience difficulty in school is the **socialization mismatch hypothesis.** This hypothesis "predicts that children are more likely to succeed in school when the home language and literacy socialization patterns are similar to those that are used and valued in school" (Faltis, 1998, p. 23). This hypothesis applies to children who are learning a second language and children who speak a non-standard English dialect. Home language socialization patterns may differ from those favored in the school classroom in the following ways (Faltis, 1998):

(1) the amount of talk directed to preschool children

(2) the participation of young children as conversation partners with adults

(3) opportunities children have to explain or give a personal interpretation of events

(4) the types of questions teachers ask of children during storybook sharing; and

(5) the forms of narrative which are used (e.g. fiction, nonfiction, or ongoing narratives).

In addition, the social interaction patterns used in the classroom may vary from the home culture's with respect to expectations for competitive versus collaborative or cooperative activities.

The following section will address dialect diversity and related issues. Subsequently, issues in second language acquisition and bilingual education will be discussed. This will be followed by implications for classroom instruction that concern both dialect and second language students.

DIALECT DIVERSITY

Some language differences represent diverse **dialects.** Cultural and social differences and geographic locality influence the development of a dialect. Dialects develop in settings where a group of people communicate within their group more frequently and for a longer period of time than they do with outside groups. As a result of this geographic or social isolation, a specialized form of language develops that is unique to that context or cultural setting. For example, adolescent peer groups often develop their own dialect.

All dialects and languages are characterized by distinctly different systematic features with respect to the five aspects of language knowledge: phonemic, semantic, syntactic, morphemic, and pragmatic. According to Labov (1995), nonstandard English dialects "show slightly different versions of the same rules [as standard English], extending and modifying the grammatical processes which are common to all dialects of English" (p. 54). A dialect is usually represented only in oral language, whereas many languages have both oral and written expression. In the United States, regional dialects and social dialects are present. People speaking a southern dialect are distinguishable from people speaking a Bostonian or New York dialect; however, people speaking different dialects of the same language generally can comprehend each other's speech. Even though a region or a cultural group may be characterized by a commonly used dialect, it is inappropriate to automatically assume that any speaker of that region or that cultural group will use that dialect. There are considerable variations among geographic regions and cultural groups with respect to dialect use.

In some areas of the United States, regional dialects have linguistic aspects that came from *pidgin languages.* A **pidgin** is a language that developed in response to the interaction of two groups of people who did not initially share a language (Crystal, 1987). Typically pidgin languages have a small vocabulary, simple grammatical structure, and a narrower range of functions than the languages from which the pidgin was developed. Pidgin language use decreases and may even disappear when one group learns the language of the other or if the original reason for communicating, such as trading or selling goods, has ceased. In some situations, the pidgin develops into a **creole** language. This occurs when a pidgin language has been used across two generations so that the children of the initial speakers of the pidgin learn or acquire the new language as their "mother tongue." As use of this language becomes more widespread and stabilized, it becomes a creolized language. When a pidgin is creolized, linguistic features of the language are expanded, especially with respect to grammar/syntax, vocabulary/semantics, and function/style/pragmatics. Some examples of pidgins and creoles in the United States are listed in Figure 3.1.

Although some pidgins/creoles are no longer used as a language, certain vocabulary and characteristic accents or pronunciations may have been incorporated into English and are still in use today. Teachers should be aware of the pidgins or creoles historically used in their communities since the current dialect of English in use may have words, accents, or other linguistic features from those earlier languages.

Dialects of the same language typically use the same written language system. Dialects of the same language base are generally understandable by all speakers of the base language; however, communication between speakers of different dialects may be more effortful since the dialects may differ in one or more of the aspects of language, including semantics, syntax, morphology, pragmatics, or phonetics.

Phonetic differences are heard in the way words are articulated. For example, the word *creek* may be pronounced with the long *e* sound (as in *beet*) or with the short *i* sound (as in *pick*) as *"crick."* Semantic differences occur when different labels are used to refer to the same object or action. In some locales, a drinking fountain is referred to as a *bubbler.* Syntactic differences involve differences in the way sentences are structured. For example, "I don't got no time to help" and "I have no time to help" reflect syntactic differences. Morphemic differences are found in the way verb endings or other inflectional endings are used, such as *gonna* or *goin'* compared with *going to* and *going.*

When people are communicating in different dialects, these differences may result in communicative efforts that require more negotiation or clarification.

Standard American English (SAE) is a dialect in itself (Durkin, 1995). It is the dialect most widely used across the United States and is the dialect commonly used in the workplace and in educational settings. It is "standard" for our current time and place in history. Throughout history, one variety of language has typically been used to communicate more broadly within any given culture (Gadda, 1995). This is not surprising since language plays a significant role in the development and advancement of any culture.

Educational activities involve specific types of communication and interaction. To be successful in academic settings, children must learn how to communicate effectively in those settings with respect to which language is used and how it is used. They must learn the language of school, or academic register. The term *register* refers to all "linguistically-distinct activities" (Crystal, 1987, p. 52). This does not mean that children must unlearn their home language or dialect;

FIGURE 3.1
Examples of Pidgins and Creoles in the United States

Pidgin/creole	Locality	Language base	Time/era	Initial purpose
Hawaiian Pidgin/ Creole	Hawaii	English-based with Chinese, Japanese, Hawaiian, Portuguese, and Philippine	Still in use	Trading and early settlements
Chinook Jargon	Alaska	Chinook-based with English, French, Nootka, and Salishan dialects	Late 19th century, now nearly extinct	Trading
Pidgin Eskimo	Alaska	Eskimo-based	Early 1900s, still in use	Trading
Pachuco (Pochismo)	Arizona and southern California	Spanish-English	1800–1900s, decreasing	Spanish-English contact
Trader Navaho	Southwest United States	Navaho-based	1900s	Used by traders to Navahos; but not reciprocal use
New Jersey Amerindian	New Jersey settlement area	Combination of Indian dialects with English-like grammar	Precolonial times; now extinct	English and Dutch traders and New Jersey Indians
Gullah	Coastal area from Florida to South Carolina	English-based creole spoken by African-Americans	Still in use	General communication

Source: Hancock, I. (1971). A survey of the pidgins and creoles of the world. In D. Hymes (Ed.), *Pidginization and creolization of languages* Cambridge University Press. New York: (pp. 509–512). Reprinted with the permission of Cambridge University Press.

instead it means they must develop linguistic flexibility and acquire the register of academic language used in school settings.

Academic Register

Academic register refers to the decontextualized language that is used in educational settings. This concept has also been labeled "literate register" (Cox, 1994; Cox & Dixey, 1994; Cox, Fang, & Otto, 1997). Academic register involves not only semantic, morphemic, and syntactic features, but also includes pragmatic features as well. Wong-Fillmore (1999) characterizes academic English as having a more technical, precise vocabulary; specific "grammatical constructions and devices, rhetorical conventions, and discourse markers" (p. 15). The complexity of academic register and its decontextualized nature is evident in the types of learning activities present in educational settings (Grant, 1995). Chamot & O'Malley (1995) identified three types of learning strategies that involve specific language competencies, or academic register:

1. Cognitive strategies—using language to interact with written and hands-on materials, using a range of cognitive processes, such as summarizing, deduction/induction, transfer, and inference.

2. Metacognitive strategies—using language to plan, monitor, and evaluate one's own learning.

3. Social-affective strategies—using language to interact with others (peers or teachers) in the learning process, such as asking questions for clarification or working collaboratively.

The emphasis placed here on the academic register is not meant to imply that all of the language used in the classroom is academic register. Indeed, in many classrooms, informal conversations and regional or cultural dialects are used in varying degrees; however, the main focus, particularly at the higher grade levels, will be on the academic register. This specific way of using language for cognitive and metacognitive learning strategies is critical for school success. Academic register is also the language used in educational materials and texts. As grade levels increase, so does text-based instruction; thus, it becomes critical that children can effectively use the academic register in both oral and written language.

"Literate register or discourse" has also been identified as the "language of power" since it is used in many corporate and governmental environments (Delpit 1988, 1992). For our nation's students to be successful as adults, many educators and community leaders contend, the school's job is to be sure all students can use standard English in written and oral communication. **Standard American English's** literate/academic register is necessary for all children regardless of the dialect they use. Children who use a regional dialect or a cultural dialect like Black English need to acquire Standard American English/literate register to maximize their educational opportunities.

Differences in achievement in our schools may not only reflect differences in academic potential but complex differences in children's familiarity with the language of instruction, the academic register, as well. Rather than judging children whose primary language is not standard English as being unintelligent or of low potential, teachers must recognize the nature of children's linguistic confusions and provide an environment where they can develop flexibility and competency in using a variety of dialects and languages in various settings. Children who acquire receptive and productive knowledge of the academic register will be better able to participate in the learning opportunities offered in schools and other educational institutions.

Acquisition of the academic register, like the acquisition of any other language or dialect, is based upon a child's first language or dialect. The main obstacle young children face appears to be a general lack of understanding from the educational community of the authenticity of all languages and dialects and the role of one's home language/dialect as a base from which knowledge of other languages and dialects is assimilated and accommodated (Cummins, 1995; Luke & Kale, 1997; Tough, 1985). Language differences are a disadvantage only when the school/classroom environment assumes or recognizes only standard English as *the* real, authentic language (Gray, 1984, cited in Luke & Kale, 1997). Children whose home environments do not use standard English may be confused and even alienated by classroom settings that expect fluency in the academic register of standard English, but do not provide explicit, guided opportunities and supporting materials to develop knowledge of that register.

Teacher's Role in Encouraging Acquisition of Academic Register

Classroom teachers play a critical role in encouraging students to acquire the academic register (Wong-Fillmore, 1999). Throughout the early childhood years, developmentally appropriate language activities can gradually foster children's awareness of the academic register. As language is used to accompany learning activities, initially through hands-on activities and increasingly through use of written materials with decontextualized language, children begin to acquire academic register. It is crucial that classroom teachers encourage children to begin to examine their own uses of language for different purposes and in different settings. Children who speak a dialect need to be encouraged to become aware of the ways in which they use their own dialect and the linguistic features of that dialect. This awareness will provide a base upon which knowledge of the academic register of standard English can be acquired.

In encouraging children to become more familiar with academic English, Wong-Fillmore (1999) advocates a continuous focus on "how language is being used and how it works" as well as providing opportunities for students to "use the language (oral and written) in more and more sophisticated ways in instructional activities" (p. 17). Fillmore cautions that although academic English is learned in the classroom, it will not be learned unless there are specific opportunities for students to focus on the features of academic English.

In the section that follows, some of the characteristics of African American English/Black English are described. This description is included as an example of the richness and linguistic complexity of a dialect used by many Americans.

African American English Dialect

African American English (AAE) is a dialect used by a significant number of people of African American descent. Varieties of AAE reflect urban and rural locales and regional dialects. The concern with dialect diversity in the classroom focuses on the role of dialect in influencing the educational opportunities and achievements of dialect speakers. As indicated earlier in the chapter, the work of Labov and his colleagues (1979) contributed to a more accurate understanding of African American English as a linguistically complete, authentic dialect. For any language or dialect to endure, it must be functionally complete to support the communication needs of the community using it. African American English has endured in various areas of the United States for many decades. Its existence is evidence that it has served and continues to serve communicative needs. Examples of some of the syntactic features of AAE contrasted to Standard American English are listed in Figure 3.2.

African American English also has characteristic modes of discourse or verbal interaction. Smitherman (1995) describes five distinctive modes of discourse found among AAE speakers (see Figure 3.3).

FIGURE 3.2
Examples of Syntactic Contrasts Between Standard American English and African American English

Standard American English		**African American English**	
Possessive -'s	Get Uncle's coat	Not required if word position indicates possession	Get Uncle coat.
Plural -s	She has ten dollars.	Not required with adjective indicating number	She get ten dollar.
Irregular past tense	This afternoon she came home.	Verb uninflected	This afternoon she come home.
Regular past tense	Yesterday I walked to town.	Not needed	Yesterday I walk to town.
Pronouns	Momma is sad.	Pronoun follows noun in apposition	Momma she sad.
Negation	I don't have anything.	Triple negation and use of *ain't* for don't, haven't, hasn't, isn't, and didn't	I ain't got nothing.

From Owens, R.E., Jr., (2001). *Language Development* (5th ed.), p. 419. Copyright © by Allyn & Bacon. Adapted with permission.

FIGURE 3.3
Examples of Discourse Modes in Black English

Discourse Mode	Characteristic(s)	Examples
Call-Response	Verbal or nonverbal interaction between a speaker and a listener; contingent upon speaker's speech segments	Example responses to speaker's "calls": *Verbal:* Amen! Tell it! Yessuh! Rap on! *Nonverbal:* rolling eyes, clapping hands, shaking head
Signification	Verbal art of insult; also known as dropping lugs, joanin, capping, sounding	In addressing his congregation, Reben Nap said, "everybody talking bout Heaven ain goin there."
"The Dozens"	Set of responses in verse	Insult focuses on a person's relatives; typically person's mother as in 'yo mamma . . .'
Tonal Semantics	Voice rhythm and vocal inflection are used to convey meaning, including the use of repetition and alliterative word play	Rhythmic pattern to speech illustrated in speeches by Martin Luther King Jr., and Jesse Jackson
Narrative Sequencing	Forms: folktale, trickster tale, "toast." All forms involve an abstract point or general message within a concrete story; events are not objectively reported but are dramatized through voicing the facts along with the teller's personal emotional and social perspective on the facts.	"Brer Rabbit"—underdog animals who succeed in outsmarting their much larger enemies

Adaptation from *Language Issues: Readings for Teachers*, pgs. 316–327 by Diane Bennett Durkin. Copyright © 1995 by Longman Publishers USA. Reprinted by permission of Addison-Wesley Educational Publishers, Inc.

These modes of discourse are part of African American English's pragmatic knowledge of how language is used differently in different situations. In each of these modes, the speaker is encouraged to use language creatively, symbolically, and figuratively while observing the established formulaic structure. These discourse structures are not found in Standard American English or in other English dialects. By recognizing and including these creative discourse structures in classroom activities, linguistic diversity is encouraged and validated. It can also provide a basis for examining other types of discourse structures.

Controversy regarding African American English has occurred in settings where assumptions have been made that AAE is an obstacle to learning. In a court case in 1978, *Martin Luther King Junior Elementary School Children* v. *Ann Arbor School District Board,* parents charged that their children were being denied equal educational opportunities because the school was not helping their children to overcome the language barrier, since the children spoke Black English (Scott, 1995). The court decision required the school district to help teachers to acknowledge the home BE language and to incorporate this awareness and knowledge into reading instruction.

Responses to the court's decision have included providing in-service training for teachers in Black English, directly teaching Standard American English, and teaching only Black English. However, the decision acknowledged that students' use of Black English in school settings often elicited negative attitudes from teachers. From these teachers' attitudes further negative assumptions developed into low achievement expectations for BE speakers, which then became a self-fulfilling prophecy (Scott, 1995).

Recognition of Black English as a separate but authentic dialect of English is important in understanding the language background of many African American children. This understanding is critical for teachers in the development and implementation of curricula that will provide children with optimal learning opportunities. It is also important for teachers and parents to acknowledge the importance for children to develop the linguistic flexibility to be able to comprehend and use the academic register of Standard American English. Children who are more linguistically flexible will be able to communicate effectively in a wide variety of settings and interactions.

LANGUAGE DIVERSITY AND SECOND LANGUAGE ACQUISITION

During the last two decades, concern has increased in the United States over the educational needs of young children from non-English speaking families. The challenge for educators is twofold: provide opportunities for students to learn the necessary knowledge and skills and provide opportunities for children to develop language competencies that will enhance and facilitate their opportunities to learn. Since the predominant language used in American schools is English, it is critical that nonnative speakers of English have opportunities to develop English competencies in both oral communication and the academic register.

The way in which nonnative speakers are encouraged to learn English is also an issue of controversy. Should separate programs be established apart from the regular classroom curricula? Should second language learners (L2) be submersed in regular classrooms? What considerations should be given to the child's first language? What role does the child's first language (L1) fluency have in acquisition of the second language?

Bilingualism may be acquired simultaneously if children acquire two languages prior to age three (Baker, 1996; Goodz, 1994). This type of bilingualism is usually centered in linguistic experiences in homes where parents speak two (or more) languages. **Successive bilingualism** refers to instances when children acquire their second language after age three.

In the past, bilingualism was thought to be an educational handicap, especially prior to 1960. It was believed that children could not learn a second language while still using their first language. Thus, children were strongly discouraged from speaking their first language and in many instances were made to feel ashamed of speaking a language different than English (Cummins, 1995). For some children, learning a second language also meant that they would lose the ability to speak their first language (Evans, 1994; Wong-Fillmore, 1991). This phenomena has been termed *subtractive bilingualism* since the result of acquiring a second language results in the loss of the child's first language. This result may have a negative impact on families as communication is disrupted. Transmission of cultural beliefs and parenting interactions require a shared language.

Prior to the late 1970s, bilingual children's academic failures were considered to be due to their bilingualism. Since that time, research has increased our understanding of the factors involved in second language acquisition, ways in which second language acquisition can be facilitated and enhanced, and ways in which the first language can be maintained. According to Wong-Fillmore's (1991) research,

> "the timing and the conditions under which they [children] come into contact with English, however, can profoundly affect the retention and continued use of their primary languages as well as the development of their second language." (p. 323)

We are also now more aware of the benefits of bilingualism. Children who have acquired a level of fluency in both languages have been reported to have higher levels of metalinguistic awareness, greater and earlier awareness of language structure, wider perspectives, and more social skills (Ben Zeev, 1977; Genesee, Tucker, & Lambert, 1975; Goodz, Legare, & Bilodeau, 1987; Ianco-Worrall, 1972). The acquisition of fluency in more than one language is accompanied by a greater awareness of the linguistic features of languages and the cultural ways in which the respective languages are used in various interactions. This body of recent research supports the conclusion that children acquire language knowledge not only at the linguistic level, but at the metalinguistic knowledge level and level of metalinguistic knowledge verbalization as well.

Becoming Bilingual

Students who have a first language (L1) other than English are faced with the challenge of learning a new language distinctly different from their native or first language. The syntactic, semantic, morphemic, phonetic, and pragmatic aspects of different languages may be significantly distinct. Languages from the same "language family" have similar characteristics and features, whereas languages from different language families will be dissimilar (Crystal, 1987). For example, Spanish and French are both in the Indo-European (Romance) language family and have some similarities, such as the use of an alphabetic writing system and similar cognates/word stems. In contrast, Spanish and Chinese belong to different language families and are distinctly different in not only the writing system used, but in other aspects of language as well, including syntactic, semantic, pragmatic, and morphemic. The ways in which aspects of language knowledge are similar or distinctly different between the two languages influences second language acquisition. Children who are attempting to learn a language from a different language family will find it more difficult than if they were attempting to learn another language from the same language family. The processes of assimilation and accommodation are part of second language acquisition. As the second language is learned, children build upon their knowledge of language by making connections and comparisons between the home language and the target language. Target languages distinctly different from the home language will require more effort to learn. The following example of the assimilation and accommodation required of Spanish-fluent children learning English illustrates the complexity involved in second language acquisition.

Distinctions Necessary Between Spanish and English

Spanish-fluent children who are learning to read English are faced with the task of distinguishing between the two systems of sound-symbol correspondences. In Spanish, the correspondence between the symbol and the sound it represents is regular (see Figure 3.4). English entails no such regularity. In fact, some vowel symbols and their corresponding sounds are distinctly different.

It is important to note that not only are English vowels more varied or irregular in the ways in which they are pronounced, but specific sounds associated with some English vowel symbols are in direct contrast to the Spanish pronunciation. For example, Spanish letter *i* has the sound of the English long *e,* and the Spanish letter *e* has the sound midway between the *e* in *let* and the *a* in *late.*

Spanish-fluent children also must learn that English differs syntactically from Spanish. For example, in Spanish, the descriptive adjective is usually placed after the noun it modifies—as in mesa redonda = table round—whereas in English the adjective is placed before the noun. The second language learner needs to be aware of this difference when speaking, reading, and writing English. The Spanish language also uses specific endings and spelling changes to indicate not only verb tense but also the subject (*I, you, he, we, you*-plural, *they*) associated with the verb in that particular sentence. This difference, too, must be considered by the second language learner when using English since English morphology has a different system for indicating subject-verb agreement and verb tense.

Second language learners' efforts in distinguishing between the relevant language knowledge in two different systems is sometimes evident in their use of English in composing oral stories (Otto, 1987). Preschool children who are in the process of acquiring English language knowledge and distinguishing that knowledge from their first or home language may produce stories that are less fluent

FIGURE 3.4
Pronunciation of Spanish Vowels *(Las vocales)*

In Spanish the vowels have a consistent pronunciation. There are only slight variations depending upon the vowel's location in the phrase or word. Vowel pronunciation remains the same whether the vowel is stressed or unstressed.

Letter-Vowel	Example English words having the same sound as the vowel as pronounced in Spanish words	Example words in Spanish
A	a in *ha-ha* o in *pop*	*papa, mama, casa, alma, mapa*
E	the sound is midway between the e in *let* and a in *late*	*pelo, tela, mesa, pena, lengua*
I	ee in *see*	*si, dia, mina, piso, sino, mismo*
Y	if Y is used alone or as a final letter in a word, its pronunciation is like I in Spanish, though said more quickly	*y* (means *and*) *ay, ley, muy*
O	o in *go*	*gitano, como, loco, sombrero, hombre*
U	u in *fluid*	*cuyo, luna, laguna, nunca*

Adapted with permission from Da Silva, W. (1987). *Beginning Spanish: A Concept Approach* (6th ed.) New York: Harper & Row, pp. 4–5.

and/or less cohesive. As a result, their stories might be judged as indicative of lower academic ability and language competency, when in fact a complex process of distinction between the various aspects of each language is occurring.

In many respects, second language acquisition in successive bilingualism resembles first language acquisition. Language is acquired through active hypothesizing of rules, analyzing rules, making errors, and revising the rules. The early stages of language acquisition are similar for first and second language learners, with one-word utterances appearing initially, followed by two-word utterances and then multiword utterances (Genesee & Nicoladis, 1995). The rate of acquisition of vocabulary (semantic knowledge) of L2 learners is somewhat slower only during the preschool years (Bialystok, 1988; Genesee & Nicoladis, 1995).

Bilingual children are challenged to acquire two languages, which requires that they differentiate between the two languages with respect to the five aspects of language knowledge for both oral and written forms of each language. Some researchers have documented what they call *language interference,* when children appear to confuse knowledge of one of the aspects of L1 language with L2 language. For example, a child might use the vocabulary or syntactic structure of one language when attempting to communicate in the other language. Other researchers have questioned the existence of language interference, citing evidence that bilingual children appear to be able to distinguish between two language systems early on (De Houwer, 1990; Goodz, 1994; Lanza, 1992; Meisel, 1994). Instances where children appear to be mixing the two languages (also known as "code mixing" or language mixing) may simply reflect their parents' use of two languages. It may also reflect attempts to maintain a conversation when knowledge of the second language is not sufficient to express the desired message (Baker, 1996; Goodz, 1994; Krashen, 1995). For example, if a child is attempting to communicate that she wants a drink of water in English, and she does not recall the word "water" she may instead say, "Mommy, *aqua* please," inserting a Spanish word in an English phrase to get her message across. Codeswitching is thought to be influenced by social or psychological factors, such as a desire to add emphasis or to show ethnic unity (Lessow-Hurley, 2000). In some instances, isolated words of a language are "borrowed" and inserted into the communication by second language learners. This typically occurs when a concept label is not available in the language being used (e.g., proper noun or new terminology, such as that referring to technology) (Baker, 1996; Bhatia & Ritchie, 1996; Lessow-Hurley, 2000).

Factors Influencing Second Language Acquisition

Three major factors have a significant influence on second language acquisition: learner characteristics, linguistic input, and social setting. These factors are complex and interdependent.

Learner characteristics. Age is a significant factor in second language acquisition. Children learn languages easier than adults. Before the age of five, children's acquisition of an additional language resembles the first language acquisition in both process and proficiency (Bialystok & Hakuta, 1994, cited in Lessow-Hurley, 2000). Not only do children learn language with more ease than adults, they also acquire productive phonetic knowledge at a level of near native pronounciation, whereas adults who are second language learners are likely to speak with an accent (Lessow-Hurley, 2000; Schacter, 1996). Virginia Collier's work (1987, cited in Lessow-Hurley, 2000) focused on the acquisition of second language proficiency for academic settings and concluded that children from ages 8–12 learn a second language quicker than children 4–7 years old. Possible factors responsible for this difference include the older children's higher cognitive functioning (Baker, 1996) and their more developed first language, both of which facilitate second language acquisition.

After age 12, the rate of acquisition slows down. With adults, their acquisition of a second language is also influenced by the ways in which the second language is similar to or different from their first language (Schacter, 1996). For example, it would be easier for an English-speaking adult to learn German than to learn Russian, due to the greater similarity between German and English. The more similar the two languages are with respect to the five aspects of language knowledge, the easier an adult will learn the second language.

Additional individual learner variables that affect second language acquisition include learners' cognitive abilities, personality, motivation, self-confidence, and home language competencies (Cummins, 1994; Tabors, 1997). A learner's

Children learn additional languages easier than do adults.

cognitive abilities influence how language input will be processed. Personality, motivation, and level of self-confidence determine the ways in which the learner will engage in language interactions. A shy child who lacks self-confidence will be less active in a language interaction than will an outgoing, confident child.

A child's first language serves as a foundation upon which the second language is acquired (Cummins, 1979). Without this threshold of first language competencies, second language acquisition is difficult. As described in Chapter 1, children first acquire a receptive knowledge of oral language; in other words, comprehension of oral language through listening and observing, followed by expressive knowledge which enables them to use language to communicate. Second language learners typically have a "silent" period (Krashen 1981, 1982, 1995; Tabors, 1997) during which time they appear to be working on acquiring receptive language knowledge. This can be seen among six- and seven-year-old second language learners who do not speak spontaneously for several months, except for memorized phrases or sentences (Krashen, 1995).

Optimally, the acquisition of a second language will follow the same sequence as the first language with receptive and expressive knowledge of the oral language developing first, followed by knowledge of the written language; however, learning difficulties may occur in classrooms where the curriculum expectations do not acknowledge the need to first acquire target language oral competency before instruction in target written language. A child who is orally fluent in his first language, but not orally fluent in his second language (English) will have more difficulty learning to read in English than will a child who is orally fluent in both languages. Similarly, a child who can comprehend and read written academic language in his first language will learn to read academic language more successfully in the second language than will a child who cannot read in his first language (Cummins, 1994). Thus, a linguistic interdependence exists between first and second language acquisition.

Linguistic input. The quality and quantity of exposure to the target language is also a significant variable in second language acquisition. Exposure to a second language is not sufficient for acquisition. The language input must be comprehensible to the learner. Comprehensible input is a critical factor in second language acquisition (Cummins, 1994; Krashen, 1995). Comprehensible input occurs when the target language is used at a level that is just beyond the learner's current level (Krashen, 1995). Whether or not the linguistic input is comprehensible is a result of the interaction between the amount and quality of the target language received by the second language learner and the learner's individual attributes, such as age, cognitive abilities, home language competencies, personality, motivation, and self-confidence (Cummins, 1994).

Social setting. The social setting where interaction occurs with speakers of the target language is also an important factor in second language acquisition (Hatch, Peck, & Wagner-Gough, 1995; Krashen, 1995). This social setting can be described in terms of three sets of variables. These variables include the second language learner's role in the setting as a listener or active participant, the presence of concrete referents which contributes to symbol formation and conceptual development, and the person who is modeling the target language. Through the interaction of these three sets of variables children acquire proficiency in a second language. Thus, in situations where there is a focus on text-based instruction, lack of linguistic awareness by the teacher, lack of experiential learning, and a more complex level of English fluency and academic register, second language learners are not able to receive the comprehensible input needed for language learning.

In the following sections specific contexts and language programs for second language acquisition will be described. Each of these settings varies in the way learner characteristics, language input, and social interactions are recognized and integrated.

Bilingualism at Home

Children who are exposed to two languages at home acquire both languages as "first languages" (Piper, 1998). In some homes, each parent speaks a different language with the child; in other homes, the parents use one language with the child while grandparents or other caregivers use the second language. Still in other homes, both parents speak both languages to the child, mixing the two languages. It appears that children acquire bilingualism with less confusion when the languages are kept separate by the parent or caregiver who speaks them (Piper, 1998).

Bilingualism at School

When second language learners are enrolled in school, decisions are made regarding their English language proficiency and the appropriate classroom placement at the end of each academic year. These placement decisions are critical to each child's success at school; however, the ways in which these decisions are made are complex and sometimes controversial. In many schools, English language proficiency is determined by a simple assessment of a child's oral English language fluency. These language proficiency tests may measure only a small amount of the language competencies involved in academic settings (Chamot & O'Malley, 1995).

Cummins (1994) has identified two aspects of language proficiency for second language learners: conversational and academic. Conversational proficiency enables children to engage in social conversations effectively. Academic proficiency involves higher cognitive demands and is related to conceptual and academic development, or academic register. The differentiation of these two types of proficiency acknowledges that oral fluency in English is not a valid index of overall language proficiency. Academic proficiency in English enables children to engage in academic tasks where they must rely on linguistic cues to develop meaning. In contrast, in everyday conversations, the language is embedded in a context that provides support for developing the meaning of the communication. In Cummins' (1994) review of research, he concludes that ESL learners need two years to acquire age-appropriate conversational proficiency, while five to seven years are needed to acquire academic proficiency. Thus, it is important for second language learners to receive language program support for several years after they have achieved conversational fluency in English.

PROGRAMS FOR SECOND LANGUAGE LEARNERS

Language acquisition refers to unconscious learning of language in naturalistic settings with a focus on meaning; in contrast, **language learning** refers to conscious rule learning in formal instructional settings with an emphasis on the form of language (Krashen, 1995). Specific programs for bilingual children can embody characteristics of language acquisition or language learning. Research on such programs indicates that those incorporating more naturalistic features of language acquisition settings are more successful than those focusing on language learning (Altwerger & Ivener, 1994; Krashen, 1995; Wong-Fillmore, 1995).

American schools' responses to the challenge of educating nonnative speakers have taken several different approaches. These approaches reflect the social values placed on the native language and English and also reflect an expectation of the value of those respective languages to the students' futures. The major educational approaches to linguistically diverse students include bilingual education, English as a second language (ESL), submersion, immersion, and dual language. These approaches focus on students' acquisition of English to enhance and facilitate their success in educational settings.

Research on past programs has documented the critical impact of such programs on family culture and communication. When young L2 students focus only on learning English and have little opportunity to use their native language, and when little value is placed on their first language in the larger culture, they lose their ability to speak their first language. In such settings, tragic disruptions of family relations have been reported (Wong-Fillmore, 1991). When children can no longer communicate with their parents or extended families in their first language, social relationships break down.

Bilingual Education

In bilingual approaches, acquisition of both the first language and the second language is emphasized, though in differing degrees. A *transitional bilingual approach* has as its goal the gradual transition from the student's first language to English. This approach is used in self-contained classrooms where children are taught by a teacher who is fluent in both languages. Initially, content area instruction is in the child's first language. English is taught as a separate subject. Then, English is gradually introduced and used during instruction. Over a period of two to three years, the amount of English used in classroom instruction increases.

The bilingual transitional approach recognizes the need to begin instruction in the language in which children are fluent. The first language is not considered valuable to the children's long-term education; only English is valued. This approach does not consider the value of children's first language to their family culture or to the larger society's culture.

Maintenance bilingual education is similar to transitional bilingual education in that both languages are also used in instruction; however, the similarities end at that point. Maintenance bilingual education emphasizes both languages throughout children's education, so that fluency in both the first language and English are developed and maintained. This type of instruction also occurs in self-contained classrooms where the teacher is fluent in both languages and where all of the students have the same first language. This approach acknowledges and emphasizes the value and need for fluency and competency in using both the first language and English. Children who experience this approach to bilingual education develop *authentic bilingualism.* They are equally able to use both languages for purposes of learning and in their social environments.

To implement bilingual education programs successfully, schools must have a large enough number of students who speak the same first language and are at the same educational level, and they must employ professionally trained teachers who are fluent in both the first language and English. Some states, including Illinois and California, mandate bilingual programs for schools with 20 or more students who speak the same first language. Financial considerations often arise in schools with small numbers of students at different educational levels, which re-quires bilingual programs involving only five or six students at each level. This dramatically increases the cost of implementing a bilingual program.

English as a Second Language (ESL)

ESL programs focus only on teaching English. Students' first languages are not a consideration, nor are their languages used in any aspect of classroom instruction. Teachers in ESL programs may not have any knowledge of, or fluency in, students' respective first languages. The goal of this approach is to foster the acquisition of English so that students can participate in English-only instruction. In most schools, ESL programs involve intensive English instruction for part of the day and placement in regular classrooms for the rest of the day. Gradually students transition to English-only classrooms, while still receiving assistance from an ESL resource room in a pull-out program schedule. A "push-in" support program may also be used (J. Villegas, personal communication, October 9, 2000). This involves the ESL instructor working in the regular classroom along with the classroom teacher in meeting the needs of the language diverse students. When successful, students are phased out of ESL assistance and are able to participate in English-only classrooms on a full-time basis. One of the main challenges posed by the ESL approach is to develop and implement instructional strategies and techniques that foster English acquisition among students from diverse linguistic backgrounds. In some urban areas, ESL classrooms are composed of students coming from a wide range of linguistic diversity: Spanish, Russian, Polish, Greek, Chinese, French-Vietnamese, and Arabic. Specially trained ESL instructors are critical to the success of these classrooms. ESL programs are usually found in schools where there is a wide linguistic diversity without sufficient numbers of students to mandate bilingual education programs.

The Cognitive Academic Language Learning Approach (CALLA)

CALLA is designed for ESL students and focuses on developing academic language skills in English (Chamot & O'Malley, 1995). It is most appropriate for upper elementary and secondary students. The theoretical perspective of this approach recognizes the cognitive complexity of language learning. A grade-appropriate content curriculum, academic language development, and learning strategy instruction are components in this approach. By focusing on grade appropriate content curriculum, ESL students are prepared to enter the regular classroom with the same content knowledge. An emphasis on academic language development provides ESL students with an opportunity to develop competencies in using the literate register found in the written materials used for instruction. Learning strategy instruction is critical since it teaches ESL students to consciously use specific strategies for comprehending and organizing written texts, locating and summarizing information, solving problems, and cooperative learning.

Although CALLA was developed for ESL classrooms, the three components of CALLA can be easily integrated into regular classrooms as well. Since this approach is based upon research about how students acquire conceptual knowledge and skills, regardless of language, all students can benefit from this approach's emphasis on content area knowledge, academic register acquisition, and learning strategy instruction (Chamot & O'Malley, 1995). In addition, when regular teachers implement this approach in classes where ESL students are integrated, students receive support for continued language development.

Submersion

The third main approach to educating children of linguistic diversity is *submersion.* In this approach, second language learners are placed in English-only classrooms along with other students who have English as their first language. The teacher may not be bilingual and may not have received any special training. The second language learners in the room may not all speak the same first language. Some may speak Spanish, others Polish, Chinese, Cambodian, Korean, or Russian. The rationale for this approach relies on second language learners' capacities to gradually acquire English through participating in an English-only environment. By their participation in this environment, it is expected that they will be able to acquire English, having heard it used in various learning activities/settings. No value or consideration is given to their first language. Submersion programs have been described as having a "sink or swim" approach (Baker, 1996; Faltis, 1998; Krashen, 1995), where the learner is likened to someone who, without knowing how to swim, is thrown in the deep end of a pool and is expected to either sink or struggle to swim. Submersion programs alone do not facilitate comprehensible input. Typically, the level of language used by both the teacher and the other students far exceeds the linguistic competencies of the second language learner. However, when a separate ESL pull out class is added to a submersion program, second language learners are more likely to experience target language at a level they can comprehend (Krashen, 1995).

Immersion

In immersion programs children are grouped according to their first language. Teachers in immersion classrooms must have fluency in both languages. Instruction in the language arts is provided in their first language. Instruction in all other areas of the curriculum is in the second language (Krashen, 1995). Typically there is no formal instruction in the second language. While most immersion programs have been for majority language children, such as English-fluent children learning Spanish, immersion programs can also be used with non-English proficient students. For example, a class of Spanish-fluent children would receive instruction in language arts in Spanish with content-area instruction—math, science, and social studies—in English.

Immersion programs vary with the grade level at which they are introduced (Piper, 1993). *Early immersion* programs begin in kindergarten, *delayed immersion* begins in third or fourth grade, and *late immersion* begins at sixth grade or later.

Foreign Languages in the Elementary School (FLES)

In contrast to bilingual and ESL programs where the target language is used in content instruction, some elementary schools have a language program where English-speaking students are taught another language with the focus on the language as a subject. The most frequently taught languages in these programs are Spanish, German, and French (McLaughlin, 1985). FLES programs range from 50 minutes of direct language instruction each day to 20 minutes of instruction three times a week (Piper, 1993). These programs have met with varying degrees of success in facilitating children's acquisition of a second language. Programs with an emphasis on rote, pattern drills and grammatical lessons have had less success than programs emphasizing cultural awareness and oral communication. One of the key factors in FLES programs is the opportunity for students to use the target language in communicative settings at school and in their community environment. This contributes to fluency; unless a language is used functionally in daily conversations and learning activity dialogues/discussions, fluency cannot be achieved. An increase in FLES programs in the United States in recent years indicates an awareness of the importance of linguistic diversity to our students' futures.

Dual Language Instruction or Two-way Bilingual Education

The term *dual language instruction* has recently developed as a way of referring to instructional programs that recognize the goal of educating children to have linguistic competency in more than one language. Half of the students come from homes where English is the home language and half from homes where a different language (e.g. Spanish) is spoken as the home language.

Dual language programs, in contrast to FLES programs, typically provide instruction for half of the day in one language and half of the day in another language (Baker, 1996). Students in each group serve as language models for each other (Cummins, 1998). In some situations, the entire school follows a dual language program, while other dual language programs may involve specific grade levels, mostly at the primary level. Some schools institute a three-phase dual language program where the proportion of time the target language is used (e.g. English) gradually increases until each language is used 50% of the day (J. Villegas, personal communication, October 9, 2000). For example, in grades K-3 the Spanish-English proportion is 80/20; grades 4-6, 60/40; and 7-8, 50/50.

Instructional Approaches

Second language programs also vary in the instructional approach used. Not all bilingual programs use the same instructional strategies or approaches. ESL programs vary in the way in which language acquisition is encouraged. Likewise, immersion and submersion programs differ in the specific teaching strategies and activities implemented. The various approaches can be represented by three categories: audiolingualism, subskill-based, and holistic-communicative.

Audiolingualism

This instructional approach is used in various programs for second language learn-ers (Chamot & O'Malley, 1994; Corder, 1995; Krashen, 1995). It is characterized by rote repetition without focusing on meaning or learning how to manipulate sen-tence segments. Although this approach has been discredited through research over the past three decades, some programs continue to use this approach. Read-ing and writing are emphasized only after extensive oral drills have been mastered. Second language learners would benefit from learning the rote phrases if they also learn the meaning of the rote phrases and develop an awareness of when to use the phrases in greetings, simple requests, and other routine communication.

Subskill-based

This approach focuses on directly teaching the semantic, syntactic, morphemic, and phonetic knowledge of the target language. It emphasizes the form of the language rather than the meaning communicated. In this approach, reading is taught from a phonics or decoding emphasis, neglecting comprehension (Chamot & O'Malley, 1994). Although this approach has been discredited as be-ing too fragmented, isolating language units rather than developing communi-cation competencies, some researchers contend that this approach may provide the necessary knowledge to L2 learners to help make linguistic input compre-hensible (Krashen, 1995).

Holistic-communicative

In this approach the emphasis is on using language to communicate. Compre-hension of the second language and the ability to use the second language for communication are primary concerns. Specific activities used in this approach that focus on communication and concept development include language ex-perience stories, cooperative group activities, content area learning centers, reading-writing centers (including journaling and creative writing), literature sharing, thematic units, and problem-solving activities. Throughout these vari-ous activities is an emphasis on the development of conceptual knowledge through hands-on, concrete experiences, a thematic emphasis integrating con-tent across subject areas, and a focus on acquiring receptive and expressive knowledge of English in both oral and written modes.

WAYS OF ENHANCING DEVELOPMENT OF LINGUISTIC DIVERSITY

Offering bilingual programs, ESL, or submersion programs is an administrative decision, outside of the realm of the classroom teacher. However, the classroom teacher has a critical role in creating opportunities for students to develop and maintain their linguistic diversity. In addition to examining their own perspective towards diversity, teachers need to create a positive classroom environment, build on first language competencies, create a literacy community, and incorporate a multicultural approach into the classroom curriculum.

Teacher's Perspective

Classroom teachers have a significant role in determining their students' attitudes toward linguistic diversity and in enhancing students' motivation to learn (Cary, 2000; Saracho & Spodek, 1995; Scott, 1995). Initially, it is important for teachers to be aware that a child's home language is closely tied to the child's personal identity and culture (Delpit, 1990). When a teacher or a school implies that a child's home language is "wrong," the negative feeling extends to the child's family and culture. Instead, teachers should acknowledge and value the linguistic diversity that children bring to the classroom.

In the United States, most teachers are monolingual, with English as their only language. While they may speak more than one dialect, they may be unaware of issues related to language diversity. Unless they have traveled extensively to other countries or regions, lived in areas where another language is used, or formally studied another language, they may be unaware of the role of language in other cultures and of the cognitive, linguistic, and social demands of acquiring a second language.

As a first step to addressing the needs of children of linguistic and cultural diversity, teachers must seriously reflect on their own attitudes and perspectives toward linguistic and cultural diversity. Recognition of the need to change one's own attitude is an initial step (Scott, 1995). This recognition must be followed by taking advantage of opportunities to learn more about the languages and cultures represented in the classroom. A next step involves teachers monitoring their own behavior for direct or indirect behaviors that might indicate low expectations for linguistically diverse students. Scott (1995) recommends that small groups of teachers work together, "meeting periodically to discuss their observations, evaluations, and progress with monitoring [their] behaviors that communicate low expectations" (p. 277). Another step in the process of attitude change involves examining the ways in which linguistically diverse students are assessed. Scott (1995) proposes that a "balanced data bank" be developed on each students' performance, including both strengths and areas of needed emphasis and resulting in a more complete profile of each student.

To become aware of the ways in which cultures may be similar or different, teachers are encouraged to examine their own culture and their students' culture with respect to these aspects: family structure, life cycle, interpersonal role/relationships, discipline, time and space, religion, food, health/hygiene, and history/tradition/holidays.

Teachers who have examined their own attitudes toward linguistic and cultural diversity and acquired information about the respective cultures and languages represented in their classrooms are better able to create classroom environments that enhance the learning opportunities of all children. (See the appendix at the end of this chapter for a listing of teacher resources.)

Creating a Positive Classroom Environment

One of the major ways in which teachers can facilitate the development of linguistic diversity is in creating classroom environments that acknowledge the value of that diversity. Guidelines for creating a linguistically diverse classroom environment are:

1. *Including literature from different cultures and dialects in the classroom.* During the last two decades, many high-quality trade books have been published on the folktales, legends, and customs of diverse cultures. Using diverse literature increases the cultural awareness of students and encourages acceptance of diversity.

2. *Emphasizing that language use is determined by the culture in which it is used.* Bring examples of other languages into your classroom in the form of books, newspapers, and other written materials as well as in songs.

3. *Focusing on the pragmatics of language: how language is used differently in different situations and settings.* Talk about the ways we use language in various social routines and settings, such as ordering at a fast-food restaurant, participating in a church service, making a purchase at a store, and seeking information from a government office. Pragmatic knowledge of written language can be emphasized in exploring the ways language is used differently in fairy tales, mysteries, nonfiction, and/or poetry.

4. *Modeling a curiosity and interest in other languages and dialects.* Show your interest in other languages by bringing other languages into your classroom. Invite speakers of other languages to come to your class to share their language with your students. Encourage children to share their diverse language knowledge with you and their classmates.

5. *Learning basic greetings and expressions in a variety of languages and dialects.* Ask native speakers of those languages in your classroom to help you with the articulation and inflection. Teach the greetings/expressions to your students. Use these greetings and expressions in communication in your classroom orally and in writing.

6. *Encouraging students in monolingual classrooms to develop an awareness of linguistic diversity through literature, guest speakers, media, and field trips.* Students in classrooms that are monolingual can also benefit from opportunities to explore linguistic and cultural diversity. Such opportunities enhance students' conceptual development and their social/ cultural awareness.

Building on First Language Competencies

Teachers need to facilitate second language learners' use of their first language as a basis for developing English oral competency and academic English register. This can be accomplished by:

1. *Acknowledging the student's first language or dialect as a valid form of communication.* By sharing your positive attitude toward the student's dialect or language, you are enhancing the child's self-esteem and confidence.

2. *Learning about the student's home language or dialect so that you are aware of potential language interference with respect to phonology, morphology, syntax, semantics, or pragmatics.* This knowledge will help you assist the student in differentiating between the two language systems.

3. *Acknowledging the student's need to develop receptive knowledge of standard English before using English expressively.* Provide many opportunities for students to hear storybooks and nonfiction books read aloud. Select books with illustrations that support the text by providing clear referents to the concepts presented. Be aware that second language learners will experience a "silent period" during which time they will be actively listening but rarely will participate verbally in class interactions.

4. *Providing many opportunities for students to engage in conversation/discussion.* This will enhance their productive/expressive language. When these opportunities involve only two or three children in a conversation or discussion, L2 students are more likely to participate.

5. *Allowing students to respond in their home language first, and then to focus on translating their responses into English.* This does not mean that the monolingual teacher must be able to assist L2 students in making the translation; however, the teacher should allow time for L2 students to process the message in both languages.

6. *Providing second language learners with cues, letting them know when to anticipate being called on or when their turn will be.* If L2 students can anticipate their turn and are aware of the type of response needed, they will be able to participate more successfully in class discussions and recitations.

7. *Providing content area books that have clear illustrations of the main concepts presented in the text.* With the main concepts illustrated, second language learners can identify concepts they already have in their first language and then learn the concept label in the second language. Second language learners can also benefit from being encouraged to use the illustrations to predict the upcoming text.

8. *Providing opportunities for students to work together with other ESL students and with English-fluent students.* Through group activities, students learn how to focus on a task, how to use language to accomplish the task, and how to work together. Cooperative learning opportunities will often draw out students' conceptual knowledge and cognitive competencies, which can be shared through problem-solving strategies.

9. *Using songs, nursery rhymes, and finger plays to emphasize the sound-symbol system and phonemic awareness.* These activities facilitate children's awareness of sound similarities and differences. The rhythm of the language also promotes a memory for the song or rhyme.

10. *Providing opportunities to learn through hands-on, exploratory, experiential activities.* As discussed in Chapter 2, concept development is enhanced through hands-on activities. As concepts develop, conceptual schemata develop and the child acquires the new language labels for the concepts. Hands-on experiences stimulate conceptual development and subsequent language acquisition.

Creating a Literacy Community

Another way in which teachers can facilitate positive attitudes toward cultural-linguistic diversity is by creating a literacy community in their classrooms. This can be accomplished by:

1. *Encouraging all students to participate verbally in class discussions in a nonthreatening, supportive manner.*

2. *Responding positively to each student's contribution.*

3. *Making expectations for behavior and responses during large and small group discussions explicit so that everyone understands what behavior is appropriate.*

4. *Encouraging students to use written text as a source of their knowledge during oral discussions and in opportunities for critical thinking.*

5. *Providing a variety of opportunities for students to engage in small group activities within formal and informal settings.*

6. *Encouraging students' creativity through open-ended activities.*

7. *Welcoming parents to visit your classroom for open house and informal visits and to participate in class field trips.* (See Chapter 14 for additional information on school-home connections.)

8. *Encouraging parents to share their cultural knowledge with your classroom.*

Through encouraging students to communicate with each other in a wide variety of ways and for a wide variety of purposes, teachers can enhance students' understanding of each other by developing shared experiences and interactions.

Incorporate a Multicultural Approach in the Classroom Curriculum

Learning activities which incorporate a focus on cultural diversity contribute to a classroom community where each student's culture is valued and respected. Specific guidelines include:

1. Provide activities and experiences that encourage an awareness and respect for other cultures.
2. Select literature to share with children that support cultural diversity.
3. Incorporate a multicultural approach throughout the curriculum each day, not just a one-time unit or seasonal "tourist" approach.
4. Avoid activities that perpetuate the concept that all people from a particular cultural group are the same (Derman-Sparks & A.B.C. Task Force, 1989).

SUMMARY

Linguistic diversity in languages and dialects is a common characteristic of urban American settings and some rural areas where groups of recent immigrants have settled. Different languages and dialects represent authentic and valid forms of communication for specific cultures, locales, and families. To be successful in American schools, children need to become fluent in the literate register, which is a form of Standard American English.

Acquisition of a second language involves the same processes, interactions, and aspects of language knowledge as does first language acquisition. Programs for second language learners differ in the goal of the approach, content of the instruction, length of the program, and value placed on the first language. The acquisition of linguistic diversity among children can be enhanced by modeling positive teacher perspectives, building on first language competencies, and developing a literacy and learning community and incorporating a multicultural curricular approach. First and second language acquisition is a life-long process (Collier, 1995). Language knowledge continues to be acquired long after basic conversational fluency is attained as children experience and participate in more complex educational tasks and varied social situations.

✳ ✳ ✳ CHAPTER REVIEW

1. Terms to review:
   socialization mismatch hypothesis   pidgin
   dialects   bilingualism

successive bilingualism
creole
academic register
Standard American English

African American English (AAE)
language acquisition
language learning

2. Describe three specific issues involving linguistic diversity in early childhood education.

3. Explain the "deficit model" perspective on linguistic diversity.

4. What was the significance of the *Martin Luther King Junior Elementary School Children* v. *Ann Arbor School District Board* court case?

5. What are the benefits of bilingualism?

6. What necessary distinctions must Spanish speakers learning English make between the two languages?

7. How is acquisition of a second language related to first language acquisition?

8. List/explain factors influencing second language acquisition.

9. What are the two aspects of language proficiency for L2 learners identified by Cummins?

10. Distinguish between the following program approaches: bilingual education, ESL, submersion, immersion, and dual language.

11. Distinguish between transitional and maintenance bilingual education. What value is placed on the first language in each approach?

12. Distinguish between these instructional approaches: audiolingualism, subskill-based, and holistic-communicative.

13. What is the role of the teacher's perspective in a culturally and linguistically diverse classroom?

14. List several ways teachers can create a positive classroom environment.

15. In what ways can teachers build on children's first language competencies?

✳ ✳ ✳ CHAPTER EXTENSION ACTIVITIES

1. Observe in a bilingual preschool or primary classroom for 1 1/2 to 2 hours. Describe how first and second languages are used in formal and informal communication.

2. Survey your local public library for children's books that are in languages other than English.

3. Select a children's tradebook (fiction or nonfiction) that focuses on a non-English language or culture. Review the book. Explain how you would use this book in an early childhood classroom.

4. Interview a primary teacher who teaches culturally diverse students. Ask the teacher to describe several techniques she or he has found valuable in enhancing students' linguistic competencies.

❄ ❄ ❄ REFERENCES

Altwerger, B., & Ivener, B. (1994). Self-esteem: Access to literacy in multicultural and multilingual classrooms. In K. Spangenberg-Urbschat & R. Pritchard (Eds.), *Kids come in all languages: Reading instruction for ESL students* (pp. 65–81). Newark, DE: International Reading Association.

Baker, C. (1996). *Foundations of bilingual education and bilingualism.* (2nd ed.). Philadelphia, PA: Multilingual Matters, Ltd.

Ben Zeev, S. (1977). The influence of bilingualism on cognitive strategy and cognitive development. *Child Development, 48,* 1009–1018.

Bereiter, C., & Englemann, S. (1966). *Teaching disadvantaged children in the preschool.* Englewood Cliffs, NJ: Prentice Hall.

Bernstein, B. (1971). A sociolinguistic approach to socialization with some reference to educability. In B. Bernstein (Ed.), *Class, codes and control* (Vol. I, pp. 165–192). London: Paladin.

Bhatia, T., & Ritchie, W. (1996). Bilingual language mixing, universal grammar, and second language acquisition. In W. Ritchie & T. Bhatia (Eds.), *Handbook of second language acquisition* (pp. 627–688). San Diego, CA: Academic Press.

Bialystok, E. (1988). Levels of bilingualism and levels of linguistic awareness. *Developmental Psychology, 24,* 560–567.

Blank, M., Rose, S., & Berlin, L. (1978). *The language of learning: The preschool years.* New York: Grune & Stratton.

Brisk, M. (1998). *Bilingual education: From compensatory to quality schooling.* Mahwah, NJ: Lawrence Erlbaum Associates.

Cary, S. (2000). *Working with second language learners: Answers to teachers' top ten questions.* Portsmouth, NH: Heinemann.

Chamot, A., & O'Malley, J. M. (1994). Instructional approaches and teaching procedures. In K. Spangenberg-Urbschat & R. Pritchard (Eds.), *Kids come in all languages: Reading instruction for ESL students* (pp. 82–107). Newark, DE: International Reading Association.

Chamot, A., & O'Malley, J. M. (1995). The cognitive academic language learning approach. In D. Durkin (Ed.), *Language issues: Readings for teachers* (pp. 160–175). White Plains, NY: Longman.

Collier, V. (1995). Acquiring a second language for school. *Directions in Language & Education, 1*(4), 1–12. National Clearinghouse for Bilingual Education.

Corder, E. (1995). The significance of learner's errors. In D. Durkin (Ed.), *Language issues: Readings for teachers* (pp. 80–89). White Plains, NY: Longman.

Cox, B. (1994). Young children's regulatory talk: Evidence of emerging metacognitive control over literary products and processes. In R. B. Ruddell, M. A. Ruddell, & H. Singer (Eds.), *Theoretical models and processes in reading* (4th ed., pp. 733–756). Newark, DE: International Reading Association.

Cox, B., & Dixey, B. (1994). Preschoolers doing "code-switching." In C. Kinzer & D. Leu (Eds.), *Multidimensional aspects of literacy research, theory, and practice.* 43rd Yearbook of The National Reading Conference (pp. 162–171). Chicago: National Reading Conference.

Cox, B., Fang, Z., & Otto, B. (1997). Preschoolers' developing ownership of the literate register. *Reading Research Quarterly, 32*(1).

Crystal, D. (1987). *The Cambridge encyclopedia of language.* New York: Cambridge University Press.

Cummins, J. (1979). Linguistic interdependence. *Review of Educational Research, 49,* 222–251.

Cummins, J. (1994). The acquisition of English as a second language. In K. Spangenberg-Urbschat & R. Pritchard (Eds.), *Kids come in all languages: Reading instruction for ESL students* (pp. 36–64). Newark, DE: International Reading Association.

Cummins, J. (1995). Underachievement among minority students. In D. Durkin (Ed.), *Language issues: Readings for teachers* (pp. 130–159). White Plains, NY: Longman.

Cummins, J. (1998). Linguistic enrichment in dual-language Spanish/English programs. *Leadership Letters: Issues and Trends in Bilingual Education.* Glenview, IL: Scott Foresman.

Da Silva, W. (1987). *Beginning Spanish: A concept approach.* (6th ed.) New York: Harper & Row.

Delpit, L. (1988). The silenced dialogue: Power and pedagogy in educating other people's children. *Harvard Educational Review, 58*(3), pp. 280–298.

Delpit, L. (1990). Language diversity and learning. In S. Hynds & D. Rubin (Eds.), *Perspectives on talk and learning* (pp. 247–266). Urbana, IL: National Council of Teachers of English.

Delpit, L. (1992). Acquisition of literate discourse: Bowing before the master? *Theory Into Practice, 31*(4), 296–302.

Derman-Sparks, L. & the A.B.C. Task Force (1989). *Anti-bias curriculum: Tools for empowering children.* Washington, DC: National Association for the Education of Young Children.

De Houwer, A. (1990). *The acquisition of two languages from birth: A case study.* New York: Cambridge University Press.

Durkin, D. B. (Ed.). (1995). *Language issues: Readings for teachers.* White Plains, NY: Longman.

Evans, C. (1994). English-only children from bilingual homes: Considering the home-school connection. In C. Kinzer & D. Leu (Eds.), *Multidimensional aspects of literacy research, theory, and practice.* 43rd Yearbook of The National Reading Conference (pp. 172–179). Chicago: National Reading Conference.

Faltis, C. (1998). *Joinfostering: Teaching and learning in multilingual classrooms.* (3rd ed.). Upper Saddle River, NJ: Merrill/Prentice Hall.

Gadda, G. (1995). Language change in the history of English: Implications for teachers. In D. Durkin (Ed.), *Language issues: Readings for teachers* (pp. 262–272). White Plains, NY: Longman.

Genesee, F., & Nicoladis, E. (1995). Language development in bilingual preschool children. In E. Garcia & B. McLaughlin (Eds.), *Meeting the challenge of linguistic and cultural diversity in early childhood education* (pp. 18–33). New York: Teachers College Press.

Genesee, F., Tucker, G., & Lambert, W. (1975). Communication skills of bilingual children. *Child Development, 46,* 110–114.

Goodz, N. (1994). Interactions between parents and children in bilingual families. In F. Genesee (Ed.), *Educating second language children* (pp. 61–81). New York: Cambridge University Press.

Goodz, N., Legare, M., & Bilodeau, L. (1987). The influence of bilingualism in preschool children. *Canadian Psychology, 28,* 218.

Grant, R. (1995). Meeting the needs of young second language learners. In E. Garcia & B. McLaughlin (Eds.), *Meeting the challenge of linguistic and cultural diversity in early childhood education* (pp. 1–17). New York: Teachers College Press.

Hancock, I. (1991). A survey of the pidgins and creoles of the world. In D. Hymes (Ed.), *Pidginization and creolization of languages.* New York: Cambridge University Press.

Hart, B., & Risley, T. (1995). *Meaningful differences in the everyday experience of young American children.* Baltimore, MD: Paul H. Brookes.

Hart, B., & Risley, T. (1999). *The social world of children learning to talk.* Baltimore, MD: Paul H. Brookes.

Hatch, E., Peck, S., & Wagner-Gough, J. (1995). A look at process in child second language acquisition. In D. Durkin, (Ed.), *Language issues: Readings for teachers* (pp. 212–223). White Plains, NY: Longman.

Hayes, C., Ornstein, J., & Gage, W. (1987). *The ABCs of languages and linguistics.* Lincolnwood, IL: National Textbook Company.

Heath, S. (1983). *Ways with words: Language, life, and work in communities and classrooms.* New York: Cambridge University Press.

Ianco-Worrall, A. (1972). Bilingualism and cognitive development. *Child Development, 43,* 1390–1400.

Krashen, S. (1981). *Second language acquisition and second language learning.* London: Pergamon Press.

Krashen, S. (1982). *Principles and practice in second language acquisition.* New York: Pergamon Press.

Krashen, S. (1995). Bilingual education and second language acquisition theory. In D. Durkin (Ed.), *Language issues: Readings for teachers* (pp. 90–115). White Plains, NY: Longman.

Lanza, E. (1992). Can bilingual two-year-olds code-switch? *Journal of Child Language, 19,* 633–658.

Labov, W. (1979). The logic of nonstandard English. In J. Alatis (Ed.), *Report of the Twentieth Annual Round Table Meeting on Linguistics and Language Studies* (Monograph Series of Languages and Linguistics, No. 22). In D. Durkin (Ed.), *Language issues: Readings for teachers* (pp. 281–313). White Plains, NY: Longman.

Labov, W. (1995). The study of nonstandard English. In B. Power & R. Hubbard (Eds.), *Language development: A reader for teachers* (pp. 50–54). Upper Saddle River, NJ: Merrill/Prentice Hall.

Lessow-Hurley, J. (2000). *The foundations of dual language instruction* (3rd ed.). New York: Longman.

Luke, A., & Kale, J. (1997). Learning through difference: cultural practices in early childhood language socialization. In E. Gregory (Ed.), *One child, many worlds.* New York: Teachers College Press.

McLaughlin, B. (1985). *Second-language acquisition in childhood: School-age children.* (Vol. 2, 2nd ed.). Hillsdale, NJ: Lawrence Erlbaum.

Meisel, J. M. (1994). Code-switching in bilingual children. *Studies in second language acquisition* (Vol. 16, pp. 413–440).

Otto, B. (1987). Unpublished research notes. Chicago: Northeastern Illinois University.

Owens, R. (2001). *Language development: An introduction* (5th ed.). Upper Saddle River, NJ: Merrill/Prentice Hall.

Peregoy, S., & Boyle, O. (1993). *Reading, writing, & learning in ESL: A resource book for K–8 teachers.* White Plains, NY: Longman.

Piper, T. (1993). *Language for all our children.* Englewood Cliffs, NJ: Prentice Hall.

Piper, T. (1998). *Language and learning: The home and school years* (2nd ed.). Upper Saddle River, NJ: Merrill/Prentice Hall.

Saracho, O., & Spodek, B. (1995). Preparing teachers for early childhood programs of linguistic and cultural diversity. In E. Garcia & B. McLaughlin (Eds.), *Meeting the challenge of linguistic and cultural diversity in early childhood education.* New York: Teachers College Press.

Schacter, J. (1996). Maturation and the issue of universal grammar in second language acquisition. In W. Ritchie & Tej Bhatia (Eds.), *Handbook of second language acquisition* (pp. 121–158). San Diego, CA: Academic Press.

Scott, J. (1995). The King case: Implications for educators. In D. Durkin (Ed.), *Language issues: Readings for teachers* (pp. 273–280). White Plains, NY: Longman.

Slobin, D. (1979). *Psycholinguistics* (2nd ed.). Glenview, IL: Scott, Foresman.

Smitherman, G. (1995). "The forms of things unknown": Black modes of discourse. In D. Durkin (Ed.), *Language issues: Readings for teachers* (pp. 314–330). White Plains, NY: Longman.

Tabors, P. (1997). *One child, two languages: A guide for preschool educators of children learning English as a second language.* Baltimore, MD: Paul H. Brookes.

Tough, J. (1977). *The development of meaning: A study of children's use of language.* New York: John Wiley & Sons.

Tough, J. (1985). *Talk two: Children using English as a second language.* London: Onyx Press.

Winch, C. (1990). *Language ability and educational achievement.* New York: Routledge.

Wong-Fillmore, L. (1991). When learning a second language means losing the first. *Early Childhood Research Quarterly, 6,* 323–346.

Wong-Fillmore, L. (1995). Individual differences in second language acquisition. In D. Durkin (Ed.), *Language issues: Readings for teachers* (pp. 224–247). White Plains, NY: Longman.

Wong-Fillmore, L. (1999). Reading and academic English learning. Paper presented at the 1999 Regional Conference of Improving America's Schools, Chicago, IL.

Appendix

✳ ✳ ✳

Teacher Resources for Linguistic and Cultural Diversity

Cary, S. (2000). *Working with second language learners: Answers to teachers' top ten questions.* Portsmouth, NH: Heinemann.

deMelendez, W. R., Ostertag, V., & Peck, J. (1997). *Teaching young children in multicultural classrooms: Issues, concepts, and strategies.* Albany, NY: Delmar Publishers.

Diamond, B., & Moore, M. (1995). *Multicultural literacy: Mirroring the reality of the classroom.* White Plains, NY: Longman.

Faltis, C. (1997). *Joinfostering* (2nd ed.). Upper Saddle River, NJ: Merrill/Prentice Hall.

Garcia, E., & McLaughlin, B. (Eds.). (1995). *Meeting the challenge of linguistic and cultural diversity in early childhood education.* New York: Teachers College Press.

Gregory, E. (Ed). (1997). *One child, many worlds: Early learning in multicultural communities.* New York: Teachers College Press.

McCaleb, S. (1997). *Building communities of learners.* Mahwah, NJ: Lawrence Erlbaum Associates.

Perez, B., & Torres-Guzman, M. (1996). *Learning in two worlds: An integrated Spanish/English biliteracy approach.* White Plains, NY: Longman.

Spangenberg-Urbschat, K., & Pritchard, R. (Eds.). (1994). *Kids come in all languages: Reading instruction for ESL students.* Newark, DE: International Reading Association.

Swiniarski, L., Breitborde, M., & Murphy, J. (1999). *Educating the global village: Including the young child in the world.* Upper Saddle River, NJ: Merrill/Prentice Hall.

Tabors, P. (1997). *One child, two languages: A guide for preschool educators of children learning English as a second language.* Baltimore, MD: Paul H. Brookes.

✻ ✻ ✻

4

Language Development of Infants and Toddlers

Miriam looked at her newborn as she held him in her arms. He was alert, his eyes were open, and he seemed to be looking intently at Miriam's face. "Hello there, little one," Miriam said. "What a handsome boy you are. The nurse even put a blue bow on your hair. And such a tight grip you have. . . . Uh-oh! Was that a hiccup I heard?"

Miriam's verbal interactions with her newborn illustrate the beginning of communication for many young infants. Through their interactions with adults and older children, infants learn how language works. Language acquisition begins when language speakers assume that an infant is a participating partner in conversational settings, even though it is months before the child is able to begin speaking a "language." In this chapter, we will focus on language development of infants and toddlers in each area of the five aspects of language knowledge: phonetic, semantic, syntactic, morphemic, and pragmatic. Each of these aspects first develops in oral language and then gradually develops in written language knowledge.

INFANTS' PERCEPTUAL ABILITIES

Research on children's perception of speech and the development of the auditory system *in utero* has determined that it is functional beginning with the 25th week of gestation (de Boysson-Bardies, 1999). A fetus hearing acuity is at a level similar to an adult's at 35 weeks gestation. Thus, during the last months of pregnancy, a fetus can hear her mother's voice and perceive other sounds in the environment.

Children are born with specific predispositions to pay attention to language and people in their environments. Infants can perceive differences in sound (Wolff, 1966) and have been found to prefer the human voice over any other sound, including environmental sounds (Condon & Sander, 1974; Eisenberg, 1976; Jensen, Williams, & Bzoch, 1975). This indicates a biological readiness to perceive and process the sounds of language (Reich, 1986). In addition, research has documented infants' ability to distinguish their mother's voice from other voices within three days after birth, even showing a preference for their mother's voice over other female voices (DeCasper & Fifer, 1980). DeCasper & Spence (1986) also found that infants show preference for the acoustic characteristics found in a speech recited by the mother when pregnant rather than an unfamiliar speech not read during pregnancy.

Further evidence of children's predisposition to attend to and process language comes from research that has documented children's ability to distinguish between specific sounds of language (phonemes) as early as one month of age (Aslin & Pisoni, 1980). Thus, children can evaluate and compare auditory stimuli from early infancy. This perceptual ability facilitates children's responses in their interactions with people in their environment.

EARLY COMMUNICATION CONTEXTS

The interaction patterns described in Chapter 2 are embedded in a variety of contexts that enhance language acquisition during infancy and toddlerhood: eye contact and shared reference, establishing and maintaining a communication loop, verbal mapping, adult-to-child speech, linguistic scaffolding, and questioning. Newborns begin learning about communication shortly after birth, although they will not acquire an oral language for almost a year. A critical aspect of communication that children experience as newborns is the pattern of turn taking or interactive dialogue (Tronick, Als, & Adamson, 1979). Adults and older children talk to and interact with infants from the day they are born. Underlying these interactions is the assumption on the part of adults and older children that infants' behavioral responses and spontaneous verbal utterances are meaningful. This assumption initiates and sustains communicative interaction between infants and their families and other caregivers.

For example, when Miriam held her newborn in the hospital, and heard him hiccup, she responded as if he had spoken, saying, "Oh, was that a hiccup I heard?" In response to her voice her newborn turned his head slightly, reestablishing eye contact. After patting him gently on the back, she said, "There, there. Are you feeling better now? Did you get rid of those hiccups?" After a short pause in which no more hiccups occurred, Miriam said, "Yes, all better now. No more hiccups." It is common when adults are verbally interacting with infants that they take the verbal role of the child, in effect answering their own questions.

This process of getting an infant's attention and maintaining that attention in a communicative interaction is critical to creating a setting in which linguistic exchanges can occur. As infants participate in turn taking, the focus of taking turns is on the meaning of the message embedded in the exchanges. The ways in which caregivers direct young children's attention to ongoing events and the meaning of those events has an important role in language acquisition (Zukow-Goldring & Ferko, 1994).

ASPECTS OF INFANTS' AND TODDLERS' LANGUAGE DEVELOPMENT

Each of the five aspects of language knowledge and awareness is present in children's expressive and receptive language behaviors. In the chapter sections that follow, each of the aspects of language will be described along with examples of oral language behaviors that illustrate the receptive and expressive behaviors of each aspect during infancy and toddlerhood. Within each section, an overview of the development of **emergent literacy** will also be presented, high-lighting how oral language development and written language development are interrelated in literate cultures. The examples and approximate ages given in the sections throughout this chapter and the next are offered to illustrate language development and/or emergent literacy behaviors; they should not be used as benchmarks for measuring or judging specific children in teachers' or care-givers' classrooms. While developmental patterns may exist, universal ages for achieving those stages are nonexistent for the most part and are highly influenced by environmental settings and the sociocultural interactions therein. It is also important to remember that variations in the acquisition of language (both oral and written language) have been observed within the same child, fluctuating from day to day within a variety of contexts, and between children of the same age or level of maturation.

INFANTS' PHONETIC DEVELOPMENT

Receptive Phonetic Knowledge

Research with very young infants has concluded that they can distinguish nearly all of the phonetic contrasts represented in natural language (Jusczyk, 1985). Children can distinguish specific phonemes as early as 1 month of age (Aslin & Pisoni, 1980). In addition, at 5 months, infants recognize/categorize the same phonemes regardless of changes in the speakers and intonation (de Boysson-Bardies, 1999). Babies can also distinguish between sequences of syllables (Bijeljac-Babic, Bertoncini, & Mehler, 1993). Between 8 and 10 months, infants begin to pay more attention to phoneme-sound contrasts that exist in their own language, while they pay little or no attention to phoneme-sound contrasts found in other languages (Werker & Tees, 1984, in de Boysson-Bardies, 1999).

The role of *prosody* in infants' language perception has also been explored. Prosody refers to the pitch, loudness, tempo, and rhythm of speech (Crystal, 1987). In research conducted by Mandel, Jusczyk, and Kemler-Nelson (1994), 2-month-old infants were found to better detect changes in phonemes when the phonemes were part of short sentences rather than in word lists. de Boysson-Bardies (1999) concludes that prosody is "a perceptual glue that holds together sequences of speech" and that "the natural prosody of the language of infants' mothers commands their listening attention" (p. 28). Thus, prosody appears to have a significant role in attracting the attention of infants to process speech sounds.

Productive Phonetic Knowledge

Although infants perceive a wide range of phonemes and environmental sounds, their production of speech sounds is limited by their immature physiology. Speech requires coordination of the vocal tract, including the larynx, glottis, hard and soft palate, jaw, lips, and tongue, in addition to the coordination of breathing so that sufficient air is available for speech production. Maturational changes in the curve of the vocal track (from a slant to the right-angle curve found in adults) occur during the first 4 months of infancy (de Boysson-Bardies, 1999).

Infant vocalizations are of two types: reflexive and nonreflexive (Stoel-Gammon, 1998). Reflexive vocalizations are those that come from the infant's physical state (cries, coughs, hiccups). Nonreflexive vocalizations include cooing and babbling. Between 6 to 8 weeks, many infants begin to produce **cooing** sounds (Reich, 1986; Wolff, 1966). These sounds are extended vowel sounds such as *ooo*, *ahhh*, *eee*, and *aaaa* and are often made in relative isolation of each other. These sounds involve less complex production than consonants that involve the lips and teeth, such as *b*, *p*, *t*, *m*, and *c*. Later on, cooing sounds are "strung together, often 10 or more at a time. These strings are not pronounced in a rhythmical way; there are no clear intonational contours" (Crystal, 1987, p. 236). The cooing stage is important because during this time infants begin to manipulate their tongues and mouths in producing sounds. These actions are precursors to those required for later speech production.

Cooing is followed by a period of vocal play, during which the vocalizations begin to show a wider range of consonants and vowels and a range of articulation aspects (e.g., a nasal quality) and day-to-day variations (Crystal, 1987). Infants appear to be exploring and practicing how to produce, repeat, and vary sounds.

A little later, around 4 to 6 months, babbling appears (Clark & Clark, 1977; Reich, 1986; Sachs, 1989; Segal, 1983; Stoel-Gammon, 1998). **Babbling** refers to the production of consonant-vowel sounds of varying intonation. Babbling is essentially reduplicated sounds, such as *ba-ba-ba-ba*. In contrast to the variations observed in vocal play, babbling involves the production of less varied sounds with greater frequency. Some of the sounds produced in early babbling have been found to be representative of phonemic distinctions different than those found in the specific language culture of the infant (Reich, 1986). Sachs (1989) cites evidence that infants also produce a relatively small subset of sounds that are similar across different languages, such as English, Arabic, and Chinese. Only when longer babbling segments with intonational cues were analyzed could listeners accurately identify which infants were from specific language cultures. Around 8 to 10 months, a child's babbling develops an **echolalic** quality. This type of babbling appears to echo the rhythm and phonation of adult speech in a child's environment (de Boysson-Bardies, 1999). It may sound as if the infant is carrying on a conversation with someone. This type of babbling has also been described as **jargon** (Sachs, 1989) or **intonated babble** (Stoel-Gammon, 1998).

The universality of the babbling stage is underscored by research with deaf infants (de Boysson-Bardies, 1999). Prior to 6 months of age, a deaf child vocalizes the same as hearing children. After 6 months, deaf children do not progress on to vocalizing syllables or a series of syllables, and vocalization decreases. When a deaf baby is a year old and has developed some muscular control over lip movements, vocal babbling reoccurs. Further evidence of babbling as a stage in language acquisition is documented by research indicating that deaf babies raised with sign language babble with their hands at 8 to 10 months of age (de Boysson-Bardies, 1999; Lillo-Martin, 1999).

An infant's exploration and production of vocal sounds is often accompanied by encouragement from the infant's family and caregivers. In some early face-to-face interactions the adult imitates the sound made by the infant and then pauses, waiting for the infant to respond. It resembles a follow-the-leader vocal game. Occasionally, as a child produces a different sound, the adult responds with an imitation of the new sound. **Selective reinforcement** occurs when children are encouraged to produce and repeat the sounds that are appropriate and necessary for the language of those people in their environment, though Sachs (1989) cautions that the use of this term may be an oversimplification of the language acquisition process that is actually occurring.

In literate cultures, awareness of phonemic distinctions may develop as infants engage in storybook sharing activities with parents or caregivers (Baghban, 1984). Interactions between parents and infants when sharing a storybook may include wide variations in sounds through intonation, animal sounds ("The cow says, 'mooooo' "), rhyming text, songs, and environmental sounds (fire trucks, train engines). Phonemic awareness related to spoken and written language is fostered during storybook sharing. As an adult reads to an infant, auditory perception is stimulated. In a case study of an 11-month old child, Otto (1994) describes the young child's attempts to reproduce her mother's varied intonation and expressive sounds during the infant's independent storybook interactions. These early storybook reading experiences appear to stimulate a child's awareness of the sounds of language and to develop an association between the sounds of language and picture books. This association is the beginning of a child's emergent literacy, a gradual acquisition of knowledge about written language and the process of reading.

TODDLERS' PHONETIC DEVELOPMENT

Children's perception of phonemes becomes even more evident during toddler years as the range of words they produce increases. At first, pronunciation of a child's first words is not stable, varying from day to day or even more often (Clark & Clark, 1977; Reich, 1986). Variations between children as to the sounds mastered have also been documented (Reich, 1986).

Toddlers are aware of speech sounds they cannot make (Ferguson, 1978) and may avoid or refuse to pronounce words containing those sounds. Children appear to have several ways of dealing with words whose sounds are too difficult to pronounce. Menn (1989) provides a detailed, linguistic description of the ways children approach the pronunciation of difficult phonetical patterns. One of these ways is by reducing the sounds of consonant clusters (e.g., <sp>, <bl>, <st>) to one sound. Thus, instead of *spill* the toddler says *pill,* and *store* becomes *tore.* When one child changed *blanket* to *banke,* she omitted the initial consonant cluster and left off the last consonant. Toddlers' avoidance of difficult sounds is also evident when adults ask them to imitate or repeat someone's name. If the toddlers perceive difficulty in pronouncing the sound, they may refuse, either verbally by remaining silent or nonverbally by shaking their head or looking away.

Literacy-related phonemic awareness begins to develop during toddlerhood when children begin to associate sounds and sound patterns with print in their environment. This acquisition is based on a child's general level of phonemic perception and production. When toddlers express delight and/or respond nonverbally with body movement while poetry or rhythmic prose is read, they are indicating their receptive awareness of sound similarities and patterns.

Let us consider two examples of toddlers' productive speech in which specific sounds are associated with letters. In the first example, Jonathan indicates he is aware that specific sounds accompany each alphabetic letter. Although he cannot produce the matching sounds, he is aware each letter has a sound. *Richard Scarry's Word Book* was a favorite book of Jonathan's when he was 21 months old. While sharing the book with his mother one day, Jonathan pointed to letters of the alphabet in the cover pages and verbalized. Then his mother started to give the correct phoneme as he pointed to it. He continued to point to letters randomly and his mother gave the corresponding phoneme.

In the second example, Glynnis has begun to use her productive language in figuring out sound/symbol relationships. When she was 18 months old, Glynnis, following the activity introduced by her parents, began placing magnetic letters on the refrigerator. Placement of some of the letters was accompanied by labeling, "/d/ daddy," "/b/ bee." When encouraged to repeat other letters that were not yet part of her verbal competencies, such as /q/, /v/, and /r/, she was silent.

EAR INFECTIONS/OTITIS MEDIA AND PHONETIC DEVELOPMENT

A child's speech and hearing mechanisms are sometimes affected by health problems during the early years. The onset and reoccurrence of ear infections is an all-too-frequent health problem of young children that can significantly impair language and speech development. Young children are more likely to have ear infections than older children or adults because of the angle of their **eustachian tubes** (see the appendix at the end of this chapter for further information). Early childhood teachers and caregivers need to be aware of the characteristics and significance of this illness so that they may assist parents in safeguarding the health and development of young children.

Prevalence

Otitis media refers to inflammation of the middle ear (Allen, 1993; Williams, 1994). Middle ear infections and fluid in the middle ear represent a common illness among young children; 90 percent of all children in the United States experience at least one ear infection before they are 6 years old (Williams, 1994). Otitis media is the second most frequent illness among children in the United States, second only to the common cold (Strauss, 1993). Almost 70 percent of all U.S. children will develop otitis media while they are toddlers (Brooks, 1994). Some children experience few ear infections; others have recurring, chronic infections during their toddler and preschool years. Children who attend any type of group care or preschool during their early years experience more ear infections as they are exposed to more respiratory viral infections (Allen, 1993; Daly, 1997; O'Neill, 1999).

Effects of Ear Infections

Severe, chronic cases of otitis media have long-term effects. It is the most common cause of acquired hearing loss among young children and is also associated with impairment in learning and language skills (Brooks, 1994). Cognitive development is influenced by stimulation from each of the senses. According to Allen (1993), "Sensory input may stimulate a greater number of interconnections between neurons in the brain" (p. 3). Allen further indicates that in instances where sensory loss is extended, delays in speech and reading acquisition occur and general intelligence is affected, even though the hearing loss is eventually corrected.

Longitudinal studies of children with varying degrees of otitis media have documented the long-term effects of ear infections in young children in the domains of language and cognition and behavioral effects (Paradise, 1997; Teele, Klein, Chase, Menyuk, & Rosner, 1990; Vernon-Feagans, Manlove, & Volling, 1996; Wallace & Hooper, 1997). These areas involve many of the important behaviors in which children must be able to engage in order to learn: listening, comprehending, speaking, getting along with others, attending, concentrating, reading, writing, and following directions.

Symptoms of Ear Infections

Symptoms of otitis media that teachers, caretakers, and parents should watch for include fever, complaints of ear pain, irritability, lethargy, inattention to verbal stimuli or lack of perception of sounds previously known (indicating loss of hearing), and frequent loss of balance or gross motor clumsiness (indicating inner ear malfunction due to fluids in the middle ear). Children may pull at their ears or rub them. Children's hearing may be impaired by fluid, which may be retained in the ear for several months after the earache and fever have gone away. Thus, it is important for teachers and caregivers to watch for behavior that may indicate hearing difficulties, such as irritability, listlessness, or intermittent inattention (Denk-Glass, Laber, & Brewer, 1982).

When children have recurring ear infections during these early years, special attention should be paid to a child's hearing and speech responsiveness. Chronic ear infections make it difficult for a child to acquire language and especially important phonetic knowledge, since both expressive and receptive processes are affected. Additional information about the physiology, causes, and prevention of ear infections is included in an appendix to this chapter.

Specific malformations in the speech mechanism such as a cleft palate, cleft lip, or a tongue abnormality hamper a child's acquisition of specific speech sounds. In many of these cases, corrective surgery is appropriate and effective. In some instances, speech therapy is needed for the "catch-up" period following surgery (Bellenir, 1997). (See Chapter 13 for further information on cleft palate/lip and tongue abnormalities.)

INFANTS' SEMANTIC DEVELOPMENT

Young infants' crying and fussing occurs as an expression of their physiological and emotional status. Infants do not initially intend to communicate meaning when first crying or fussing; however, sociocultural responses to their crying and fussing exposes children to the ways in which meaning is developed and communicated. Although infants' stable use of speech units with meaning will not occur until around age 1, infants begin to participate in communicative settings shortly after birth. Young infants' cries have been studied by various researchers; however, there is no conclusive evidence that different cries result from different stimuli (Reich, 1986). Our discussion of semantic development begins here with the topic of infants' cries because their cries elicit a parental or caregiver response that nearly always involve language and the assumption that the cries "mean" something. This assumption of meaning leads to the inclusion of children in interactive dyads (adult and child), which promote communication.

When caregivers or parents interact with crying infants, they assume that the infants have a particular need. Often the context of the crying provides a clue. Perhaps a fire engine speeds by, noisily blasting its siren and waking the infant from a nap. An adult might presume the child was startled by the noise and attempt to calm the infant. The soothing behavior of the adult most likely would include speech low in volume and terms of endearment.

If the infant is not quieted, the caregiver/parent tests other possible sources of discomfort, such as a soiled diaper, hunger, change of position, or temperature of the sleeping area. These attempts also are accompanied by speech directed to the infant. The infant's verbal and nonverbal responses in this situation are carefully monitored by the parent/caregiver and interpreted as indications of the child's continued need or satisfaction thereof. In these early infant-adult interactions, children are introduced to meaningful communication.

The pairing of the oral symbol, or word, with the object, action, or attribute in the environment has been previously described from Werner & Kaplan's theory of symbol formation (see Chapter 2). This pairing has also been described as a **mapping** of the language to a specific meaning (Hirsh-Pasek & Golinkoff, 1996). Infants appear to be using this principle of reference as they develop semantic knowledge.

Two types of interactions are important to children's acquisition of conceptual knowledge and vocabulary: turn taking and shared reference. The turn-taking process (described in Chapter 2), involving an adult or older child engaging the child in a conversation-like interaction, encourages the child to attend to the object or action and to respond to the speaker's verbal behavior and/or actions. Another important type of interaction is shared reference of an object or action by both the child and adult (also described in Chapter 2), which enhances concept development and vocabulary. Gradually, as a child matures cognitively, the verbal symbol (word) for an object elicits the concept without the presence of the actual referent.

For example, a mother holds her 5-month-old infant while standing at a window in their home, looking at the bird feeder out in the yard. A cardinal comes to the feeder. The mother says to the infant, "Oh, look at the bird! It's a pretty red birdie. See, he's coming to eat. Look at the birdie! Oops, he flew away. Bye-bye birdie." This scene is repeated throughout the following months in varying settings with varying verbal descriptions: seeing a bird fly by as they are riding in a car, seeing birds in the park, and seeing birds in the trees in the back yard. Verbal descriptions provided by adults and older children enhance the infant's awareness of birds—what they are and what they do.

Semantic development, then, first occurs in a child's understanding of other's words and actions and object associations. Between 8 and 12 months, most infants can comprehend numerous words (Jewell & Zintz, 1990; White, 1978). An infant's perception of **suprasegmental elements** of language (i.e., **intonation**: stress, pitch, and juncture) also adds to semantic development as meaning, attitude, and emotion are communicated through these elements before the words themselves are comprehended (Stewig, 1982). As children enter the one-word (holophrasic) stage around 12 months of age, these suprasegmental elements are used by children to add meaning to their words. For example, the word "mama" may convey a variety of messages when spoken with varying stress and pitch. It may very well be intended to communicate any of the following:

1. "Come pick me up!"
2. "I'm scared."
3. "Oh, I'm glad you're back home."
4. "I'm uncomfortable."

Around age 1 year, children begin to use distinct vocal units to refer to specific objects or actions with some degree of consistency. Menn (1989) refers to children's early invented words as **protowords** while others refer to them as **idiomorphs** (Reich, 1986; Werner & Kaplan, 1963). According to Reich (1986) idiomorphs develop from four different sources: (1) straining sounds that accompany gestures of need; (2) imitation of environmental sounds such as keys, motors, and animals; (3) self-imitation sounds that occur naturally and then are

Verbal descriptions provided by adults enhance a child's awareness of her environment.

repeated when a certain outcome is desired, such as "Achoo" meaning "I need a handkerchief," and (4) imitation of adult speech.

The development of idiomorphs is important for three reasons:

1. Idiomorphs are children's first consistent sound patterns that have relatively stable referents.

2. Idiomorphs are evidence of children's ability to create and develop their own language.

3. Parents and caregivers who learn the meaning of children's idiomorphs encourage verbal interaction by, in effect, learning the children's unique language.

As a child makes the transition from idiomorphs to more standard words, the idiomorphs may be used with adultlike inflection, combined with other adult words to make compound words, or combined with an adult form of the same word (e.g. /ba/ sheep; /muh/ cow). Some children switch back and forth for a period of time between using idiomorphs and adult forms (Reich, 1986).

In a review of research describing children's first words, Owens (1988) notes that most of their words refer to people or animals in their immediate environment or objects young children can manipulate. Nouns are usually acquired before verbs (de Boysson-Bardies, 1999). Most young children develop a core vocabulary of frequently used words (Shatz, 1994).

The development of semantic knowledge related to emergent literacy occurs as infants and adults participate in storybook interactions. During this activity, adults typically use gesture and finger pointing to establish a shared reference before labeling the person or object pictured. Adults select for naming and labeling those pictured items that are entities in the child's environment and often those whose referents are visible at that time, such as a ball, chair, cat, or train. In repeated readings of storybooks, adults encourage greater participation from young children in labeling concepts pictured and in expanding the number of items (concepts) named. In some instances the adult reading the storybook emphasizes the sound made by the item picture, such as a growling lion, and the child develops an idiomorph for the lion pictured based on the growling sound.

Children who have been included in storybook sharing events since early infancy, beginning at about 4 to 5 months, often show they are predicting the meaning of upcoming text by their verbal and nonverbal behavior. In a case study of emergent reading among infants, Otto (1995) documented an 11-month-old girl's anticipation of upcoming story text. In this study, a mother and her 11-month-old daughter were sharing a book together that they had shared repeatedly over previous months. The text pattern on successive pages was "touch your nose," "pat your head," and "wiggle your toes." Just seconds before the mother read "pat your head," the little girl reached up and patted her own head. When the mother turned to the page where the text was "wiggle your toes," the little girl's toes began to wiggle. During this interaction the little girl's attention was focused on the storybook, and she appeared to be listening to her mother's reading. In another instance, this same pair was sharing a book about animals whose pictures were under small flaps on successive pages. The mother had established a routine of making noises for each animal pictured. When they came to the lion page and the monkey page, the little girl made the respective sounds slightly ahead of her mother. In both of these examples, this 11-month-old was attributing meaning to specific content in a storybook, an early form of emergent literacy.

SEMANTIC DEVELOPMENT OF TODDLERS

Between 1 and 2 years of age, children have 20 to 50 words in their productive vocabulary (Biehler, 1976; Morrow, 1989; Owens, 1988) but understand many more. Toddlers are busy people. Having achieved locomotion through crawling and walking, they eagerly investigate all aspects of their environment. Once they discover that everything has a name, they often eagerly seek names for objects and people in their environment. Toddlers may also use language in ways that increase their opportunities to learn about their world by repeating what others say, asking questions, or using repetition to clarify meaning (Shatz, 1994).

Toddlers may also show an increased interest in staying close to their primary caregiver and bringing objects to her for comment on a frequent basis (Cawlfield, 1992). A typical interaction involves a child's question, "What's that?" pronounced quickly as "whadat?" or "whadis?" or more simply "dis?" with rising intonation. When the adult responds with the label, the child may repeat it spontaneously. The child may then continue by asking about another entity in the environment.

As children's environments are repeatedly labeled, both receptive (listening) and expressive (productive) vocabularies increase; however, the listening vocabulary is still larger than the productive vocabulary (Owens, 1988). The productive vocabulary of older toddlers (18 to 24 months) ranges from 200 to 300 words with a much more extensive listening (receptive) vocabulary. A toddler usually maintains only one word in their productive vocabulary per referent. A child may experiment with a specific word and switch to another if the first word is not successful in referring to the desired object, action, or event (Reich, 1986).

Children appear to learn some words quickly with only a few exposures and without specific feedback reinforcement. This is known as **fast mapping** (Carey, 1978), and it has been documented in research with toddlers, preschoolers, and older children (Bloom, 2000; Crais, 1992; Markson, as cited in Bloom, 2000; Markson & Bloom, 1997).

One aspect of semantic development involves children's acquisition of categories, which organize phenomena into groups of shared characteristics. Gelman's research (1998) indicates children as young as 21/2 years old are starting to make "broad generalizations about categories . . . these generalizations increase rather dramatically between two-and-a-half and four years" (p. 24). These generalizations may be evident in toddlers' semantic overextensions and underextensions.

Some adults, aware of children's increasing comprehension, start spelling words to communicate with another adult without the children comprehending, as in "Shall we go for a r-i-d-e?" This works for a while, though through repeated exposures children quickly learn what the spelling sequence means. It is important for teachers and caregivers to realize that although children's speech production is limited, comprehension of others' speech is much higher.

When talking, toddlers rely on suprasegmental elements—the stress, pitch, and juncture of intonation—and gestures to get their message across in their one- and two-word utterances. In responding to toddlers, parents and teachers also rely on contextual factors to assist them in interpreting the child's message. For example, a child's statement, "Mommy milk," can have a variety of meanings based on different pauses, intonation, and gestures, such as:

1. "Mommy, you're drinking milk, too."
2. "My milk's all gone, Mommy."

3. "Oh, look Mommy, I spilled the milk."

4. "Mommy, I want some milk."

The sociocultural context of the speech provides clues to the intended meaning of a child's one- and two-word utterances.

Semantic knowledge related to emergent literacy continues to expand during the toddler years, as children develop an awareness of environmental print and meanings, such as stop signs, McDonald's logos, and labels on food packaging. If you observe a mother and her toddler as they shop for the family groceries, you will often see that the toddler can easily pick out the cereal package she wants even though the specific print is not yet read. Further semantic development also occurs during storybook reading as words and their referents are paired and emphasized in narrative and nonfiction books.

Among some children of toddler age, exploration of drawing and writing occurs. Detailed study of the emergence of writing has been described by various researchers (Baghban, 1984; Clay, 1987; Sulzby, Barnhart, & Hieshima, 1989; Temple, Nathan, & Burris, 1982). Early on, children seem to begin to distinguish between drawing and writing in both form and function, indicating that writing is "read." The attachment of meaning to graphic representations is an important development in children's interactions with written language. By observing adults as they use paper and pencil and interact with print in the environment, children learn that graphic marks carry meaning. As toddlers make marks of their own on paper, they may turn to an adult to ask or confirm what meaning their writing has or may label it themselves (Baghban, 1984).

Children's awareness that written symbols carry meaning is often evident in the way they interact with printed or written materials in their home environments. For example, Ryan (1 year, 9 months) picks up a letter from his grandmother (written in cursive). As he looks at it, he begins to verbalize /ladeladelada/. Similar verbalization occurs when Ryan picks up and looks at informational brochures, his parents' mail, or food cartons. Occasionally, he asks one of his parents to read the print, "Wha da say?"

The dynamics involved in young children's explorations of written language and meaning are illustrated in this example of a toddler who participates in creating his family's grocery list. One day Jon (age 2 years, 11 months) approaches his mother while she is writing her grocery list. When asked what he wants from the store, he replies "raisins." She writes it down on her list. A few moments later she asks Jon if he needs anything else from the store. He says, "raisins" again. His mom replies that she's already written it down. At that point, Jon takes the pencil from her hand and says, "Me write raisins." He makes some marks on the grocery list, along with some dots. Then he hands the paper back to his mother.

Throughout infancy and toddlerhood children are active learners in building their conceptual knowledge and vocabulary. Daily interactions with people, objects, and actions in their environment provide direct and vicarious experiences that enhance children's development of semantic knowledge. When children have opportunities to observe parents and teachers interacting with written language and to participate in those interactions (via storybooks, grocery lists, mail, and newspapers), semantic knowledge related to written language is also enhanced.

Research suggests that children's sensitivity to the way in which words are ordered in language—syntax—also impacts semantic development (Gleitman & Gilette, 1999). For example, verbs occupy a systematic or set place in English sentences. Children appear to perceive this "special place" as indicating that words used in this manner indicate actions and not objects. In this way, syntactic knowledge narrows down possible meanings of new words, thus facilitating semantic development.

SYNTACTIC DEVELOPMENT IN INFANCY

Syntactic development during infancy is not readily evident since infants do not begin to use productive/expressive language until the later part of infancy and then only in the form of idiomorphs and single words. However, children's receptive knowledge of syntax is developing during infancy as they observe and begin to participate in the communicative contexts around them. Although children may be at the one-word stage in their productive language, research suggests they are perceiving and processing language in five- to six-word segments. Children at the one-word stage appear to indicate "that words presented in strings are not isolated units, but are part of larger constituents" (Hirsh-Pasek & Golinkoff, 1996, p. 73). This early awareness facilitates syntactic knowledge development. Comprehension of speech requires that children be able to process words, phrases, and sentences. They must be aware of the role of phrases and word order in determining meaning from speech. Research also indicates that infants may be attending to acoustic properties (prosody) in distinguishing phrasal units (Jusczyk, 1997).

Children develop receptive knowledge of syntax through speech directed to them and by being a listener/observer in adult-adult interactions. The specific ways in which adult-to-child speech differs from adult-adult speech has been detailed in Chapter 2. Syntactically, adult-to-child speech is shorter in length and less complex grammatically. It contains repetitions, uses fewer subordinate clauses, contains fewer modifiers and pronouns, and has more content words but fewer verbs.

Mother speech to children has been studied more extensively than father or caregiver speech since mothers have more frequently been the primary caregivers. There is some indication that mother speech to children changes syntactically during infancy (Clark & Clark, 1977; deVilliers & deVilliers, 1978; Harris, 1992; Snow, 1977). When speaking to 8-month-old children, mother speech is as long as it is to 28-month-old children; however, when a child enters the one-word stage, shortly after age 1, mother speech becomes shorter and focuses on eliciting verbal interaction from the child. Thus, it appears that as children begin to talk, mothers simplify their speech and focus on encouraging their children to verbally participate. Then, after children reach a higher level of verbal production around two years, mother speech again becomes more complex. This is further evidence of mothers' sensitivity to their children's linguistic competencies and zone of proximal development.

Older infants' receptive knowledge of syntax is evident in their behavioral and nonverbal responses to questions or directions such as "Where is your cup?" or "Go get the ball." or "Where is your nose?" When the child retrieves the cup or ball or points to his nose, comprehension of the question or command is evident.

Although infants' productive speech may involve single idiomorphs or one-word utterances, often an implied grammatical structure conveys sentence type. Through the use of intonation and gesture, children's one-word utterances are often perceived to be "questions," "statements," or "commands" (Crystal, 1987).

Infants who are involved in storybook interactions and are read to are exposed to more complex syntactic structures than those that occur in daily conversational settings. As infants near their first birthday, they begin to participate verbally more during storybook interactions. Adults intuitively appear to alter the exact text to fit the comprehension and linguistic competencies of children. They shorten the text, increase repetitions, ask questions, and add sound effects. These adaptations encourage more responses from children. For example the written text, "A is for apple" from an alphabet book might become simply "apple" when directed to a 1-year-old. This labeling might be followed with a short conversation about a child's experiences with apples. One-word labels simplify the text and focus on the main meaning or message of the text. Storybook interactions with infants who are at the one-word stage may be more of a conversation about what is pictured rather than an actual reading of the text.

SYNTACTIC DEVELOPMENT IN TODDLERHOOD

Between the ages of 1 and 2 years, children develop **telegraphic speech.** Telegraphic speech is defined as the child's use of two or three content words in an utterance, with no function words such as conjunctions articles, prepositions, and inflections (Tager-Flusberg, 1997). Simple sentences or sentence fragments involving two or three words are created, such as "Daddy come" and "Mommy coat." Grammatical (syntactic) relationships are implied in these two-word combinations. Although telegraphic speech appears to be syntactically simple, detailed research exploring the contextual meaning of the two-word utterance has indicated that word order expresses semantic relationships not captured by simply identifying the part of speech used by the child (Brown, 1973; Schlesinger, 1971; Slobin, 1979).

Children's telegraphic speech represents both syntactic and semantic language knowledge. Syntactic knowledge is represented in the word order patterns found in telegraphic speech; however, the word order patterns are closely tied to a child's semantic knowledge. Because we cannot directly ask these young children how they decide to combine words in utterances, we must analyze their utterances to see what syntactic patterns are present.

For example, in "Daddy come," a noun and a verb are used in sequential order. The noun functions semantically as an agent and the verb functions to show action. Thus, the semantic relations in "daddy come" are *agent + action.* Children appear to use this syntactic-semantic knowledge as they create other utterances, such as "kitty come," "dog go," and "bird fly."

In addition to the agent + action pattern, several other syntactic/semantic patterns are evident in the telegraphic speech of toddlers (Brown, 1973, cited in Tager-Flusberg, 1997):

action + object	drink milk
agent + object	mommy hat
action + location	go bed
entity + location	sock floor
possessor + possession	daddy shoe
entity + attribute	cookie big
demonstrative + entity	dis coat

Although these syntactic-semantic patterns are found in children's telegraphic speech, no specific order of acquisition has been documented (Braine, 1976, cited in Tager-Flusberg, 1997).

Even though children may be using multiple word utterances as toddlers, they may have difficulty with pronoun use. Pronoun use is semantic in the sense that pronouns take the place of nouns in an utterance; however, the way in which pronoun reference works in a sentence or utterance involves syntactic structure because a pronoun refers to a noun used earlier in the utterance/ sentence in a specific syntactic position.

For example, in the sentence, "The girl was riding her bike when it broke," both *her* and *it* are pronouns referring to nouns. We can identify the referent for *her* because the noun *girl* precedes the pronoun; likewise for *it,* preceded by *bike.* When children learn to use pronouns, they learn how to identify the appropriate referent in the utterance/sentence by using both syntactic and semantic information.

The acquisition of pronouns begins during the toddler years and extends through preschool (Owens, 2001). This long period of acquisition reflects the complexity of pronoun use. Children need to learn that the form of the pronoun must reflect the syntactic position within the utterance. For example, a pronoun may indicate the subject of an utterance (*I, he, she*) while a different form is used to refer to the utterance's object *(him, her, me).*

The acquisition of the pronouns *I* and *you* is particularly complex for toddlers because the use of these pronouns depends on the role of the listener (*you*) and speaker *(I)* (Owens, 2001; Warren & McClosky, 1997). In a conversation the roles of speaker and listener are constantly changing so that the referents for *I* and *you* are also constantly changing. Further, it is difficult for an adult to model the appropriate use of *I* and *you* without adding to the confusion. This confusion may explain why parents and caregivers use labels for objects like *Daddy's* or *baby's* instead of *my* or *your*.

Gradually toddlers learn to use the *I* and *you* pronouns appropriately; however, it is important for early childhood teachers to be aware of the initial confusion toddlers experience in acquiring these pronouns.

When toddlers participate in storybook activities with adults, they are exposed to more complex sentence structure than in conversations; however, adults may intuitively continue to adapt story text to fit the comprehension and attention span of toddlers. This adapted text often models simple syntactic structures similar to adult-to-child speech. When sharing the story *Are You My Mother?* (Eastman, 1960), the text "A mother bird sat on her egg" may be adapted as "Look at the bird. See the nest" and accompanied by gestures, pointing, and eye contact between adult and child to ensure a shared reference. In the example that follows, Allison (1 year, 6 months) and her mother are engaged in reading an alphabet book (Otto, 1996):

Mom:	*(holding book in front of Allison) What are those?*
Allison:	*a*
Mom:	*a, Un-huh (points to letters **ABC** on cover; Allison follows with her own pointing to the letters) b, ABCs (turns page)*
Allison:	*apple*
Mom:	*apple*
Allison:	*bu (points to illustration)*
Mom:	*bug*
Allison:	*(points to letter A)*
Mom:	*and there's the A*
Allison:	*a (pointing to letter)*
Mom:	*that's A*
Allison:	*a*
Mom:	*big A and a little a*
Allison:	*a apple (pause, points to airplane pictured)*
Mom:	*that's an airplane*
Allison:	*mama*
Mom:	*Oh, that's the mama bear, that's a B, mama bear*
Allison:	*bear (points to picture)*
Mom:	*giving the baby bear a bath. Baby bear has a bath. (p. 13)*

This focused conversation about an alphabet book's illustrations exhibits the interaction patterns of shared reference, adult-to-child speech, linguistic scaffolding, verbal mapping, mediation, and the communication loop. It also shows the way in which a child may learn that an alphabet book has a particular type of text structure, as in "a is for apple."

Sometimes toddlers develop a clear sense that text is stable. Parents, teachers, and caregivers are often reminded of this when they are rereading a familiar storybook and fail to recreate the same adapted text they used during prior readings. Realizing the change in the text, a toddler may stop the adult's reading and insist that specific language or sound effects be included that were previously part of the story.

MORPHEMIC DEVELOPMENT IN INFANCY

The development of the morphemic aspect of language is influenced by phonemic awareness (Owens, 1988; 2001). The ability to perceive sound distinctions associated with inflectional morphemes (e.g., plurals, tense markers, and possessives) is necessary for the development of morphemic knowledge. As infants listen to language around them (spoken and read), they begin to develop receptive knowledge of the meaning-changing aspects of morphemes. For example, "You may have one cracker" v. "You may have these crackers" signals significant differences for the young child.

MORPHEMIC DEVELOPMENT IN TODDLERHOOD

Pronoun usage begins during this time, with the use of *I, mine, my, it*, and *me*. This is important to the development of morphemic knowledge in the sense that noun-verb agreement in English influences the use of inflectional morphemes. For example: *I go. He goes. We go.* Verbs are usually expressed in present tense or present progressive (e.g. go-go*ing*) during the early toddler period. At the end of the second year, children usually begin regularly using plural forms of nouns (Bellugi & Brown, 1964; Brown, 1973; Owens, 1988; 2001).

Research on the emergence of English morphemic knowledge among children has documented the order in which 14 specific grammatical morphemes develop during the toddler-primary years (Brown, 1973; deVilliers & deVilliers, 1973) (See Figure 4.1) The first grammatical morphemes to appear are the use of present progressive verbs (go-go*ing*) and two prepositions (*in* and *on*). This sequence of morpheme acquisition does not appear to be influenced by the frequency of parents' use of specific morphemes; instead, acquisition is thought to be related to the linguistic (syntactic and semantic) complexity involved in using the specific morpheme (Brown, 1973).

FIGURE 4.1
Average Order of Acquisition of 14 Grammatical Morphemes

Morphemes by Three Children Studied by Brown

	Morpheme	Example
1.	present progressive	(sing*ing;* play*ing*)
2/3.	prepositions	(*in* the cup; *on* the floor)
4.	plural	(book*s,* doll*s*)
5.	irregular past tense	(*broke; went*)
6.	possessive	(*Mommy's* chair; *Susie's* teddy)
7.	copula, uncontractile	(This *is* my book)
8.	articles	(*The* teddy; *A* table)
9.	regular past tense	(he climbed; Mommy cooked)
10.	third person, present tense, regular	(he climbs; Mommy cooks)
11.	third person present tense, irregular	(John *has* three cookies)
12.	auxiliary, uncontractible	(She *was* going to school; Do you like me?)
13.	copula, contractible	(*I'm* happy you are special)
14.	auxiliary, contractible	(*Mommy's* going shopping)

From Tager-Flusberg, H. "Putting words together: Morphology and syntax in the preschool years." In J. Berko Gleason, (Ed.), *The Development of Language* (4th ed.) (c) 1997 by Allyn & Bacon. Reprinted by permission.

PRAGMATIC DEVELOPMENT IN INFANCY

Through infants' interactions with their world, actions of others come to be perceived as related to outcome or intent (e.g., mother's appearance means baby will be fed). As speech accompanies action, the intent associated with the action becomes associated with the speech. Then as children acquire the ability to sit up independently and reach out to objects and people in their environment (around 6 to 7 months), their gestures are accompanied by vocalizations. Although infants may initially produce gestures and vocalizations without intention, adults may interpret their behavior as meaningful. For example, if an infant waves her arm toward an object and produces a sound, an adult may say, "Oh, you want to play with this?" and give the object to the infant. At 10 months, many infants begin to use specific types of gestures to indicate intent (Bates, Camaioni, & Volterra, 1975; Menyuk, 1988). Somewhat later, around one year of age, idiomorphs or words accompany gestures in expressing intent or purpose.

Infants' intent appears to focus on need satisfaction and control, corresponding to Halliday's (1975) instrumental and regulatory functions (described in the toddler section that follows). During infancy, children's early interactions with adults and older siblings become dialogic in nature with clear turn-taking and shared reference. This dialogic turn-taking contributes to children's awareness of how language is used in specific contexts. They begin to develop an awareness or understanding of how language is used and whether the outcome or intent was achieved. For example, did certain gestures and vocalizations result in being fed, comforted, or entertained? Social routines involving greetings and farewells and ritualized games of peek-a-boo and pat-a-cake also contribute to infants' developing pragmatic knowledge of language.

When infants and parents or caregivers enjoy storybooks together, their joint focusing on the book develops an awareness that books have meaning communicated through language and the process of reading (Joyner and Ray, 1987). In this context, oral language may be used by the parent/adult and the child to regulate, to develop interaction, and heuristically to ask questions about the book's content. A child may learn that his vocalizations accompanied by rising intonation ("questioning") resulted in further speech from the parent or caregiver.

PRAGMATIC DEVELOPMENT IN TODDLERHOOD

Gradually, as infancy ends and toddlerhood progresses, children begin to use language for a variety of purposes (Halliday, 1975; Menyuk, 1988). Initially, language is used *instrumentally* to satisfy a need. Then the child also begins to use language in *regulation* of others' behavior. "No" is a frequently used word by some toddlers to influence others. The *interactional* function of language can be seen as toddlers begin and/or maintain a dialogue. A child's exclamation to "look!" after building a block structure is an example of the *personal* function, drawing attention to his uniqueness or abilities. Language serves a *heuristic* function as children ask questions (e.g., "What's this?" "Why?"). The *imaginative* function of language is observed as children pretend and role play. The last developing function of language used by children is *informative.* Children who relate information to others ("I have a turtle") are using language in an informative way.

Conversations

When they are toddlers, children begin to respond more verbally in conversational settings and take a few turns in maintaining the interaction (Owens, 1988). Older toddlers introduce or change the topic of conversation. In addition, toddlers may use some attention-getting words and gestures (Owens, 1988). Gestures are used to increase the semantic content of what is said; however, as children's productive vocabulary increases during toddlerhood, they begin to rely less on gestures and gesture less during conversations.

Emerging Written Language Knowledge

In literate cultures where children interact with print and texts, their behaviors may indicate they are becoming aware of certain ways in which pragmatic aspects of written language are used to communicate (Phillips & McNaughton,

Toddlers learn how to handle books and turn pages by having frequent opportunities to explore books.

1990; Snow, 1983). Toddlers may crawl up on a parent's or caregiver's lap as the adult is reading a newspaper or book and begin to ask questions or comment (e.g., "Whada write?" "Whada say?" "Whada name?"). Other toddlers eagerly bring the mail to parents, asking them to read it. One mother reported that her toddler hurried over to her with a book, crawled on her lap, and asked her to "talk to the book, Mommy."

During toddlerhood children may also be learning how to hold a book and turn the pages. When Ryan was about 11/2 years old, he was observed experimenting with how to hold a book. On several occasions, after first holding a book upside down, he turned the book right side up before continuing to page through it. Ricky, another toddler, also indicated his awareness of print and reading in his interactions with storybooks by jabbering with a "reading" intonation and pointing to specific letters (Shatz, 1994). Shatz also describes Ricky's "reading" of a fortune from a fortune cookie. Toddlers may also be learning what books are not used for in their environments (throwing, chewing, tearing). These are all parts of developing pragmatic knowledge of literacy and literacy-related events.

The way in which parents interact during the storybook sharing may also influence a child's awareness that books contain information and knowledge. In a storybook sharing, a zone of proximal development may be created between the adult and child. DeLoache (1984; DeLoache & DeMendoza, 1985) explored mothers' storybook interactions with their toddlers (12 to 18 months of age) and documented the following ways in which mothers focused on meaning while supporting and facilitating the interactions. Mothers adjusted their comments and questioning to reflect the linguistic and cognitive level of their children. With younger children, they focused on vocabulary acquisition, while older children were encouraged to respond to questions. In situations where the child's response was not completely correct, the mothers typically used indirect ways to hint at the correct answer or responded positively to what the child said while providing the correct answer. Some mothers referred to real-life events and objects as a way of relating to a pictured object or action. Mothers also added gestures or dramatizations as a way of explaining the meaning of the book text to their children. The supportive scaffolding provided by the mothers in this research provided their children with the opportunity to engage in enjoying books at a level the children would not be able to engage in independently. The children could not access the information and knowledge of the book independently, but with the scaffolding provided by their mothers, children became more aware of the value of books and enjoyment of reading.

Toddlers may also pick up printed items (cards, brochures, books, and junk mail) and verbalize as if they were reading the print, though their reading is best described as imaginative jargon. Parents have described children's spontaneous participation in other literacy events such as grocery list making and letter writing. When Ryan was 1 year, 7 months and his mother was busy writing a letter, he went to his mother, crawled up on her lap, grabbed the pen, and scribbled on the letter. His mother then took his hand and the pen in hers and helped him write a short message. As this occurred, he watched as the message appeared on the page. In this example, Ryan was welcomed as an "emergent writer," contributing to the letter in his own manner and with mediation from his mother. As infants and toddlers participate in contexts where oral and written language are used, they begin to develop their pragmatic knowledge of how language is used in various settings and for various purposes.

Toddlers' responses to print may also indicate an awareness that "print is different from pictures and is associated with meaning in a particular way" (Walton, 1989, p. 52). For example, a toddler who indicates that her wavy line scribble says her name is indicating this awareness, as is a toddler who hums when she sees a page with music printed and vocalizes on a text-only page (Shatz, 1994).

SUMMARY

During infancy and toddlerhood, children's language competencies develop in five areas of language knowledge: phonetic, semantic, syntactic, morphemic, and pragmatic. Developments in each area form the foundation for later, more complex acquisition of language knowledge. During infancy receptive knowledge of language occurs with productive/expressive language usually appearing at the end of infancy. Due to increased mobility, toddlerhood is characterized by energetic exploration of the surrounding environment and the language present in those environments. Significant growth of language knowledge occurs in each of the five aspects of language knowledge as toddlers become more active participants in a wider variety of communicative contexts.

✳ ✳ ✳ CHAPTER REVIEW

1. Terms to review:

emergent literacy	otitis media
cooing	mapping
babbling	suprasegmental elements
echolalic babbling	intonation
jargon	protowords
intonated babble	idiomorphs
selective reinforcement	fast mapping
eustachian tubes	telegraphic speech

2. How may ear infections impact language acquisition of infants and toddlers?

3. Describe an infant's auditory perceptual competencies.

4. What is the value in parent-toddler storybook sharing?

5. When does language acquisition begin?

6. Why is the *I-you* distinction difficult for toddlers?

7. At what age do children typically begin to use words?

8. How is adult-to-child speech adapted syntactically to the needs of the toddler?

9. What is the role of experience in the development of semantic knowledge?

10. What are the causes of ear infections?

✳ ✳ ✳ CHAPTER EXTENSION ACTIVITIES

1. Divide the class into groups of four or five students. Each group will write a description of a child's behavior that illustrates development of one of the aspects of language development. Each group then selects a member to read the description to the whole class. Other groups decide which component was described.

2. Bring a familiar storybook to class, one for every small group. Examine the storybook for each of the five aspects of language. For example, what phonological knowledge can be stimulated by using the book? What value does the book have in promoting semantic knowledge? One member from each small group then presents the analysis to the whole class.

3. Develop a chart summary based on the information in the chapter using the following chart. The class could be divided into five groups with each group developing the chart summary for one of the five aspects of language knowledge. For an example, see the following chart:

	Infant	Toddler
Phonetic		
Semantic		
Syntactic		
Morphemic		
Pragmatic		

✳ ✳ ✳ REFERENCES

Allen, P. (1993). *Understanding ear infections*. Whangarei, New Zealand: Dr. Peter Allen. Available from: Hear You Are, Inc., 4 Musconetcong, Ave. Stanhope, NY 07874.

Aslin, R., & Pisoni, D. (1980). Some developmental processes in speech perception. In G. Yeni-Komshian, J. Kavanaugh, & C. Ferguson (Eds.), *Child phonology: Vol. 2. Perception.* New York: Academic Press.

Baghban, M. (1984). *Our daughter learns to read and write: A case study from birth to three.* Newark, DE: International Reading Association.

Bates, E., Camaioni, L., & Volterra, V. (1975). The acquisition of performatives prior to speech. *Merrill-Palmer Quarterly, 21,* 205–216.

Bellenir, K. (Ed.). (1997). *Congenital disorders sourcebook.* Vol. 29, Health Reference Series. Detroit, MI: Omnigraphics, Inc.

Bellugi, U., & Brown, R. (1964). The acquisition of language. *Monographs for the Society for Research in Child Development, 29*(92).

Biehler, R. (1976). *Child development.* Boston: Houghton-Mifflin.

Bijeljac-Babic, R., Bertoncini, J., & Mehler, J. (1993). How do four-day-old infants categorize multisyllabic utterances? *Developmental Psychology, 29,* 711–721.

Bloom, P. (2000). *How children learn the meanings of words.* Cambridge, MA: MIT Press.

Brooks, A. (1994, November 19). Middle ear infections in children: Brouhaha over treatment leads to consensus—for now. *Science News, 146*(21), 332–334.

Brooks, D. (1978). Impedance screening for school children: State of the art. In E. Harford, F. Booss, C. Blueston, & J. Klein (Eds.), *Impedance screening for middle ear disease in children.* New York: Grune & Stratton.

Brown, R. (1973). *A first language: The early stages.* Cambridge, MA: Harvard University Press.

Carey, S. (1978). The child as word-learner. In M. Halle, J. Bresnan, & G. Miller (Eds.), *Linguistic theory and psychological reality.* Cambridge, MA: MIT Press.

Cawlfield, M. (1992, May). Velcro time: The language connection. *Young Children,* 47(4), 26–30.

Childhood ear infections: Treatments worse than disease. (1995, April). *HealthFacts, 20*(191), 1–3.

Clark, H., & Clark, E. (1977). *Psychology and language.* New York: Harcourt Brace Jovanovich.

Clay, M. (1987). *Writing begins at home.* Portsmouth, NH: Heinemann.

Condon, W., & Sander, L. (1974). Neonate movement is synchronized with adult speech: Interactional participation and language acquisition. *Science, 183,* 99–101.

Crais, E. (1992). Fast mapping: A new look at word learning. In R. Chapman (Ed). *Processes in language acquisition and disorders* (pp. 159–185). St. Louis: Mosby Year Book.

Crystal, D. (1987). *The Cambridge encyclopedia of language.* New York: Cambridge University Press.

Daly, K. (1997). Definition and epidemiology of otitis media. In J. Roberts, I. Wallace & F. Henderson (Eds.), *Otitis media in young children: Medical developmental and educational considerations* (pp. 3–42). Baltimore, MD: Paul H. Brookes.

de Boysson-Bardies, B. (1999). *How language comes to children: From birth to two years.* Cambridge, MA: MIT Press.

DeCasper, A., & Fifer, W. (1980). Of human bonding: Newborns prefer their mothers' voices. *Science, 208,* 1174–1176.

DeCasper, A., & Spence, M. (1986). Prenatal maternal speech influences newborns' perception of speech sounds. *Infant Behavior and Development, 9,* 133–150.

DeLoache, J. (1984). What's this? Maternal questions in joint picture book reading with toddlers. Paper presented at the annual meeting of the American Educational Research Association, New Orleans, LA. ED 251 176.

DeLoache, J., & DeMendoza, O. (1985). Joint picturebook interactions of mothers and one-year-old children. Technical Report No. 353. Champaign: University of Illinois, Center for the Study of Reading.

Denk-Glass, R., Laber, S., & Brewer, K. (1982, September). Middle ear disease in young children. *Young Children,* 51–53.

deVilliers, J., & deVilliers, P. (1973). A cross-sectional study of the acquisition of grammatical morphemes. *Journal of Psycholinguistic Research, 2,* 267–278.

deVilliers, J., & deVilliers, P. (1978). *Language acquisition.* Cambridge, MA: Harvard University Press.

Eastman, P. D. (1960). *Are you my mother?* New York: Random House.

Eisenberg, R. (1976). *Auditory competence in early life: The roots of communicative-behavior.* Baltimore, MD: University Park Press.

Ferguson, C. (1978). Fricatives in child language acquisition. In V. Honsa & M. Hardman-de-Bautista (Eds.), *Papers in linguistics and child language: Ruth Hirsch Weir Memorial Volume.* The Hague, Netherlands: Mouton.

Food allergies linked to ear infections. (1994, October 8). *Science News, 146*(15), 231.

Gelman, S. (1998). Categories in young children's thinking. *Young Children, 53*(1), 20–26.

Gleitman, L., & Gilette, J. (1999). The role of syntax in verb learning. In W. Ritchie & T. Bhatia (Eds.), *Handbook of child language acquisition.* San Diego, CA: Academic Press.

Halliday, M. A. K. (1975). *Learning how to mean: Explorations in the development of language.* London: Edward Arnold.

Harris, M. (1992). *Language experience and early language development: From input to uptake.* Hillsdale, NH: Lawrence Erlbaum Associates.

Henderson, F. (1997). Medical management of otitis media. In J. Roberts, I. Wallace, & F. Henderson (Eds.), *Otitis media in young children: Medical, developmental and educational considerations* (pp. 219–244). Baltimore, MD: Paul H. Brookes.

Hirsh-Pasek, K., & Golinkoff, R. (1996). The origins of grammar: Evidence from early language comprehension. Cambridge, MA: MIT Press.

Jensen, P., Williams, W., & Bzoch, K. (1975, November). Preference of young infants for speech vs. nonspeech stimuli. Paper presented to the annual American Speech and Hearing Association Convention, Washington, DC.

Jewell, M., & Zintz, M. (1990). *Learning to read and write naturally.* Dubuque, IA: Kendall/Hunt.

Joyner, R., & Ray, E. (1987). Reading behavior in infancy: Developmental and attitudinal implications. Paper presented at the annual conference of the Association for Childhood Education International, Omaha, NE. ED 292 068.

Jusczyk, P. (1985). On characterizing the development of speech perception. In J. Mehler & R. Fox (Eds.), *Neonate cognition: Beyond the blooming, buzzing confusion.* Hillsdale, NJ: Erlbaum.

Jusczyk, P. (1997). *The discovery of spoken language.* Cambridge, MA: MIT Press.

Lillo-Martin, D. (1999). Modality effects and modularity in language acquisition: The acquisition of American sign language. In W. Ritchie & T. Bhatia (Eds.), *Handbook of child language acquisition* (pp. 531–568). San Diego, CA: Academic Press.

Mandel, D., Jusczyk, P., & Kemler-Nelson, D. (1994). Does sentential prosody help infants organize and remember speech information? *Cognition, 53,* 155–180.

Markson, L., & Bloom, P. (1997). Evidence against a dedicated system for word learning in children. *Nature, 385,* 813–815.

Menn, L. (1989). Phonological development: Learning sounds and sound patterns. In J. Berko Gleason (Ed.), *The development of language* (2nd ed., pp. 59–100). Columbus, OH: Merrill.

Menyuk, P. (1988). *Language development: Knowledge and use.* Glenview, IL: Scott Foresman/Little, Brown.

Morrow, L. (1989). *Literacy development in the early years.* Upper Saddle River, NJ: Prentice Hall.

O'Neill, P. (1999, September 25). Acute otitis media. *British Medical Journal* [Online], *319* (7213), 833–836. Database: Academic Search Elite; Item number: 2345312.

Otto, B. (1994). Emergent reading among infants and toddlers. Paper presented at the Illinois Day Care Action Council Annual Conference, Rosemont, IL.

Otto, B. (1995, February). Emergent reading behaviors among infants and toddlers. Paper presented at the Chicago Association of the Education of Young Children Conference, Chicago.

Otto, B. (1996). Let's read a story: The role of storybook reading in young children's literacy acquisition. *Illinois Schools Journal, 76*(1), 5–18.

Owens, R. (1988). *Language development.* Columbus, OH: Merrill.

Owens, R. (2001) *Language development.* Boston: Allyn & Bacon.

Paradise, J. (1997). Developmental outcomes in relation to early-life otitis media: Present and future directions in research. In J. Robert, I. Wallace, & F. Henderson (Eds.), *Otitis media in young children: Medical, developmental, and educational considerations* (pp. 287–306). Baltimore, MD: Paul H. Brookes.

Phillips, G. & McNaughton, S. (1990). The practice of storybook reading to preschool children in mainstream New Zealand families. *Reading Research Quarterly, 25*(3), 163–250.

Pulec, J. (1998). Treatment of otitis media: A step backwards. *ENT: Ear, Nose, & Throat Journal* [Online], 77(10) p. 800. Database: Academy Search Elite; Item Number: 1298562.

Reich, P. (1986). *Language development.* Upper Saddle River, NJ: Prentice Hall.

Roberts, M. (1976). Comparative study of pure tone, impedance, and otoscopic hearing screening methods. *Archives of Otolarynology, 102,* 690–694.

Ryval, M. (1995). "Mommy, my ear hurts!" *Chatelaine,* (68)3, 24.

Sachs, J. (1989). Communication development in infancy. In J. Berko Gleason (Ed.), *The development of language* (2nd ed., pp. 35–58). Columbus, OH: Merrill.

Schlesinger, I. (1971). Production of utterances and language acquisition. In D. Slobin (Ed.), *The ontogenesis of grammar.* New York: Academic Press.

Segal, M. (1983). *Birth to one year.* White Plains, NY: Mailman Family Press.

Shatz, M. (1994). *A toddler's life: Becoming a person.* New York: Oxford University Press.

Slobin, D. (1979). *Psycholinguistics* (2nd ed.). Glenview, IL: Scott Foresman.

Snow, C. (1977). Mother's speech research: From input to interaction. In C. Snow & C. Ferguson (Eds.), *Talking to children: Language input and acquisition* (pp. 31-50). New York: Cambridge University Press.

Snow, C. (1983). Literacy and language relationships during the preschool years. *Harvard Educational Review, 53*(2), 165–189.

Stewig, J. (1982). *Teaching language arts in early childhood.* New York: Holt, Rinehart & Winston.

Stoel-Gammon, C. (1998). Role of babbling and phonology in early linguistic development. In A. Wetherby, S. Warren, & J. Reichle (Eds.), *Transitions in prelinguistic communication* (pp. 87–110). Baltimore, MD: Brookes.

Strauss, R. (1993, May). Otitis media with effusion in children: Telltale clinical patterns, helpful diagnostic procedures. *Consultant, 33*(5), 85–88.

Sulzby, E., Barnhart, J., & Hieshima, J. (1989). Forms of writing and rereading from writing. In J. Mason (Ed.), *Reading and writing connections* (pp. 31–64). Needham Heights, MA: Allyn & Bacon.

Tager-Flusberg, H. (1997). Putting words together: Morphology and syntax in the preschool years. In J. Berko Gleason (Ed.), *The development of language* (4th ed., pp. 159–209). Boston: Allyn & Bacon.

Teele, D., Klein, J., Chase, C., Menyuk, P., & Rosner, B. (1990). Otitis media in infancy and intellectual ability, school achievement, speech and language at age 7 years. *The Journal of Infectious Diseases, 162,* 685–694.

Temple, C., Nathan, R., & Burris, W. (1982). *The beginnings of writing.* Boston: Allyn & Bacon.

Tronick, E., Als, H., & Adamson, L. (1979). Structure of early face-to-face communicative interactions. In M. Bullowa (Ed.), *Before speech: The beginning of interpersonal communication* (pp. 349–372). New York: Cambridge University Press.

Vernon-Feagans, L., Manlove, E., & Volling, B. (1996). Otitis media and the social behavior of daycare-attending children. *Child Development, 67,* 1528–1539.

Wallace, I. & Hooper, S. (1997). Otitis media and its impact on cognitive, academic, and behavioral outcomes: A review and interpretation of the findings. In J. Roberts, I. Wallace, & F. Henderson (Eds.), *Otitis media in young children: Medical, developmental and educational considerations* (pp. 163–194). Baltimore, MD: Paul H. Brookes.

Walton, S. (1989). Katy learns to read and write. *Young Children, 44*(5), 52–57.

Warren, A., & McCloskey, L. (1997). Language in social contexts. In J. Berko Gleason (Ed.), *The development of language* (4th ed., pp. 210–258). Boston: Allyn & Bacon.

Werker, J., & Tees, R. (1984). Cross-language speech perception: Evidence for perceptual reorganization during the first year of life. *Infant Behavior and Development, 7,* 49–63.

Werner, H., & Kaplan, B. (1963). *Symbol formation: An organismic approach to language and the expression of thought.* New York: John Wiley & Sons.

White, B. (1978). *The first three years of life.* New York: Avon Books.

Williams, R. (1994, December). Protecting little pitchers' ears. *FDA Consumer, 28*(10), 10–15.

Wolff, P. (1966). The natural history of crying and other vocalizations in early infancy. In B. Foss (Ed.), *Determinants of infant behavior IV.* London: Methuen.

Zukow-Goldring, P., & Ferko, K. (1994). An ecological approach to the emergence of the lexicon: Socializing attention. In V. John-Steiner, C. Panofsky, & L. Smith (Eds.), *Sociocultural approaches to language and literacy: An interactionist perspective.* New York: Cambridge University Press.

APPENDIX

✳ ✳ ✳

EAR INFECTIONS: PHYSIOLOGY AND TREATMENT

PHYSIOLOGICAL SYMPTOMS AND CONDITIONS

To understand the nature of this illness, it is necessary to become familiar with the structure of the ear and nose area. Ear structure is composed of three main areas: the ear canal, the middle ear, and the inner ear. The eustachian tube connects the middle ear area with the nose. The eustachian tube functions to allow air to pass up or down the tube and to allow secretions in the middle ear to drain down into the nose and to prevent fluid from flowing back up into the middle ear (Allen, 1993). In young children the eustachian tube is shorter and almost horizontal, whereas an adult's is longer and has a vertical slant. Thus, in young children the fluids may not drain as well and fluids may flow back up into the middle ear area. When fluids are in the middle ear, the eardrum cannot vibrate normally and hearing is affected. Normal vibration of the eardrum only occurs when both the middle ear and the ear canal are full of air. When the middle ear becomes infected, children experience painful earaches. Depending upon the severity of the infection and the length of time the infection is present, children's hearing may be impaired.

The term *otitis media with effusion* refers to a condition where fluid is present in the middle ear for over three months without indications of an infection (O'Neill, 1999). There is no fever and little discomfort. Though the fluid may not be infected, hearing is still affected since the eardrum cannot function normally with fluid present in the middle ear. This condition may be short term or it may last for many months. *Acute otitis media* is the condition where the middle ear has an active infection; the eardrum is inflamed (red and swollen) and is accompanied by pain and fever (Allen, 1993). In severe cases the eardrum may rupture due to the high level of infection (O'Neill, 1999). In these instances, hearing is greatly affected and recovery takes much longer. When otitis media occurs during the preschool years, particularly ages 1 to 3 when children are acquiring their phonetic knowledge both receptively and expressively, significant language impairments or delays can occur.

CAUSES AND PREVENTION

Several factors have been identified as contributing to the presence of fluid in the middle ear. One of the most frequent causes is a respiratory infection (common cold). Viral respiratory infections cause the lining of the nasal cavity to swell, which also involves the eustachian tube. When this fluid and infection reach the middle ear, otitis media develops. Children of large families and those attending preschool or day care are more likely to be exposed to viral respiratory infections due to the number of people with whom they are in contact. Preventive measures should be taken to reduce the transmission of bacteria and viral infections by thorough hand washing by caregivers and children as well as monitoring children who have colds or other respiratory infections.

Other conditions associated with the onset of otitis media include bottle-feeding, secondhand smoke, allergies, and birth defects. Infants who are breast-fed have less incidence of otitis media. Breast milk may contain antibodies that reduce susceptibility to infections. Additionally, bottle-fed babies may be fed while in a horizontal position; particularly if they are given a bottle while laying in a crib. This increases the chance that milk will be forced into the middle ear through the eustachian tube (Allen, 1993). Both bottle-fed and breast-fed infants should be held in a slanted position with the head tilted upwards, not laid horizontally.

Children whose parents smoke have three times the number of incidents of otitis media than children whose parents do not smoke. These children also take longer to get well (Williams, 1994). With this in mind, parents, caregivers, and teachers of young children should not expose children to secondhand smoke.

Recent research indicates food allergies are associated with incidents of otitis media ("Food Allergies Linked," 1994; Strauss, 1993; Williams, 1994). T. M. Nsouli and his colleagues at Georgetown University School of Medicine in Washington, D.C. (cited in the "Food Allergies" article) studied children who had recurring ear infections and found 77 percent of the children were allergic to a frequently eaten food. Milk and wheat allergies were the most common. When the children did not eat the specific food for four months, nearly 70 percent were healthier. Then the foods were added back to the children's diets. Within four months, 63 percent of the children again showed fluid in the ears. While research continues in to the role of allergies in causing otitis media, parents and teachers should carefully monitor children's reactions to specific foods, particularly reactions that involve nasal congestion or watery mucous.

Ear infections are also associated with enlarged "tonsils and adenoids and chronic tonsilitis" (Pulec, 1998, p. 800). In addition, birth defects are also associated with a higher incidence of otitis media. Children with cleft palate, Down's syndrome, or nervous system abnormalities are more susceptible to middle ear infections and ear fluid. These birth defects involve impaired muscular control of the eustachian tube and abnormal physical conditions in the ear, mouth, and/or nose area that increase the likelihood of fluid entering the eustachian tube. Parents and teachers of children with these birth defects need to be especially vigilant in monitoring the health of these young children.

TREATMENT

Technological advances in the diagnosis of ear infections have increased the medical profession's ability to diagnose and treat middle ear infections (Brooks,

1978; Henderson, 1997; O'Neill, 1999; Roberts, 1976); however, there is little universal agreement as to which treatment is the most appropriate.

Antibiotics are the most common form of treatment for middle ear infections. Children typically take an oral antibiotic for approximately 2 weeks, followed by an additional visit to the doctor to check on the condition of the ear(s). Recent research has called into question the use of antibiotics since it has been associated with varied rates of successful treatment and additional side effects "Childhood Ear Infections," 1995; Henderson, 1997; O'Neill, 1999; Williams, 1994).

Another type of treatment for chronic middle ear infection involves surgically inserting tiny tubes into the middle ear, through the ear drum (tympanostomy) (Allen, 1993; Strauss, 1993). This type of treatment is often done when ear infections recur frequently. These tubes usually stay in the eardrum from several months to two years. Sometimes the tubes fall out on their own; in other instances they are removed by a surgeon. The tubes do not prevent future occurrences of otitis media; instead, the tubes provide drainage of the fluid that accumulates during any future episodes of otitis media. Tube insertion, however, does decrease the incidence of acute otitis media: since the fluids are drained away, severe infection is less likely to occur.

More than 1 million ear tube placement operations occur annually in the United States ("Childhood Ear Infections," 1995). The high number of these operations has been the subject of debate among medical professionals (Williams, 1994). Critics contend that tube placement and antibiotic treatment are too frequently recommended when middle ear fluid (not infected) goes away on its own within 3 months in 60 percent of the cases and in 85 percent of the cases, fluid goes away in 6 months (Ryval, 1995). Additional concerns stem from complications arising from the surgical placement of the tubes (Allen, 1993; Brooks, 1994). Recommendations now suggest that surgery be performed if the child's condition shows no improvement for 4 to 6 months and if there is a significant hearing loss (Brooks, 1994; Williams, 1994).

While the medical profession continues to debate the ways in which otitis media is best treated, teachers and parents can continue to monitor the health and hearing of young children so that medical advice is sought at the first sign of otitis media. Teachers and parents should attempt to minimize children's exposure to respiratory ailments, secondhand smoke, and foods associated with allergies. Additionally, teachers and parents of infants should not allow infants to bottle-feed while lying horizontally in their cribs. When teachers and parents are aware of the potential threat of otitis media to the normal auditory and cognitive development of young children, they can better monitor children's health, reduce the risk factors, and seek medical attention early.

5

ENHANCING LANGUAGE DEVELOPMENT IN INFANTS AND TODDLERS

The toddler room is busy with activity. Marc is at the table putting the large snap beads together into a "snake." Robin is building in the block center and announces she's making a house. Teddy is in the writing center. He "writes" vigorously, stops, and takes his paper to his teacher, saying, "Read it." Sarah is in the drama corner, putting on a hat and stuffing a scarf into her big purse. As she leaves the drama corner and walks around the room, you hear her say "goin' shoppin'."

Children's language development is influenced by their surrounding environment. One of the basic tenets of early childhood education involves the planning and implementation of learning environments for young children that enhance their development. In this chapter, we will consider specific aspects of early childhood curriculum and their roles in enhancing language development among infants and toddlers. An emphasis will be placed on the rationale for selecting certain activities and teachers' roles in facilitating the activity/experience. Use of the terms *infants* and *toddlers* is not meant to indicate only chronological age; instead, *infant curriculum* describes the appropriate learning activities for young, nonwalking children, and *toddler curriculum* focuses on children from the time they are walking until they are around 2 1/2 to 3 years old.

As described in Chapter 4, infants develop receptive language as they begin to interpret and comprehend the messages communicated by people around them. Children also begin to participate in communicative interactions through their use of gesture and preword vocalizations. Thus, during infancy learning activities should focus on developing receptive language and establishing communication with infants through the use of gesture and preword vocalizations.

Toddlers begin to use language in two- or three-word utterances for a variety of purposes and are beginning a period of rapid growth in all aspects of language knowledge. Thus, toddlers need a curriculum that provides them opportunities to explore and interact within their environment in a range of activities.

The learning environment of infant and toddler settings is critical. It is important to consider all aspects of the environment—the physical environment, the cognitive environment, and the social-emotional or interpersonal environment—when seeking to enhance language development.

DEVELOPMENTAL APPROPRIATENESS OF CURRICULA

Developmentally appropriate curricula that focus on language development are characterized by the following:

- recognition of the developmental levels of children,
- incorporation of language development activities throughout the curriculum,
- embedded conceptual development in a predominance of hands-on activities with authentic materials, and
- flexibility in meeting the needs of individual children (Bredekamp & Copple, 1997).

Curricula for infant and toddler settings are not just simplified versions of curricula for preschool rooms; instead, each curriculum has specific, unique features that meet the specific developmental needs of infants and toddlers (Lowman & Ruhmann, 1998).

Infant and toddler rooms need to have flexible curricula that provide opportunities for meeting the unique needs of each young child. As a result there may be a tendency not to plan any specific learning experiences and instead assume that all learning activities will develop spontaneously. To a certain extent this is true: an appropriately prepared environment provides a setting in which children's spontaneous activities are beneficial and meet the needs of the children involved. However, in some cases, infant and toddler rooms are prepared only intuitively rather than from a thoughtful analysis of the developmental appropriateness of the anticipated activities and events.

Teachers guide children in engaging in learning activities by carefully selecting the materials present in the classroom. This planning needs to include a specific focus on the ways in which the activities provided will enhance the acquisition of language knowledge. By engaging in this type of planning, teachers become more aware of the value of particular activities in infant and toddler rooms and can then provide specific curricular information to parents and/or administrators. Preplanning also enhances a teacher's role as a facilitator, guide, and observer, rather than someone who just leads the activities.

Early childhood classrooms for infants and toddlers may be located in day-care centers or other child care settings. In these settings, caregivers, staff, and state-certified teachers all serve as children's "teachers," preparing the learning environment and serving as mediators and guides for infants and toddlers as they explore and interact with children and adults in that environment. With that in mind, the term *caregiver* will refer to both center staff and formally trained, or certified, teachers.

INFANTS

General Guidelines for Interactions Between Caregivers and Infants

Four of the interaction patterns described in Chapter 2 are particularly relevant for interactions with infants: eye contact and shared reference, communication loops, verbal mapping, and adult-to-child talk. Caregivers should frequently engage infants in one-to-one conversations, using simple language and establishing eye contact and shared reference. Engaging infants in conversation-like turn-taking establishes the patterns of future, more complex conversations. Through eye contact and shared reference, caregivers engage infants in communication about an event or object. In establishing eye contact, caregivers need to hold infants close enough so the infants can see their faces as they talk.

Timing the interaction with infants is also important. This is "key to helping the infant see the connection between language labels and the things they refer to (referents)" (Fowler, 1990, p. 26). For example, if you are showing a new object to an infant and labeling it, you first establish eye contact and then manipulate the object to draw the child's attention while labeling the object. You also need to monitor the infant's verbal and/or nonverbal responses to the object. Does the infant attempt to reach for the object? Does the infant vocalize or attempt to imitate the object label? Does the infant turn away and look at another event in the room? By monitoring the infant's response, you can determine whether the interaction can be extended or whether it should be discontinued.

In addition, timing is important in a broader sense. Infant caregivers need to be sensitive to each infant's approach to learning (Honig & Lally, 1981). Some infants thrive with more frequent stimulation from their caregivers while other infants need periods of "free time" to explore the environment on their own, at their own pace, without constant adult interaction.

It is also important that caregivers listen and respond to the sounds that infants make, encouraging them to participate in a turn-taking communication loop. When conversing with infants, it is important to use speech that is expressive and varied in intonation because it extends the child's attention and interest. In addition, adult speech that is more syntactically simple is easier for the infant to understand. By repeating words or phrases, infants' understanding is increased. Caregivers should also use consistent concept labels, rather than calling a cat *cat* one time and *kitty* the next (Fowler, 1990).

Verbal mapping occurs when the caregiver talks to the infant about what is going to happen, what is happening, and/or what has happened. When verbal mapping is appropriately provided when the child is alert, it can enhance an infant's receptive language by stimulating attention to the caregiver's speech and the ongoing events or actions. It is important for caregivers to be sensitive to individual children's responses to verbal mapping. Continuous or too frequent verbal mapping may be overwhelming to some infants. By monitoring an infant's eye contact, shared reference, and verbal and nonverbal responses, caregivers can determine whether the verbal mapping is too frequent and overstimulating.

Infants' cries or calls of distress should always be given a quick response. Infants need the security of knowing that their physical and emotional needs will be met by their caregivers. This sense of security builds a trusting relationship between infants and their caregivers and provides a foundation for positive personality and social development that are essential for optimal cognitive development (Wortham, 1998).

Caregivers should praise infants for sitting up, shaking a rattle, vocalizing, and other accomplishments. This increases their positive feelings and encourages them to continue to respond to their environment.

General Guidelines for Infant Classroom Settings

A room that is cheerful and contains a variety of colorful pictures of familiar objects, friendly animals, and people's faces displayed at the child's level provides interest to infants' visual environment. The room should be "rich in sensorimotor and social experiences" (Weiser, 1991, p. 21) without being overwhelming. Toys should focus on the sensorimotor needs of infants. For example, bells,

Bright-colored, soft rattles provide infants with auditory and visual stimulation.

balls, large snap-locking beads, nesting bowls, music boxes, or squeeze toys should be easily accessible. Toys should be safe for infants to explore through grasping, chewing, or manipulating. Books should be of heavy cardboard or padded plastic. They should have bright pictures of familiar objects. A variety of music should be played to enhance listening through exposure to a range of rhythm, pitch, and musical tone.

INFANT CURRICULA

Three types of activities predominate in a developmentally appropriate infant room: exploratory activities, caregiver-mediated activities, and routine activities. Each of these activities embodies informal instruction by the caregiver and a thoroughly and thoughtfully prepared environment. The daily schedule is planned around infants' physical needs and is individualized to accommodate each child's needs for eating, sleeping, and physical care, along with activities to engage children during their "alert" time. Exploratory activities and caregiver-mediated activities take place during infants' alert time. Eating, arrival, departure, and physical care activities compose routine activities.

Exploratory Activities

The focus of exploratory activities at this level is on encouraging children to engage independently in sensorimotor activities. These activities are based in sensory perception, involving sight, sound, taste, touch, and smell. According to

Piaget (Brainerd, 1978), infants develop cognitively through their sensory and movement experiences while interacting in various settings. Piaget's description of the sensorimotor stage focuses on the importance of children exploring objects and their actions upon those objects. From those experiences children develop ways of organizing sensory information so that it makes sense (Goodman, 1993). These activities are critical for concept formation as firsthand, direct experience provides the basis for the development of concepts. During the course of a child's first year, labels for concepts begin to become attached to this experiential basis. As discussed in Chapter 2, these experiences provide the basis for symbol formation and receptive language knowledge.

Exploratory activities for infants are accompanied by more caregiver monitoring and mediating guidance than activities for older children due to the necessary concern for infants' safety and well-being. Additionally, caregiver mediation can provide labeling and linguistic mapping, which is important to children's developing receptive language knowledge (Fowler, 1990). However, caregivers should not feel compelled to engage in constant labeling or linguistic mapping. Infants need time to explore on their own and at their own pace.

Crib-Based Activities

Young infants in group care settings spend some alert time each day in their cribs, though it is not recommended that children be left alone in their cribs when awake for extended periods of time. Crib time should be accompanied by opportunities to explore a variety of objects. Manipulative toys or toys that are visually engaging and safe are appropriate for crib-based activities, such as mobiles, crib activity centers, and other appropriate objects.

Mobiles. Some crib mobiles are visually engaging due to the movement of the items and the color contrasts and patterns of the items on the mobile. When deciding to use a mobile, be sure to examine it for safety features and to view the mobile from the child's perspective. High-quality mobiles are generally easily attached and removed so that when caregivers want to provide this type of visual and cognitive stimulation, the mobile can be mounted on the crib for a specific time period. When placing a mobile, consider the view from the child's line of sight. Some mobiles are only effective when viewed from a sitting position and are not interesting when viewed from underneath. Young infants benefit from their own observations and interactions with mobiles; however, it is also appropriate for caregivers to occasionally provide basic labels for the items on the mobile and to describe the movement of the items. When labeling or talking about an item, the caregiver should touch the item in question and check to be sure the child is also focusing on the item, engaging in shared reference.

Crib activity centers. Crib activity centers are similar to mobiles in that they provide visual/perceptual stimulation. These activity centers are generally designed to be safer than mobiles, so if they are securely attached to the side of the

When placing a mobile, consider the view from the child's line of sight.

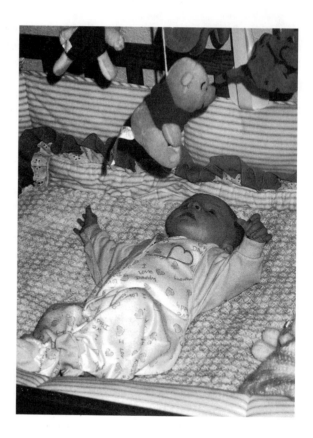

crib, they may be left up for an extended time, provided they are checked on a daily basis for safety. When infants are interacting with an activity center, caregivers may occasionally mediate infants' interactions similar to the way interactions with a mobile are mediated.

Crib-appropriate objects. Crib toys need to be visually or perceptually engaging so that the infant is interested and attempts to reach for and manipulate the object (Maxim, 1990). The caregiver should verbally introduce the item by labeling it and show any appropriate action. For example, a caregiver would shake a rattle and pause, then repeat the action several times before leaving it in the crib. Plastic balls or other shapes with bells or noisemakers inside are appropriate crib toys. However, caregivers must make sure that the object is securely made so it will not come apart. When an infant seems to have tired of the object, exchange it for another similar or slightly familiar object or move the object to a different position. Changing the position of the object is particularly important if perception of the object changes with the position. Placed in different positions, many objects take on new shapes and perspectives.

Stuffed animals are not always included in infant centers since they are difficult to sanitize and thus may increase the spread of illness. For this reason, some states have restrictions against the use of stuffed animals in child care facilities.

With older infants who are able to sit up and move around independently by crawling or scooting, crib-based activities should involve objects they can hold and manipulate. Selecting objects that have a variety of textures, shapes, colors, and functional properties provides opportunities for important conceptual development and receptive language acquisition. Objects with properties of sound such as rattles and balls with bells or squeakers inside encourage infants to repeat actions that create those sounds. All of the items used in crib-based activities should be easily sanitized so that illnesses will not be spread when the objects are used from crib to crib.

Young infants also benefit from being placed in an infant seat for short periods of time so that they can observe people and activities in the room and the environment in general (Wortham, 1998). During the time an infant is positioned in an infant seat, the caregiver needs to monitor the child's comfort level frequently and occasionally engage the infant in a conversation or short interaction.

Room-Based Exploratory Activities

When infants can sit up independently and move around by scooting or crawling, exploratory activities are more appropriately room-based. This increases the perceptual range for infants. The infant room needs to be arranged and furnished so that all items within children's reach or mobility are appropriate and free of safety hazards. Since crawling infants are exploring their environment at the floor level, it is important to prepare the floor space to be safe and interesting (Maxim, 1990). A colorful floor rug provides visual interest to crawling infants. Furniture cushions and pillows also add to infants' exploration. Large pictures of people, animals, or storybook characters can be mounted on the lower part of walls to increase visual interest. An unbreakable mirror mounted near the floor also stimulates exploration.

Infants need time and opportunity to interact with objects at their own pace. The role of the caregiver in this instance is to provide an appropriate environment and then to monitor and mediate children's interactions, providing verbal mapping and labeling in a way that is sensitive to each child's individual learning approach.

Balls and push-pull toys. Toys that move when touched or pulled encourage infants to move with or after the toy. These toys also encourage children to use their hands to move the toy. This helps children learn cause-and-effect relationships and figure out how to repeat actions to create the same results. Caregivers' verbal mapping and affective responses to children's actions stimulate conceptual development and encourage verbal (preword) interactions.

Music. During exploratory times, children's auditory perception can be stimulated by playing a variety of music. Instrumental music and vocal music are appropriate. Music should be played at a moderate-to-low volume and only for short periods (10- to 15-minutes). Music with simple instrumentation, such as piano music or flute music, is more appropriate than full orchestration with complex interwoven melodies and rhythms. Vocal music should feature distinct voices. Using instrumental or vocal music during exploratory activity time has value for older and younger infants. Older infants who are moving around more independently may indicate their perception of rhythm and tone by their body movements. In addition, older infants are more responsive verbally and may babble or vocalize in response to vocal music. Music that has become familiar to them may evoke stronger responses.

Exploratory infant activities enhance language development through stimulating conceptual development, which leads to semantic knowledge. Infancy is a time of receptive language development, as children hear language used by adults and begin to establish communication routines through shared reference and communication loops. Children begin to learn that all objects have a name. They also learn that certain actions on objects produce certain results: if you push a ball, it will roll; if you pick up a ball and throw it, it will go far away fast. Through their sensorimotor explorations, children develop conceptual knowledge. The caregiver's verbal mapping and mediation facilitate children's receptive knowledge of each of the five aspects of language development.

Caregiver-Mediated Activities

Many of the exploratory activities described in the previous section involve caregiver mediation in which the caregiver verbally interacts with a child while an object is being contemplated or manipulated (Weiser, 1991). Caregiver interaction in these instances also involves verbal mapping and labeling, linguistic scaffolding, and an adult-to-child speech register.

Music

When caregivers sing simple songs to infants, they provide opportunities for children to become more aware of sound and rhythm through auditory sequencing, imitation, and anticipating outcomes from repetitive rhythms (Maxim, 1990). In addition, listening skills are encouraged. Children may also begin to associate word labels with objects in their surroundings (Maxim, 1990). Action songs, also known as *finger plays,* are simple melodies that are accompanied by rhythmic gestures and movement. In singing to infants, caregivers should "exaggerate the sounds and speak slowly" while using gestures or soft clapping in rhythm with the song (Honig & Brophy, 1996). Infants enjoy songs such as "Itsy, Bitsy Spider" or "Open Them, Shut Them." Although not always set to music, chants and nursery rhymes are also enjoyable because of the rhythmic language. (For a collection of chants, see Coglin, 1982, in the list of reference books for toddler activities at the end of this chapter).

Objects

Another type of caregiver-mediated activity occurs when a caregiver selects a particular object or activity to be used with a specific child or several children based on their developmental needs. This interaction is more didactic in nature, with the caregiver specifically selecting the learning materials and providing a flexible structure for the interaction. For example, to stimulate an infant's hearing, a caregiver might select a rattle and hold it near the infant and shake it briefly, establishing eye contact and shared reference. Then the caregiver would pause, waiting to see if the infant has any response, and then shake the rattle again, and pause. The caregiver should respond enthusiastically to the child's perception of the sound. Labeling and verbal mapping are appropriate during this activity, such as, "Look at this rattle. It makes this sound (shake it). Did you hear it? (Baby waves arms, looks at rattle intently, or smiles.) Yes, you did!" This should be followed with time for the infant to interact with the rattle alone without caregiver mediation.

Remember that an infant's curiosity and interest in objects or events is influenced by the way in which the selected object can be assimilated or accommodated into previous experiences. The child's interest is the greatest for objects or events that are only slightly different from previous experiences. Totally new experiences may be too overwhelming, resulting in the infant ignoring the object or event or simply withdrawing (Weiser, 1991).

Object permanence is an important cognitive achievement of infancy. Caregivers can provide experiences that will enhance this acquisition with games such as peek-a-boo and uncovering a hidden object. The hidden object activity involves tying a brightly colored ribbon onto a small toy (Wortham, 1998). Then the toy is hidden under a small blanket or cloth. The caregiver shows the infant how to find the toy by pulling the ribbon. By repeating these actions several times and praising the infant's responses and attempts to find the toy, the infant is encouraged to become actively involved in the game.

Caregivers should also carry infants about the room and talk to them about interesting objects or pictures in the room, using labeling and verbal mapping (Wortham, 1998). This verbal and visual stimulation encourages children to respond to objects and events in the room while in close contact with a watchful adult.

Books

Infants enjoy sharing and "contemplating" books with their caregivers and parents. Book sharing with infants provides rich opportunities for both receptive and expressive language development; however, recent research has indicated that infants and toddlers in group care may have only limited opportunities for book sharing (Honig & Shin, 2001). The emphasis of the interaction is on describing what is pictured rather than on reading the story (Honig & Lally, 1981; Honig & Shin, 2001). Books for infants should be made of a durable material, such as cardboard, plastic, or cloth. The illustrations should be simple and large (Maxim, 1990). Caregivers can make infant books by mounting magazine pictures on cardboard or cloth (Honig & Lally, 1981). These books should be short, about four pages long, and can be on a single subject, such as foods, toys, or animals.

Honig and Brophy (1996) offer specific guidelines for caregivers to follow in sharing books with infants.

1. Select a quiet area in which to read, free of other sound or visual distractions.
2. Sit comfortably with the infant in your lap.
3. Talk slowly, enjoying each page of the book.
4. Monitor the infant's eye gaze and any gestures to determine his attention to a particular picture. Take more time talking about pictures in which he is interested.
5. Talk with expression, providing labels, adding sound effects, and using variations in intonation to encourage responses.
6. Continue the book sharing until the infant shows a lack of interest. Do not be concerned about finishing the book.

Routine Activities

At the infant level, the children's developmental needs determine that significant portions of the day be devoted to feeding, sleeping, and other physical care routines. During these times, caregivers can engage infants in conversation-like interactions and provide verbal mapping.

Feeding times can be accompanied by a caregiver's talk about the types of food and encouragement for the child's efforts in feeding. For very young infants, bottle feeding should be accompanied by being held by their caregiver in a semi-upright, slanted position. Caregiver talk should accompany the feeding and burping sequence. With older infants, caregivers can verbally encourage their hand-feeding attempts and talk about the food being served.

Diaper-changing and dressing times should also be accompanied by caregiver talk or singing. Since the child and caregiver are face to face, these activities provide a good opportunity to establish eye contact and conversational turn-taking through imitation of the infant's cooing and babbling responses and through verbal mapping, labeling, or singing. It is also an opportunity for the infant to observe up close the caregiver's facial expressions and hear the variations in intonation of the caregiver's speech and singing.

Incorporating an infant's name into a simple melody about dressing or incorporating the names of body parts, such as foot, arm, head, nose, and hand, also provide infants an opportunity to begin to associate word labels with themselves or parts of their bodies. Music can also be used to cue routines such as cleanup time or mealtime (Honig & Brophy, 1996).

Arrival and departure routines are also important times of verbal and non-verbal communication (Wilson, Douville-Watson, & Watson, 1995). These transition times are critical for children's feelings of security and comfort. At arrival, caregivers should touch, hold, and talk with each infant for a few minutes during the departure of the parent and for a few minutes after. Caregiver talk can center on ongoing events, familiar toys, or a favorite picture in the room along with what is observed from a window and what the child is wearing. In this way, a caregiver mediates or supports a child's reentry into the classroom/center environment. Greetings such as "Hello, how are you?" or "Good morning" exchanged with parents serve to expose children to verbal social routines, developing their receptive pragmatic knowledge. A smile, giggle, or gesture from a child during these routines can be interpreted as a response, or turn-taking, and verbally reinforced.

Departure routines should also incorporate verbal interaction with infants and their parents. Sharing the significant and positive aspects of their infants' day with parents helps children transition back into parents' care and often provides a topic of conversation (though verbally one-sided) for the parent and child.

TODDLERS

Guidelines for Enhancing Language Acquisition Among Toddlers

The toddler age begins when a child achieves walking and ends when the child is 2 1/2 to 3 years old. Children in this age span still enjoy sensorimotor play, such as touching, hearing, tasting, smelling, pushing, lifting, pulling, and dropping. They are also developing more complex ways of playing (Maxim, 1993), using speech as a way of organizing their play and engaging in symbolic play.

Toddlerhood is a time of energetic exploration of the environment and of dramatic changes in receptive and productive language. Classrooms need to be furnished and activities planned with the active explorer in mind. The curriculum should reflect toddlers' increasing independence and their need for opportunities to practice and refine their newly acquired skills. Hands-on experiences within a variety of learning activities foster continued growth in conceptual development, which supports language acquisition. More specific learning activities may occur occasionally when caregivers interact with a small group of toddlers at one time.

Three types of activities compose a typical day in a toddler room: exploratory activities, caregiver-mediated activities, and routine activities. In each type of activity it is important that toddlers not be rushed through the activity or pressured to respond in a particular way. Because toddlerhood is a time of developing autonomy, it is critical that the curricula in toddler rooms provide for sufficient time and opportunity for children to be more independent (Trawick-Smith, 1997).

Exploratory Activities

Exploratory activity time should provide toddlers with an opportunity to engage in hands-on activities and to interact creatively with a variety of materials and objects. The materials selected should be multipurpose in the sense that children can use them for a variety of purposes. Many caregivers and parents comment that their toddlers often appear more interested in the box than the toy that came in the box. This behavior illustrates toddlers' developmental needs to have the opportunity to structure their own activities, to explore the possibilities of using basic items, and to engage in symbolic play. A large box can become a car, a train engine, a house, a store, or an airplane.

Exploratory time provides toddlers with time to investigate their prepared environment. This time of hands-on conceptual development provides opportunities for both receptive and productive language development. Toddlers do more than just "play." They engage in trial-and-error learning, they test hypotheses about how things work, and they explore cause-and-effect relationships.

Time allotted for exploratory activities depends on the developmental level of the children involved. Generally the range of time for each exploratory activity period is about 30 minutes. Sufficient time should be allotted for children to engage in a variety of activities without feeling rushed; however, the time period should not extend beyond toddlers' energy levels. Depending on the total time in the program, there may be several exploratory activity periods, such as in day-care programs that run for 10 to 12 hours.

During exploratory activity time, caregivers should actively monitor individual children's behavior and involvement in the various activities. Caregivers should circulate the room and occasionally engage children in conversation and dialogue about their respective activities. Taking this active role is a positive way for caregivers to monitor, model, and mediate children's interactions with materials and with each other.

The listening skills of caregivers are also a factor in children's language acquisition. Caregivers should listen actively, establishing eye contact with the toddler who is speaking and giving interested attention to what is being communicated (Honig, 1982). By listening carefully to toddlers' comments and questions, caregivers can provide the linguistic scaffolding needed to help toddlers express themselves. This active listening by the caregiver also serves as a model to the child.

Active monitoring and conversation with children provides caregivers with an opportunity to anticipate difficulties that may arise and to deal with them before the problem has reached a crisis stage. However, caregivers should avoid becoming too intrusive with their verbal mediation, remembering that too much interference with children's exploratory activities can have a negative effect.

In the sections that follow, specific exploratory activities appropriate for enhancing language acquisition among toddlers are described, along with guidelines for caregiver implementation and mediation.

Blocks and Manipulatives

Blocks and other manipulatives provide unlimited opportunities for symbolic play. Blocks for toddlers should be sturdy, lightweight, and free from sharp corners or wooden slivers. Cardboard or plastic blocks are appropriate if they stack easily and maintain their shape through continued use. Occasionally, children can be encouraged to talk about what they are building.

Manipulatives should be of moderate size. Small items should be avoided since toddlers are not able to coordinate their small muscles to handle tiny pieces. In addition, small items add to the time it takes to put away the materials at the end of the activity, and they can easily be lost or misplaced. Items should not be small enough for children to put in their mouths, since some toddlers may still have a tendency to attempt to put items in their mouth.

A caregiver should be available to monitor this area and enhance children's social-verbal relationships through mediation and by participating in child-initiated dialogue.

Book Corner

Toddlers enjoy looking at familiar books on their own, especially when the books are durable and have pages that are easily turned. Cardboard books with thicker pages usually work well. Familiar books should be used to allow children to enjoy revisiting a story through looking at pictures and remembering when it was read by a caregiver. Multiple copies of the same book reduce the issue of taking turns or sharing, which is difficult for some toddlers.

Books should be stored within children's reach and on shelves that encourage children to return books to their place. This allows children to select books of their choosing and to return them and pick additional books as they wish. Book racks or shelves that allow book fronts to be displayed will be more visually enticing than if only the book spine is visible. Toddlers will be able to quickly locate familiar or favorite storybooks (Post & Hohmann, 2000). Comfortable seating areas near the books, such as pillows or small chairs, with a rug on the floor will encourage children to share books with each other (Post & Hohmann, 2000). Occasionally, a caregiver may sit in the storybook area and be available for impromptu story sharing.

Writing Center

Toddlers often show an interest in writing and drawing. This appears to stem from their observations of adults and older siblings writing. Providing an area with large sheets of paper and water-soluble colorful markers encourages toddlers to write. Adult supervision may be necessary to ensure their writing goes

Toddlers enjoy looking at familiar books on their own.

on the paper and not on the tabletop or walls. It is important to remember that children's early writing is exploratory in nature. They are exploring how writing is made and how it has meaning. Research has established that children gradually construct their knowledge of written language through these explorations (Temple, Nathan, Burris, & Temple, 1988).

Toddlers may fill a whole sheet with their scribblelike writings or may only have a small amount on the sheet. They may announce the content/meaning of the writing or take it to a caregiver to "read." When this happens, a caregiver can instead request the child to read it for her. If the child insists that the caregiver read, the caregiver can make something up based on what is known about the context for the writing. The important consideration here is to provide positive feedback for a child's attempts and not to discourage this exploration by telling the child the writing is not "real" writing. When the child is finished with her piece of writing, a caregiver should write the child's name on the front, modeling for the child the writing process and saying aloud each letter of the child's name.

Discovery Centers

Discovery centers are specific areas that have been designed and developed to facilitate experiences supporting the acquisition of specific concepts related to math, science, or social studies as well as general language knowledge. Discovery centers enhance semantic development and general verbal communication. Even at the toddler level, discovery centers can be effective; however, the discovery centers are less structured and more exploratory than centers are for children at older ages.

For example, a discovery center equipped with a magnifying glass and a small basket of sea shells would encourage children to observe the detailed textures of the shells and the delicate shapes. Another toddler discovery center could involve a collection of different types of rocks (moderate in size) along with a magnifying glass. Caregivers should provide opportunities for children to talk about their experiences in a discovery center.

Drama Corner

An area provided with dress-up clothes and accessories affords children opportunities to engage in symbolic, pretend play and use language as a part of that play. Clothes and other items should represent both genders so that this area is not gender restrictive. Both boys and girls need to participate in this area.

The drama corner should include appropriate props such as a telephone, telephone book, empty boxes, chairs, and/or a table. Some caregivers may decide to create themed drama corners on a rotating basis. A grocery store, home kitchen area, or post office are typical themes for toddlers. These are contexts with which they may be familiar. Their respective experiences provide the creativity and frames of reference for engaging in this dramatic play.

Children this age usually do not play cooperatively but may engage in parallel play. Caregivers monitoring the dramatic activity area need to keep in mind that these children are just beginning to interact with each other. There may be times when a child is trying to engage in solitary play although she is in an area with other children. For this reason, only two or three children should be in the drama corner at one time.

In assuming specific roles, children may communicate verbally with that specific role in mind. For toddlers, caregivers may need to initiate a conversation ("Good Morning Mr. Mail Carrier. What letters do you have for me today?") and then extend that conversation to include other children in the area, thereby encouraging those children to respond verbally and become a part of the dramatic activity: "Thank you for my letters. What letters do you have for Jennifer today? Jennifer, come see what mail you have."

In dramatic activities, children also learn to verbally negotiate the roles they want to play relative to the roles others around them want to play. With toddlers, you may expect that all of them will want to be mail carriers or that all of them want to be the mother. Caregivers then model for the children how to settle the issue verbally. For example, "We need to have a mother in the kitchen area to re-ceive the mail. Beth, would you like to get the mail that Julie has for you?" or "We have two mail carriers. Let's pretend that each of you are on a different route. Pick someone different to deliver mail to."

Sand and Water Table Activities

Sand and water tables allow children to have tactile experiences that contribute to their conceptual development. Toddlers need only a few accessories while at sand and water tables. Utensils for stirring and pouring encourage children to manipulate the sand/water. Using their hands to move the sand/water provides them with a better understanding of the basic properties of each of the medi-ums. Toddlers need room to explore during this activity; thus, only two or three children should use the sand/water table at the same time. Similarly to other exploratory activities, the caregiver's role is to initiate conversation occasion-ally with the children about their activities and to encourage the children to talk with each other. In this way children's receptive and productive language will be enhanced.

Art Activities

At the toddler level, art activities involve initial exploration of various media. The focus is on the process rather than on the product. Pseudo art activities that involve children pasting precut pieces onto patterned paper or attempting to color predrawn designs have little value to the goals for conceptual develop-ment and creative expression. In such preformed activities, the focus is defi-nitely on the product rather than the process.

Children's curiosity in exploring painting and other artistic media will dominate their activities such that they often will not show an interest in nam-ing or identifying what they have created. Some toddlers may resist painting or art activities that appear to be overly messy; others seem to relish those activi-ties. By providing a variety of activities, caregivers can meet the needs of both types of children.

When children's artwork is displayed in the room or sent home, caregivers can help parents and other adults in interpreting the value of the activity and the product by focusing on the role of exploration in conceptual development and the process in using the specific media. A child's name should be written (printed) on the front (if possible) or on the back of the art paper. This models written language for the child and gives the child a sense of ownership.

Outdoor Activities

Toddlers are physically active and need regular times to be outside. Safe, de-velopmentally appropriate playground equipment is crucial. There should also be room for exploration and space for movement activities (running, walk-ing, trike riding). The outdoor area should be away from traffic and separate

Opportunities to explore outdoors provide toddlers sensory experiences that contribute to conceptual and semantic knowledge.

from older children's activities. A boundary fence eases monitoring children's movements.

Outdoor activities provide opportunities for children to see and experience activities not present in the classroom. Caregivers who are aware of this potential make themselves available for spontaneous conversations with children while outside.

Caregiver-Mediated Activities

Caregiver-mediated activities at the toddler level involve the caregiver interacting with two or three children at a time, while reading a book or sharing a new object or collection of objects, such as seashells. Large group activities are not appropriate because toddlers need to be actively engaged with the materials or books used and have limited attention spans. These activities are open-ended and exploratory, sensitive to the interests and comments of the toddlers participating. Caregiver-mediated activities are of short duration, reflecting the limited attention span of toddlers for any group activity. As opportunity presents itself, caregivers can use some verbal mapping or linguistic scaffolding techniques. As toddlers' attention spans increase, group time and size can be gradually increased.

Book Sharing

Book sharing with toddlers enhances acquisition of phonetic, semantic, syntactic, morphemic, and pragmatic language knowledge. Through shared reference with teachers or caregivers, toddlers develop both receptive and expressive language knowledge. Sharing books with young toddlers focuses on labeling and commenting on the objects and events pictured in the book. Children should be encouraged to participate in the book sharing, contributing their spontaneous comments and responding to their caregiver's comments and questions. Younger toddlers may show a preference for randomly paging through a book, attracted by the pictures (Lawrence, 1998), or they may want to spend a long time looking at one particular picture (Honig & Brophy, 1996).

Books should be selected that have clear, colorful illustrations of familiar objects and/or events. A variety of cultural/ethnic groups should be represented and portrayed positively within them. Books with nursery rhymes or poems are enjoyed for their rhythmic, patterned language, which becomes memorable to toddlers. Books with simple plots can be used; however, the initial reading of these books may focus only on labeling and commenting. Small amounts of text may be read, depending on the listening comprehension level of the toddlers involved. If children have participated in book sharing since infancy, they will have a higher level of listening comprehension than if they are inexperienced in book sharing interactions.

A developmental sequence for sharing books with infants and toddlers (Fowler, 1990) begins with labeling and describing pictures, with a focus on the objects pictured. This may be followed by describing the actions or events pictured. Because young toddlers may be interested in book sharing for only short periods of time, there is no initial attempt to go from the beginning to the end of a book or even from front to back. As a toddler becomes more familiar with books, caregivers extend the discussion and questioning to pay more attention to a story line that goes from page to page. At this point the caregiver may say, "Look what's happening here. It looks like . . . " and "Oh, now, see where . . . ". Gradually, over repeated interactions and with a child's evident interest and comprehension, increasing amounts of the exact text can be read and discussed. As teachers begin to include more text reading, they should continue to use dramatic intonation, eye contact, and simple questioning, along with text elaboration, to keep toddlers engaged in the book sharing (Honig & Shin, 2001).

Toddlers may request the same book be shared over and over again. With repeated sharings, toddlers may begin to verbally participate more in describing the pictures or the story events. Requests for repeated book sharings indicate toddlers' appreciation for the predictability of familiar pictures or the story text as well as their developing memory for story sequence and story language.

Language acquisition is also enhanced when caregivers coordinate the topics of books to actual events (Fowler, 1990). For example, if the street outside the toddler center is being repaired, books on trucks or building roads could be shared. A trip to a nature center could be followed up with a book about animals. Or it may be as simple as talking about the apples served for lunch when sharing a book that has an apple pictured, as shown in these caregiver's questions: "That's an apple. What did we have for lunch today? Yes, we had apples" (Honig & Brophy, 1996, p. 61). Conceptual knowledge is enhanced when this coordination between book topics and real events takes place, and it sets the stage for content-rich conversations between toddlers and caregivers.

Songs and finger plays. Group action songs and finger plays enjoyed at small group time or during routine activities enhance toddlers' language development by encouraging active listening, imitation, and attention to rhythm, repetition, and expressive intonation (Squibb and Deitz, 2000). Toddlers enjoy short, rhythmic songs and nursery rhymes. Introduce only one verse or song at a time. Through repeated opportunities to hear a song or rhyme, toddlers will begin to anticipate upcoming words and actions. Toddlers can also be encouraged to begin to mark the rhythm of a song with sound shakers or clapping. In a group of toddlers, there will be a range of involvement, from simply listening to full verbal participation. Teachers' enthusiasm, eye contact, and clear enunciation of the song or rhyme will encourage toddlers' participation.

Activity Boxes

Another type of caregiver-mediated activity involves **activity boxes** (Wilson, 1988). This type of activity centers on the manipulation and labeling of items contained in boxes with removable lids. Caregivers facilitate children's interactions with items in the boxes by using verbal mapping, labelling, as well as linguistic scaffolding (extension and expansion) techniques. This activity is best done with only 1–2 children at a time, which allows each child to have more direct involvement in the activity.

For example, a Peek-a-Boo Box encourages children to label what they see in the box's window (in the lid). After the toy is labelled (e.g. cat) it is removed and held by the child. Then the caregiver can encourage further receptive and productive language by asking questions or making simple requests: "Point to the cat's ears." "Where is the cat's tail?" "Point to the cat's eyes."

A *movement box* can be used to familiarize children with action concept labels. For example, place a medium-sized soft ball and a long, colorful scarf in the box. Remove the ball and bounce it a couple times. Talk briefly with the children about the ball going up and down. Then suggest, "Let's jump like the ball bounces." Put the ball back in the box and remove the scarf. Wave the scarf in the air. Then hand the scarf to a child and ask him to show the others how he waves it. Reinforce the child's actions verbally. Then the scarf can be given to another child and the request maybe repeated.

Action songs and finger plays enhance children's awareness of rhythm and rhyme.

A *feely box* is another type of activity box that toddlers will enjoy (Honig, 1982). This activity also enhances conceptual development and children's ability to label and describe objects, which are important components of semantic and syntactic development. A feely box may be constructed of a shoe box that has a hand-sized hole cut into the top of the box. Items of various textures and shapes are placed in the box. The toddler reaches into the box and talks about what she is touching. The caregiver supports the child's description of interactions with items in the boxes by using verbal mapping, labeling, and linguistic scaffolding (extension and expansion) techniques. This activity is best done with only one or two children at a time, which allows each child to have more direct involvement in the activity.

For example, a peek-a-boo box encourages children to label what they see in the box's window (in the lid). After the toy—for example, a cat—is labeled, the child removes it from the box and holds it. Then the caregiver asks questions such as, "What are you touching? Does it feel hard or soft? Is it smooth or bumpy?" Then the child takes the object out of the box. The activity can be continued until all the items are guessed. Incorrectly guessed items can be returned to the box for additional description and guessing. Caregivers should praise toddlers for their descriptions and their guesses.

Additional caregiver-mediated activities are described in the resource books listed at the end of this chapter.

Routine Activities

Routines provide toddlers with a sense of security. Routines provide toddlers with a predictable event and because of their familiarity with the routine, toddlers feel secure. In contrast to infants, toddlers are now able to participate more independently in some of the routines of eating, dressing, hand washing, and toileting. Additionally, toddlers can participate more actively in arrival and departure routines. The aspect of language knowledge encouraged in routines is pragmatic knowledge, which is an awareness of how language is used differently in different situations.

Arrival

During arrival time, caregivers should be sure to call the child by name and to speak directly to the child and to his parent. Caregivers should encourage children to respond to their greetings, and caregivers should respond to any verbalization or gesture from the children. While holding the toddler briefly during the transition time, the caregiver should engage the child in a conversation about a familiar object or event occurring in the room.

Snack/Mealtime

Toddlers enjoy feeding themselves, though their appetite may decrease during this time. Caregivers should sit with toddlers as they eat, encouraging conversation and social routines of saying "please" and "thank you" and passing food around the table. This is also a good time for children to become aware of new words. Caregivers should talk about food, describing the appearance or texture, color, and/or taste (Wortham, 1998): "Your applesauce is *lumpy, bumpy,* and *cool.*" "Your mashed potatoes are *warm* and *white.* They stick to your spoon" (Honig & Brophy, 1996, p. 26).

Caregivers should show interest in each child's contribution to the table conversation, regardless of how limited it might be (Fowler, 1990). It is important that each child feel included in the social-verbal interaction during snack/mealtime. Toddlers should also be encouraged to help clean up their eating area when they have finished. This encourages toddlers to learn to follow verbal directions.

Departure

At departure time, caregivers should hold each child briefly or sit at the child's level, talking with each child about events of the day. Information about the child's day should be shared with parents. Caregivers need to keep this sharing informative and positive. Toddlers' listening comprehension is at a higher level than their speech production and they may comprehend and be influenced by a caregiver's or parent's comments about them. These end-of-day conversations between caregivers and parents set the stage for children's transitions back home. It is important that these transitions be positive and reassuring.

SUMMARY

The planning and implementation of developmentally appropriate curricula in infant and toddler rooms is important to a child's future development. Curricula for both levels focuses on facilitating the development of receptive and expressive/productive language. Sensorimotor, hands-on experiential activities are the basis for children's development of conceptual knowledge and for the acquisition of language labels (words) for those concepts. Opportunities to explore in a safe, well-planned environment with caring, observant caregivers form the basis of developmentally appropriate classrooms for infants and toddlers. Caregivers are children's guides and facilitators in exploring their classroom and center environments. Language acquisition is facilitated by caregivers using a variety of techniques, including verbal mapping, labeling, linguistic scaffolding, questioning, and shared reference. Caregivers communicate with parents daily, sharing information about their children's developing competencies. Developmentally appropriate infant and toddler activities enhance the acquisition of each of the five aspects of language knowledge.

✳ ✳ ✳   CHAPTER REVIEW

1. Terms to review:

   verbal mapping   discovery centers
   object permanence   activity boxes

2. Describe three exploratory activities for an infant. Explain the way in which each activity enhances language development. Mention the specific aspects of language knowledge involved.

3. Explain how routine activities in an infant classroom can enhance language acquisition.

4. Explain the value of object labeling and verbal mapping to toddlers' language acquisition. State the specific aspects of language knowledge involved. Give two examples.

5. State three criteria for selecting books to place in a toddlers' book corner.

6. Describe caregiver techniques for sharing books with infants and toddlers.

7. Explain why discovery centers enhance semantic development. Give an example.

8. Describe the way in which conversations during snack or mealtime enhance language acquisition.

9. Select a caregiver-mediated activity. Explain how it should be conducted and how that activity enhances language acquisition.

✳ ✳ ✳ CHAPTER EXTENSION ACTIVITIES

1. Develop your own activity box to foster language development. Write up a procedure or plan for using the box. If possible, visit a toddler classroom to try it out. Share your experiences with your fellow students.

2. Select a book to be used with an infant. Explain why you selected the book, detailing the characteristics of the book that make it appropriate for sharing with an infant. Explain how you would use the book with an infant.

3. Observe outdoor time in a toddler center, focusing on the verbal interactions between the caregivers and the children. Pay attention to the characteristics of caregivers' talk to children. Describe whether it follows the characteristics of adult-to-child speech first mentioned in Chapter 2.

4. Plan three activities for an infant room. Using the chart format presented in the appendix to this chapter, analyze the activities for ways in which the curricula enhances acquisition of the five aspects of language knowledge.

5. Plan three activities for a toddler room. Using the chart format presented in the appendix, analyze the activities for ways in which the curricula enhances acquisition of the five aspects of language knowledge.

✳ ✳ ✳ REFERENCES

Brainerd, C. (1978). *Piaget's theory of intelligence.* Upper Saddle River, NJ: Prentice Hall.

Bredekamp, S., & Copple, C. (Eds.). (1997). *Developmentally appropriate practice in early childhood programs.* Washington, DC: National Association for the Education of Young Children.

Fowler, W. (1990). *Talking from infancy: How to nurture and cultivate early language development.* Cambridge, MA: Brookline Books.

Goodman, K. (1993). *Phonics phacts.* Portsmouth, NH: Heinemann.

Honig, A. (1982). *Playtime learning games for young children.* Syracuse, NY: Syracuse University Press.

Honig, A., & Brophy, H. (1996). *Talking with your baby: Family as the first school.* Syracuse, NY: Syracuse University Press.

Honig, A., & Lally, J. (1981). *Infant caregiving: A design for training.* Syracuse, NY: Syracuse University Press.

Honig, A., & Shin, M. (2001). Reading aloud with infants and toddlers in child care settings: An observational study. *Early Childhood Education Journal, 28*(1), 193–197.

Lawrence, L. (1998). *Montessori read & write: A parents' guide to literacy for children.* New York: Three Rivers Press.

Lowman, L., & Ruhmann, L. (1998, May). Simply sensational spaces: A multi-S approach to toddler environments. *Young Children,* 11–17.

Maxim, G. (1990). *The sourcebook: Activities for infants and young children* (2nd ed.). Upper Saddle River, NJ: Merrill/Prentice-Hall.

Maxim, G. (1993). *The very young: Guiding children from infancy through the early years* (4th ed.). Upper Saddle River, NJ: Merrill/Prentice Hall.

Post, J. & Hohmann, M. (2000). *Tender care and early learning: Supporting infants and toddlers in child care settings.* Ypsilanti, MI: High/Scope Press.

Squibb, B. & Deitz, S. (2000). *Learning activities for infants and toddlers.* Washington, DC: Children's Resources International.

Temple, C., Nathan, R., Burris, N., & Temple, F. (1988). *The beginnings of writing* (2nd ed.). Boston: Allyn & Bacon.

Trawick-Smith, J. (1997). *Early childhood development: A multicultural perspective.* Upper Saddle River, NJ: Merrill/Prentice Hall.

Weiser, M. (1991). *Infant/toddler care and education.* Upper Saddle River, NJ: Merrill/Prentice Hall.

Wilson, L. (1988, January). What's inside the box? Activity boxes that foster language development. *Scholastic Pre-K Today, 2*(4), 38–39.

Wilson, L., Douville-Watson, L., & Watson, M. (1995). *Infants and toddlers: Curriculum and teaching* (3rd ed.). Albany, NY: Delmar.

Wortham, S. (1998). *Early childhood curriculum: Developmental bases for learning and teaching* (2nd ed.). Upper Saddle River, NJ: Merrill/Prentice Hall.

❋ ❋ ❋ RESOURCE BOOKS FOR TODDLER ACTIVITIES

Coglin, M. (1982). *One potato, two potato, three potato, four: 165 changes for children.* Mt. Rainier, MD: Gryphon House.

Honig, A. (1982). *Playtime learning games for young children.* Syracuse, NY: Syracuse University Press.

Honig, A., & Brophy, H. (1996). *Talking with your baby: Family as the first school.* Syracuse, NY: Syracuse University Press.

Lawrence, L. (1998). *Montessori read and write: A parents' guide to literacy for children.* New York: Three Rivers Press.

Maxim, G. (1990). *The sourcebook: Activities for infants and young children* (2nd ed.). Upper Saddle River, NJ: Merrill/Prentice Hall.

Maxim, G. (1993). *The very young: Guiding children from infancy through the early years* (4th ed.). Upper Saddle River, NJ: Merrill/Prentice Hall.

Miller, K. (1984). *Things to do with toddlers and twos.* Chelsea, MA: Telshare Publishing Co.

Miller, K. (1999). *Simple steps: Developmental activities for infants, toddlers, and two year olds.* Beltsville, MD: Gryphon House.

Post, J., & Hohmann, M. (2000). *Tender care and early learning: Supporting infants and toddlers in child care settings.* Ypsilanti, MI: High/Scope Press.

Squibb, B., & Deitz, S. (2000). *Learning activities for infants and toddlers: An easy guide for everyday use.* Washington, DC: Children's Resources International.

Wilson, L., Douville-Watson, L., & Watson, M. (1995). *Infants and toddlers: Curriculum and teaching* (3rd ed.). Albany, NY: Delmar Publishers.

APPENDIX

❋ ❋ ❋

ENHANCING LANGUAGE DEVELOPMENT

The charts provided in this appendix can be used to plan for exploratory, mediated, and routine activities in infant and toddler classrooms. An example chart for a toddler classroom is also included.

Enhancing Language Development Among Infants

Activity	Description/Steps	Materials	Rationale and Language Knowledge Focus	Guidelines
Exploratory				
Mediated				
Routine				

Enhancing Language Development Among Toddlers

Activity	Description/Steps	Materials	Rationale and Language Knowledge Focus	Guidelines
Exploratory				
Mediated				
Routine				

ENHANCING LANGUAGE DEVELOPMENT AMONG TODDLERS

(SAMPLE RESPONSE FROM PAT CLEVELAND, NEIU STUDENT)

Activity	Description/Steps	Materials	Rationale and Language Knowledge Focus	Guidelines
Exploratory	Sand Table Exploration: Stock sand table with objects for pouring, measuring, and scooping. Three children may explore at the sand table at any given time. Observe types of play and verbal interactions with peers.	Sand table with sand. Objects: plastic cups, measuring spoons, small plastic hand shovels, plastic containers with and without holes	Concept development: conservation/change in form, observation skills, sensory exploration, language interactions. Children engage in purposeful exchange with peers. They participate in a communication loop that includes receptive and expressive sharing.	Watch for symbol and concept formation as child physically explores his/her environment. Listen for language development and patterns of communication. No sand throwing!
Mediated	Water Table: Float vs. sink. Discuss with child concepts of float and sink. Have child predict which items will float and which will sink. Explore child's reasons. Experiment.	Water table w/water Objects: cork, shell, leaves, crayons, plastic spoons, pebbles, pieces of wood, plastic bottle with lid, plastic sieve, smocks/ towel.	Concept formation: cause and effect. Encourages higher order cognitive processing. Language is embedded in the experience. Child develops ideas and observations through expressive language. Other skills used: observation skills, problem-solving, comparison, weight:heavy/light.	Use adult-to-child speech. Use open-ended questions that encourage expressing ideas and reasoning strategies through verbal expression. Provide towels and smocks.

148

ENHANCING LANGUAGE DEVELOPMENT AMONG TODDLERS

(SAMPLE RESPONSE FROM PAT CLEVELAND, NEIU STUDENT) (*CONTINUED*)

Activity	Description/Steps	Materials	Rationale and Language Knowledge Focus	Guidelines
Routine	Pre-snack transition song. Fingerplay-song: "open-shut them" or fill-in "Down by the Bayou." Involve the children in a song designed to purposely bridge into the snack time.	No specific materials needed.	Transitioning from one activity to another is often difficult at this age. Songs can be incorporated into the routine as a bridging function. Participating in song aids in the development and auditory reception, auditory sequencing, auditory discrimination, voice projection/control, and rhythm. All of these attributes are integral to language development.	Encourage participation of each child; encourage expressive sharing in "fill-in" places in song where each child can contribute something unique.

6

LANGUAGE DEVELOPMENT IN PRESCHOOLERS

Eric and Dylan were on trikes near each other. Dylan said, "Mine's outa gas and gotta flat tire!" Eric added, "Mine, too!" Then Eric pantomimed filling the tires with air and filling the trike with gas. He said, "Pump, pump, pump" while filling the gas tank.

During lunch, Tammy identified many of the letters present in her alphabet soup. Several times she asked her teacher what they spelled.

While playing at the table with the small shape blocks, Maria picked up a star shape and said, "Twinkle, twinkle, little star."

During the preschool years language increases in both complexity and volume, building on the acquisition achieved during the infancy and toddler years in each of the five aspects of language knowledge. Preschool children who are surrounded by literacy-rich environments continue to develop in their knowledge of written language. Children's use of language is individualized during infancy and toddlerhood. In a way, children have their own private language, so that they are often most easily understood by their parents or primary caregivers. Unfamiliar adults may have a hard time understanding what a toddler is trying to communicate. This situation changes as children approach age 3. At this time, their use of language is more easily understood by outsiders (Clay, 1991). They can more accurately produce phonemes of their culture's language and observe adult word meanings, using a larger vocabulary. Preschool children's syntax is more complex and conveys more precise communication than that of toddlers. In these ways children's language knowledge continues to be acquired during the preschool years. These increased language competencies provide children with greater facility in interacting with their environment.

Preschoolers continue in their exploration of language: how it sounds, as they perceive patterns of sound; how language communicates meaning; how the way words are sequenced influences meaning; what significance word endings have; how language is used differently in different settings; and what the relationships are between oral language and written language. Children's explorations of language occur simultaneously with explorations of their environment. A dynamic interaction connects these two types of exploration. Language exploration and environmental exploration influence each other. Children's ability to ask questions and to use follow-up questioning to clarify others' communication enhances their explorations of language and their world.

HOME ENVIRONMENT

The importance of parents' interactions with their children and the learning contexts created for children at home has been documented by various researchers (Berk & Spuhl, 1995; Payne, Whitehurst, & Angell, 1994). Of particular importance is the way in which parents teach their children through scaffolding or supporting the learning within zones of proximal development. Scaffolding involves parents supporting children's learning by helping their children engage in verbal and nonverbal tasks that children cannot perform alone. Parents adjust the amount of help provided to children, taking into consideration their current level of performance (Moerk, 1974). As a child increases in competence in the task, his parent gradually decreases the amount of assistance. Gradually, the child can engage successfully and independently in performing the task. Critical features of parental teaching behavior have been identified to include "warmth,

responsiveness, patience, and an appropriate degree of structure and control"
(Berk & Spuhl, 1995, p. 165).

Through these scaffolded interactions, children's inner speech begins to develop. Language and actions are the components of the scaffolding. Learning is
supported or assisted both by what the parent says to guide the child's thinking
and actions and by what the parent does in gesture or action to support or assist the learning. Scaffolded interactions often occur in problem-solving settings, such as putting together a puzzle; in daily routines, such as putting on a
child's shoes; and in establishing and sustaining conversations.

When parents are engaged with their preschoolers in conversations, they
support or scaffold the conversation through questioning, expansion, and extension (see Chapter 2). Gradually, as a child takes a more active role in conversations, parents reduce the level of verbal support. Dinner table conversations are an example of scaffolding.

Mother:	Mark, let's tell Tommy (older brother) what we did today? (pause) Where did we go today, Mark?
Mark:	To the park.
Mother:	And what did we see the workers doing at the park?
Mark:	Tree?
Mother:	Yes, that's right, they were planting a big tree.

In countless conversations such as this, his mother creates a scaffolding by
using questioning, expansion, and extension, and Mark gradually learns how to
assume a more active role in sharing information. As his conversational competency increases, his mother reduces her support, so that Mark's dinner table
conversation might sound like this:

Mother:	Let's tell Tommy what we did today, Mark.
Mark:	We went to the park. Wow, guess what? They have a big slide now. Do you want to go with me?

In a longitudinal study of literacy development and home-school experiences, Dickinson and Tabors (1991) report that mealtime talk, whether it was
explanatory or narrative, was positively associated with increased vocabulary
scores. In addition, mealtime narratives were associated with children's ability
to respond to comprehension questions (on an unfamiliar storybook). Thus, it
appears that oral language experiences at home contribute to literacy-related
competencies.

The role of the home literacy environment in contributing to later language
and reading competencies has been documented by numerous research inves-
tigations (Mason, 1980; Ricciuti, White, & Fraser, 1993; Teale, 1986). A critical
activity appears to be shared picture/storybook reading. Payne, Whitehurst, and
Angell (1994) report that preschool children's receptive and productive vocab-

When parents share storybooks with children, they use language to describe the actions pictured and to tell or "read" the story, enhancing children's receptive language.

ulary was correlated with the following specific aspects of children's individual literacy environments: "frequency of reading with child, child's age when shared reading began, number of picture books in the home, frequency with which child asks to be read to, and frequency of trips to the library with child" (p. 435). Similar findings have been reported for bilingual children, indicating that storybook reading at home is closely associated with higher linguistic and cognitive competencies (Santiago, 1994).

When parents share storybooks with preschoolers, they use language to describe the actions pictured and to tell or "read" the story, enhancing children's receptive language. When children have opportunities to participate frequently in the storybook sharing, their productive language is enhanced as they ask questions, comment, or even attempt to recreate the specific language of the text. Children's involvement in storybook sharing increases as the storybook becomes more familiar (DeTemple & Beals, 1991); thus, it is important for children to have opportunities to experience repeated readings of their favorite storybooks.

Throughout children's daily experiences at home and in the community, contexts occur in which language is used in a variety of communications. Going to a grocery store, participating in food preparation at home, visiting a doctor's office, riding on a bus or subway, going to a library, washing clothes at home or at the laundromat, or playing in a park or backyard are examples of settings in which preschool children develop experiential bases for concepts and for the language accompanying those concepts. The preschool years are characterized by children's active exploration. The way in which their home and community environments support and guide their explorations influences not only children's language development but their cognitive development as well.

CLASSROOM ENVIRONMENT

The preschool years are also a time when many children begin to spend part of their day in a group with other preschoolers, either in an all-day child care setting or in a nursery school (partial day) setting. The school setting varies from the home environment in several ways, most noticeably in the number of children and adults present and in the type of interactions that occur.

In a preschool classroom, children no longer have an adult's undivided attention, since a group of children interacts with one or two adults. Tizard (1981) reported finding many more adult-child conversations occurred at home and lasted twice as long as adult-child conversations at school. When attending school, children must learn to wait their turn and observe specific rules (implied or explicit) for talking and interacting.

Classroom environments vary in the amount of talking encouraged during different times of the day and the tolerance for children's verbal interruptions or infractions of rules for talking. In their study comparing the expectations for young children's verbal participation in preschool and kindergarten, Hadley, Wilcox, and Rice (1994) reported that talking was usually encouraged during arrival and learning center activities and was discouraged during story time. Teachers who were "encouragers" were more tolerant of children's interruptions during teacher-directed activities. Teachers also showed more variations in their support for children's verbal participation in teacher-directed activities than in child-directed (independent) activities. Preschool teachers were found to have higher levels of encouragement for children's talking than did kindergarten teachers, particularly during activities that were teacher-directed.

For example, "sharing time," or show-and-tell, is an activity that is structured and directed by the teacher. Children must observe specific expectations when taking turns and asking and answering questions (Hadley, Wilcox, & Rice, 1994).

In a detailed study of storybook sharing in nursery schools, Cochran-Smith (1984) describes the unique speech event known as "rug time." Although book readings were almost always a part of rug time, other language-related activities also took place: children's show-and-tell; teacher-led discussions about art, craft, or story projects; discussions of past or future classroom events; and/or sound filmstrips. Rug time was governed by specific rules for participation that required that all children participate; they could not come and go as they desired. Children were expected to be physically inactive but participate verbally with the group. However, they were not allowed to engage in conversations with individual children seated nearby.

Other research has indicated that group size, teachers' theoretical perspectives and classroom goals (e.g., fostering early literacy development), and specific classroom circumstances (e.g., length of day) appear to influence the language environment of the classroom (Smith & Dickinson, 1994). When part of a group, children are likely to have fewer opportunities to engage adults in conversation. In addition, verbal interaction may be limited due to issues of group control and focus on a specific activity. However, teachers who have specific language-related goals and theoretically based perspectives of language acquisition appear to have a positive impact on the type of linguistic interactions occurring in the classroom.

Within these environmental settings, at home and at school, children are directly and indirectly encouraged to learn the rules for participating in conversations. At home and in classroom settings, children's language acquisition continues at a rapid pace during the preschool years. Significant advances occur in language knowledge in each of the aspects of language: phonetic, semantic, syntactic, morphemic, and pragmatic. While much of the language knowledge is acquired at the level of linguistic usage, some preschool children may begin to reflect on language metalinguistically. In the sections that follow, preschool children's development of language knowledge of each of the five aspects will be discussed.

DEVELOPMENT OF PHONETIC KNOWLEDGE

Preschool children's receptive awareness and production of language-related sounds (phonemes) is fairly well developed. While general patterns of acquisition have been identified, considerable variation exists among children of similar ages. Little agreement exists among researchers as to the universality of the onset of specific speech sound production prior to age 3; however, in research on children after age 3, some consensus has been reached. As noted in Chapter 4, children who have had a history of chronic ear infections may experience some difficulty in speech sound perception and discrimination.

Figure 6.1 summarizes the development of production for phonemes in the English language (Owens, 2001) that typically are acquired during the preschool years. As with all developmental charts, the ages of acquisition are approximate and should be used as a point of general reference rather than as the sole vehicle for determining developmental achievements. Researchers do not agree about the order of acquisition prior to the age of 3. Owens (1988) notes that research studies on phoneme acquisition often differ in the way data was

FIGURE 6.1
Overview of Phoneme Production

Three-year-olds	All vowel sounds
	/p/ /m/ /h/ /n/ /w/ /b/ /k/ /g/ /d/
	*p*ig su*m h*appy su*n w*att *b*ig *c*oat *g*oat *d*ot
50% also produce:	/t/ /ŋ/ /f/ /j/ /r/ /l/ /s/
	*t*ot su*ng f*ace *y*acht *r*ot *l*ot *s*ea
Four-year-olds	/p/ /m/ /h/ /n/ /w/ /b/ /k/ /g/ /d/
	/t/ /ŋ/ /f/ /j/
50% also produce:	/r/ /l/ /s/ /tʃ/ /ʃ/ /z/
	*ch*oke *sh*oe *z*eal
	na*t*ure mi*ss*ion
Five-year-olds	/p/ /m/ /h/ /n/ /w/ /b/ /k/ /g/ /d/ /t/ /ŋ/ /f/ /j/ /r/ /l/ /s/ /tʃ/ /ʃ/ /z/ /dʒ/
	*j*oke *g*entle
50% also produce:	/ð/ *th*y, *th*is *th*ere
Some still have difficulty with consonant blends: *str*eet *cl*ean	
Six-year-olds	
Also produce /θ/ as in *th*in and /ʒ/ as in trea*s*ure	
Eight-year-olds	
Also produce consonant clusters	*str sl dr*

From Owens, R. E., Jr., (2001). *Language Development* (5th ed., pp. 99–102, 105, 464). Copyright ©
by Allyn & Bacon. Adapted with permission.

collected. In some studies the language data was based on spontaneous utterances. In others the language data was elicited speech. Criteria for determining
whether the speech sound had been acquired also differed. Some studies used
attainment by 50 percent of those children sampled as the criteria for conclud-
ing that the sounds had been acquired; other studies had a criteria of 90 percent.
This variability in research methodology and the validity of developmental expectations based on that research contribute to the cautions in using developmental stage/sequence charts such as the one in Figure 6.1. Additional generalizations about phonemic development are provided in the appendix to this
chapter.

Preschool children's growing awareness of phonemes is often evident in
their language play. One of the types of language play identified by Schwartz
(1981) is *sound play,* which consists of children manipulating the phonemic elements and prosodic features of pitch, stress, and juncture. As noted in Chapter 4, children engage in sound play when they are infants. Sound play also oc-

curs when they are at preschool age. This type of language play occurs when children are playing alone and with others.

Spontaneous rhyming is a type of phonemic sound play. As children play, rhyming chants may be expressed, as in "cat, fat, bat, mat, sat." When children listen to stories or to poetry readings, they may indicate their awareness of sound patterns and phonemic relationships by anticipating upcoming text or contributing additional rhyming words.

During this time some children develop a more conscious awareness of speech perception and sound production. This awareness of a specific feature of language and the ability to focus on it is a part of **metalinguistic knowledge.** Maclean, Bryant, and Bradley (1987) studied the development of phonological awareness in young children. They reported that children as young as 3 years old are aware of rhyme and alliteration and can respond to tasks requiring them to orally identify words that rhyme and words that start the same as a target word (e.g., "pin, pig, tree," p. 261).

Metalinguistic knowledge also develops when children begin to focus on print in literacy-rich environments. As preschool children interact more with written language formally as adults read stories and informally (e.g., environmental print: road signs and restaurant or store signs), they begin to associate initial letters with specific sounds (Clay, 1983). Ryan's mother, Barb, reported that whenever he would see the letter *B* present in print in his environment, he would say, "*B* starts your name, Mommy." This occurred when he saw the words *bible* and *bank,* and also when he saw the letter *B* in an alphabet book. Although it is not clear whether Ryan was focusing on the sound of *b* or just the visual association, Ryan's comments indicated he was beginning to pay attention to words and the graphic system for representing words in print. It is also possible that Ryan was remembering what his mother had told him previously when the letter *B* was singled out and associated with her name.

In a similar example, Grant, at age 4 1/2, spotted the letter *G* engraved on the bottom of a flower pot. After asking what the letter stood for, and being told it was the potter's name, he said, "I know *G,* 'cause that's what my name starts with."

Some preschool children begin to try to match speech to print and to explore ways of sharing ideas on paper (Bissex, 1980; Purcell-Gates, 1996; Schickedanz, 1981; Schickedanz, York, Stewart, & White, 1990; Shatz, 1994; Sulzby, 1983; Temple, Nathan, Burris, & Temple, 1988). These exploratory, hypothesis-testing behaviors are seen in monolingual classrooms and in bilingual classrooms (Ballenger, 1996). As preschoolers attempt to figure out which letters to use for their names and messages and how to "say" what they have written or what someone else has written, their developing awareness of relationships between sounds and print becomes evident. Through experiences with language embedded in their environments, called *functional print*, along with oral language activities focusing on phonetic features of speech, teachers and parents encourage children to begin to segment speech into individual sounds (Purcell-Gates, 1996; Schickedanz, York, Stewart, & White, 1990).

DEVELOPMENT OF SEMANTIC KNOWLEDGE

Children's vocabulary expands and also begins to be more refined or precise during the preschool years. Children begin to develop more complex concepts and schemata for related concepts. As children encounter new experiences, they have opportunities to expand their language to include ways of referring to and responding to these new experiences. Receptive and expressive vocabulary grows rapidly. A preschool child's expressive vocabulary has been estimated to range from 800 to 1,000 words (Crystal, 1987; Morrow, 1989; Owens, 2001).

Children develop concepts for those entities and ideas that are part of their cultural environment (Nelson, 1973). As discussed in Chapter 2, concepts develop through direct experiences and through vicarious experiences. Semantic knowledge develops through the processes of assimilation and accommodation. In assimilation a new concept is incorporated into an existing conceptual schema. In accommodation, a cognitive structure or schema is changed to incorporate the new concept (Brainerd, 1978).

For example, a child has a concept of *cow* as having four legs and a long tail, making the sound "moo," eating grasses, and being brown in color. On a trip to the zoo, this child sees a brown cow and a black and white cow. She learns from her parent that this differently colored animal, too, is a cow. This new semantic knowledge is assimilated into the child's existing conceptual structure, within the color feature. The remaining features (tail, four legs, eats grass, says "moo") stay the same.

At the same zoo is a horse next to the cow pen. When the child calls this new animal a cow, her parent responds, "No, that's a horse. See how tall the horse is. And look at the hair at its neck. Horses have manes." Now the child realizes that a *horse* is not a *cow* and must alter her cognitive structure to incorporate or accommodate this new concept. Her new schema for "four-legged animals" might look like Figure 6.2:

Gradually, through firsthand and vicarious experiences children become aware of additional features that distinguish a cow from a horse. In this way, through assimilation and accommodation, children's conceptual knowledge is expanded and refined. Accompanying this expansion and refinement is the acquisition of language to allow more precise talking about the newly acquired concepts and their relationships. Children's semantic knowledge develops as

FIGURE 6.2
Example Schema for Four-legged Animals

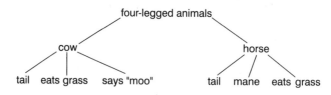

they communicate with adults and other children who expose them to new words.

As children are developing their semantic knowledge, overextensions and underextensions may occur. Overextensions occur when children use the same label or word to apply to referents that may resemble the actual, appropriate referent in some way. For example, a child learns the concept of *candy* and begins using the word only to refer to candy. When he extends the use of that term to cherries or anything sweet, overextension has occurred. Another example is when a child first uses the word *kitty* to refer to a cat but later extends that term to refer to rabbits and other small, furry animals. Underextension, in contrast, occurs when the label or word is inappropriately restricted. For example, the word *cat* is used only to refer to the neighbor's cat and not when the child sees other cats in the neighborhood. Preschool children's verbal interactions with adults and other children gradually refine the use of words and concept labels, reducing instances of overextension and underextension.

In this way, environmental contexts, including people, objects, or events in the environment, are critical for semantic development. Children need to have the actual referent of the concept present in the immediate context (either in real life or pictured in a book) to enhance semantic knowledge. In addition, the word representing a concept needs to be introduced in these meaningful, supportive contexts, or vocabulary will not develop.

When asked to create an adventure story, Nicole (4 years old) responded orally with this story about "going down to a museum":

> The story of going down to a museum. A museum has so many words. It has some dinosaurs. It shows some moons of Jupiter. Jupiter was the big one, the biggest of all. I knew, because of school, and because the museum told me. Don't you know that museums can tell you stuff? (pause) That's the end.

Nicole's concept of museums appears to be that museums are full of words, dinosaurs, and planets. Museums also can tell people "stuff." Since Nicole is not yet reading independently, we know that her concept of museums is based on her own direct or mediated experiences. Perhaps she has visited a museum displaying dinosaurs and models of the solar system, or perhaps she had had a book on museums read to her. Regardless of whether her museum experiences were direct or vicarious, it is clear that her experiences and interactions with other people have provided her with the appropriate language to talk about museums.

Conceptual development and vocabulary are also increased through book sharing with fiction and nonfiction texts (Elster, 1994). The written language of storybooks exposes children to more precise and varied vocabulary than they may experience otherwise. For many children, the appeal of storybooks and nonfiction books is in the variety of ways in which language is used to communicate a story or real-world information.

In school and home contexts, adult-child discussions during and after sharing books expand and refine children's semantic knowledge. These discussions enhance children's semantic development and also provide adults with a way of becoming familiar with children's developing conceptual knowledge. Children not only learn the literal meanings of words used in written texts but acquire more subtle meanings as well. They often are exposed to figurative language found in similes and metaphors.

When Ryan was 3, his mother had been reading him *Gus and the Baby Ghost* (Thayer, 1972) for several months. One night he spontaneously acted out a scene from the book in which Mr. Frizzle runs down the stairs "with his bathrobe flying" (p. 7). That night after Ryan had finished getting ready for bed and was wearing his bathrobe, his mom tried to tie it closed. He twisted away and hurried for the stairs. When his mom asked him where he was going, he replied, "I gotta run down the stairs with my bathrobe flying. Like Mr. Frizzle." Ryan proceeded to run down the stairs quickly so that his bathrobe "flew" out behind him, grinning all the while. In fact, he repeated this scene several times that night.

Where the Wild Things Are (Sendak, 1963) is a favorite book of many preschoolers. The language used in this book and the relationship of the illustrations to that language creates a vivid context for children and demonstrates how language is enhanced through storybook interactions. In this text, the following words are used and supported by dramatic illustrations: *gnashed, roared, mischief, world, tumbled, lonely, blinking, terrible, rumpus*. These words are not typically used in children's daily oral conversations, yet within the context of this memorable story, children become acquainted with specific words that can be understood and incorporated into their receptive, and eventually productive, semantic knowledge. A preschool teacher once described how several of her students first announced, and then began, their own "wild rumpus" while outside at the playground.

Preschool children's understanding of metaphoric or figurative language is also seen in the following instance. A mother who was getting her son ready to leave for preschool one day said to him, "Hop on over here and let's put on your shoes." He responded by hopping on both feet over to where his mother was sitting. He had a big grin on his face that seemed to indicate he knew she was not expecting him really to "hop" over.

In these instances, young children are showing their awareness of figurative language and showing how they are refining their semantic knowledge by incorporating more specific vocabulary into their verbal interactions and responding to others' use of metaphoric language.

As children begin to create their own stories, they use their semantic knowledge, acquired through direct and vicarious experiences. Children may incorporate specific phrases or vocabulary in their own stories that most likely come from their experiences with storybooks. Ariel B.'s (age 4 years, 7 months) story included the following: "When I stood before my eyes, I saw twinkling in the twilight, I saw a beautiful, handsome prince . . ." Another child, Ariel F., created a fairy tale in which the queen told the king to go to the "parlor" to get his food. In both of these instances, the impact of storybook experiences upon children's developing semantic knowledge is evident.

The development of semantic knowledge is closely related to the development of syntactic knowledge. Children's understanding of how words convey meaning is closely related to their knowledge of how to interpret or comprehend speech directed to them and how to arrange words in creating the messages they want to communicate to others.

DEVELOPMENT OF SYNTACTIC KNOWLEDGE

During the preschool years, syntactic development occurs in significant ways: increasing noun and verb phrase complexity, using negation (no, not), producing interrogative sentences (questions), and beginning to use passive forms of sentences (O'Grady, Dobrovolsky, & Aronoff, 1989). Each of these new structures enhances the linguistic complexity of the way a preschool child uses language.

Noun and Verb Phrase Complexity

Noun and verb phrase development occur as sentence structures become more complex. Children begin to use subject-verb-object structure for sentences as well ("I ride train"). Auxiliary verb use may appear, as in "I am going." As children's ability to engage in monologues, or *extended speech,* develops, they begin to create and recall short stories, imaginary characters, and imaginative personal experience accounts.

And is used as an all-purpose conjunction to string speech together in children's monologues; the use of *because* typically develops toward the end of the preschool years. Michael (age 4) created this story using *and* to join his ideas together.

> Once there was a little mouse that can run fast *and* the cat was running after him because he took the cheese *and* he was too fast for the cat *and* he got to the mousehole.

Negation

Preschool children begin to use the word *no* at the beginning of an utterance; next, the negative word/element appears within the sentence, as in "*I no want milk.*" Gradually, contractions such as *don't* or *can't* appear. By the end of the preschool years, children are using negatives internally in sentences along with auxiliary verbs, such as *am, is, will, do* (e.g., "I'm not singing a song." or "It's not cold.").

Interrogatives

At first, preschool children create their questions by using rising intonation and/or a *wh* word, such as *where, what,* or *why,* while still keeping subject → verb order. Gradually preschoolers begin to use questions that have inverted order and auxiliary verbs (auxiliary verb → subject → verb). For example, a young preschooler might ask *"Mommy pinch finger?"* using rising intonation to indicate that a question is being asked, while an older preschooler would ask, *"Did Mommy pinch her finger?"* For a while during the preschool years, *wh* words are used in questions without the inversion of the subject-verb order. Toward the end of the preschool years, children use inversion along with the *wh* words, as in "Where did my hat go?"

Passive Sentences

In passive sentence construction, word order is changed from that typically used so that instead of the sentence being constructed as *agent-action-object* (The girl threw the ball), the order is now *object-action-agent* (The ball *was* thrown *by* the girl). Preschool children are beginning to be able to comprehend passive sentences, though not consistently (O'Grady, Dobrovolsky, & Aronoff, 1989; Tager-Flusberg, 1997). Preschoolers' comprehension appears to be related to whether or not the verb is an action verb. In most research that has explored children's understandings of passive sentences, comprehension was determined by children's responses when asked to act out the meaning of the sentence. Children seemed to be more influenced by the order of the words in the sentences and ignored *was* and *by* in comprehending the passive sentence. Spontaneous production or expressive use of passives by preschool children has been only rarely documented by researchers (Owens, 2001).

During the preschool years, significant changes occur in children's syntactic knowledge. At the beginning, children are likely to be using simple two- and three-word sentences, while at the end of the preschool years, children are using a wider variety of sentence types (statements, questions) characterized by greater complexity and having embedded clauses ("because. . .") and cojoined clauses ("and . . ."). Sentence complexity is also related to the development of morphemic knowledge. As children acquire morphemic knowledge, their sentences also increase in complexity. In the next section, preschoolers' increasing morphemic knowledge and indications of greater linguistic complexity are described.

DEVELOPMENT OF MORPHEMIC KNOWLEDGE

Acquisition of morphemic knowledge contributes to young children's linguistic competencies in providing a way of communicating meaning more precisely. By knowing how to change word structures to change meanings, children can communicate more effectively. In English, certain word endings indicate specific grammatical meanings. For example, -ed on the end of a verb signals past tense; -s or -es on a noun indicates plurality; -'s is used to indicate possession. Comparatives are regularly formed by adding -er or -est, as in *fast, faster, fastest.*

The preschool years are a time of significant development in morphemic knowledge. As toddlers (see Chapter 4), children begin to use the present progressive verb form (-*ing),* the regular plural (*/s/, /z/, and /Iz/ as in bridges*), along with the prepositions *in* and *on.* Between the ages of 2 and 4 years, children gradually develop mastery over other types of morphemes, including irregular past tense, possessives, regular past tense (-*ed*), regular third person noun-verb agreement ("*Kathy hits.*"), and verb use with irregular third person (*does, has*). They are using the verb *is* in response to questions ("Who is wearing your hat?" "He is.") and in subject-verb contractions ("*Daddy's* drinking juice.") (Owens, 2001).

Researchers have concluded that children do not learn morphology by simple imitation of adult speech; instead, children appear to experiment actively with language to determine how word endings are used to influence the meaning of a sentence. Children's experiments with language can be observed as they use language to tell stories or in their conversations. Overgeneralization occurs when children use their morphemic rules for words that are not regular (Owens, 2001), creating, for example, *falled, goed, eated.*

When preschool children create their own stories, they may use a variety of verb tenses. Gradually, only past tense is used in storytelling. In Jonathan's (age 4) story, he used past tense fairly consistently for both regular and irregular verbs, except for the irregular verb *fall:*

> The queen wanted to fly, but actually she couldn't. For a few years she tried but she always *fall* down the mountain. But one day, she was on a side mountain and she flew. She thought of the other town with many windows, but then she decided to make a new town.

An analysis of Jonathan's story shows that considerable morphemic knowledge is developing. Plural forms of nouns are used (*years, windows*). Two irregular verbs have correct past tense forms (*flew, thought*). One conjunction is used (*couldn't*). Three regular verbs had appropriate past tense markers (*wanted, tried, decided*). There were two instances of infinitives (*to fly, to make*) and one example of using a form of *to be* as a main verb (*was*). Jonathan's mother reported that he had just "made up" the story; to her knowledge it was not based on a story that had been read to him.

Preschoolers also begin to use comparatives. Children are not yet able to determine which comparatives are regular and which are irregular, so overgeneralization may occur, as in *good, gooder,* and *goodest.* Similarly, in the following story Erica (age 4) made *upper* a comparative of *up* as a way of describing the further distance traveled by her spaceship:

> The spaceship was going *up* and then the spaceship starting to go *upper.* And that is the end.

Significant evidence of children's developing morphemic knowledge was documented by Berko (1958; cited in Genishi & Dyson, 1984). This procedure, known as "the Wug Test," elicited children's morphemic knowledge by using nonsense nouns and verbs which the children had to change to fit within a particular meaning/context. Preschool and first-grade children were shown picture cards with novel creatures and specific actions. A linguistic context was then provided, and the children filled in the linguistic gap. For example, "This is a wug. Now there is another one. There are two of them. There are two _____ (wugs)" (Berko, 1958; cited in Genishi & Dyson, 1984, p. 135). Berko concluded that children's ability to create the correct forms indicated they had internalized morphemic rules and had not just learned them through simple imitation or memorization.

Dialect variations in the use of morphemes also are acquired by young children as they interact with adults and other children during the preschool years.

DEVELOPMENT OF PRAGMATIC KNOWLEDGE

Facilitated by increasing semantic, syntactic, phonetic, and morphemic knowledge, preschool children begin to use language for a wider range of purposes. During the preschool years, children begin to use language to request permission, to invoke social rules, to express emotions, and to make judgments (Owens, 1988). Language may also be used for jokes and teasing or to make an indirect request. Preschoolers do not sustain conversation long, usually only one to two turns per topic (Hulit & Howard, 1993). If asked to clarify a point when in conversation, a preschooler may just repeat what was said or may use a different word.

Research has indicated that preschool children can engage in tailoring their speech appropriately when addressing young infants or older siblings (Berko Gleason, 1973; Shatz & Gelman, 1973). This awareness of a listener's needs is part of children's growing metalinguistic awareness, a conscious awareness that language can be manipulated to achieve a certain goal and that language is used differently in different situations and with different audiences. For example, parents may be surprised when their child's teacher reports their child is polite and does not whine at preschool, even though at home the child will resort to whining to achieve a certain goal.

The use of pragmatic language knowledge is evident when a 4-year-old wants a toy another child is currently using. This message may be communicated in a variety of ways using different levels of pitch, loudness, and tempo and nonverbal behaviors:

1. "It's mine." (grabs toy)

2. "Let's share." (suggests cooperative interaction with toy)

3. "Are you done with that?" (implying turn taking)

4. "Can I play with you?" (suggesting activity together of which the toy is a part)

5. "I want it!" (direct assertion of goal)

6. "Give me it!" (direct order, no negotiation)

The particular way in which the child communicates the message and the resultant success of the message further develops the child's pragmatic knowledge of language. Throughout frequent interactions with others, children gain receptive and productive experience in using language differently in different settings.

Children's dramatic play can provide a further look at children's developing pragmatic knowledge as they assume various roles and corresponding speech. These different ways of speaking in different settings and assuming different roles are referred to as **registers.** Anderson (1992) explored in detail the pragmatic knowledge of a group of 18 children between ages 4 and 7. Five different registers were studied: babytalk, foreignertalk, classroom language/teachertalk, doctortalk, and gendertalk. Children were asked to provide the oral language for role-specific puppets in selected settings. The three settings included a family or home setting, a doctor's office, and a classroom. The classroom setting included a teacher puppet and two student puppets; one of the student puppets was described as a child who had just come to the United States and did not speak English well.

Anderson concluded that children's competence in language use was not consistent across settings. Children in her study seemed to acquire the family register the easiest, followed by the doctor register, and then the classroom register. The hardest register appeared to be the foreigner register, which involved assuming the role of someone who did not speak English well.

Within the doctor setting, children used a register marked by technical jargon. Anderson also noted that the role play by older children indicated status differences between the doctor and nurse and between the medical staff (doctor and nurse) and patient.

In the classroom context, how the children assumed the various roles differed according to age. The youngest children avoided the teacher role. The foreigner role was assumed only by the oldest children.

Anderson found that the children indicated the various roles first through prosodic features. Distinctions between the roles were indicated by voice pitch. Louder voices were used for male roles. When children assumed the foreigner role, they talked with a slower tempo and used syncopated speech (syllable-timed).

Another interesting finding was that the context of the interaction in the setting was distinguished through children's choices in the topic of conversation and in the vocabulary or lexicon used. The oldest children had larger vocabularies and selected terms that were more appropriate for the setting than did the younger children. Role differences were also indicated by differences in the average length of the utterance.

In some instances children even corrected the experimenter's role-playing language to fit the register. Children also made self-corrections spontaneously. Most of these corrections were adjustments in pitch, so that their pitch would fit the character role they were assuming. Self-corrections in vocabulary were not as frequent and were more characteristic of older children. Older children also made more self-corrections in syntax, such as changing a request from an imperative statement to a more polite question.

Gender differences were indicated as girls assumed more roles, spoke more, and modified their speech more to fit the specific contexts. Anderson speculated that boys were just as aware of gender register differences as girls, but boys consciously avoided assuming inappropriate sex-typed language since they had been socialized against speaking like girls in any context.

Although Anderson's study is limited in its generalizability to all children due to its small sample and the sample's lack of ethnic and economic diversity, the study does provide evidence that children are acquiring pragmatic language knowledge during the preschool-primary years. This ability to tailor one's speech to fit the social and linguistic context is an important development in becoming able to communicate effectively in a variety of contexts.

Heath (1983) conducted an ethnographic study of two communities in the Piedmont area of the southeastern United States. Her 10-year study explored the ways in which children learned to use language in various settings: home, school, and community. Roadville was a white working-class community and Trackton was a black working-class community; however, the focus was not on racial differences, but on the ways in which cultural beliefs, practices, and social institutions influence children's acquisition of language. From infancy on, children in these two communities learned the specific ways in which language was used within their respective cultural settings. Heath's detailed account of children's experiences in acquiring language and learning how to use that language in various settings provides a wealth of evidence that pragmatic knowledge is an important aspect of language acquisition. According to Heath,

> Flexibility and adaptability are the most important characteristics of learning to be and to talk in Trackton. Children learn to shift roles, to adapt their language, and to interpret different meanings of language according to varying situations. [For example] In the elementary grades, children take this ability into their "mamma" games, in which they exchange insults, usually including references to "yo 'mamma." (1983, pp. 111–112; reprinted with permission of Cambridge University Press)

Heath also documented differences in the way in which children from the two communities created and told stories. What constituted a "good" story was defined differently by each community. Children's stories reflected the aspects of "storyness" valued by their respective communities. Trackton stories, while based on a real event, contained exaggeration and elaboration developed through the storyteller's creativity and entertaining manner. In contrast, the stories valued in Roadville were those retold from a book's story, a factual account of a real event, or a traditional story adapted to fit the situation (to make a moral or ethical point). While the findings from Heath's study were unique to the two communities involved, her study increased our awareness of the ways in which language learning is shaped by the cultures in which it is used. As participants in specific cultures and their communities, children learn not only what to say but how and when to say it.

Research on the development of storytelling among young children provides a picture of how children develop language competency in using language to create monologues. Prior to the preschool years, children's linguistic behaviors occur in predominately dialogic interactions or short conversations. Preschoolers gradually begin to engage in **monologues,** or settings where they are the main speaker to a listening audience. This shift between dialogue and monologue represents a significant change in the way language is used (Temple, Nathan, Burris, & Temple, 1988). Environmental support for this change is found in groups such as those described in Heath's study, where children's early stories occur in scaffolded settings and gradually become more independent as the child acquires more monologic competency.

Miller & Mehler (1994) describe young children's participation in personal storytelling events, from being a listener to a co-narrator to solo narrator. In this way children are involved in zones of proximal development as stories are told around the children, about them, and with them.

PRAGMATIC KNOWLEDGE AND EMERGENT LITERACY

The pragmatic component of language development also involves knowledge of the pragmatic aspects of written language. As children interact with written language in their world, inside and outside of school settings, they learn how written language is used for various purposes. Pragmatic knowledge of written language builds upon children's pragmatic knowledge of oral language. Children are active explorers in this process.

The shift from dialogic interactions to monologues is also related to the acquisition of pragmatic knowledge of written language. Written language and oral monologues are similar in their use of decontextualized language. When a child develops the ability to engage in oral monologues, she is learning to use language in a manner closer to the way written language is used. The nature of the relationship between dialogue, oral monologue, and written text can be thought of as a continuum of decontextualization (shown in Figure 6.3).

Oral monologues contain features of context specificity. When someone is telling a story orally, their intonation, gestures, and references to the physical surroundings (there, that, this) contribute to the meaning of the message. The oral words alone do not totally communicate the story; however, there is more

FIGURE 6.3
Continuum of Decontextualization of Language

Dialogue	Oral Monologue	Written Text
Comprehension tied to immediate context, negotiated through speaker-listener interaction	Comprehension aided through speaker's use of intonation, gesture, and the physical setting	Comprehension independent of immediate context through precise wording

specificity and precise, descriptive language than is typically used in dialogic conversations. Written text, however, "stands alone" in terms of being specific and not dependent on an immediate context *outside of the language used in the text.* Thus, as preschool children begin to use monologues in telling stories or recounting personal experiences, they develop language competencies that will also enhance their pragmatic knowledge of written language.

Children's interactions with written language occur in three ways: as an *observer* of how written language is used in their environments, as a *questioner* of adults who are engaged in literacy-related tasks, and as an active **explorer/ experimenter** with written language. In homes where literacy-related events occur frequently or daily, children's observation of how written language is used may begin in infancy or toddlerhood (see Chapter 4). Often these children become questioners of adults while toddlers. Some toddlers begin to explore and experiment with how it feels to read and write by approximating the literacy-related behaviors of their parents and older siblings. Observation and questioning continue during the preschool years with increased energy, particularly in environments where literacy-related events occur frequently. Preschoolers also actively engage in exploring and experimenting with what it is like to read and write.

Preschool children's curiosity about written language is evident when they see print in their environment and question their parents or teachers about it. When Ryan (age 3 years) and his mother went to a carnival and he got a balloon with words printed on it, he asked, "What does that say?" Earlier that day, Ryan was getting dressed and was putting on shorts that had the word "PRO" printed on them. When he first put them on, he said, "Have name on" and looked for the word. When he located it he said, "Mom, what that say?" She replied, "PRO. P-R-O, PRO." Ryan then turned to his father, and pointing to the word he said, "Dad, that say PRO, that say PRO." His dad said, "Yes, it does!"

One day, Jon (3 years, 3 months) and his mother were looking at his baby album. On several pictures his mother had written captions. Jon noticed the writing and asked, "What that say?" His mother asked him to point to what he meant. He pointed to the writing, again asking, "What that say? Why that there?" She read a couple of the captions for him, and said, "I wrote it there so we'd know what the picture was about." Interactions such as these two examples show children's beginning understanding of how written language is used in different settings and what it means. In each case, a parent responded to the child's inquiry by explaining how print was used and what it "meant."

Children's early explorations of writing often involve their creating some writing and then giving it to an adult to be "read" (Schickedanz, York, Stewart, & White, 1990). Preschool children who are exploring the writing process have been described as having different purposes or intentions for their writing. Clay (1975) describes children's writing that was like an inventory listing letters or words they could write. Other children have made signs for their school rooms or homes to tell certain specific information, such as "keep out." Clay (1987) describes a preschool child who wrote jokes for her dad and stories. Baghban's (1984) daughter wrote letters to everyone she knew and wanted to mail them.

Preschool children's responses to other literacy-related activities also indicate they are acquiring pragmatic knowledge about written language. Young children have a growing awareness of how written language is used in classrooms and in out-of-classroom contexts. In their work, Morrow and Rand (1991), Vukelich (1990), and Neuman and Roskos (1990, 1991) have explored dramatic play behaviors for evidence of literacy-related knowledge. These researchers have documented a wide range of literacy-related behaviors in prepared dramatic play environments. Young children are acquiring important information about the ways in which written language (reading and writing) is used in various settings such as a doctor's office, business office, kitchen, and retail shop.

Vukelich (1990) describes how children interacted in a dramatic play corner that was equipped as a "postal service center":

> As Jason receives a package from Jonathon (he had prepared the mailing label noting whom the package was to and from), Michael asks, "Are you stamping that package and getting his money? Be sure to write receipt." Jason stamps and stamps and stamps the package. Michael directs, "That's enough! Look, you're holding up the line! Write the receipt!" Jason doesn't know how to spell Jonathon's name. Allen tells Jonathon to turn around so Jason can copy his name from his name tag. The package is weighed, the weight is recorded on the receipt and the money collected. Michael calls, "Hey, driver, get this package delivered. It's going to Canada." Jessica drives off toward "Canada."(p. 207)

In this setting, children were experimenting and exploring how written language (both reading and writing) is used in specific contexts. Some children took more of a directive role in the interactions, while others followed their leads.

PRAGMATIC KNOWLEDGE OF STORYBOOKS

For many preschool children, storybook interactions are a frequent event. Through preschoolers' experiences as observers and participants in shared book interactions, they develop knowledge of how written language is used in books.

They become aware of the left-right, top-down progression of texts. They learn how to orient a book and proceed through the book from the front to the back. They also become aware that the print carries the real message of the story rather than the pictures. Children with frequent storybook experiences also learn that the text is stable; what it says one day, it will say the next day. Parents and teachers often find this out when they do not read the text exactly the same way or with the same intonation during repeated readings. Their preschoolers will stop them, letting the adult reader know that what was said was not "right."

Children's early attempts to track print may be accompanied by their metalinguistic comments about the way written language works, providing further evidence of developing pragmatic knowledge. When 4-year-old Robbie was attempting to read *Where the Wild Things Are* (Sendak, 1963), he experienced difficulty in matching up the title he had memorized with his pointing to print. After trying several times unsuccessfully, Robbie concluded, "This book's not working right" (Schickedanz, 1981, p. 18).

Children's attempts at recreating or "reading" storybooks involves pragmatic knowledge as it indicates what a child knows about how language is used in the process of reading. These reading attempts appear to follow a general developmental sequence. In Sulzby's (1985) study of 2-, 3-, and 4-year old chil-

Preschool children's attempts at recreating or "pretend reading" familiar storybooks indicates their developing pragmatic knowledge.

dren's attempted readings of familiar storybooks, she documented the ways in which preschool children begin to explore the process of reading, from simple labeling and commenting on the pictures to strategy-based reading.

Nicole's story of going to a museum (see the "Semantic Knowledge" section of this chapter) was actually the text of a storybook she created. Although her story was not represented phonetically in her storybook, what she did write indicates her growing awareness of written language as well as her knowledge of how storybooks work (see Figure 6.4).

Nicole's written story indicates that she is aware that storybooks have letters in them, as well as illustrations. She also is using some known words (probably family names), and some word-like units that have consonant-vowel-consonant patterns. However, the phonetic relationship present in written language is still at an early stage of development. She also knows that books have titles, i.e. "the story of going down to a museum" as well as an "end" and "pages." Except for the conversational aside, Nicole's intonation indicated that she was "reading," which further demonstrates her pragmatic knowledge of written language.

Through understanding the significance of children's early explorations and experimentations in reading and writing, teachers and parents will have a better awareness of the complex ways in which children's language knowledge is developing. Parents and teachers can enhance children's further development by being available to answer preschoolers' questions and to welcome preschooler's participation in literacy-related events.

SUMMARY

The preschool years are characterized by rapid development of each aspect of language knowledge. Children's articulation of speech becomes more understandable, more likely to be understood by people outside the family. Their semantic knowledge increases; many more words are added to their receptive and productive vocabularies. Sentence structure becomes more complex, allowing them to be more precise in what they are trying to communicate. Acquisition of morphemes also contributes to preschool children's increasing competencies in creating more precise messages. Pragmatic knowledge is evident in preschool children's flexibility as they begin to use language differently in different situations.

Acquisition of knowledge of written language occurs for children who are in environments where literacy-related events occur frequently and where adults respond to children's inquiries about written language. Children begin to develop an awareness that letters can be associated with specific sounds and with particular words/meanings. Children's interactions with environmental print and their storybook interactions with parents and teachers provide contexts for supporting children's observations of how written language works and how one goes about reading.

FIGURE 6.4
Nicole's Storybook

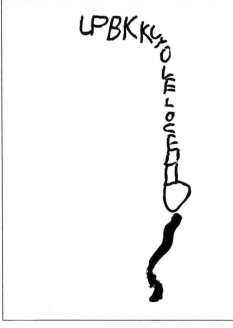

(Cover Page)

(Page 1)

(Page 2)

(Read with word-by-word reading intonation) The story of going down to a museum. (turns page) A museum has so many words. It has some dinosaurs. It shows some moons of Jupiter (laughs). Jupiter was the big one, the biggest of all. I knew, because of school and because the museum told me. (turns page) Don't you know that museums can tell you stuff? (pause, conversational tone) That's the end. And the rest of the pages are all blank.

(Nicole's "reading")

Each of the five aspects of language knowledge is an important aspect to consider in understanding language acquisition among preschool children. This understanding of language development forms the basis for planning and implementing early childhood language curricula. Chapter 7 will explore the ways in which preschool curricula can support and enhance children's developing language knowledge.

✳ ✳ ✳ CHAPTER REVIEW

1. Terms to review:
   - metalinguistic knowledge
   - registers
   - monologues
   - explorer/experimenter

2. Describe five concepts about written language that preschool children can learn when storybooks are shared with them on a regular basis.

3. How is the preschool classroom language environment different from the home language environment? Describe at least three differences.

4. What specific sounds are more difficult for 4-year-olds to produce? Give an example of several words that contain those specific sounds.

5. Define and give an example of an *overextension* and an *underextension*.

6. In what way does storybook sharing enhance preschool children's semantic development?

7. Explain several specific ways in which preschool children's syntactic knowledge becomes more complex. Give an example.

8. Give two examples of evidence that preschoolers are experimenting with, and acquiring, morphemic knowledge.

9. How did Heath's research increase understanding of the development of pragmatic language knowledge and competencies?

✳ ✳ ✳ CHAPTER EXTENSION ACTIVITIES

1. Record a preschool child's oral monologue. Analyze the child's speech for the presence of morphemic knowledge.

2. Describe two activities that would foster the development of the pragmatic language knowledge at the preschool level.

3. Bring a familiar storybook to class. Examine the storybook for each of the five components of language. For example, what phonetic knowledge can be enhanced by reading the book? What value does the book have in promoting semantic knowledge or syntactic knowledge? Share your conclusions with your class.

✳ ✳ ✳ REFERENCES

Anderson, E. (1992). *Speaking with style: The sociolinguistic skills of children.* London: Routledge.

Baghban, M. (1984). *Our daughter learns to read and write: A case study from birth to three.* Newark, DE: International Reading Association.

Ballenger, C. (1996). Learning the ABCs in a Haitian preschool: A teacher's story. *Language Arts, 73*(5), 317–323.

Berk, L., & Spuhl, S. (1995). Maternal interaction, private speech, and task performance in preschool children. *Early Childhood Research Quarterly, 10*(2), 145–169.

Berko Gleason, J. (1973). Code switching in children's language. In T. Moore (Ed.), *Cognitive development and the acquisition of language.* New York: Academic Press.

Bissex, G. (1980). *GNYS AT WRK: A child learns to read and write.* Cambridge, MA: Harvard University Press.

Brainerd, C. (1978). *Piaget's theory of intelligence.* Upper Saddle River, NJ: Prentice Hall.

Clay, M. (1975). *What did I write?* Auckland, New Zealand: Heinemann.

Clay, M. (1983). *Reading begins at home.* Exeter, NH: Heinemann.

Clay, M. (1987). *Writing begins at home.* Portsmouth, NH: Heinemann.

Clay, M. (1991). *Becoming literate: The construction of inner control.* Auckland, New Zealand: Heinemann.

Cochran-Smith, M. (1984). *The making of a reader.* Norwood, NJ: Ablex.

Crystal, D. (1987). *The Cambridge encyclopedia of language.* New York: Cambridge University Press.

DeTemple, J., & Beals, D. (1991). *Family talk: Sources of support for the development of decontextualized language skills.* Paper presented at the American Educational Research Association annual conference, Chicago.

Dickinson, D., & Tabors, P. (1991). *Early literacy: Linkages between home, school and literacy achievement at age five.* Paper presented at the American Educational Research Association annual conference, Chicago.

Dixon-Kraus, L. (1996). *Vygotsky in the classroom: Mediated literacy instruction and assessment.* White Plains, NY: Longman.

Elster, C. (1994). "I guess they do listen": Young children's emergent readings after adult read-alouds. *Young Children, 49*(3), 27–31.

Genishi, C., & Dyson, A. (1984). *Language assessment in the early years.* Norwood, NJ: Ablex.

Hadley, P., Wilcox, K., & Rice, M. (1994). Talking at school: Teacher expectations in preschool and kindergarten. *Early Childhood Research Quarterly, 9*(1), 111–129.

Heath, S. (1983). *Ways with words.* New York: Cambridge University Press.

Hulit, L., & Howard, M. (1993). *Born to talk: An introduction to speech and language development.* New York: Merrill/Macmillan.

Maclean, M., Bryant, P., & Bradley, L. (1987). Rhymes, nursery rhymes, and reading in early childhood. *Merrill-Palmer Quarterly, 33*(3), 255–281.

Mason, J. (1980). When children do begin to read: An exploration of four-year-old children's letter and word reading competencies. *Reading Research Quarterly, 15,* 203–227.

Miller, P., & Mehler, R. (1994). The power of personal storytelling in families and kindergartens. In A. Dyson & C. Genishi (Eds.), *The need for story: Cultural diversity in classroom and community* (pp. 38–54). Urbana, IL: National Council of Teachers of English.

Moerk, E. (1974). Changes in verbal child-mother interactions with increasing language skills of the child. *Journal of Psycholinguistic Research, 3*(2), 101–106.

Morrow, L. (1989). *Literacy development in the early years: Helping children read and write.* Upper Saddle River, NJ: Prentice Hall.

Morrow, L., & Rand, M. (1991). Promoting literacy during play by designing early childhood classroom environments. *The Reading Teacher, 44*(6), 396–402.

Nelson, K. (1973). Structure and strategy in learning to talk. *Monographs of the Society for Research in Child Development, 38* (1-2, Serial No. 149).

Neuman, S., & Roskos, K. (1990). The influence of literacy-enriched play settings on preschoolers' engagement with written language. In J. Zutell & S. McCormick (Eds.), *Literacy theory and research: Analysis from multiple paradigms* (pp. 179–187). Chicago: National Reading Conference.

Neuman, S., & Roskos, K. (1991). Peers as literacy informants: A description of young children's literacy conversations in play. *Early Childhood Research Quarterly, 6,* 233–248.

O'Grady, W., Dobrovolsky, M., & Aronoff, M. (1989). *Contemporary linguistics: An introduction.* New York: St. Martin's Press.

Owens, R. (1988). *Language development* (2nd ed.). Columbus, OH: Merrill.

Owens, R. (2001). *Language development* (5th ed.). Boston: Allyn & Bacon.

Payne, A., Whitehurst, G., & Angell, A. (1994). The role of home literacy environment in the development of language ability in preschool children from low-income families. *Early Childhood Research Quarterly, 9*(3-4), 427–440.

Purcell-Gates, V. (1996). Stories, coupons and the *TV Guide:* Relationships between home literacy experiences and emergent literacy knowledge. *Reading Research Quarterly, 31*(4), 406–428.

Ricciuti, H., White, A., & Fraser, S. (1993). Maternal and family predictors of school readiness and achievement in black, Hispanic, and white 6–7 year olds. *Society for Research in Child Development Abstracts, 9,* 567.

Santiago, R. (1994). The interdependence between linguistic and cognitive performance among bilingual preschoolers with differing home language environments. In

D. MacLaughlin and S. McEwen (eds.), *Proceedings of Boston University Conference on Language Development,* 19, 511–520. Somerville, MA: Cascadilla Press.

Schickedanz, J. (1981). "Hey! This book's not working right." *Young Children,* 18–27.

Schickedanz, J., York, M., Stewart, I., & White, D. (1990). *Strategies for teaching young children.* Upper Saddle River, NY: Prentice Hall.

Schwartz, J. (1981, July). Children's experiments with language. *Young Children,* 16–26.

Sendak, M. (1963). *Where the wild things are.* New York: Harper & Row.

Shatz, M. (1994). *A toddler's life: Becoming a person.* New York: Oxford University Press.

Shatz, M., & Gelman, R. (1973). The development of communication skills: Modifications in the speech of young children as a function of listener. *Monographs of the Society for Research in Child Development, 38* (Serial No. 152).

Smith, M., & Dickinson, D. (1994). Describing oral language opportunities and environments in Head Start and other preschool classrooms. *Early Childhood Research Quarterly, 9*(3-4), 345–366.

Sulzby, E. (1983). *Beginning readers' developing knowledges about written language.* Final Report to the National Institute of Education. Evanston, IL: Northwestern University.

Sulzby, E. (1985). Children's emergent reading of favorite storybooks: A developmental study. *Reading Research Quarterly, 20*(4), 458–481.

Sulzby, E. (1991). Assessment of emergent literacy: Storybook reading. *Reading Teacher, 44*(7), 498–500.

Tager-Flusberg, H. (1997). Putting words together: Morphology and syntax in the preschool years. In J. Berko Gleason (Ed.), *The development of language* (4th ed., pp. 159–209). Columbus, OH: Merrill.

Teale, W. (1986). Home background and young children's literacy development. In W. H. Teale & E. Sulzby (Eds.), *Emergent literacy: Writing and reading* (pp. 110–121). Norwood, NJ: Ablex.

Temple, C., Nathan, R., Burris, N., & Temple, F. (1988). *The beginnings of writing* (2nd ed.). Boston: Allyn & Bacon.

Thayer, J. (1972). *Gus and the baby ghost.* New York: William Morrow.

Tizard, B. (1981). Language at home and at school. In C. Cazden (Ed.), *Language in early childhood education* (Rev. ed.). Washington, DC: National Association for the Education of Young Children.

Vukelich, C. (1990, Summer). Where's the paper? Literacy during dramatic play. *Childhood Education,* 205–209.

Vygotsky, L. (1962). *Thought and language.* Cambridge, MA: M.I.T. Press.

Vygotsky, L. (1978). *Mind in society: The development of higher psychological processes.* Cambridge, MA: Harvard University Press.

Wertsch, J. (1984). The zone of proximal development: Some conceptual issues. In B. Rogoff & J. Wertsch (Eds.), *Children's learning in the zone of proximal development* (pp. 7–18). San Francisco: Jossey-Bass.

Appendix

✳ ✳ ✳ ✳ ✳ ✳

Generalizations on the Order of Phoneme Acquisition

1. Vowels are acquired earlier than consonants.
2. The order of acquisition is based upon the type of production:

    nasals—degree of closing of the oral cavity (/m/ /n/)
    plosives—explosive release of sound (/p/ /b/ /t/)
    approximates—produced without turbulence (/w/ /j/)
    lateral approximates—produced with lateral air flow (/l/)
    fricatives—sound produced by friction, narrow constriction of the sound passage (/f/ /v/ /θ/ /s/)
    affricatives—combination of plosive and fricative (choke, joke)

3. The order of acquisition is based upon the location of the sound produced:

    glottals—at the glottis, the opening to larynx (happy)
    bilabials—lips together (/p/ /b/)
    velars—back of tongue touches the soft palate (/k/ /g/)
    alveolars—tongue to upper gum ridge (/t/ /d/ /s/)
    post aveolars—tongue barely reaches back of upper gum area (shoe, visual)
    dentals—teeth; tongue tip between upper and lower incisors (thigh, thin, this)
    labio dentals—upper incisor teeth are touched by lower lip, (face, vase)
    palatals—hard palate (choke, nature, gentle)

4. Sounds in the initial position within words are acquired first.
5. Consonant clusters and blends are acquired around ages 7 or 8. Some consonant clusters may appear as early as age 4.
6. Wide variations exist among children of the same ages. In some instances, the acquisition of sound production may vary by as much as 3 years.

❋ ❋ ❋

7

ENHANCING LANGUAGE DEVELOPMENT IN PRESCHOOLERS

"It is the way language is used in the classroom that is important in influencing educational achievement."

Cazden (1996, p. 94)

Based upon the growth in language knowledge during the preschool years, described in Chapter 6, this chapter will focus on the ways in which preschoolers' language development can be enhanced. Critical aspects of encouraging growth in preschoolers' language involves teachers who provide many opportunities for children to talk and who listen thoughtfully to children's speech (Bredekamp & Copple, 1997). In addition, it is important that teachers use supportive linguistic scaffolding and expansions to enhance children's communicative efforts. The following section describes basic teacher-child interaction patterns appropriate for preschool classrooms. This section is followed by a description of specific curricula and activities that enhance language development.

INTERACTIVE PATTERNS

The ways in which teachers and caregivers interact with young children influence children's growth and development. Basic patterns in which adults interact with young children were described in Chapter 2. These basic patterns of interaction are also effective *teaching strategies* in enhancing children's learning and development in a classroom environment. This section describes four teaching strategies, which are grounded in the basic patterns of interaction first described in Chapter 2. These strategies can be used throughout the preschool curriculum to facilitate and nurture the acquisition of language competencies:

1. Questioning
2. Linguistic scaffolding
3. Mediation
4. Conflict resolution

Some of these strategies are also appropriate for interaction with children at other ages; however, because of the differences in developmental levels, the use of each strategy differs with the level. In this chapter, the focus will be on using the strategies with preschool children.

Questioning

While this strategy composes a major part of the discussion dialogue between teachers and students at the primary level, it can also be used at the preschool level to encourage language development. Since questions serve to elicit answers, the way in which a question is worded or developed influences the language used in the response.

Questions can vary with the level of knowledge required in the answer. At the preschool level, teachers' questions focus on two main levels: low-level questions involving rote recall or literal information and high level, involving interpretative or inferential responses. When children respond to high-level questions, they are "most actively involved mentally" and "use their language most powerfully for learning" (Lindfors, 1987, p. 314).

A teacher's decision to use low-level or high-level questioning is influenced by the educational goal or purpose of the activity. Literal or low-level recall questions can be used to establish a basic level of comprehension or understanding. These questions can help determine if the child is perceiving the same information in the environment or shared point of reference.

For example, in the following dialogue the teacher begins with literal questions and then progresses to higher-level questioning in line 5:

1. T: What animal do you see on the ground by the tree?
2. C: A squirrel.
3. T: What is the squirrel doing?
4. C: Picking up an acorn.
5. T: Why do you think he is doing that?

The teacher's use of *why* asks the child to speculate a reason for the squirrel's actions. If squirrels and nut gathering had been mentioned earlier in the class (at story time, for example), the teacher's question would have also elicited a comparison of the squirrel outside with the information about the squirrel they read about in the book.

More elaborate systems of classifying questions have been developed (e.g., Bloom, 1956). While it is important to include a variety of the higher-level questions, such as those that support synthesis, evaluation, and application, most preschool teachers find it more useful to think in terms of two broad categories, low- and high-level questioning (Genishi & Dyson, 1984).

While many questions are asked "on the run" during routine and exploratory activities, teachers need to take time to develop some questions for group activities in advance so that they can monitor the level and quality of the questions they ask. In preplanning questions to ask, it is valuable to develop sample answers to the questions and to determine if the activity has sufficient information for the child to answer the questions. Then when activities are conducted and children are asked the questions, teachers are well prepared. Having questions and sample answers prepared also helps teachers remain focused or return to the activity should any classroom disruption or unexpected events occur.

Questions are more effective if they require a more complex answer than just "yes" or "no." If yes-no questions are used, they can be followed up with a more open-ended question sequence. When children compose their answers, they incorporate their knowledge of all five aspects of language knowledge.

Questions may also be developed to reflect the Socratic method. This type of questioning involves developing a series of questions that leads up to a logical conclusion or target answer. The initial questions in a Socratic series are simple and provide a basis for the subsequent questions.

Questions can also vary in terms of the teacher's purpose for questioning. *Clarification questions* are used when a teacher needs to understand more clearly the message or meaning of what a child said. This type of question reelicits part of a previous response in order to clarify what was originally said, as in "What did you say happened next?" Sometimes clarification questions have an echolike format, such as in the following example:

> *Child:* I going owa nah.
> *Adult:* You're going where?
>   (Reich, 1986, p. 97)

Recitation questions are asked when teachers want children to indicate their level of knowledge or awareness of a specific topic, such as "What is your name?" or "What color is this?" These questions are recitational because the teacher already knows the answer but is checking to see whether the child can produce the correct response to the question. Many of the questions teachers ask are recitational and are asked to check the comprehension or understanding by children on a particular task or about a specific event.

Information questions elicit information from a child that the teacher does not know but needs to know. For example, "Where did you put your coat?" "In what center do you want to work today?" Information questions can also be open ended, such as "What do you think happened next in the story?"

Another type of questioning that occurs in preschools focuses on things or events that are not present in the immediate context, called *there-and-then questions* (Genishi & Dyson, 1984). These questions encourage children to think about past and future events and thus encourage their use of different verb tenses. This type of question also encourages children to use language to express their recall or to hypothesize what might happen.

Throughout a typical day, there-and-then questions can be used at arrival time, departure, and story time, as well as in conversations at snack time or on the playground. Children's original stories can also be elicited by there-and-then questions such as, "How did you learn to ride a bike?" (Sulzby, 1981).

Another way in which teachers may use questions at the preschool level is to stimulate children's curiosity by modeling wondering about the world around them (Lindfors, 1987). In this way teachers communicate to their children exciting possibilities in learning about their environment and help children become aware of the teacher as a learner, someone who asks questions to find out new information.

Wait Time

A critical aspect in using any questioning strategy is to provide an appropriate **wait time** for the child to respond. Questions that are asked too quickly or impatiently discourage children from giving careful thought to the question and to their respective answers.

Responding to Children's Answers

In acknowledging children's responses, teachers need to monitor their implied and direct evaluation of what children have said. To encourage children to participate in individual and group conversations (discussions), teachers should acknowledge each child's response positively. When necessary, teachers can encourage additional clarification through follow-up questioning. When a child's responses/contributions are repeatedly ignored, a signal is sent that those responses are not valued, and often the child begins to feel that the teacher does not want her to participate.

Positive feedback to children's responses should be more than just "That was a good answer" or "Yes, that's right." A teacher should confirm for the child (and the other children listening) the aspect of the answer that was appropriate and confirm the comprehension strategy used by the child. For example, in the following group discussion of *Are You My Mother?* (Eastman, 1960), the specific feedback to Matt's response confirmed for Matt why his response was correct.

> *Teacher:* Why do you think the baby bird thought the airplane was his mother?
>
> *Matt:* Because it has wings, flies.
>
> *Teacher:* Yes, Matt, both birds and airplanes do have wings and can fly.

In summary, the role of questioning as a teaching strategy is to stimulate the use of receptive and expressive language. The effectiveness of questions should be carefully monitored. When preschoolers appear unable to comprehend what the question is asking, the question should be restated or reworded. For example, in a group setting, if the teacher's question elicits two or more incorrect responses, the question needs to be revised. To continue to call on other children is simply "fishing" for an answer. It takes away from the activity's focus and can lead to inattention on the part of young students. Poorly formed discussion questions rarely occur when teachers prepare questions and sample answers ahead of time.

The types of questions used by a teacher and the way in which questioning occurs have a significant impact on the learning environment of the classroom. Asking too many questions may result in class discussions becoming only times of recitation rather than times of sharing thoughts and developing knowledge. The key to successful questioning is to use a balance of questioning types and purposes, while constantly monitoring the impact the questioning has on the discourse patterns in the classroom.

Linguistic Scaffolding

The linguistic scaffolding appropriate for interacting with preschool children is different from that used with infants and toddlers due to increased language competencies. However, the basic approach still involves creating a zone of proximal development. The teacher's interaction supports the child's participation at a higher level than the child could have alone. As with the use of this strategy at other levels of development, linguistic scaffolding provides support for children as they communicate so that messages are sent and received effectively.

Linguistic scaffolding may include the use of questioning, expansion, and/or repetition. The questioning used during the linguistic scaffolding strategy serves to lead the child ahead in the dialogue or discourse as a way of maintaining the verbal interaction. In maintaining the dialogue, the teacher is sensitive to the child's utterances and formulates her response based upon what the child said (Trousdale, 1990) in both content and form. For example, in the following dialogue between Scott and his teacher during share-and-tell time, the teacher uses questioning to maintain the dialogue. Without the use of this scaffold of questioning, the interaction would have stopped.

Teacher:	Scott, it's your turn to share.
Scott:	(stands up, walks to front of the semicircle, stands near his teacher; he holds up a toy fire truck; long pause)
Teacher:	Scott, what do you have?
Scott:	A truck. (long pause)
Teacher:	What kind of truck is it?
Scott:	A fire truck. (long pause)
Teacher:	Yes, it is a bright red fire truck. (Teacher motions to the ladders on the truck) Scott, tell us what these are.
Scott:	Ladders.
Teacher:	Why do firefighters need ladders?
Scott:	To help people.
Teacher:	Yes, firefighters use ladders to rescue people from tall buildings.

Through the use of contingent questioning, the teacher engages the child in sharing more complete information about the truck he brought to share-and-tell. Without the questioning and linguistic scaffolding, Scott's verbal participation would have been limited.

Expansion is another part of linguistic scaffolding. It is used to "fill out" what a child says (Reich, 1986). Expansion is also a way to model more complex syntax, morphology, semantics, and correct pronunciation. In the following dialogue, expansion enhances syntax and morphology by creating complete sentences and adding inflectional endings and correct past tense forms:

Cameron and Mark are playing at the outdoor sandbox. Their teacher Sandy is seated near the sandbox.

Mark:	(finds a ladybug crawling in the grass near the sandbox) Oh, a bug!
Teacher:	That looks like a ladybug.

> *Cameron:* Look, it flied.
>
> *Teacher:* Yes, it flew over to the dandelion.

Repetition is also a part of linguistic scaffolding. In the previous example the teacher repeated specific words to reinforce pronunciation and to confirm the meaning of what was said.

Mediation

This strategy focuses on simplifying the learning stimulus or task to facilitate the language interaction with, and comprehension by, the child. The nature of **mediation** appears to be influenced by an adult's awareness of a child's level of comprehension (receptive language) and ability to respond (expressive language). A teacher is in the middle, a go-between for the child and the learning stimuli.

In mediation, the teacher's focus is on understanding the way in which children's responses to the activity indicate, or fail to indicate, their ability to learn from the task or activity. Blank (1973) emphasizes the role of tutorial dialogue initiated by a teacher when interacting with a child. Through specific techniques involving both questions and comments, a teacher can determine the errors a child may be making in reasoning or in cognitive perception. Then, the teacher can attempt to lead the child through a verbal exchange that increases the child's understanding of the activity or task. In this type of interaction the child's response determines how the teacher will proceed in the dialogue. The teacher continuously seeks to determine what confusions the child may have and how the focus of the interaction can be further elaborated.

At the preschool level, mediation can occur in situations where a preschooler is putting a puzzle together or working at the water table and experimenting with objects that float or sink. Mediation may also be seen in altered texts as storybooks are shared. When teachers encounter a concept in the text they feel is too difficult for children to understand, they change the text to fit their understanding of their children's semantic and syntactic knowledge. Sometimes teachers may mediate the text by pausing after a new concept/label is introduced in the text and explain the concept through questioning or commenting in terms that children can comprehend.

When presenting conceptual information to children, teachers need to decide what information to present and how to present it so that it is comprehensible to children. In deciding how to present the information, teachers need to have an awareness of their children's prior knowledge and current conceptual understandings. Specific conceptual terms are not usually introduced until children are familiar with the general term; for example, the word *dog* is used to identify the larger class of animals before the specific term *cocker spaniel* or *labrador* is used.

It is also important to consider children's prior experiences when selecting a book to read. Sharing a book about collecting seashells would require different mediation and presentation to a group of children who have vacationed at or live near an ocean beach than it would to a group of urban or rural children who have never been to the seashore.

Conflict Resolution

Usually **conflict resolution** is considered a strategy for classroom management and discipline (Maxim, 1993), not language development. Yet, when conflict resolution is employed to encourage children to use language to express themselves and to solve or ameliorate social disagreements, it is another way of increasing language knowledge among young children.

At the preschool level, most children have acquired sufficient language competencies so that teachers can begin to use verbal conflict resolution strategies. In disagreements over toys or turn taking, teachers can help children verbalize their intents and wishes and lead them to some form of consensus or compromise.

For example, in a dramatic play area, two girls who want to be the mother have resorted to pushing each other. When the teacher intervenes, she suggests that one girl be the mother and the other one an aunt. By providing the children with alternative roles and helping them begin their role playing, the learning and communicating value of the activity is enhanced. Without conflict resolution strategies the two girls probably would have chosen separate activities, ending their verbal role-playing interaction.

An important part of conflict resolution is active listening (Maxim, 1993). In active listening, teachers acknowledge and accept what children are communicating. Children are encouraged to verbalize their feelings and identify other's feelings. When the nature of the conflict is identified, teachers help children become aware of alternatives or possible compromises. As an active listener, a teacher acknowledges the emotional state of children while keeping a positive and balanced approach to resolving the conflict. The goal of conflict resolution is to have both sides of the disagreement accept the outcome/solution as a fair way to reduce the conflict while recognizing their individual needs and wishes.

Each of these interaction strategies (questioning, linguistic scaffolding, mediation, and conflict resolution) can be used throughout the preschool curriculum. The specific way in which each strategy is implemented depends on the particular curricular goals and the aspect of language knowledge involved.

CURRICULAR ACTIVITIES FOR ENHANCING PRESCHOOLERS' LANGUAGE

A well-balanced preschool curriculum provides learning opportunities that enhance acquisition of phonetic, syntactic, semantic, morphemic, and pragmatic language knowledge. More specific language goals are usually developed at the classroom level by teachers after they have determined the individual needs of children in their classrooms.

As teachers plan and implement their curricula, each learning activity should have a clear, educational rationale or purpose. Many sources of curriculum ideas and activities describe how to conduct specific activities but do not indicate why these activities should be used. As a result, teachers may implement activities without a full awareness of the potential for fostering language development. When teachers have a strong educational rationale for each learning activity, implementation of each activity is more focused and assessment of the learning outcome is more direct. When activities are implemented without a clear rationale or objective, the focus may simply be on keeping the children busy.

In the sections that follow, preschool learning activities and their potential for fostering language development are described in three categories of activities:

1. **Exploratory activities**—Independent, unstructured activities that are open ended and provide opportunities to explore ways of interacting with the materials provided.
2. **Teacher-directed activities**—Structured, teacher-led activities for small and whole class groupings.
3. **Routine activities**—Activities that may occur on a daily basis in the classroom, such as attendance taking, arrival and departure routines, and snacks and mealtimes.

In each of these areas, specific activities are described and analyzed for their potential contributions to language acquisition. Guidelines for implementing the activities incorporate questioning and linguistic scaffolding and other successful interaction strategies.

Encouraging Language Development Through Exploratory Activities

During the day, a developmentally appropriate preschool program has several time blocks in which children can select from a number of unstructured, open-ended activities. While initially planned for by teachers, these learning opportunities allow children to decide how they will interact with the materials provided.

Examples of exploratory activities include blocks and manipulatives, a drama corner (housekeeping, store, health office), book center, listening center, writing center, learning centers, and art center. Outdoor play is another unstructured activity during which time specific aspects of language development can be encouraged. In each of these areas, it is important to remember that the exploratory nature of the activity requires that the children have an opportunity to interact independently with the materials with only a minimum of adult guidance or intervention. The guidelines for teachers' interactions in each of the areas should be implemented sensitively as opportunity arises and not as required teacher behavior for each time the activity is conducted.

In the following sections, language goals for these activities will be discussed, along with guidelines for teachers.

Blocks and Manipulatives

Blocks and manipulatives, such as Legos®, beads, and Duplos®, are an important part of a preschool curriculum. Educational goals inherent in blocks and manipulatives involve enhancing physical development, social interaction and collaboration, conceptual development, and problem solving (Bredekamp & Copple, 1997; Lindberg & Swedlow, 1980). Language development is embedded within these educational goals when language communication accompanies children's actions in manipulating and talking about their creations and in working in collaboration with other children.

When a block/manipulative area contains a wide variety of building materials, language development can be stimulated in several ways. A teacher who visits with children as they build encourages them to describe verbally what they are building through extending, expanding, and repeating important segments of the children's comments.

Specific language goals for this learning area include helping children learn to describe and label what was built and how they built it, helping children use language to solve problems, and encouraging the children to ask questions about what they are building and how it relates to real-life structures or events. As they communicate in their situations, children use both receptive and expressive language.

Teachers can encourage and facilitate block/manipulative play in several ways. Silent support is given when teachers plan for sufficient time, space, and materials for block/manipulative play. The presence of a teacher in the block/manipulative area shows the teacher is interested in that area (Lindberg & Swedlow, 1980).

When children need direction, a teacher might make a suggestion or ask a question as a way of providing or clarifying an idea related to the building activity. It is critical, however, that the teacher balance his involvement so that it enhances, but does not interfere with, children's exploration and creativity. There is a fine line between positive intervention and interference. Too much teacher direction, or too many questions and/or comments, may result in the children losing interest in the activity. Teachers must be sensitive to children's needs for independent exploration and creativity, along with possible benefits from teacher intervention and verbal interaction.

Drama Corner

For people who have no background in early childhood education, the drama corner looks like a lot of fun but has no relationship to "real school learning." In reality, the drama corner has an important part in a preschool curriculum. Dramatic play activities provide opportunities for children to practice using language in a variety of contextual situations. Dramatic activities also provide opportunities to engage in problem solving. Language is used during the negotiation of specific roles and common purposes that occur during the beginning of the dramatic play and throughout the joint interaction (Berk & Winsler, 1995).

Gender neutral roles should be encouraged, such as "server" rather than "waitress" and "mail carrier" rather than "mailman," since this opens up dramatic roles to both boys and girls (Sheldon, 1990).

Language goals for drama areas include helping children learn to use language to communicate or converse in their assumed roles and helping children learn to negotiate the role they want to assume. All five aspects of language knowledge are involved as children use receptive and expressive language to carry out their role playing. Semantic knowledge is used to communicate the concepts conveyed in their conversations. Phonetic knowledge is used in articulation. Syntactic knowledge is evident in the grammatical structures used in their speech. Plural word endings and verb tenses indicate morphemic knowledge. Pragmatic knowledge is evident as children tailor their speech to fit the dramatic setting, whether it be a restaurant, post office, or dinner table at home.

In preparing a drama corner, teachers should attempt to include realistic materials, keeping in mind children's needs for safety and self-esteem. Sufficient amounts of drama materials are needed to allow several children to participate. Materials should be representative of both genders and promote multicultural diversity and acceptance.

Themed drama corners encourage children to begin to translate into behaviors their understandings of complex concepts involving written language (see Morrow & Rand, 1991; Neuman & Roskos, 1990). For example, an office area, complete with a telephone, typewriter, phone books, calculator, message pads, file folders, writing utensils, desks, and chairs, draws on children's understanding of specific careers, literacy skills needed for office work, and adult communication skills. A post office would have letters ready to be processed, envelopes, stamps, a zip code book, and postcards. Children's interactions in this post office area would draw on their understandings of how written communications are sent in the mail. Examples of specific themes for dramatic play areas are located in Figure 7.1 (Morrow & Rand, 1991).

When providing materials for dramatic play, a teacher needs to consider the cultural background of children in his classroom and be sure that children are comfortable and familiar with the materials and arrangement (Nourot & VanHoorn, 1991). In addition, both high-realism and low-realism props are needed to accommodate the range of children's symbolic play (McLoyd, 1986, as cited in Nourot & VanHoorn, 1991).

Even in classrooms where creative drama props are provided, some children may engage in noisy, stereotypic "monster" play, using growling sounds and limited speech. When this happens, a teacher may suggest alternative actions or speech that will stimulate more complex language. The teacher needs to redirect and discourage any running or pushing that may become part of the monster play.

In many instances, it is valuable for the teacher to model specific ways of interacting with the themed materials. For example, in a veterinarian's office setting, the teacher could remind children to fill out appointment forms or prescription forms, to read to their pets in the waiting area, and to provide directions for the medications (Morrow & Rand, 1991).

FIGURE 7.1

Ideas for Themed Dramatic Play Corners

Theme	Props/Equipment
Fast-food restaurant	Order pads, pencil/markers, a cash register, recipes, lists of items/menu, newspapers for customers to read
Gas station/car repair shop	Sales receipts, repair orders, road maps, repair manuals, posters advertising equipment, newspapers for sale
Airport	Arrival and departure signs, tickets, boarding passes, safety messages, name tags for luggage, name tags for airline staff, magazines and newspapers for passengers
Supermarket/grocery store	Food packages, a cash register, shopping lists, receipts, coupons, advertising flyers, labeled shelves and sections
Newspaper office	Paper, pencils or thin markers, typewriter, telephone book, telephone, newspapers, pictures/photos, old camera, maps

A teacher's guidance in dramatic play is often based upon careful observation of children's interactions in that area. Through this observation a teacher can become aware of the need for an additional prop or piece of equipment. Through monitoring dramatic play, a teacher may take advantage of the opportunity to encourage cooperation between children and facilitate their negotiation of purposes and/or roles (Berk & Winsler, 1995). A teacher can also become aware of questions or misconceptions children might have about a particular concept or person's role. It is important not to interrupt a child's thinking (Lindberg & Swedlow, 1980) or to provide too much direction to children in the dramatic play area.

Dramatic play activities are most beneficial when children can engage in a variety of roles and have sufficient time to explore the materials provided within that theme. Children need repeated opportunities to engage in dramatic play. From these repeated opportunities, children gradually begin to elaborate upon the dialogues and interactions within that dramatic setting. When children's interest in a specific theme decreases, fewer children choose to interact in the dramatic play corner. A new theme should then be selected and prepared. Teachers have found it valuable to introduce the new theme gradually so that children become familiar with the resources and props available in the new setting.

Book Center

Most preschools have an area where children can interact with storybooks. However, in some classrooms, children are given only discarded books, and the better-quality books are tucked away on a high shelf or on the teacher's desk for "safekeeping." For children to gain the most benefit from a book corner, high-quality, interesting books must be present and accessible for all children. These books should be changed periodically, approximately every two to three weeks, to maintain interest in the area. Comfortable pillows or chairs, such as beanbag chairs, contribute to children's interest in relaxing with a book. This area should have enough room for two to four children to encourage literature sharing.

Specific language goals for this area include orally recreating stories via pictures and memory for story texts, increasing vocabulary development, and learning to discuss or share a book with another child. Both receptive and expressive language knowledge are enhanced through children's storybook interactions.

Books placed in the book corner should be familiar, having been read previously at group story time. This provides children with an introduction to the book so that they can build upon this introduction when they interact with the book independently in the book corner. A range of genres should also be provided: poetry/nursery rhymes, narratives, alphabet books, fairy tales, and nonfiction. This range provides children with a wide variety of language structures and vocabulary. A range of genres also will enhance children's development of pragmatic knowledge of language since they will be exposed to the way in which language is used differently in poetry, fairy tales, nonfiction, and alphabet books.

Vocabulary development is also enhanced by books that are clearly illustrated and whose illustrations are directly related to the book's text. Picture dictionaries, wordless books, and concept books encourage children to look closely at the illustrations and to label the items or actions illustrated.

Teachers support and facilitate children's interactions in the book corner by providing a variety of books and comfortable seating and by monitoring children's book interactions. In keeping with the exploratory nature of the book center, teachers' monitoring should involve observing which books are used more frequently and the ways in which children interact with the books. For example, do they look only at the pictures when recreating the story? Do they have a memory for the text or story line? Do they talk with each other about the story events or the illustrations? Informal conversations about the books provide opportunities to further develop children's expressive language and listening skills.

Listening Center

In another part of the room, where quiet activities are planned, a tape player and headphone set can be placed along with storybooks and accompanying tapes. Language goals for this area include increasing children's listening comprehension and vocabulary and expanding children's ability to sequence story events. The storybooks used in this area should be familiar so children can follow the story easily. Predictable stories and rhyming texts (poetry and nursery rhymes) provide opportunities for children to hear the patterns of text and sound patterns in rhyme. Teachers can make their own audiotapes of storybooks by tap-ing a group story time in their classroom. In this way children will hear the familiar voice of their teacher reading the storybook and they will hear the other students' comments and questions as the storybook is read. This repetition enhances their familiarity with the story and with the language in the text.

Be sure the tape recorder is a durable model and the controls are easily operated by children. Teachers should take time to demonstrate how to use the tape player and headphones on several occasions so that children are comfortable and confident in how to use the equipment.

Teachers need to monitor this area, noting whether children are having any difficulty using the equipment. Occasionally, they may also engage children in brief, informal conversations about the taped stories.

Writing Center

Since exploration of written language is the goal of this center, teachers should expect (and encourage) children to use a wide range of preconventional forms of written communication: drawing, scribbling, letter strings, copied environmental print, and invented spelling. Children should be encouraged to use illustration and print for a variety of purposes: story creation and sharing, list making, notes to others, greeting cards, thank-you notes, and invitations. Teacher suggestions as to the format or purpose of children's writing in a writing center should remain as only optional suggestions; the decision to create should remain entirely within each child. In the writing center, children explore ways of communicating through pictures and print. Some writing-related materials may already be included in themed learning centers (see next section); however, a writing center is devoted to the general exploration of written communication. Through their attempts in communicating on paper, children will gradually acquire receptive and expressive knowledge of how written language works.

The writing center should be stocked with ample supplies of paper and writing implements (pencils, small felt-tip markers, and crayons), along with writing-related materials such as envelopes, pretend stamps, alphabet letter stamps, and ink pads. A bulletin board in this area encourages children to share their creations with the class. Coloring books and/or reading readiness workbooks should not be a part of the writing center since neither activity encourages exploration and creative communication.

A writing center needs to have a low table and several chairs, along with shelving units where the supplies are kept. There should be room for several children to use this center at the same time. Their conversations with each other often help them clarify and develop their explorations.

A teacher may decide to visit the writing center to informally observe children's explorations, to model writing behaviors, or to offer encouragement (Neuman & Roskos, 1990). The emphasis should be on children's creative explorations of a wide range of preconventional forms rather than on insisting that children begin to "learn" to write with conventional spelling, penmanship, and grammar. If children insist that they cannot "read" what they have written, teachers should then ask them to tell about what they have written or drawn, or what they wanted their writing to say or picture to show.

Learning Centers

Learning centers contain exploratory and gamelike activities that one or more children may use independently. Specific learning centers are planned and implemented based upon the current needs of the students in the classroom (Schickedanz, York, Stewart & White, 1990). General language goals for learning centers include increasing children's conceptual development and vocabulary through hands-on activities, increasing children's ability to describe or verbalize concepts, using language in problem-solving tasks, and increasing children's question-asking behaviors.

Some learning centers provide open-ended activities that are process-oriented, while others have activities that are more product-oriented. For example, a science center on magnetism might encourage children to test the magnetic properties of a variety of metal and nonmetal items. In contrast, another science center might have students match pictures of baby animals with pictures of adult animals. Learning centers may present specific content information, such as math, science, and social studies, or may have integrated content, such as math-science or social studies-language arts.

A learning center can also be designed and developed to focus on concepts within classroom curricular themes. For example, for a seasonal theme of autumn, a learning center could provide a collection of leaves that children could examine with a magnifying glass; they could also complete a texture rubbing of the leaves and/or assemble a leaf collage.

Learning center activities should be self-correcting or open ended so minimal monitoring by the teacher is needed. Simply worded directions or illustrated steps should be provided. A tape recorder can be placed in the learning center to record children's responses to the learning center activities and to record any specific questions they might have for the teacher. By providing a tape recorder, children have an opportunity to use language to describe and record what they have learned or what questions they have. It is important to monitor the children's interest level for each center so that a new center can be introduced when the current learning center no longer serves their needs. Teachers also need to monitor the organization and equipment in the learning center to be sure the center is appropriately ready. As teachers visit learning centers, they should respond to children's questions and comments by using the interaction strategies of questioning, linguistic scaffolding, and mediation.

Learning centers are usually designed for only one child at a time since 3- and 4-year-olds developmentally are transitioning between solitary and parallel interaction patterns and are usually not ready for activities requiring cooperation. When children can interact cooperatively, learning centers may be designed for two or three children. In these situations, the learning center task may involve problem solving or another task requiring verbal interaction among children.

Art Center

Although art activities are visually expressive and communicative by nature, they also provide opportunities to enhance language development. Language goals for art activities focus on encouraging children to develop conceptual knowledge related to art and to be able to verbally describe the colors, textures, or shapes with which they are working. Children should also learn the concept name of the particular technique they are using. Rather than labeling the technique as simply "painting," a teacher should explain the type of painting involved, such as sponge painting, string painting, finger painting, block painting, or brush painting. Semantic development is furthered as children learn other art-related concepts and vocabulary involving textures, shapes, and colors. When children have opportunities to share their comments and questions during the artistic process, they continue to develop in the five aspects of language knowledge.

Art activities are an opportunity for children to explore independently the various mediums of artistic expression. Teacher direction in art activities should be minimal; however, opportunities for conversation may occur during the creative process. Teachers should respond to children's comments and questions during art activities, using expansion and verbal scaffolding to clarify concepts or processes involved in the ongoing activity. At the same time, too much teacher direction or conversation may interfere with a child's art experience.

Outdoor Play

Outdoor play provides many opportunities for exploratory activities. Children can be encouraged to use language during their outdoor experiences to describe, to negotiate, and to question. With different types of outdoor play equipment, an all-weather play surface, and shade trees and other vegetation, preschool children can explore and experience a wide variety of activities.

Language goals for outdoor play include encouraging children to describe natural events, such as rain, snowfall, and wind, and cause-and-effect relationships. Children should also be encouraged to use language to negotiate the use of equipment and to carry on conversations with peers and adults. Semantic development also occurs as children explore and ask questions about their environment. Specific activities can be provided during outdoor play such as using a sandbox, a water table, parachute play, and big wheels and other riding toys. Each of these activities is an opportunity to encourage children to use language to describe what they are experiencing and to comment and question during their exploration.

A sandbox provides opportunities to explore a variety of concepts and vocabulary related to temperature, texture, shape, size, and processes. Figure 7.2 focuses on sandbox activities and illustrates the wide variety of concepts related to sandbox experiences. Mediation provided sensitively by a teacher can encourage children to focus on these concepts and vocabulary without impinging on the spontaneity of their exploration.

Building a snowman can provide opportunities to expand vocabulary and conversation skills.

Another outdoor activity appropriate for preschool children is a parachute group activity. In this activity, a group of about 8 to 10 children, with their teacher(s), hold onto the edges of a circular parachute. A teacher leads the children in raising and lowering the parachute, catching currents of air. While this is a group activity, it is exploratory in the sense that the activity explores how a parachute moves, responding to currents of the air and specific manipulation. The activity contributes to conceptual and language development as a hands-on activity that provides opportunities to feel and see concepts such as *up, down, high, low, wavy, twisting, floating, rising,* and *falling.* Teacher talk here directs children's actions and should be minimal since the important focus of this activity is to experience the concepts through visual and tactile perception, developing receptive semantic knowledge.

It is important to remember that outdoor activities are most beneficial for preschool children if the activities remain exploratory, with only limited

FIGURE 7.2
Concepts Related to Sandbox Activities

Temperature	Texture	Shape	Size	Processes
hot	rough	round	tall	filling
warm	grainy	square	small	dumping
cool	smooth	pointed	big	packing
cold	bumpy	hilly	short	pouring
		flat	tiny	patting
			huge	shaking
				spooning
				pushing
				smoothing

teacher direction. However, by being aware of the concepts and vocabulary related to specific activities, a teacher can enhance semantic development during informal conversations with children in outdoor activities or in recalling outdoor events during classroom discussions. During outdoor activities, spontaneous conversations between teachers and children and between children may be longer and involve more conversation turns than conversations in the classroom, which further enhances language acquisition.

Encouraging Language Development Through Teacher-Directed Activities

In preschool settings, teacher-directed activities occur during large or small group times. Large groups generally involve all students; small groups usually involve three to five children. Small groups are more appropriate for this age group since the children have more opportunities to participate and can better see illustrations or objects involved in the activity. Both large and small group activities are designed and directed by the teacher. The length and frequency of large group or whole class activities need to be limited for this age group since children at this age have a wide range of attention spans. Preschool children also vary in their listening comprehension skills and may not be able to attend to a teacher's speech directed to the whole group. Children's participation in large group activities should remain voluntary. Children should be encouraged to join the group activity; however, they should not be disciplined if they choose not to join in, or stay with, the group. Four types of group activities will be discussed here with respect to encouraging language development: share-and-tell time, story time, oral storytelling, and poetry/music time.

Share-and-Tell

This activity involves children taking turns to describe orally or comment upon an object they have brought to share with their class. According to Stewig (1982), this activity is one of the most abused practices when not planned and implemented with language development goals in mind.

Language-related goals for share-and-tell time include increasing listening comprehension and vocabulary, learning to focus on a topic/object and to describe its distinguishing features, and learning to relate a sequence of events. Other goals are to encourage children to learn to take turns in this group setting and to generate their own questions about the object or topic being presented.

The share-and-tell activity potentially enhances development of each of the five aspects of language knowledge in both receptive and productive modes. Receptive phonetic knowledge is enhanced as children come to understand others' speech and articulation patterns. Expressive phonetic knowledge is encouraged when children have the opportunity to communicate to a group of other children, speaking so that the volume and articulation of their speech contributes to clear communication. Receptive semantic knowledge is enhanced through hearing other children describe what they have brought, while expressive semantic knowledge is encouraged as children describe their own contributions. Morphemic knowledge is enhanced as children hear another's speech and contribute verbally to the discussion of the items brought to share-and-tell. A child's acquisition of syntactic knowledge is fostered by the exposure to various syntactic structures present in the verbal interaction occurring during share-and-tell. Pragmatic knowledge is enhanced as preschoolers learn how to use language in this specific setting: sharing an object or event of interest to the class and engaging in verbal interaction focusing on the object or event. Children's discourse in this activity may be monologic or may have the characteristics of a dialogue as they interact with those in the audience. Share-and-tell time embodies the use of language to share information as a speaker and to obtain information as a listener.

Teachers should give a carefully planned share-and-tell activity their undivided attention (Stewig, 1982). They should provide the framework, scaffold, or mediation needed to help children share and talk about what they have brought. Teachers ask questions to stimulate further description by the children. Teachers should use expansion and linguistic scaffolding to support children's verbal interactions. Summarizing and/or repeating what the children say is another way to enrich the verbal interaction of this activity.

Since preschool children's attention span may be limited to 10 or 15 minutes for group activities, many teachers have found it is better to have five or fewer children participate as speakers in share-and-tell each day. The class is divided into groups so that over the course of a week, each child has an opportunity to participate as a speaker.

Storybook Time

For many teachers and children, storybook time is a favorite part of their school day, as they share the ideas and images created through literature. The benefits of including storybook reading in the curriculum are many and have been well documented in studies of language acquisition and emergent literacy research. Storybook sharing is a social interaction routine that supports language development and "bridges the development of oral language skills and the emergence of print literacy" (Rice, 1995, p. 8). Children who have had early story sharing experiences also have "greater success in learning to read and write" (Slaughter, 1993, p. 4). Morrow (1989) attributed these benefits to children from storybook sharing:

1. increased interest in reading;
2. increased familiarity with written language;
3. increased vocabulary development; and
4. awareness of story structure.

Children's knowledge of each of the five aspects of language is enhanced through storybook sharing (Otto, 1996). As stories are read aloud and shared, children:

1. learn that language is used differently in different types of stories (pragmatic knowledge);
2. become more aware of the sound-aural system and the sound-graphic system of language (phonetic knowledge);
3. develop receptive knowledge of how morphemes influence word meanings (morphemic knowledge);
4. increase in vocabulary knowledge through the rich and varied language in literature (semantic knowledge); and
5. increase in knowledge of how thoughts are organized into sentences and phrases of book language, or literate register (pragmatic and syntactic knowledge).

Language-related goals for storybook time reflect our current knowledge of the benefits of storybook experiences for preschool children. These goals include increasing children's listening comprehension and vocabulary, helping children become aware of the relationship between speech and print, and encouraging children to learn to sequence events and to recall sequences of events.

Selecting Books to Share

Characteristics of the books chosen to share at storybook time influence the success and value of this activity. Book choices should reflect the developmental needs of children in the classroom and the ongoing curriculum. Three main criteria for book selection include subject content, language complexity, and quality of illustrations.

Subject content. Books for preschool children should initially have subject content that concerns familiar concepts, actions, places, and people. Young preschool children need to draw on their current conceptual knowledge and oral language (receptive) to comprehend the story or book's content. Gradually, as their listening comprehension and receptive vocabulary increase, books can be selected that introduce new concepts as well as refine and/or elaborate upon existing concepts and vocabulary. Preschoolers enjoy both fiction and nonfiction.

Language complexity.   Young preschool children with limited previous storybook experiences need to have simple labeling books for their initial storybook interactions. With frequent story sharing experiences and greater listening comprehension, more complex text (and story lines) can be introduced. Teachers need to constantly monitor the language complexity of the books read and determine whether children's listening comprehension can accommodate the level of syntactic complexity found in the chosen book.

Quality of illustrations.   In evaluating the quality of the illustrations, teachers should determine whether the illustrations support the concepts, ideas, actions, and/or events portrayed in the text. Vocabulary acquisition is facilitated when illustrations directly and accurately support the text. Books for young children need to have simpler illustrations since complex illustrations make it difficult for children to determine the context or referent for the concept/vocabulary introduced in the story. Illustrations need to be large enough to be visible when shared during group story time. Not being able to see the illustrations clearly interferes with children's comprehension of the story.

In addition to considering subject content, language complexity, and illustration quality, teachers should also consider whether a book's format will have benefits for children. Three special book formats are often used with preschool children: predictable books, big books, and alphabet books.

Predictable books.   This special book category includes books that have one or more of the following patterns of language (Slaughter, 1993): repetition of phrases or sentences (*The Gingerbread Boy*), cumulative structures that repeat and expand phrases and/or sentences (*The House That Jack Built*), rhythmic language and/or rhyme (*The Cat in the Hat* by Dr. Seuss), and sequential episodes (*Brown Bear, Brown Bear* by Bill Martin). The characteristic patterns of language in predictable books encourages children to focus on the language. Memory for the text and content is enhanced by the predictability of these books.

Big books.   Books in this category are oversized, usually about 14 inches by 20 inches. This larger size enables children to see the illustrations and the print more clearly and encourages greater involvement in the story. Children can see the print better if the text is written at the top of each page, rather than at the bottom. In selecting a big book, teachers also need to evaluate the book for its quality of illustrations, language complexity, and subject content.

Alphabet books.   Alphabet books represent a genre of children's literature that was first used in America in the late 1600s (Smolkin & Yaden, 1992). The format of alphabet books focuses on pairing each letter with a word or words that begin with that letter. Illustrations represent the concept conveyed by the target word(s). In a longitudinal study of preschool children and their parents' interaction with alphabet books, Smolkin & Yaden (1992) concluded that children were actively constructing six kinds of information about graphic systems:

1. Metalinguistic terms, such as *letter* or *word,* and using phrases such as "starts with" or "is for."
2. Directional concepts, such as left to right, top to bottom, and front to back.
3. Letter orientation, distinguishing between *M, N,* and *W.*
4. Feature analysis of letters: "This is *E,* with the three lines."
5. Letter symbol system and number symbol system, distinguishing between "numbers" and "letters."
6. Conventional sound-symbol relationships, as in "D is for dog."

Smolkin and Yaden concluded that parents' interaction with their children was critical for the development of this knowledge of letter-sound relationships.

When selecting alphabet books for preschoolers, review the text to see if the labels used represent general concepts and not more specific concepts. For example, "F for flower" represents a general label while "R for rose" is more specific and requires that a child have a conceptual hierarchy including both flowers and roses. Illustrations should also provide strong support for the concepts selected. For example, if "Y is for yogurt," the yogurt illustrated should not look like an ice cream cone, or children may become confused.

Teacher's Role

The way in which a teacher reads and shares the storybook with preschoolers influences the value of the experience. The focus of storybook sharing at the preschool level should be on developing listening comprehension, which is based upon receptive knowledge of each of the five aspects of language knowledge. Books should not be read simply to take up class time.

Teachers need to prepare to share storybooks with children so that they are familiar with the book's content and language. The teacher should sit on a low chair and hold the book so that all children can clearly see the illustrations in the book. When reading, the teacher should use a conversational tone of voice, clear pronunciation, and varied intonation reflecting the characters or events in the story.

In anticipating and monitoring children's storybook comprehension, teachers often do not read the text word for word. Instead they mediate the text for their young learners, rephrasing and rewording the text to fit their students' level of understanding. When they read, teachers also enhance comprehension by drawing upon children's prior knowledge. For example, when reading the book *Snowy Day* by Ezra Jack Keats, the teacher could begin by asking, "What do you like to do on a snowy day?" as a way to encourage children to activate their prior knowledge and to predict what the child pictured on the cover of the book will do in the story.

In repeated readings of a storybook, children's responses can be elicited to predict upcoming events or book language. By reading a segment of text and pausing for a group response, teachers can encourage children to predict upcoming text based on their memory of text from previous readings. Through repeated readings, children become familiar with book language (literate register) and gradually may begin to focus on letter-sound relationships.

Group story time may provide a setting in which children are encouraged to create their own version of storybooks through dictation. For example, after reading *Goodnight Moon* by Margaret Wise Brown, children can create their own version, replicating the pattern of the original text (Glazer, 2000). After the teacher takes their story and puts it into a big book format the story can be enjoyed at group story time.

Oral Storytelling

Oral storytelling also enhances the development of language knowledge among preschoolers. It shares many of the same benefits of story reading; however, story reading and storytelling have distinct differences. In storytelling the story is communicated through speech and nonverbal behaviors without supporting written text or illustrations. This places different demands on students and teachers. Since there are no illustrations to provide context for the story, children must rely on listening along with their interpretation of the speaker's gestures, facial expressions, and other nonverbal behaviors to comprehend the story.

Oral storytelling is an art. It requires some different skills from teachers than does story reading. More preparation time is required to tell a story since the story must be rehearsed until it can be told without using a text. Since there are no illustrations to create the mood, characters, and setting, a storyteller needs to communicate these facets of the story through thoughtful and dramatic use of language, intonation, and gesture. In storytelling, the teacher/storyteller establishes and maintains direct eye contact with the audience. This allows the storyteller to closely monitor the audience's comprehension of the story and, with young children, their attention span. When the story appears to be longer than children's attention span, it can be shortened.

Oral storytelling can be accompanied by hand or finger puppets, felt-board characters, props, and musical instruments (Morrow, 1989). Each of these creative accompaniments helps to create a visual context for the story and communicate the story events or characterizations to the children, enhancing listening comprehension. It is important to rehearse the use of these accompaniments along with the actual story so that the storytelling event will be coordinated.

With repeated experience in oral storytelling, a teacher can build up her repertoire and confidence. When storytelling occurs frequently in the classroom, the teacher's storytelling behaviors become an example for the children in their storytelling attempts.

As an extension of a teacher's story reading and storytelling, children can be encouraged to begin participating in retelling a story, such as *The Little Red Hen* (Trousdale, 1994). After the children have become familiar with the story, they can be asked to provide sound effects or join in on the repeated refrain of the text. Stuffed animals or stick puppets can be handed to individual children to use when retelling their particular part of the story.

Poetry and Song

Sharing nursery rhymes, rhyming story texts, and songs in small or whole group settings provides children with an opportunity to become aware of words that have sound similarities (Schickedanz, Pergantis, Kanosky, Blaney, & Ottinger, 1997). Sometimes a teacher may share the poetry or song using oral storytelling techniques; at other times, a book version of the rhyme or song may be used. Poetry and song activities are beneficial to preschool children in two basic ways. The rhythmic quality of the language enhances children's receptive knowledge of the sounds and patterns of sound. In addition, the rhythmic language encourages movement, which enhances comprehension of the poem or song.

When selecting a poem or song to use with preschool children, a teacher should look for poetry with a subject familiar to the children and for simple syntax. The selection should feature a strong rhythm or rhyme. In preparing to present the poem or song to children, a teacher should also decide which actions or movements should accompany the poem or song.

After preschool children have enjoyed the same poems and songs on repeated occasions, they may begin to pay attention to the print of the song or poem, attempting to match their oral memory of text with the actual text. In this way, sharing poetry and song with young children provides opportunities to develop knowledge of how oral and written language are related.

Encouraging Language Development During Routines

Language enhancement opportunities in daily routines often go unrecognized. Routine activities are those activities that occur on a regular basis in preschool and serve an organizational (e.g., attendance) or physical need (e.g., snack time and dressing to go outside). These activities are often excluded from consideration when planning curricula as they may not be credited with any opportunity for important learning. To the contrary, routine activities provide opportunity for acquiring important language knowledge. Specific language goals for routines may focus on developing conversational skills (pragmatic knowledge) along with enhancing the other four aspects of language knowledge (phonetic, semantic, morphemic, syntactic) through the communication that occurs during daily routines.

Arrival

During the time preschoolers are arriving at school, various language competencies can be encouraged. Pragmatic knowledge is enhanced as children participate in using oral language in routine greetings and in conversations with teachers and with peers. When children engage in routine greetings ("How are you?" "I am fine."), they are learning appropriate syntactic structures and common uses of language in social settings. Teachers who greet each child by name (appropriately pronounced) and encourage children to address the teacher and each other by name are fostering an awareness of the role individual names have in the process of communication. Phonetic knowledge is enhanced when children learn to distinguish and pronounce each other's names.

Pragmatic aspects of written language can be introduced when children's names appear on coat racks or cubbies. Labeling the coat rack with children's names indicates where their coats should be hung. Attendance-taking procedures illustrate another function of written language—to record information. A procedure in which children check in by selecting their name card and placing it on a display board or pocket chart also helps children learn to recognize their name in print and begin to recognize others' names. During arrival time, short previews of the day's upcoming events can be mentioned. For example, "We're going on a walk today." "Today Matt is going to bring his rabbit to visit class." Such statements model various sentence structures and provide semantic and morphemic information for children. As children respond verbally to the preview of upcoming events, they have an opportunity to use their expressive language knowledge.

Snack/Lunch Time

Many opportunities for language development can occur when children and teachers are gathered around a table to enjoy a snack or lunch. Conversational skills, one aspect of pragmatic knowledge, are encouraged during snack/lunch time as teachers and children talk informally about events or happenings in the classroom and in the outside world. Children's reception of others' speech and the expression of their responses foster their syntactic and morphemic knowledge. Phonetic knowledge is also enhanced as children listen to each other and express their responses. When teachers expand and extend children's utterances, they are encouraging the development of syntactic knowledge by modeling more complex language structures.

Snack/meal time also provides a good opportunity to introduce new vocabulary. Teachers may do this by expanding or extending the speech of the children, incorporating the new concepts/vocabulary. For example, when the children are eating sliced apples, a teacher could begin a conversation about apples, reminding them of the story they had shared about picking apples. Depending on student interest and response, a teacher may go on to visit with the children about the parts of the apple (peel, stem, seeds), as well as its shape, color, and taste.

Teachers may also encourage children to elaborate on their comments. For example, a child says, "I saw a train today." The teacher responds, "Where did you see a train?" eliciting further response from the child. Teachers should avoid asking questions that can be answered by a simple yes or no. All of the other children at the table should be encouraged to participate by observing their interest in the topic and in contributions made by another child or the teacher. In this activity, a teacher facilitates conversation but should not dominate the conversation or turn it into a "lesson."

By participating in group discussions/conversations, preschool children begin to learn how language is used in informal group interactions. Conversations at snack/meal time are less directed than in a teacher-led group discussion about a storybook or event. In fact, it is natural for conversations to develop between pairs of student during snack time and with the whole table of children.

Departure

Additional opportunities to extend their language knowledge arise when children get ready to go home. Pragmatic aspects of language can be emphasized through routine good-byes. In addition to a routine "Good-bye. See you tomorrow!", children can be encouraged to label and talk about items they are taking home, such as artwork and books. Departure time is also a time when children appropriately communicate any specific need they have. For example, "I can't find my mitten." or "Where is my picture?"

At departure time, teachers may briefly review the highlights of the day and share them with children and their parents or primary caregivers. This allows parents and caregivers to be included in a conversation with their children about their experiences at school that day, easing the transition between school and home. Such conversations reinforce semantic information and may encourage children to express themselves in more syntactically complex utterances. The teacher may also use this time to relate the day's events and learning with future planned events. For example, "Today we wrote a story about our trip to the apple orchard. Tomorrow we will be making pictures to go with our story."

A teacher's awareness of the potential for language development in routine activities will contribute to children's opportunities to see language in use: for communication, to find out information, to share information, and to engage in patterned social dialogues.

CURRICULUM PLANNING

To maximize the enhancement of preschool children's language acquisition, the curriculum throughout the day should have a consistent theme and a focus on language-rich activities. One example of a comprehensive language-theme curriculum focuses on "The World of Communication," developed by Schickedanz, Pergantis, Kanosky, Blaney, and Ottinger (1997). This curriculum is composed of five specific units that incorporate a focus on oral and written communication and other forms of communication (sign language, gesture, and Morse code). In addition, stories and linguistic diversity are emphasized. A wide variety of suggested activities are included that enhance acquisition of each of the five aspects of language knowledge.

The "Language-Focused Curriculum" developed at the Language Acquisition Preschool at the University of Kansas (Bunce, 1995; Rice & Wilcox, 1995) is also a comprehensive curriculum for enhancing language development. The curriculum incorporates child-centered and teacher-directed activities along with routine activities and changing activities that focus on various aspects of receptive and productive language acquisition. These and other resources for curriculum planning are listed as **"Teaching Resources"** at the end of this chapter.

SUMMARY

Important language knowledge develops during the preschool years. The curriculum of the preschool classroom can foster language development through a wide range of exploratory, teacher-directed, and routine activities.

A teacher's awareness of the potential for enhancing language development in all areas of the preschool curriculum provides many opportunities for children to see language in use. Specific teaching strategies that are effective in encouraging language development include questioning, linguistic scaffolding, mediation, and conflict resolution. Activities that incorporate books, poetry, and song encourage children to develop receptive and expressive knowledge of written language and to further develop their receptive and expressive knowledge of oral language.

✳ ✳ ✳ CHAPTER REVIEW

1. Terms to review:

   wait time
   mediation
   conflict resolution

2. Explain the role of the questioning process in enhancing language acquisition among preschool children.

3. Differentiate between recitation questions, information questions, and clarification questions.

4. Define *linguistic scaffolding*.

5. How is language knowledge involved in conflict resolution?

6. State three goals for language acquisition at the preschool level.

7. Explain the value of themed dramatic play areas to enhancing language acquisition.

8. In what ways does a writing/drawing center enhance the acquisition of language knowledge at the preschool level?

9. Why is it important for preschool children to have opportunities for exploratory activities? How do these activities in general enhance language acquisition?

10. How can language development be enhanced during informal outside activities?

11. What criteria are used in selecting books to share with preschoolers?

12. What is the value in using predictable books to enhance language development?

13. What is the value in using alphabet books to enhance language development?

✳ ✳ ✳ CHAPTER EXTENSION ACTIVITIES

1. Select a storybook that is appropriate for preschool children. Develop a lesson plan that identifies the language goals for using the book. Also develop five to eight discussion questions, including both high-level and low-level questions.

2. Plan a learning center, describing the activity involved and the materials needed. Identify language goals for the learning center.

3. Plan a themed drama area for a preschool classroom. List the materials needed. Indicate the language goals appropriate for this activity.

4. Observe in a preschool classroom for a total of 30 minutes. Observe both unstructured and structured activities. Record in writing questions used by the teachers or teacher aides. Categorize the questions as low- or high-level questions. Come to class prepared to discuss what you observed.

5. Observe in a preschool during unstructured activities for a 20-minute period. Describe how language was used by the children based on Halliday's classification of language functions (see Chapter 2).

6. Tape record your reading of a favorite storybook appropriate for preschool children. Put the audiotape and a copy of the book in a listening corner of a preschool classroom. Observe children's use of the tape. Analyze the potential of this activity for developing specific language knowledge.

7. Observe in a preschool classroom for 30 minutes. Describe what teaching strategies (from this chapter) were used in the classroom by either the teacher or the teacher aides.

✳ ✳ ✳ REFERENCES

Berk, L. & Winsler, A. (1995). *Scaffolding children's learning: Vygotsky and early childhood education.* Washington, DC: National Association for the Education of Young Children.

Blank, M. (1973). *Teaching learning in the preschool: A dialogue approach.* Columbus, OH: Charles E. Merrill.

Bloom, B. (Ed.), (1956). *Taxonomy of educational objectives: The classification of educational goals.* (Volume 1 & 2). New York: David McKay.

Bredekamp, S., & Copple, C. (Eds.). (1997). *Developmentally appropriate practice in early childhood programs. Revised Edition.* Washington, DC: National Association for the Education of Young Children.

Bunce, B. (1995). *Building a language-focused curriculum for the preschool classroom: Vol. II. A planning guide.* Baltimore, MD: Paul H. Brookes.

Eastman, P. (1960). *Are you my mother?* New York: Random House.

Genishi, C., & Dyson, A. (1984). *Language assessment in the early years.* Norwood, NJ: Ablex.

Glazer, J. (2000). *Literature for young children.* (4th ed.). Upper Saddle River, NJ: Merrill/Prentice Hall.

Lindberg, L., & Swedlow, R. (1980). *Early childhood education: A guide for observation & participation.* (2nd ed.). Boston: Allyn & Bacon.

Lindfors, J. (1987). *Children's language and learning.* (2nd ed.). Upper Saddle River, NJ: Prentice Hall.

Maclean, M., Bryant, P., & Bradley, L. (1987). Rhymes, nursery rhymes, and reading in early childhood. *Merrill-Palmer Quarterly, 33*(3), 255–281.

Maxim, G. (1993). *The very young: Guiding children from infancy through the early years. (*4th ed.). Upper Saddle River, NJ: Merrill/Prentice Hall.

Morrow, L. (1989). *Literacy development in the early years: Helping children read and write.* Upper Saddle River, NJ: Prentice Hall.

Morrow, L., & Rand, M. (1991). Promoting literacy during play by designing early childhood classroom environments. *The Reading Teacher, 44,* 6, 396–402.

Neuman, S., & Roskos, K. (1990). The influence of literacy-enriched play settings on preschoolers' engagement with written language. In J. Zutell & S. McCormick (Eds.), *Literacy theory and research: Analyses from multiple paradigms* (pp. 179–187). Chicago: National Reading Conference.

Neuman, S., & Roskos, K. (1992). Literacy objects as cultural tools: Effects on children's literacy behaviors in play. *Reading Research Quarterly, 27*(3), 202–225.

Nourot, P., & VanHoorn, J. (1991). Symbolic play in preschool and primary settings. *Young Children, 46*(6), 40–50.

Otto, B. (1996). Let's read a story: The role of storybook reading in young children's literacy acquisition. *Illinois Schools Journal. 76*(1), 5–18.

Reich, P. (1986). *Language development.* Upper Saddle River, NJ: Prentice Hall.

Rice, M. (1995). Children's language acquisition. In B. Power & R. Hubbard, (Eds.), *Language development: A reader for teachers.* Upper Saddle River, NJ: Merrill/Pentice Hall.

Rice, M., & Wilcox, K. (1995). *Building a language-focused curriculum for the preschool classroom: Vol. I. A foundation.* Baltimore, MD: Paul H. Brookes.

Schickedanz, J., Pergantis, M., Kanosky, J., Blaney, A., & Ottinger, J. (1997). *Curriculum in early childhood: A resource guide for preschool and kindergarten teachers.* Boston: Allyn & Bacon.

Schickedanz, J., York, M., Stewart, I., & White, D. (1990). *Strategies for teaching young children* (3rd ed.). Upper Saddle River, NJ: Prentice Hall.

Sheldon, A. (1990, January). "Kings are royaler than queens": Language and socialization. *Young Children, 45*(2), 4–9.

Slaughter, J. (1993). *Beyond storybooks: Young children and the shared book experience.* Newark, DE: International Reading Association.

Smolkin, L., & Yaden, D. (1992). *O* is for *mouse:* First encounters with the alphabet book. *Language Arts, 69,* 432–441.

Stewig, J. (1982). *Teaching language arts in early childhood.* New York: Holt, Rinehart & Winston.

Sulzby, E. (1981). *Kindergartners begin to read their own composition: Beginning readers' developing knowledges about written language project.* Final report to the Research Committee of the National Council of Teachers of English. Evanston, IL: Northwestern University.

Trousdale, A. (1990). Interactive storytelling: Scaffolding children's early narratives. *Language Arts, 67*(2), 164–173.

Trousdale, A. (1994). Tell me that one; Now let's tell it together: Sharing stories with Tim. In A. Trousdale, S. Woestehoff, & M. Schwartz (Eds.), *Give a listen: Stories of storytelling in school* (pp. 19-27). Urbana, IL: National Council of Teachers of English.

✳ ✳ ✳ TEACHING RESOURCES

Barbour, N., Webster, T., & Drosdeck, S. (1987). Sand: A resource for the language arts. *Young Children, 42* (2), 20–25.

Beaty, J. (1994). *Picture book storytelling: Literature activities for young children.* Fort Worth, TX: Harcourt Brace.

Bunce, B. (1995). *Building a language-focused curriculum for the preschool classroom: Vol. II. A planning guide.* Baltimore, MD: Paul H. Brookes.

Fields, M., Spangler, K., & Lee, D. (2000). *Let's begin reading right: Developmentally appropriate beginning literacy.* (4th ed.). Upper Saddle River, NJ: Merrill/Prentice Hall.

Glazer, J. (2000). *Literature for young children* (4th ed.). Upper Saddle River, NJ: Merrill.

Honig, A. (1982). *Playtime learning games for young children.* Syracuse, NY: Syracuse University.

Lawrence, L. (1998). *Montessori read & write: A parents' guide to literacy for children.* New York: Three Rivers Press.

McGee, L., & Richgels, D. (1990). *Literacy's beginnings: Supporting young readers and writers.* Needham Heights, MA: Allyn & Bacon.

Rice, M., & Wilcox, K. (1995). *Building a language-focused curriculum for the preschool classroom: Vol. I. A foundation.* Baltimore, MD: Paul H. Brookes.

Salinger, T. (1996). *Literacy for young children* (2nd ed.). Upper Saddle River, NJ: Merrill/Prentice Hall.

Schickedanz, J., Pergantis, M., Kanosky, J., Blaney, A., & Ottinger, J. (1997). *Curriculum in early childhood: A resource guide for preschool and kindergarten teachers.* Boston: Allyn & Bacon.

Schickedanz, J., York, M., Stewart, I., & White, D. (1990). *Strategies for teaching young children* (3rd ed.). Upper Saddle River, NJ: Prentice Hall.

Sheldon, A. (1990). "Kings are royaler than queens": Language and socialization. *Young Children, 45*(2), 4–9.

Stewig, J. (1982). *Teaching language arts in early childhood.* New York: Holt Rinehart & Winston.

8

※ ※ ※

LANGUAGE DEVELOPMENT IN KINDERGARTNERS

The kindergarten year marks a transition from home to school for most children. Even for children who have attended preschool or were in day care during the preschool years, kindergarten is their first experience in a larger educational system. The school setting differs from preschool in the wider range of children's ages and greater number of teachers and school staff. Such changes in children's social environments are accompanied by changes in the way children are expected to communicate and the opportunities that occur for their continued language acquisition.

Within this new context, kindergarten-age children continue to refine and expand their current knowledge of each of the aspects of language in both receptive and productive/expressive modes. Children come from their preschool years with increased phonetic knowledge, a rapidly expanding vocabulary, a greater understanding of syntactic and morphemic structure, and increased knowledge of how to use language differently in different settings. During this year, children may also become aware that different dialects and/or languages are spoken in different settings. Kindergarten children's knowledges of the five aspects of oral and written language reflect the dialects and/or languages that are used in their home and school environments (see Chapter 3).

The language acquisition of kindergartners is also characterized by increasing metalinguistic awareness. They become more aware of language as an object and language as a process (Rowe & Harste, 1986). Chapter 6 described ways in which preschool children were reflecting on oral and written language as they engaged in story time and play. In the kindergarten setting, children continue to reflect upon how language works, both in speech and in writing.

DEVELOPMENT OF PHONETIC KNOWLEDGE

Phonetic Knowledge of Oral Language

At kindergarten age, children are easily understood by most adults, having mastered the production of many phonemes (Allen & Marotz, 1994). A range of successful phonetic production, however, is still represented in any classroom. It is important for teachers to remember that age-correlated information such as that presented in Chapter 6 (see Figure 6.1 and the Chapter 6 appendix) should only be used as a general guide. Teachers do not need to be concerned when children's acquisition of speech sounds does not precisely follow that given in developmental charts; slight variations in developmental rates of acquisition should not alarm teachers or parents.

Children's awareness of sound similarities and contrasts, and their ability to focus on sound similarities and contrasts in creative expression, are evident in the verbal games playing with sound that kindergartners enjoy in school and when playing informally with peers. Children may spontaneously focus on verbal rhyme and rhythm when engaged in play with blocks, art materials, or other manipulatives. Chants, rhymes, action poems, and word games are a source of enjoyment and increase children's awareness of sound patterns and distinctions (Buchoff, 1994; Colgin, 1991).

The acquisition of phonetic knowledge is also evident in kindergarten children's ability to distinguish similarities in beginning and ending sounds (Kirtley, Bryant, MacLean, & Bradley 1989). Children's awareness of alliteration (similarities of beginning sounds) and rhyme contribute to the acquisition of reading in two ways (Bryant, MacLean, Bradley, & Crossland, 1990): (1) perception of rhyme and alliteration are the forerunners of being able to distinguish phonemes, and (2) perception of rhyme helps children see similarities in spelling patterns.

Kindergarten children may also become aware of others' different pronunciations and may tease those children who speak differently. Likewise, children who are experiencing difficulty may become less verbal, not risking failure or embarrassment. Teachers must be aware of these situations and encourage acceptance and communication among all children.

Phonetic Knowledge of Written Language

Significant evidence of children's acquisition of phonetic knowledge of written language may occur during the kindergarten year. Over the past 20 years, emergent literacy research has documented kindergartners' acquisition of receptive and expressive knowledge of written language through close observation of early attempts to read and write (Clay, 1982; McGee & Richgels, 1990; Sulzby, 1981, 1985, 1986; Temple, Nathan, Burris, & Temple, 1988). This body of research has focused on what children *do* when attempting to read and write and what they *say* about what they are doing. Their *doing* is the linguistic behavior or use of language to communicate. Their *saying* about what they are doing is their *metalinguistic awareness* of how the alphabetic coding system language works (or doesn't work).

When kindergarten children are creating their own stories, they may comment on their process and their expectations for using print. When she was beginning to create her story, Pam announced, "Mine's gonna spell something." She then proceeded to write *THE LION* on the cover page of her book and said that was "the title." Joel, also a kindergartner, commented as he began his storybook creation, "I can write letters but they won't spell anything." He then wrote letters of the alphabet in sequence from *A* to *K*. When asked to read his story, Joel responded:

> Once the bear jumped over the log, then, he climbed a tree and fell down the tree, and picked an apple from the tree and ate it. The end.

Joel's comment prior to creating his story indicated that he knew a system for writing used letters, but he was aware that he did not know yet how to spell anything. The alphabet sequence he put to paper apparently was the "placeholder" for the story he wanted to share.

Evidence of Phonetic Knowledge in Reading Attempts

An increase in attempts to read by focusing on letter-sound relationships among kindergarten children has been reported by several researchers (Clay, 1982; Otto, 1993; Sulzby, 1983; Sulzby, Barnhart, & Hieshima, 1989). When asked to "read" a familiar storybook, some children attempt an effortful "sounding out," focusing on the print. When they encounter difficulty, some children then refuse to read, indicating that although they know the print is the source of the message, they cannot decode it: "I don't know what that word says" or "I don't know this word." These print-related refusals are thought to indicate an awareness of the importance of decoding to "real" reading (Sulzby, 1983). Other children, while unsuccessfully attempting to decode print, frequently look to the adult researcher for confirmation that their attempts are "right" (Otto, 1984).

In Rachel's attempt (Otto, 1992) to read *Mr. Gumpy's Motor Car* (Burningham, 1973), she seemed aware that reading involved decoding the print and stopped frequently to note that she could not "read that word." After reassurance that she was doing a good job, she would continue with the story, relying on her memory for the story text.

Rachel: Mr. Gumpy's Motor Car. There's his motor car. Mr. Gumpy was going for a ride in his motor car. He dr-dr-drove down the lane and out the gate. He got out—then—I can't read these words, they're too hard.

Adult: That's OK. That's OK.

Rachel: The boy and the girl asked if they could come. The goat,the cow, the sheep and the hen, too. So did the pig. I can't read that part.

Adult: OK.

Rachel: And off they went. I do not like the-the-the way those clouds look. I do not like the way those clouds look. Wait, I can't read that page either.

Rachel continued her story re-creation until the story was completed; however, she continued to pause periodically, saying she could not "read" a specific part. She seemed clearly aware that the words needed to be decoded.

Evidence of Phonetic Knowledge in Writing Attempts

Kindergarten children exhibit a wide variety of emergent writing behaviors that indicate they are beginning to focus on the way in which print represents specific speech sounds. Since the English alphabet has 26 letters and the English language is represented by approximately 44 phonemes (or standard sounds), children, not knowing standard spelling, "invent" the way in which the sounds are represented in their writing. An additional factor complicating children's early writing attempts is that the English language contains many borrowed words from other languages—French, Spanish, and Italian, to name a few—that follow a different system of sound-symbol relationships. Children deal with these inconsistencies by developing their own system to represent sound-symbol relationships through first focusing on letter-name and sound relationships and then gradually beginning to represent more complete phonemic aspects of each word. Children's early spelling attempts are rich evidence of their acquisition of phonetic knowledge about written language.

Sound and print relationships may be represented inconsistently with children appearing to select letters randomly without considering the specific sound(s) typically represented by the letter. This stage is known as *prephonemic spelling* (Temple et al., 1988).

Sharbani's story (see Figure 8.1) contains two long strings of letters; however, she assigned no specific meaning to the letters represented, telling her teacher, "I don't have to read this. It's just about spring." Her story is an example of prephonemic spelling. There are no word boundaries, just strings of letters.

Adrienne's story in Figure 8.2 is another example of prephonemic spelling. Her written story ("a fairy tale") appears to be mostly random letters. When attempting

FIGURE 8.1
Sharbani's Spring Story

FIGURE 8.2
Adrienne's Story

to read her story, Adrienne first began, "Once upon a time. . . ." Then she seemed to realize that she was not decoding what she had written and began to attempt to "sound out" what she had written. When she came to her name at the bottom of the page, she said, "Oh, that's my name, Adrienne."

Early phonemic spelling is characterized by evidence that children are attempting to encode phonemes; however, they may only represent one or two sounds per word (Temple et al., 1988). For example, Snow White is represented as "SW" and big is as "bg."

In *letter-name spelling*, each letter represents a sound; no additional letters are included. For example, when LADE is written for the word *lady,* each of the letter names corresponds to the sounds the child was trying to represent. In Ari's story (Figure 8.3), he represented some of the phonemes of the words using his awareness of letter sounds.

FIGURE 8.3
Ari's Story

Ari read his story as "The rabbit jumped over the rock." Notice that *rabbit* is spelled as *rabt,* over as *ovr,* and rock as *rac,* which are fairly complete representations of the phonemes of the specific words. Ari's spelling of jumped (*jg*), the (*hta*) and a (*ha*) also indicate his efforts in matching the speech sounds with letters.

Transitional spelling is characterized by words that, while not spelled conventionally, have conventional features and consonant/vowel patterns (Temple et al., 1988). Even when children have acquired conventional spelling for a number of words, they may use their invented spelling to overcome uncertainties they have when they are writing. In Kara's story (see Figure 8.4), she used conventional spelling for most of the words; however, *with* was spelled *weih.*

Digraphs, such as *th,* represent a special spelling challenge for children, since two letters are used to represent one sound (Temple et al., 1988). In writing words that contain digraphs, children search for letters they think represent the sounds needed. By observing how children represent digraphs in their early writing, a teacher can learn more about their phonemic awareness.

Embedded in children's early writing attempts is their concept for what makes a "word." This concept includes not only their semantic idea of words, but also their visual perceptions of what it takes to make a word (Berthoud-Papandropoulou, 1978; Sulzby, 1986). Temple, Nathan, Burris, and Temple (1988) describe the complexity of spelling for beginning writers and how a child's concept of *word* is embedded in this process:

> But for the child to be able to spell a word, the word must have some reality for him as a unit; he must be able to make it hold still in his mind while he operates on it. For in order to spell a word, the child must:
> 1. say the word mentally to himself;
> 2. break off the first phoneme from the rest of the word;

FIGURE 8.4
Kara's Story

I WENT
TOT He
PARK
WEiH
MYPAPA

3. mentally sort through his repertoire of letters and find one to match with that phoneme;
4. write down the letter he has decided on;
5. recite the word again in his mind;
6. recall the phoneme he has just spelled, subtract it from the word, and locate the next phoneme to be spelled; and
7. match that phoneme with a letter of the alphabet, and so on, until all of the phonemes are spelled. (p. 76)

When teachers are aware of the challenges facing emergent writers who are attempting to represent the specific sounds of words in their writing they can better understand the amount of concentration required. In addition, they can appreciate the value of observing children's early writing for evidence of children's developing phonetic knowledge of written language.

(From Temple, C., Nathan, R., Burris, N., & Temple, F. (1988). *The beginning of writing* (2nd ed.), reprinted with permission from Allyn & Bacon Publishing)

DEVELOPMENT OF SEMANTIC KNOWLEDGE

Kindergarten children typically have a vocabulary of 1,500 or more words (Allen & Marotz, 1994) and understand many more words than they use in their speech (Piper, 1993). Wide variations in the size of the expressive vocabulary between children may also be observed. Acquisition of semantic knowledge during the kindergarten year involves not only new words and concepts but also the further development of networks of vocabulary or schemata. Existing concepts and vocabulary are further refined. Synonyms and antonyms are added, along with shadings of specific meaning.

Storybook sharing experiences expose children to new concepts and vocabulary. Children then may use this new knowledge in their creative writing, "trying out" the words they have heard used in the storybooks. For example, after listening to a nonfiction book about peacocks in her class, Nicole created a story about a peacock during her time at the writing center. Her story did not contain any print, only illustrations. When asked to share her story, Nicole responded:

> Once there was a peacock, and, and he had, and his designs on his tail turned different colors. One day when they were all different colors, he met a brown rhinoceros and then his, his designs turned purple, and he met a purple turtle.

Defining Words

Researchers have focused on children's ability to define words as one way of exploring semantic development. Kindergarten-age children typically emphasize the function of the object when stating a definition (Allen & Marotz, 1994; Pease, Berko Gleason, & Pan, 1989). For example, in defining *ball,* children often emphasize "bounce," or the function of the ball. Definitions are now likely to change from being based on individual experiences to having a more socially shared definition; however, children's definitions do not share the elaboration of an adult's definitions (Owens, 2001).

Figurative Language

An understanding of figurative language is evident in some kindergartners' comprehension and production of similes and metaphors (Broderick, 1991; Waggoner & Palermo, 1989). Although direct, concrete similes and metaphors are most easily understood, there is some evidence that even kindergartners are beginning to understand more abstract comparisons (Waggoner & Palermo, 1989).

Humor

Kindergarten children's sense of humor is also an indication of their semantic knowledge development. The riddles and jokes they create are often based in semantic comparisons or words that have multiple meanings (Honig, 1988). "Knock-knock jokes" may begin to be popular among kindergarten children, though some children do not fully appreciate such jokes until they are in the primary grades. Kindergarten-age children's humor also may show their awareness of incongruity; a situation is funny because of the discrepancy between what is supposed to happen and what happens. Incongruity may involve exaggerations of shape or size or misnaming (Cornett, 1986).

Story Vocabulary

Kindergarten-age children's story monologues are evidence of their acquisition of semantic knowledge and may indicate areas of semantic confusion. For example, Gwen's story shows an enriched level of semantic knowledge:

> Once the fairy was getting very hot so she made the vol—, the volcano. The volcano was erupted and the sea divers didn't know the underwater volcano named Kalypsie erupted, when the sea divers did not know, know that and the sea divers were all killed, and then it stopped once second, and there was a big pool of saliva on the floor of the ocean.

Gwen's story describing an underwater volcano and what happened after it erupted indicates her acquisition of a schema for the sea and its phenomena. It is not clear whether her use of "saliva" instead of "lava" was the result of confusing the two terms or if her use of the term "saliva" was another aspect of her creativity.

When asked to create an adventure storybook, Alysoun (age 5) created the following oral text, which appears to be an inventory of what she considered to be her adventures:

> I went to the circus. A field trip, to the Art Institute, to my birthday party, to my grandma Jones at Christmas. To my birthday party.

Semantic Knowledge in Story Re-Creations

Children's attempts to recreate a familiar story also indicate their developing semantic knowledge. In their story re-creations they often use semantically equivalent words that indicate their vocabulary development. Substituting "home" for "house," "food" for "groceries," and "ran" for "scampered" all indicate an awareness of word meaning and semantic commonalities.

When children self-correct during their story re-creations, they may indicate their understanding of subtle semantic differences and schema knowledge. When Rachel, a kindergartner (Otto, 1992), was "reading" *Mr. Gumpy's Motor Car* (Burningham, 1973), she first said, " 'Not I,' said the cat. 'It will ruin my skin.' " She immediately repeated and self-corrected, saying, " 'Not I,' said the cat. 'It will ruin my *fur*.' " Her self-correction indicated that she knew that "fur" was more in keeping with the intent of the text and that "skin" was not appropriate semantically.

Since the increases in children's semantic knowledge during the kindergarten year are represented in words from many syntactic categories (e.g., nouns, verbs, adverbs, adjectives, and conjunctions), the increase in semantic knowledge occurs concurrently with an increase in syntactic knowledge.

DEVELOPMENT OF SYNTACTIC KNOWLEDGE

Kindergarten-age children can construct basic sentences with little difficulty (McNeill, 1970). The average sentence length for 5-year-olds is five to seven words (Allen & Marotz, 1994). Children understand a wider range of syntactic structures than they produce. Kindergarten-age children's acquisition of syntactic knowledge continues as they use more complex noun and verb phrase structures (Owens, 1988, 2001). Increases in syntactic knowledge allow children to communicate more complex ideas.

In Joshua's (age 5 1/2) story, the sentences are complex syntactically, containing subordinate clauses, prepositional phrases, and compound predicates. *And* and *then* are used to begin sentences and to join sentences together. Since Joshua created this story in response to a prompt to develop an "adventure story," this story also indicates the semantic events that he considered appropriate for an adventure.

> Once upon a time, I was in the desert, and I found a castle that was made out of gold. Inside there was only gold. Then I went up a ladder and found the gold. Then I found a big pile of gold next to the last that I dug up. And then when I was going back home, I met a giraffe and his hair was sticking straight up. The end.

Pronoun Usage

Acquisition of more complex noun phrase structures may involve clearer use of pronouns. Most kindergarten-age children have mastered pronoun use for indicating subjects (*I, you, she, he, they*), and objects (*me, him, her, them*); however, they are just beginning to master the use of reflexives (*myself, himself, herself, themselves*) (Owens, 1988, 2001).

The relationships between nouns and their referent pronouns are also indicated with more clarity during the kindergarten year. In Joshua's story, included previously, he used *his* to refer back to the giraffe whose hair was sticking straight up. Not all uses of pronouns are that clear, however, which indicates that some children are still working on the relationships between nouns and pronouns. *Unreferenced pronouns* are those pronouns whose noun referent is not clearly indicated by the pronoun and sentence structure. In oral speech, un-referenced pronouns may be clarified by the context in which they are used and by gesture; however, in written language, unreferenced pronouns interfere with comprehension. In Nicki's story, which follows, pronouns are clearly referenced except in the sentence, "The net was something he could stay in to bring home." It is not clear whether the *he* refers to the fisherman or the fish. Thus, in the middle of her story, comprehension breaks down.

> Once there was a goldfish and he swam all over the sea. And then there came a fisherman, and he took this fish into the net. *The net was something he could stay in to bring home.* He does have something to hold the net with, and there's food for the fish to eat. The person goes home in his car, in the purple car, he rides off and calls home. And at home is where he eats dinner and then he goes back to fishing in the sea.

Verb Phrase Expansion

Kindergarten-age children's speech is characterized by an increase in the number of adverbs. Auxiliary verbs are also increasingly used throughout in the kindergarten year, such as *have, do, will, shall, and could.*

Passive Sentences

During the kindergarten year, children typically begin to comprehend passive sentence construction, although they may only be able to produce short passives (Owens, 1988, 2001). Comprehension of passive sentences requires that children change the way in which they process a sentence. Passive sentences are arranged in a object-action-agent order ("The cat was chased by the dog"), which differs from the agent-action-object construction of most speech ("The dog chased the cat.")

As the complexity of children's sentence structures increase, children also begin to show an increase in their understanding of morphemic knowledge of both inflectional and derivational morphemes.

DEVELOPMENT OF MORPHEMIC KNOWLEDGE

Throughout the kindergarten year, morphemic knowledge increases as children become more aware of morphemes in oral language. Inflectional morphemes are acquired for indicating past tense for regular verbs (-ed, wanted, jumped). More irregular verbs are mastered, such as *went, gone, caught* (Allen & Marotz, 1994); however, overgeneralization still occurs (e.g., *gived, singed*).

One way of examining children's morphemic development is to look at their oral reconstruction of familiar storybook texts. In the example that follows, Jennifer is reconstructing *Harry the Dirty Dog* (Zion, 1956). While the original text used past tense consistently, Jennifer varied between present and past tense, as shown in the following excerpt (verbs are in italics here for emphasis):

> Then he *slept* in his favorite place, where he always *sleep.* He *took* the scrubbing brush and *hide* it under his favorite place.

Another example of kindergarten children's developing knowledge of verb tense markers comes from Saroeuth's re-creation of *Harry the Dirty Dog* (Zion, 1956). In the following segment, Saroeuth's story varies in the verb tenses used.

> . . . and he took the brush and ran out. He put it in the garden and he ran away. First he played street, then they got all mud up by the train, then he played tag with the other dogs and *slide* down. Then he was so hungry he *go* home. Then, they didn't recognize them. He do, he *do* all his tricks, flip-flop, he *singed, going to do* all over and all over again. Then they just *walk* away. . . .

In Saroeuth's story re-creation most of the verbs that were not marked/inflected for past tense are irregular verbs, which probably contributed to his decision to use the present tense (*slide, do, go, walk*) or to use the past-tense marker for regular verbs (*-ed*); however, since Saroeuth did successfully use the past-tense marker for *played* and also used some irregular verbs in the past tense (*got, ran, took, was*), it is clear that he is developing morphemic knowledge for verb tense.

Sharbani's story of a flying fairy also shows evidence that she is aware of verb tense; however, with the irregular verb of *fly,* she applied the past-tense marker of *-ed:*

> She flyed to where she got to a world full of colors. She stood there and stood there until somebody looked. She quickly flyed away.

Comparatives and Superlatives

Kindergarten-age children appear to be aware that there are two ways of making comparatives and superlatives. One way is to add *-er* and *-est* to the root word; another way is to use "more" or "most" in front of the root word. For example, re-creating *Harry the Dirty Dog* (Zion, 1956), Erika said, "Harry's bath was the superest, superest one he ever did."

Sometimes, it appears that children are trying out several hypotheses as to how comparatives and superlatives are formed. Misty, another kindergartner, re-creating the same story as Erika, said, "He got all dirty. He got even more dirtier. He played catch with the other dogs. He got more dirty." In this instance, she used both forms of making comparatives, even to the point of using both forms in the single instance, "even more dirtier."

Jennifer also showed some awareness of comparative and superlative endings though her use of them was not yet conventional. For example, Jennifer said, "He gonna get a lot of dirtiest" and "he got tired and tireder and tired."

Noun Suffix -er

By age 5, most children have receptive and productive knowledge for the noun suffix *-er* (Owens, 1988, 2001). Children know that by adding this suffix to a verb, they can make the name for the person who does the verb action, as in *teach—teacher, bat—batter,* and *catch—catcher.*

Possessives

Children's story monologues may contain evidence they are learning how to use possessive markers. In Ariel's fairy tale about a king, she used the phrase, "and he always went to people's houses." A few weeks later, her story about a snowman and a little girl contained this sentence: "Then after the girl woke up she threw lots of snowballs all over her mother's clean car."

Along with continuing to develop knowledge of the phonetic, semantic, syntactic, and morphemic aspects of language, kindergarten-age children are also continuing to acquire knowledge of how language is used differently in different settings. In many respects, this pragmatic knowledge will determine a child's competence in communicating and in participating in various social situations.

DEVELOPMENT OF PRAGMATIC KNOWLEDGE

Pragmatic Knowledge of Oral Language

Kindergartners use language for a wide variety of purposes. They use language to tell stories, direct peers, express pride, role play, engage others as a resource for help or information, and gain and hold others' attention (Owens, 1988, 2001). Language may also be used indirectly to request help or regulate another's behavior. Teachers can expect to see differences between kindergarten-age children in their awareness and use of pragmatic knowledge for oral and written language. A child's pragmatic knowledge of language is influenced not only by the variety of social settings they experience but also the frequency of those opportunities.

The various social settings that children encounter during their kindergarten year can enhance acquisition of pragmatic knowledge. Children can learn how to respond during verbal interactions with their teachers and other school staff, such as the principal, assistant principal, janitors, secretaries, older children, teachers' aides, and guest speakers. Pragmatic knowledge involves not only knowing when one can speak and to whom, but also the appropriate topics of conversation and cultural expectations for initiating, maintaining, and ending conversations.

Pragmatic knowledge has been further described as involving *social registers.* This term refers to a systematic variation of one's language based upon the speaker's awareness of to whom she or he is speaking, the topic of discussion, and the social relationship between the two speakers. Anderson (1992) studied young children's (ages 4 to 7 years) use of four different registers when role playing using puppets: babytalk, foreignertalk, classroom language/teacher talk, and doctortalk. Initially, children's distinctions for the different registers were marked phonetically through voice pitch and loudness (for the male roles). Children also showed specific register differences in the topic chosen for the conversations and for the specific vocabulary. There were age differences in their knowledge of the specific vocabulary and their ability to elaborate upon the topics.

Foreigner talk was characterized by a slower tempo and words spoken in a syllable-like manner. Older children used more linguistic devices when assuming the different roles. Older children also distinguished status differences between doctors and nurses and between doctors or nurses and patients.

Children's ease and competence in assuming roles in the various settings of Anderson's study appear to be related to their previous experiential basis. The family context appeared to be the easiest, followed by the doctor context, classroom context, and finally, foreigner talk. When assuming classroom roles, there was a big difference between the ages studied. The youngest children avoided assuming the teacher role. Young children also were less willing to participate in role playing the foreigner situation.

Anderson also noted gender differences. While such differences diminished with age, girls exhibited a wider range of roles, spoke more, and used more specific modifications than did boys. It was not clear whether boys were not aware of the range of specific linguistic modifications in specific settings or if boys had been socialized against using what might be perceived as baby talk or "sissy talk" even in a play setting.

Pragmatic Knowledge of Written Language

Kindergartners' emergent literacy behaviors also indicate a growing awareness of the pragmatic aspect of written language. Kindergarten children can identify a wide range of functions for writing, including using writing to remember something, to communicate with others, to learn, and to express one's own ideas and stories (Freeman & Sanders, 1989).

Kindergarten children's pragmatic knowledge of written language is also evident in the different ways in which they use language when telling a story and when they are dictating a story for someone (usually an adult) to write down. In Sulzby's (1982) study of kindergarten children's told and dictated stories, she noted that the told stories were generally characterized by a conversational tone and voice-continuant intonation between sentences. In contrast, dictated stories were generally characterized by unit-by-unit (words, phrases, short sentences) phrasing and segmented intonation patterns. Some of the children in the study closely observed the scribe's writing while they were dictating.

Children's competencies in dictating stories or narratives are another component of pragmatic knowledge. Vivian Paley's (1981) yearlong chronicle of her kindergarten children's stories, *Wally's Stories,* documents the growth of children's language as they dictate original imaginative stories and retell and adapt familiar storybooks.

When creating their own original stories, children's knowledge of story genre is shown by their creation of specific genre, such as fairy tales or alphabet books. When asked to create a fairy tale, many children begin their stories with "once upon a time" and some close the story formally by announcing "the end." Laura's orally told fairy tale is an example of how children's knowledge of fairy tales is incorporated into their own "tales":

> Once upon a time, a girl came up to a very large town, but it didn't look like a town. Then another . . . she saw something that . . . so she walked, and she walked over nowhere, until she came, then she came up to a frog, and he was trapped. The end.

The format children choose for their storybooks may indicate their awareness of how language is used. In creating her storybook, Sharbani (age 5) announced that it was just a picture book and therefore did not "need any words." Later on, Sharbani created an alphabet book with four pages, each containing one letter and an illustration. In sharing her book with her teacher, she said, "It's not going to be in words or anything. H for Hawaiian, another H for Hawaiian, W for water fountain, W for water fountain."

Children also acquire knowledge of how specific nonfiction texts are structured. Carlos (age 5), an avid sports fan, created a baseball story that resembles a sports page account. When putting his text on paper, he used both print and illustration. Print was used to label the opposing sides and to indicate the score: **Cubs 3, Cards 0** (Cardinals) (see Figure 8.5).

When asked to read his story, Carlos said:

> Cubs win over the Cardinals three to nothing. The Cardinals even didn't have a chance to bat. The Cardinals are the red guys. Blue are the Cubs. That's all of it.

Carlos' illustration has the quality and perspective of being a sky view of the ballpark. Perhaps his selection of words to add to the illustration came from his familiarity of watching televised games with the score appearing on the lower part of the television screen. Carlos' "reading" of his story has a nonfiction quality to it, different than fictional narratives.

Kindergarten children's re-creations of familiar storybook texts can also indicate their awareness of the different types of texts and the way in which language is used. Traditional storybooks are characterized by detailed descriptions, varied syntax, fully developed stories, and content-rich illustrations. In contrast, beginning reader texts are likely to have a reduced vocabulary, simple syntax with repeated sentence patterns, limited story plots, and artless illustrations. Through repeated opportunities to listen to these two types of text being read, kindergarten children indicate their awareness of the structural charac-

FIGURE 8.5
Carlos's Story

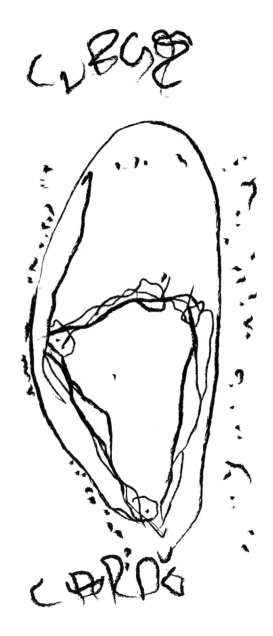

FIGURE 8.6
Misty's Re-Creation of *Stop!*

Stop, said the man, but it kept going on.
Stop, said the boy, but it kept going on.
Stop, said the dog, but it kept going on.
Stop, said the postman. It kept going on.
Stop, said the policeman. It kept going on.
Stop, said the boy, but it just went on.
All milk come, fall out. The cats are happy.

teristics of the two types of texts in their re-creations of the story (Otto, 1993). For example, compare the ways in which Misty used language in re-creating *Harry the Dirty Dog* (Zion, 1956), a traditional storybook, and *Stop!* (Crowley, 1982), a beginning reader text. Misty's re-creation of the two story texts shows that she has a strong awareness of the characteristics of the two texts. *Stop!* (Figure 8.6) is characterized by repetition and simple sentence structure. *Harry the Dirty Dog* (Figure 8.7) is characterized by more complex syntax and no repetitive pattern. Although both re-creations are only approximations of the actual texts, Misty's competency in reproducing texts with similar characteristics to the originals indicates her awareness of how language is used differently in these two storybooks.

Children's memory for text and their expectations for the type of text associated with specific storybooks are aspects of pragmatic knowledge, which may become evident during the kindergarten year in classrooms where children have numerous opportunities to interact with a wide range of storybooks.

FIGURE 8.7
Misty's Re-Creation of *Harry the Dirty Dog.*

"He heard the water running so he took the brush, ran downstairs and hid it in the backyard. And run away from house, his house. He got all dirty, he got even more dirtier. He played catch with the other dogs. He got more dirty. He turned into a dog with black, he turned into white spots in with black body. He was hungry so he went home. They said, All the family looked out the window. There's a strange dog out there. He did everything to make them see that it's dirty dog. He did his tricks, but it never worked. He even put his, then, he even singed. He even put the flower on his nose. Wait a minute, he said. He ran up the stairs, the family was way a-hind him. Give me a bath, he washed as they, the father said, why don't you and your brother give him a bath? So the kids washed. Dad, Mom! In here right now! So he didn't want any more baths so he hid the thing under his pillow."

Kindergarten-age children whose home and school environments include them in a wide range of activities related to functional literacy acquire specific pragmatic knowledge of how oral and written language are used differently in those varied settings.

SUMMARY

Kindergarten children continue to refine and expand their current knowledge of each of the aspects of language in both receptive and expressive modes. Kindergartners are easily understood by most adults; however, a range of phonetic production is still present among children this age. Children's comments when creating their own stories may indicate their awareness of the writing process and their expectations for using print. Children's use of prephonemic, early phonemic, and transitional spelling indicates their developing phonetic knowledge.

Acquisition of semantic knowledge during the kindergarten year includes learning new vocabulary and the continued development of increasingly complex schemata. Kindergartners use more complex noun and verb structures and understand a wider range of syntactic structures than they can produce. Increases in kindergartners' morphemic knowledge is evident in their use of inflectional morphemes to indicate verb tense and possession. Kindergarten children's pragmatic knowledge of oral and written language is influenced by the social settings and school interactions they experience.

✳ ✳ ✳ CHAPTER REVIEW

1. How is the kindergarten environment different from a preschool environment?

2. What sounds are not yet mastered by 5-year-olds?

3. What language knowledge is indicated by invented spelling?

4. Describe the types of invented spelling that may be used by kindergarten-age children.

5. Why are digraphs a spelling challenge to young writers?

6. How is a child's word concept related to their early spelling behaviors?

7. Give several examples of ways in which children's morphemic knowledge may increase during the kindergarten year.

8. Summarize Anderson's (1992) findings about children's use of social registers of speech.

9. Describe how children's interactions in retelling/re-creating familiar stories provides evidence of their pragmatic knowledge.
10. What is the expressive vocabulary volume of kindergartners? Is this larger or smaller than their receptive vocabulary?

❊ ❊ ❊ CHAPTER EXTENSION ACTIVITIES

1. Observe children's conversations in a kindergarten room during independent/learning center time. Identify the number of children engaged in each conversation. Record the length of the conversation and the number of turns in each conversation.
2. Observe in a kindergarten classroom's writing center. Ask children to share their writing with you. Observe whether letter-name spelling or phonemic spelling is used. In your note taking, record a sample of their metalinguistic comments while composing their stories. What aspect of language knowledge is represented in their comments?

❊ ❊ ❊ REFERENCES

Allen, K. E., & Marotz, L. (1994). *Developmental profiles: Prebirth through eight* (2nd ed.). Albany, NY: Delmar Publishers.

Anderson, E. (1992). *Speaking with style: The sociolinguistic skills of children.* London, England: Routledge.

Berthoud-Papandropoulou, I. (1978). An experimental study of children's ideas about language. In A. Sinclair, R. Jarvella, & W. Levelt (Eds.), *The child's conception of language* (pp. 55–64). New York: Springer-Verlag.

Broderick, V. (1991). Production and judgment of plausible similes by young children. *Journal of Experimental Child Psychology, 51,* 485–500.

Bryant, P., MacLean, M., Bradley, L., & Crossland, J. (1990). Rhyme and alliteration, phoneme detection, and learning to read. *Developmental Psychology, 26*(3), 429–438.

Buchoff, R. (1994, May). Joyful voices: Facilitating language growth through the rhythmic response of chants. *Young Children,* 26–30.

Burningham, J. (1973). *Mr. Gumpy's motor car.* London, England: Penguin Books.

Clay, M. (1982). *Observing young readers: Selected papers.* Portsmouth, NH: Heinemann Educational Books.

Colgin, M. (1991). *One potato, two potato, three potato, four: 165 chants for children.* Mt Rainier, MD: Gryphon House.

Cornett, C. (1986). *Learning through laughter: Humor in the classroom.* Bloomington, IN: Phi Delta Kappa Educational Foundation.

Crowley, J. (1982). *Stop!* Auckland, New Zealand: Shortland Publications.

Freeman, E., & Sanders, T. (1989). Kindergarten children's emerging concepts of writing functions in the community. *Early Childhood Research Quarterly, 4,* 342–347.

Honig, A. (1988). Humor development in children. *Young Children, 43*(4), 60–73.

Hulit, L., & Howard, M. (1993). *Born to talk.* New York: Merrill-Macmillan.

Kirtley, C., Bryant, P., MacLean, M., & Bradley, L. (1989). Rhyme, rime, and the onset of reading. *Journal of Experimental Child Psychology, 48,* 224–245.

McGee, L., & Richgels, D. (1990). *Literacy's beginnings: Supporting young readers and writers.* Boston: Allyn & Bacon.

McNeill, D. (1970). *The acquisition of language: The study of developmental psycholinguistics.* New York: Harper & Row.

Otto, B. (1984). Evidence of emergent reading behaviors in young children's interactions with favorite storybooks. (Doctoral dissertation, Northwestern University, 1984). *Dissertation Abstracts International, 45,* DA8423283.

Otto, B. (1992). [Inner-city kindergartners' storybook reading project]. Unpublished raw data.

Otto, B. (1993). Signs of emergent literacy among inner-city kindergartners in a storybook reading program. *Reading & Writing Quarterly: Overcoming Learning Difficulties, 9,* 151–162.

Owens, R. (1988). *Language development* (2nd ed.). Columbus, OH: Merrill.

Owens, R. (2001). *Language development* (5th ed.). Boston: Allyn & Bacon.

Paley, V. (1981). *Wally's stories.* Cambridge, MA: Harvard University Press.

Pease, D., Berko Gleason, J., & Pan, B. (1989). Learning the meaning of words: Semantic development and beyond. In J. Berko Gleason (Ed.), *The development of language.* (3rd ed., pp. 115–150). Columbus, OH: Merrill.

Piper, T. (1993). *Language for all our children.* Upper Saddle River, NJ: Merrill/Prentice Hall.

Rowe, D., & Harste, J. (1986). Metalinguistic awareness in writing and reading: The young child as informant. In D. Yaden & S. Templeton (Eds.), *Metalinguistic awareness and beginning literacy: Conceptualizing what it means to read and write.* Portsmouth, NH: Heinemann.

Sulzby, E. (1981). *Kindergartners begin to read their own compositions: Beginning readers' developing knowledges about written language.* (Final report to the Research Foundation of the National Council of Teachers of English.) Evanston, IL: Northwestern University.

Sulzby, E. (1982). Oral and written language mode adaptations in stories by kindergarten children. *Journal of Reading Behavior, 14*(1), 51–59.

Sulzby, E. (1983). *Beginning readers' developing knowledges about written language. Final report to the National Institute of Education.* Evanston, IL: Northwestern University.

Sulzby, E. (1985). Kindergartners as readers and writers. In M. Farr (Ed.), *Advances in writing research: Vol. 1. Children's early writing development* (pp. 127–199). Norwood, NJ: Ablex.

Sulzby, E. (1986). Children's elicitation and use of metalinguistic knowledge about *word* during literacy interactions. In D. Yaden & S. Templeton (Eds.), *Metalinguistic awareness and beginning literacy: Conceptualizing what it means to read and write* (pp. 219–233). Portsmouth, NH: Heinemann.

Sulzby, E., Barnhart, J., & Hieshima, J. (1989). Forms of writing and rereading from writing: A preliminary report. In J. Mason (Ed.), *Reading and writing connections* (pp. 31–64). Needham Heights, MA: Allyn & Bacon.

Temple, C., Nathan, R., Burris, N., & Temple, F. (1988). *The beginnings of writing* (2nd ed.). Boston: Allyn & Bacon.

Waggoner, J., & Palermo, D. (1989). Betty is a bouncing bubble: Children's comprehension of emotion-descriptive metaphors. *Developmental Psychology, 25*(1), 152–163.

Zion, G. (1956). *Harry the dirty dog.* New York: Harper & Row.

✳ ✳ ✳

9

ENHANCING THE LANGUAGE DEVELOPMENT OF KINDERGARTNERS

Teachers can enhance children's language development during the kindergarten year by providing a curriculum that is rich in opportunities for both *using* and *exploring* language. Developmentally, children of kindergarten age need a curriculum that is predominately informal, with many opportunities for independent, exploratory activities. Hands-on activities provide important opportunities for children to construct and refine their conceptual knowledge and their use of language to talk about and explore concepts. Hands-on activities also provide opportunities for problem solving and critical thinking.

The opportunity to ask questions is essential for kindergartners. Curricula and daily schedules need to provide times of informal conversation between children and their teacher, and between children. Throughout the early childhood years, a major consideration in selecting and implementing learning activities is the developmental appropriateness of the curriculum and the manner in which it is implemented.

Developmentally appropriate instruction activities are those that involve "varied, informal learning activities within a specifically prepared environment" (Lesiak, 2000, p. 213). In this developmentally appropriate curriculum, the teacher plans for specific activities to meet the individual needs of the children through a variety of informal groupings, including individual, small group, and whole group activities.

Kindergartners' increased attention spans and listening vocabularies make it possible for them to participate more in group settings; however, it is important to limit large group activities to a small part of the total schedule. Kindergarten teachers can determine the appropriateness of group size and activity length by trying out different group sizes with the different developmental levels of students present in the classroom.

GUIDELINES FOR TEACHERS' INTERACTIONS WITH KINDERGARTNERS

In addition to providing a developmentally appropriate curriculum, kindergarten teachers should also develop oral language environments in which teacher talk nourishes and supports language development. Teachers' classroom talk sets the stage for children's verbal participation and resulting language enhancement. According to Genishi (1992), "almost every activity presents an opportunity for talk when teachers allow it to" (p. 110).

Of the interaction patterns introduced in Chapter 2, the key interaction patterns for kindergarten teachers include linguistic scaffolding, verbal mapping, mediation, and questioning. By kindergarten age, shared reference via eye contact and communication loop patterns are well established. In addition, the adult-to-child language pattern found in interactions with toddlers and preschoolers is less used with kindergartners because of their increased receptive and productive language competencies. While adults may slightly simplify their speech to kindergartners in terms of syntax or vocabulary, the adult-to-child speech at the kindergarten level is much more complex than that addressed to a toddler or young preschooler and does not show the varied intonation patterns used with younger children.

Linguistic scaffolding is used by kindergarten teachers to support and expand children's participation in personal conversations and class discussions. Verbal mapping and mediation are used when a teacher demonstrates how to use a learning center or explains a particular concept to kindergarten learners. Questioning has a key role in the oral language and conceptual/cognitive environment of kindergarten. Teachers' questioning techniques stimulate and guide children's thinking and their use of language. According to Copple, Sigel, and Saunders (1984), "expertise in the use of inquiry is one of a teacher's most valuable assets. It is difficult to acquire, and its proper exercise demands considerable sensitivity and perceptiveness" (p. 223). Skillful questioning not only motivates intellectual participation and provides direction for children in thinking through complex issues, it also provides the opportunity for teachers to determine what children know and how they are thinking (Copple, Sigel & Saunders, 1984).

Questioning strategies at the kindergarten level incorporate literal and inferential questions, discussed in earlier chapters, along with recognition that some questions are asked for information, recitation, or clarification purposes. In kindergarten, questioning is increasingly used to discuss more complex and more distant (nonpresent) phenomena. Teachers should use strategies that will "expand the child's ability to think and to represent" (Copple, Sigel, & Saunders, 1984, p. 25). When children are encouraged to represent their concrete experiences through various modes of communication (oral language, written language, and art), they have the opportunity to reconstruct the experience mentally, which enhances cognitive and language development. Specific strategies that are effective in expanding children's thinking and representational competencies include asking questions, drawing attention to a puzzling situation such as a contradiction or inconsistency, and appropriately challenging children to move beyond concrete experiences (Copple, Sigel, & Saunders, 1984).

Vivian Paley's books (1981, 1990, 1997) detailing the stories and thoughts of her kindergarten children offer repeated examples of effective questioning that encourages children to represent their experiences through oral language. In her interactions with children, Paley was sensitive to their thought processes and to the role of student interactions in group discussion. In the example interaction that follows, Paley (1981) is discussing a story she has just read to the children about an enormous turnip that is stuck in the ground and is not pulled out until a whole group of characters (people and animals) combine efforts to pull it up. The last character to add his efforts to the task is a mouse, and as he joins the pulling, the turnip comes up. A discussion ensued:

Teacher: Why did the turnip come up when the little brown mouse pulled?

Warren: Because the grandfather and grandmother couldn't pull it up.

Teacher:	They couldn't. You're right. Then the mouse helped and it came up. Why?
Warren:	He was stronger.
Deana:	If all of them pulled, the enormous turnip *would* come up.
Wally:	That was only the strength they needed.
Eddie:	If just some pulled it wouldn't. But they needed all to pull.

(Reprinted by permission of the publisher from WALLY'S STORIES by Vivian G. Paley, 1-2, Cambridge, Mass.: Harvard University Press, Copyright © 1981 by the President and Fellows of Harvard College.)

Paley's continued questioning is contingent upon what the children say but also challenges the children to think out a puzzling situation. All of the children were given a chance to participate and give their perspective on the situation, which enhances their thinking by providing opportunities to use language to represent their thinking.

Throughout Paley's books are repeated examples of teacher-student interactions that take the form of "instructional conversations" (Thorp & Gallimore, 1988, cited in Hudson, Chryst, & Reamsnyder, 1994), instances where "teachers and students weave spoken and written language together with prior knowledge and experience to create new understanding" (Hudson, Chryst, & Reamsnyder, 1994, p. 266). Instructional conversations have a key role in establishing a communicative environment in kindergarten that enhances language development.

In classrooms in which instructional conversations are fostered, teachers recognize children as conversational partners who have important thoughts to offer. Teachers plan activities that draw on children's prior knowledge and present new or more complex information, challenging and guiding children's thinking and conceptual development. Teachers who engage in instructional conversations actively listen to what each child has to say, avoiding the tendency to listen only for "correct answers." While teachers may have a general idea of the questions they will use during a particular activity, the actual formulation and use of ongoing questions is contingent on the ways in which children respond to previous questions. Teachers who understand that children's responses reflect their thinking processes use this awareness to guide children's thinking and use of language through instructional conversations. Throughout kindergarten, instructional conversations play a key role in enhancing language development.

LANGUAGE-RELATED CURRICULAR GOALS

Curricular goals provide direction to teachers in selecting and implementing learning activities. The following specific goals (Otto, 1991) for enhancing language development in kindergarten incorporate the five aspects of language knowledge and both oral and written language modes.

Goal One: Increase children's ability to communicate orally in instructional and conversational settings. This goal addresses the overall language competencies of children and involves all five aspects of language knowledge. This goal places an emphasis on pragmatic knowledge of how language is used to communicate orally during instruction and in conversation.

Goal Two: Encourage an awareness of the purposes of reading and writing. Children are encouraged to become aware that reading and writing may have different purposes, such as reading for information, for enjoyment, for problem solving, and for interpersonal communication. This involves pragmatic knowledge of how language is used differently in different settings.

Goal Three: Increase listening comprehension. When children develop higher levels of listening comprehension they are also developing their semantic, syntactic, and morphemic knowledge. Phonetic knowledge is also increased as they hear new words pronounced. Pragmatic knowledge is enhanced as they become familiar with different genre.

Goal Four: Increase vocabulary through conceptual development. Direct, hands-on experiences are important in the development of conceptual knowledge. Conceptual knowledge is needed as a basis for vocabulary development, or semantic knowledge. Through concrete learning experiences inside and outside the classroom, children's conceptual knowledge and vocabulary develop.

Goal Five: Increase children's awareness of the process of communicating by using written language. Initially this goal is furthered by experiences that increase children's awareness of sound patterns and rhyme in spoken language. Poetry and rhyming story texts can be shared with kindergarten children to provide opportunities to develop more awareness of sound patterns and rhyme. More explicit learning activities can also be introduced that focus on sound patterns and rhyme (see the "Teacher-Directed Activities" section that follows). Another part of this goal is to increase children's awareness of letter-sound relationships. Through shared big books, language experiences, dictated stories, and opportunities to create written messages, children become more aware of the patterns of letter-sound relationships.

LANGUAGE-ENHANCING ACTIVITIES THROUGHOUT KINDERGARTEN

The activities suggested in this chapter resemble many of the activities discussed in the chapter on preschool curriculum. Although the activities may be similar, a difference occurs in the way in which the children engage in those activities. Since kindergarten children are at a higher level of cognitive, social, and emotional maturity than when they were in preschool and since their language knowledge is more developed, their interaction in those activities is more elaborate and complex. Kindergarten teachers who are sensitive to the ways in which children's language is developing can plan and implement learning activities that enhance children's language acquisition.

In the following section, examples of three types of learning activities will be described: exploratory activities, teacher-directed activities, and routine activities.

Exploratory Activities

Exploratory activities in the kindergarten classroom involve learning center activities, outdoor activities, and a sand/water table.

Learning Center Activities

Exploratory activities in learning centers need a generous time allotment to provide opportunities for children to fully engage in the exploration. Center activities at the kindergarten level may accommodate more than one child, since most children can successfully interact with one to two other children. The learning centers should be set up to encourage conversation. Teacher visits to the various centers can involve verbally and nonverbally modeling ways to interact with materials. The teacher should not dominate or explicitly narrow the ways in which children can interact with materials.

Learning centers at the kindergarten level can involve more problem-solving opportunities than at the preschool level. The class schedule should set aside time for children to share any outcomes of their center activities with the classroom; they could, for example, share a story they wrote or illustrated, share a piece of artwork, or show their block construction. Learning center activities at the kindergarten level may include a drawing/writing center, a storybook center, a science/math center, and a drama corner.

Drawing/writing center. Kindergarten children are active symbol makers (Dyson, 1990a). They communicate through both art and writing, symbolically representing their ideas and experiences. Teachers should expect that kindergartners will use a variety of forms of emergent writing, from scribble to letter strings to varied degrees of phonemic invented spelling. The forms used may vary from day to day or may be mixed in the same instance of writing (Casbergue, 1998; Sulzby, Teale, & Kamberelis, 1989). Hayes (1990) and Raines and Canady (1990) describe kindergarten classrooms where children are encouraged to engage in a wide range of writing-related activities throughout the curriculum for a variety of purposes. For example, in these classrooms children are encouraged to use writing in their dramatic play, in signing their names to stories and artwork, and in signing up for activities/centers. In these settings, children acquire a greater awareness of the pragmatic or functional aspects of both oral and written language.

Kindergarten writing centers should be well stocked with a variety of writing implements, such as crayons, felt-tip washable markers, pencils, and pens, along with a variety of paper, including both lined and unlined and different shapes and colors. Providing a stapler and transparent tape encourages children to make books. Other ways of writing are encouraged when the writing center

The opportunity to work with manipulatives encourages children's conversational competencies.

contains a typewriter, a chalkboard or slate and chalk, a computer, and/or magnetic letters and a display board.

In addition to having appropriate materials, kindergarten writing centers need to be organized so that children have opportunities to choose their own topic, ample time to create their stories and illustrations, and the chance to share and celebrate their stories with their classmates, teachers, and families (Merenda, 1989)

Children should be encouraged to talk with each other while they are creating their stories (Dyson, 1990b; Throne, 1988). As they draw and write, children may engage in socio-dramatic dialogue about the stories they are creating. This "talk" is important because it enhances the children's ability to manipulate and refine language and encourages them to use metalinguistic knowledge when they talk about their stories in progress. However, their final product may not clearly indicate the richness of their stories nor the discrete events that were discussed during the creation of their stories.

Giving children an opportunity to dictate stories individually at the writing center to an adult who serves as the scribe also enhances their acquisition of language knowledge. In dictating a story, children observe the relationships between speech and print as they observe the scribe (teacher's aide, teacher, or parent volunteer) writing down what they have dictated. When children dictate stories, they use vocabulary and syntactic structures they have mastered. Thus, children will be better able to reread their own dictated stories.

Classroom library center.   In preparing a classroom library, a teacher should provide a wide variety of fiction and nonfiction books. Newspapers and magazines should also be provided (Lesiak, 2000). At the kindergarten level, it is important to have wordless picture books and illustrated books with printed text. Compared to the books used at the preschool level, books selected for a kindergarten library center should have a more complex story plot and more text on each page; however, supportive, complementary illustrations that enhance children's comprehension of the story or nonfiction content remain essential. Big books should be provided because their format draws children's attention to print. Classroom big books created during circle time should also be featured in the library center, providing children with opportunities to enjoy the books individually. A few "easy reader" chapter books can be included for kindergartners who are already reading.

Books should be organized so that children have easy access. Many of the books should be stories the children have heard read at group story time. This familiarity will support their attempts to recreate the story for themselves independently (Martinez & Teale, 1988). A tape player and tapes of familiar storybook readings can also be included in this library corner, along with copies of the book. Classroom read-alouds can be taped and placed in this area for repeated listening. Audiotapes of story readings provide opportunities for children to listen to fluent reading and to become more aware of speech-print relationships.

Science/math center.   A science/math center involves hands-on exploration of concepts, with the introduction of accompanying vocabulary. This center is most effective when it is related to concepts introduced at story time through nonfiction or fiction books. For example, read *Is This a House for Hermit Crab?* (McDonald, 1990) during group story time. Then in the math/science center, set up an aquarium with a hermit crab. Plan with the children how to care for the crab. As children visit the center, have them write or draw their observations in a class journal.

Drama corner.   In the drama corner, children use language in many different ways, thus enhancing their pragmatic knowledge of language. In dramatic play, language is used to plan, develop, and maintain their interactions. Theme-related drama (such as a post office, restaurant, or grocery store) provides opportunities for children to practice and master related vocabulary and supporting concepts. Kindergarten children participate in the drama corner in a more elaborate way than they did at the preschool level. In dramatic play, children create, negotiate, and assume imaginary roles in imaginary settings through using language (Galda & Pelligrini, 1990). In doing this, words are used to change the identity of people. For example, children assuming the roles of a mail carrier and postal clerk may no longer be addressed by their real name but by a pretend name or title of their assumed role. Through language the nature of objects is also changed; for example, a book bag becomes a mail pouch, and a rubber stamp becomes the postmark.

Dramatic activities enhance language development more when children have some shared background information about the setting; when they have time, space, and props needed; and when an adult facilitates in expanding their dramatic play (Levy, Wolfgang, & Koorland, 1992). The benefits of these enriched dramatic activities include an increase in vocabulary, syntactic complexity, and the total number of words used in conversation turns (Levy, Wolfgang, & Koorland, 1992). Dramatic play opportunities also have been found to encourage greater linguistic elaboration—explicit reference and the use of adjectives/ modifiers—and expand their metalinguistic awareness as children negotiate with each other during dramatic play, deciding who should say what and how and when it should be said (Galda & Pelligrini, 1990).

While the classroom teacher carefully prepares the themed drama corner by providing the dramatic materials, her role is not to direct children's use of the materials or the roles they assume. Galda and Pelligrini (1990) reported that the presence of adult(s) in the dramatic play area may inhibit children's creativity and their use of language.

Dramatic play activities incorporating puppets provide an opportunity to use language in role playing.

Copple, Sigel, & Saunders (1984) offer these guidelines for teachers to follow when deciding whether or not to become involved in children's dramatic play:

1. Teachers should enter a child's dramatic play only when the child's play will not be disrupted.
2. When a child appears to need assistance to either enter the play or to continue in a particular role, a teacher may enter the play, giving suggestions for actions or speech.
3. If the play appears to be limited or restricted in terms of content, a teacher may enter the play, adding some information or ideas.

Children's dramatic play activities can also be enhanced by providing direct (field trips) or vicarious (storybook or nonfiction) experiences in which children will see people in various roles.

Outdoor Play

Kindergarten children need opportunities for vigorous exercise to enhance physical development; however, outdoor activities are also a time when language opportunities can be incorporated. Receptive and expressive language is encouraged in simple games with a few rules, as well as rules for using equipment and taking turns. Outdoor play offers opportunities for extended conversations between children and for teachers to talk with individual children. Encouraging children to observe weather, such as clouds and wind currents, trees, flowers, birds, and other elements in natural surroundings also helps children use language to describe what they observe.

Sand/Water Table

In the preschool classroom, a sand/water table is often available for children's explorations. In the kindergarten classroom, the sand/water table may not be available as often, but it still serves a purpose for occasional exploration. Examining the properties of sand and water enhances children's conceptual knowledge and vocabulary. Opportunities for understanding cause-and-effect relationships and predicting outcomes occur in sand and water table activities. In these activities children should be encouraged to use language to explain what they observe, feel, and predict will happen.

Teacher-Directed Activities

Teacher-directed activities in kindergarten may involve whole class or small group participation. In these activities, the teacher organizes and directs children's participation, engaging in instructional conversations with the children. The section that follows describes five types of teacher-directed activities that enhance children's language knowledge acquisition: share-and-tell, storybook time, dictated stories, calendar time, and language games.

Share-and-Tell

This activity is also frequently used at the preschool level; however, at the kindergarten level children's sharing is expected to be longer and more elaborate than at the preschool level. Sometimes the oral sharing focuses on an item the child brings to school or it may simply be an oral narrative describing an experience or event. "Y' All Know What?" is a form of sharing described by Pelligrini and Galda (1998), that may be more familiar to some young children than the share-and-tell label. In their classroom research, "Y' All Know What?" was used as a label for sharing time to encourage children to tell stories about their experiences. It draws on children's experiences in telling stories in home and community settings, where daily events are simply recounted or creatively exaggerated. Pelligrini and Galda describe this approach as a way of transitioning children from a familiar speech event to more literate discourse patterns at school.

Kindergarten children are able to ask more questions of the presenter than preschoolers. Another difference between the preschool and kindergarten levels is that kindergarten children typically need less prompting and linguistic scaffolding from the teacher when they present their share-and-tell. To provide more opportunity for discussion, a teacher may decide to schedule only three to five children each day to share rather than trying to give everyone a turn to present the same day. By keeping the sharing to only a few students each day, the audience will be more attentive and participate in the discussion more actively. Oral sharing or personal narratives may also be used as a basis for putting children's stories on paper through dictation and story illustration.

Storybook Time

When teachers read to kindergartners, they are providing children with an opportunity to learn more about language, the communication of meaning, and the varied purposes for reading (Taylor & Vawter, 1978). Frequent storybook reading has also been associated with increased knowledge of written language and of more specific concepts of letter name knowledge and phonemic awareness (Neuman, 1999; Otto, 1996). When children are from home environments where storybook reading is not routine, it is even more critical that their kindergarten teacher include storybook time in the curriculum. Children who have not had many storybook experiences prior to kindergarten will benefit from opportunities for storybook reading individually with the teacher or with only a few children, since there are more opportunities in the smaller setting for asking questions and becoming involved in responding to the story and illustrations. Since children's listening comprehension forms the basis for their later reading comprehension, storybook time is critical.

At the kindergarten level, stories are longer and more complex than the stories read in preschool classrooms. Books to include range from fiction to nonfiction and should also involve a variety of genre such as realistic fiction, fantasy (but not scary stories), poetry, fairy tales, and alphabet books. Kindergarten children should continue to have opportunities to experience literature/trade books and not be limited to listening to the teacher reading the basal or primer stories at group time. When compared to a basal reader, the language of "real literature" is more complex, the characters are more developed and realistic, and the story line is more elaborate. In this way, children's receptive knowledge of increasingly complex syntax and vocabulary is enhanced, which provides a foundation for their developing expressive language knowledge.

Teachers should add to the mix select illustrated books that involve humorous language play. This type of book further enhances and refines children's metalinguistic abilities (Zeece, 1995) because in comprehending the humorous situation, children become aware of the features of language, including multiple meanings, alliteration, rhythm, rhyme, and figurative language. Read-aloud books can also be selected to focus on sound similarities between words and phonemic awareness (Yopp, 1995), through texts characterized by rhyme and rhyming patterns, simple alliteration, and tongue twisters.

Kindergarten children may not rely as much on illustrations to understand the story as preschool children, since their vocabulary is more developed. This listening comprehension allows them to comprehend parts of a story without seeing the illustrations constantly. However, storybooks shared with kindergarten children should have high-quality illustrations that support the story and theme. When kindergarten children attempt to recreate the story independently, they may use the illustrations as a way of recalling specific language of the text.

As a book becomes more familiar, kindergarten children may eagerly participate in reconstructing the story line or sequence of events. This is an important activity since it encourages children to develop an awareness of a story event sequence and enhances their comprehension of the story. Another way to encourage children's story involvement is to use "participation stories" (Neuman & Roskos, 1993). In this activity, children participate by repeating a refrain of the text, providing sounds of animals or events, or joining in a choral response.

The use of finger puppets or flannelboard characters also enhances children's comprehension of a storybook. Puppets or flannelboard characters can be used as the storybook is initially read, or they may be used when reconstructing the story orally, without using the book. Children can participate by using the puppets to recreate characters' roles in speech and action.

Wordless picture books are also valuable to share with kindergarten children at storybook time. Because wordless books contain no text, the focus of the sharing is on talking about the characters and events illustrated and the sequence of events. When sharing this type of book, it is critical for teachers to focus on the underlying story structure to help children make connections between the events and characters from page to page (Hough, Nurss, & Wood, 1987).

Effective storybook reading techniques involve three parts: prereading, reading, and postreading (Mason, Peterman, & Kerr, 1989). Prior to reading, teachers should introduce the book to the children by talking about the title of the book and encouraging children to predict what the book is about. Teachers also encourage children to listen with a purpose. As they read the story, teachers should pause occasionally to ask comprehension questions or to involve children in predicting upcoming events or commenting on what has happened in the story. After the story reading is finished, the story events can be reviewed and children can be encouraged to make connections between the story events and their own lives.

Dictated Stories

Opportunities to dictate stories encourage children to use their oral language competencies in creating a text. Because children are not constrained by the writing process, their stories have more elaboration and structure than their stories would if they were writing them down themselves. As the children dictate a story, the teacher writes it on chart paper or on the chalkboard. Each child contributes a sentence (or thought). The teacher is careful in preserving the sentence structure or dialect of each child. After the story is completed, the teacher reads it back to the students, pointing to each word as it is read. Then the story is read a second time, with the children encouraged to join in unison or by reading their own sentences (Neuman & Roskos, 1993).

Dictated stories provide many opportunities for language growth. Watching their teacher write in response to what they dictate helps children become aware of the relationship between speech and print. Children also can watch the writing process involving the mechanics of writing such as punctuation and capitalization. Dictated stories also enhance syntactic and semantic knowledge as sentences are formed and specific vocabulary is used. Morphemic awareness is enhanced as teachers use and pronounce specific word endings to indicate verb tense or plurality of nouns. The process of creating a group story draws out children's expressive language (oral register and literate register). Children see how a narrative is constructed to share with others. The dictated story activity also provides opportunities for joint/unison reading. Repeated readings of the story foster children's memory for text and encourage them to begin to make the speech-print match. Further language opportunities arise as the storybook is laminated, bound, and placed in the reading center for individual enjoyment.

Two types of dictated story activities are used in kindergarten. In the first type of dictated story, a teacher shows children one or more related pictures and leads them in creating a story to fit the pictures. Children find it easier to construct a story from a sequence of pictures rather than from one "busy" picture. In the latter instance they are more likely to describe all of the things seen in the picture rather than focusing on a sequence of possible events or predicting what would happen next (Hough, Nurss, & Wood, 1987). Sequenced pictures can be developed by a teacher or purchased from a teacher's supply store. Wordless picture books may also be used in creating a group story.

Another type of dictated story activity is the *language experience story.* Language experience stories provide an opportunity for children to share in composing a narrative based on their common experience such as a trip to the zoo or the arrival of the classroom pet hamster. In this activity children put words to their experiences and see those words written down to be shared with others.

Calendar Time

This typically involves determining the day of the week and the number of the date, along with the month and sometimes the year. Some children may not be able to understand these temporal concepts since they are abstract rather than concrete in nature. The teacher may need to identify the day of the week with a particular activity: "Today is Tuesday. This is the day we go to the school library." "Today is Friday. Today we go to the gym." For some classrooms, a daily calendar time is not appropriate, since children cannot fully comprehend the concepts involved. While they may be able to respond in rote fashion to saying the days of the week or the number of the date, there may be little understanding of the real concept. It may be enough to have calendar time for a few weeks, take a break for a month or two, and then start calendar time again.

Language Games

Language games in kindergarten are used to consciously focus children's attention on language units, such as syllables or phonemes, and to provide opportunities to begin to manipulate those units. For example, rhyming games encourage children to recognize and produce words that have the same ending sounds. This conscious manipulation of language involves metalinguistic knowledge, which is a higher level of language knowledge. Metalinguistic knowledge is the second level represented in the hierarchy of language knowledge introduced in Chapter 1 (see Figure 1.4).

Prior to kindergarten, language acquisition involves mainly language knowledge at the linguistic or usage level; however, with the beginning of formal schooling in kindergarten, it is increasingly important for children to begin to develop metalinguistic knowledge of the aspects of language—most specifically, the phonetic, or sound-symbol, aspect. Systematic attention to a specific aspect of language knowledge, such as phonemic awareness and letter-sound relationships, has been found to enhance reading achievement (Ball & Blachman, 1991; IRA-NAEYC, 1999). Reading and writing instruction in the primary and upper elementary grades requires children to consciously manipulate units of language—units of sound (phonemes, syllables, onset-rime) and units of syntactic/semantic meaning (morphemes, phrases, sentences).

While research has not identified one specific method as being effective with all children, successful approaches with beginning readers and writers are those that involve "systematic code instruction along with meaningful connected reading" (IRA-NAEYC, 1999, p. 175). Kindergarten children are not yet ready for the formal instruction activities used in the primary grades, but they can benefit from language games that focus on phonemic awareness or letter-sound relationships in playful, interactive, and engaging ways (Yopp & Yopp, 2000) in small group or individual settings. Language games for kindergartners focus on oral language responses and encourage manipulation of units of language. Although these language games are based on informal, interactive, game-like formats, they need to be planned for and implemented in sequences that are developmentally appropriate. Initial activities should focus on developing children's listening skills since those skills are needed for subsequent later language games and more formal instruction. Listening games should encourage children to listen "actively, attentively, and analytically" (Adams, Foorman, Lundberg, & Beeler, 1998, p. 15). Listening games are followed by activities that focus on language in increasingly smaller units: syllables, initial and final sounds (onset-rime), and phonemes (Adams et al., 1998; Yopp & Yopp, 2000). Initially it is also beneficial to use language games that focus on words and sentence units, since reading and writing acquisition "depends on a relatively secure notion of what is and is not a word" (Adams et al., 1998, p. 39).

Language games involve different types of manipulation, including matching, isolation, substitution, blending, segmentation, and deletion (Yopp & Yopp, 2000). For example, children are asked whether two words start the same, focusing on syllables as in *sandbox* and *sandbag*, onset-rime as in *bat-butter*, or phonemes as in *car-catsup*. Language games that are based on children's literature, nursery rhymes, or songs provide a meaningful basis for focusing on language units. Ideas for specific language games for kindergarten teachers are found in the resources listed at the end of this chapter.

Routine Activities

Each classroom has routines that occur on a daily or weekly basis. In these routines are opportunities to enhance children's pragmatic knowledge of language and their receptive and expressive knowledge of syntactic, semantic, morphemic, and phonetic properties of language.

Arrival and Departure

When children first begin to attend kindergarten, they will have already had an opportunity to establish arrival and departure greetings in their home and community environments; however, they may not be familiar with the specific routines established in more formal settings such as classrooms. Arrival and departure routines are established during the first few weeks of school. The classroom teacher should greet children individually, calling them by name. During arrival time children can also be encouraged to talk about their experiences.

Children can also participate in attendance taking. One strategy is to provide each child with a name card in a pocket chart. When they arrive in the classroom, they select their name card and take it to the rug area for the morning circle time. Specific activities can be developed based upon children's names and the letters used in their names, such as "If your name starts with an *A*, stand up." This strategy encourages children to recognize their printed name and begin focusing on specific letters in their names and other children's names.

Another version of this attendance-taking strategy is to write the children's names on t-shirt shaped pieces of paper, and hang them with clothespins from a line draped at the children's height. When children arrive in the classroom, they pick up their t-shirt and place it on the rug. As the class assembles on the rug, the teacher leads the children in taking attendance, determining who is absent and participating in other name-related activities.

'Specials' within the School Building

Kindergarten children may go as a class to other locations in the school for art and music or perhaps to the school library. Thus, they need to learn how to move as a class through the hallways. While it is important for children to learn to pass quietly through the hallways so as to not disturb other classes, there may be occasional opportunities for children to see and read printed signs or labeled doors in the school, such as OFFICE, JANITOR, or BAKE SALE. By encouraging children to read signs in their school environment, teachers increase children's awareness of the ways in which printed language is used for information, for identifying locations, and for other functional purposes.

SUMMARY

Kindergarten children's language development is enhanced through curricular activities that provide opportunities to use and explore language. Developmentally appropriate learning environments provide hands-on, informal learning activities that engage children in social and instructional conversations. The classroom teacher has a critical role in establishing the language environment of the classroom. Key interaction patterns in kindergarten include linguistic scaffolding, verbal mapping, mediation, and questioning. A well-balanced kindergarten curriculum includes exploratory, teacher-directed, and routine activities that incorporate many opportunities for children to use their developing knowledge of oral and written language.

✳ ✳ ✳ CHAPTER REVIEW

1. What are the key interaction patterns for kindergarten teachers?
2. How are questioning strategies used at the kindergarten level?
3. Why are hands-on activities an important part of the kindergarten curriculum?

4. Define *instructional conversations.*

5. State and explain three of the language-related curricular goals for kindergarten.

6. How are learning center activities different at the kindergarten level than at the preschool level?

7. Develop four guidelines for teachers to follow when including a drawing/writing center in the kindergarten.

8. How do dramatic play opportunities enhance kindergarten children's language development?

9. Explain the value of storybook time in enhancing children's language development in kindergarten.

10. In what ways can children be encouraged to participate in storybook sharing and reading?

11. What are two types of dictated stories?

12. What are the benefits of the dictated story language experience activity for children's language development?

13. What is the value of individual dictated stories and group dictated stories?

14. Define *language game.* Give an example.

15. How can routine activities enhance language development in kindergarten?

✳ ✳ ✳ CHAPTER EXTENSION ACTIVITIES

1. Observe a kindergarten teacher reading to his or her class. Identify the ways in which the teacher focuses on vocabulary to enhance comprehension.

2. Sit near the writing center of a kindergarten classroom. Listen to children's conversations while they are writing and drawing. How do their conversations relate to their creations?

3. Select a children's illustrated storybook. Create flannelboard characters or finger/hand puppets based on the story.

4. Observe in a kindergarten during arrival time. Describe how the children and teacher participate in verbal greeting and attendance taking.

5. Observe in a kindergarten classroom during share-and-tell time. Describe how the teacher supports children's language during this activity.

✳ ✳ ✳ REFERENCES

Adams, M., Foorman, B., Lundberg, I., & Beeler, T. (1998). *Phonemic awareness in young children: A classroom curriculum.* Baltimore, MD: Paul H. Brookes Publishing.

Ball, E., & Blachman, B. (1991). Does phoneme awareness training in kindergarten make a difference in early word recognition and developmental spelling? *Reading Research Quarterly, 26*(1), 49–66.

Casbergue, R. (1998). How do we foster young children's writing development. In S. Neuman & K. Roskos (Eds.), *Children achieving: Best practices in early literacy* (pp. 198–222). Newark, DE: International Reading Association.

Copple, C., Sigel, I., & Saunders, R. (1984). *Educating the young thinker: Classroom strategies for cognitive growth.* Hillsdale, NJ: Lawrence Erlbaum Associates.

Dyson, A. (1990a). Symbol makers, symbol weavers: How children link play, pictures, and print. *Young Children, 45*(2), 50–57.

Dyson, A. (1990b). Talking up a writing community: The role of talk in learning to write. In S. Hynds & D. Rubin (Eds.), *Perspectives on talk and learning* (pp. 99–114). Urbana, IL: National Council of Teachers of English.

Galda, L., & Pelligrini, A. (1990). Play talk, school talk, and emergent literacy. In S. Hynds & D. Rubin (Eds.), *Perspectives on talk and learning* (pp. 91–97). Urbana, IL: National Council of Teachers of English.

Genishi, C. (1992). Developing the foundation: Oral language and communicative competence. In C. Seefeldt (Ed.), *The early childhood curriculum: A review of current research* (pp. 85–117). New York: Teachers College Press.

Hayes, L. (1990). From scribbling to writing: Smoothing the way. *Young Children, 45*(3), 62–68.

Hough, R., Nurss, J., & Wood, D. (1987). Tell me a story: Making opportunities for elaborated language in early childhood classrooms. *Young Children, 43*(1), 6–12.

Hudson, L., Chryst, C., & Reamsnyder, D. (1994). Goin' to grandma's house: Using instructional conversation to promote literacy and reduce resistance in minority children. In D. Lancy (Ed.), *Children's emergent literacy: From research to practice* (pp. 265–284). Westport, CN: Praeger.

International Reading Association–National Association for the Education of Young Children. (1999). Learning to read and write: Developmentally appropriate practices for young children. In K. Paciorek & J. Munro (Eds.), *Annual editions: Early childhood education* (20th ed., pp. 166–183). Guilford, CN: Dushkin/McGraw-Hill.

Lesiak, J. (2000). Research based answers to questions about emergent literacy in kindergarten. In R. Robinson, M. McKenna, & J. Wedman (Eds.), *Issues and trends in literacy education* (2nd ed., pp. 213–236). Boston: Allyn & Bacon.

Levy, A., Wolfgang, C., & Koorland, M. (1992). Sociodramatic play as a method for enhancing the language performance of kindergarten age students. *Early Childhood Research Quarterly, 7*, 245–262.

Martinez, M., & Teale, W. (1988). Reading in a kindergarten classroom library. *The Reading Teacher, 41*, 568–572.

Mason, J., Peterman, C., & Kerr, B. (1989). Reading to kindergarten children. In D. Strickland & L. Morrow (Eds.), *Emergent literacy: Young children learn to read and write* (pp. 52–62). Newark, NJ: International Reading Association.

McDonald, M. (1990). *Is this a house for hermit crab?* New York: Orchard Books.

Merenda, R. (1989). "Me and Ethan": Celebrating the writer's choice. *Childhood Education, 65*(4), 217–219.

Neuman, S. (1999). Books make a difference: A study of access to literacy. *The Reading Teacher, 34*(3), 286–311.

Neuman, S., & Roskos, K. (1993). *Language and literacy learning in the early years: An integrated approach.* Fort Worth, IN: Harcourt Brace Jovanovich College Publishers.

Otto, B. (1991). Developmentally appropriate literacy goals for preschool and kindergarten classrooms. *Early Child Development and Care, 70*, 53–61.

Otto, B. (1996). Let's read a story: The role of storybook reading in young children's literacy acquisition. *Illinois Schools Journal, 76*(1), 5–18.

Paley, V. (1981). *Wally's stories.* Cambridge, MA: Harvard University Press.

Paley, V. (1990). *The boy who would be a helicopter.* Cambridge, MA: Harvard University Press.

Paley, V. (1997). *The girl with the brown crayon.* Cambridge, MA: Harvard University Press.

Pelligrini, A., & Galda, L. (1998). *The development of school-based literacy: A social ecological perspective.* New York: Routledge.

Raines, S., & Canady, R. (1990). *The whole language kindergarten.* New York: Teachers College, Columbia University.

Sulzby, E., Teale, W., & Kamberelis, G. (1989). Emergent writing in the classroom: Home and school connections. In D. Strickland & L. Morrow (Eds.), *Emergent literacy: Young children learn to read and write* (pp. 52–62). Newark, NJ: International Reading Association.

Taylor, N., & Vawter, J. (1978). Helping children discover the functions of written language. *Language Arts, 55*(8), 941–945.

Throne, J. (1988, September). Becoming a kindergarten of readers? *Young Children,* 10–16.

Yopp, H. (1995). Read-aloud books for developing phonemic awareness: An annotated bibliography. *The Reading Teacher, 48*(6), 538–543.

Yopp, H., & Yopp, R. (2000). Supporting phonemic awareness development in the classroom. *The Reading Teacher, 54*(2), 130–145.

Zeece, P. (1995). Laughing all the way: Humor in children's books. *Early Childhood Education Journal, 23*(2), 93–97.

✳ ✳ ✳ TEACHER RESOURCES

Adams, M., Foorman, B., Lundberg, I., & Beeler, T. (1998). *Phonemic awareness in young children: A classroom curriculum.* Baltimore, MD: Paul H. Brookes Publishing.

Cecil, N. (2001). *Activities for striking a balance in early literacy.* Scottsdale, AZ: Holcomb Hathaway.

Seefeldt, C., & Galper, A. (2001). *Active experiences for active children: Literacy emerges.* Upper Saddle River, NJ: Merrill/Prentice Hall.

Yopp, H., & Yopp, R. (2000) Supporting phonemic awareness development in the classroom. *The Reading Teacher, 54*(2), 130–145.

10

LANGUAGE DEVELOPMENT IN THE PRIMARY YEARS

Duﾠring the primary school years, children's language continues to develop in the five areas of language knowledge: phonetic, semantic, syntactic, mor- phemic, and pragmatic. Children enter the primary grades with language com- petencies developed through their experiences in home and preschool/kinder- garten settings. The primary years mark changes in children's language environment in two major ways: (1) children spend more of their days in non- home settings with nonrelatives, and (2) school settings increasingly involve formal instruction. These two changes influence the variety of language styles encountered by children. In addition, the increased emphasis on formal in- struction requires that children acquire the pragmatic knowledge involved in learning how to participate verbally and to acquire the academic/literate regis- ter. Instruction at the primary level also often involves metalinguistic concepts, requiring that children consciously focus on specific linguistic concepts such as *letter, word, sentence, paragraph, punctuation, sound, blend, digraph, vowel,* and *consonant.*

Each of these changes in the linguistic environment influences the ways in which children's language development progresses. In this chapter, we will fo- cus on the ways in which children's language continues to develop during the primary years. Chapter 11 will focus on specific strategies that enhance lan- guage development during the primary years.

DEVELOPMENT OF PHONETIC KNOWLEDGE

Oral Language Knowledge

During children's 6th and 7th years, they continue to increase in their ability to produce a full range of specific language sounds. By the age of 8, most children have complete phonetic production. The 6-year-old typically becomes able to articulate /θ/ (*thin*) and /ʒ/ (*treasure*) (Sander, 1972; Owens, 2001). The acqui- sition of consonant clusters (such as *str, sl,* and *dr*) may not occur until children are 8 years old. While some children may have acquired these articulations ear- lier than the ages cited here, it is important for teachers to hold off on referring slower achieving children for speech remediation until they are well past those target ages for the respective sounds. For example, if a kindergarten child has difficulty with the /θ/ sound in *thin* or the /ʒ/ sound in trea*s*ure, speech reme- diation may not be appropriate until the child is around 7 years old.

Primary-age children also increase in their rhyming abilities and awareness of other sound patterns, such as *onset* and *rime*. **Onset** refers to the initial con- sonant (or consonant cluster) of a syllable that preceeds the first vowel of a syllable; **rime** refers to the vowel and any remaining consonants of a syllable (Harris & Hodges, 1995) (see Figure 10.1).

FIGURE 10.1
Examples of *Onset* and *Rime*

Word	Onset	Rime
cat	c	at
mat	m	at
light	l	ight
bright	br	ight
weed	w	eed
speed	sp	eed
thought	th	ought
sought	s	ought

Written Language Knowledge

Research investigating children's awareness of onset and rime patterns has documented children's use of this awareness when reading to compare known words with new words, figuring out the pronunciation and decoding the new word by creating an analogy between the old and new word (Goswami, 1986, 1990; Goswami & Mead, 1992). Children appear to use this strategy regardless of their reading level (Goswami, 1986). For children to develop onset-rime awareness that contributes to their reading strategies, onset-rime activities must have both oral and written language components. This is because the English phonetic system has many alternative spellings for the same phonemes. For example, *go, show,* and *though* all have the same vowel sound; however, the rime aspect of each syllable is spelled differently, precluding any productive analogy that might assist decoding. Only through activities that combine oral and written language will children see the function that onset and rime patterns may serve in decoding. (See Figure 10.2 for additional orthographic variations of phonemes.) Other research with first graders has indicated that "phonemic segmentation scores . . . predicted overall performance in reading and spelling" (Foorman, Francis, Novy, & Liberman, 1991, p. 456).

FIGURE 10.2
Examples of Orthographic Variations for Same Phonemes

Phoneme	Examples
[iy]	bead, weed
[a]	cot, caught, fought
[ey]	hay, hey
[ɛ]	said, dead, red

The current controversy involving phonics instruction appears to center on two questions: (1) How much phonemic knowledge is necessary for the development of conventional reading and writing? and (2) Can sufficient phonemic knowledge be acquired by children through informal, indirect instruction or is formal, direct instruction in letter-sound relationships necessary? (See Adams, 1990; Chall, 1967, 1983; Chomsky, 1972; Fields, Spangler, & Lee, 1991; Jewell & Zintz, 1990; McGee & Richgels, 2000; Menyuk, 1984; Schwartz, 1988; Teale & Sulzby, 1987). Instead of specifying a discrete body of phonemic knowledge universally necessary for conventional reading, some educators contend that individual learning styles allow children to learn to read and comprehend text successfully though their phonemic knowledge varies. Continued research in the areas of emergent literacy and formal reading instruction promises to clarify these issues.

Many variables are involved in these studies that may have influenced the outcomes of the research and the manner in which the target terms were identified. For example, what level of language knowledge was involved in the experimental task used in the research? Was the children's phonemic awareness examined at the level of linguistic knowledge or metalinguistic knowledge? Or did the experimental task require that children verbalize their metalinguistic knowledge? How did the level of language knowledge focused on in the instructional intervention match up with the level of language knowledge emphasized in subsequent classroom instruction? Research that focuses on these questions is needed for a clearer understanding of the role of phonemic awareness in learning to read.

During the last two decades, a more thorough understanding of primary children's developing phonetic knowledge has resulted from the study of children's early spelling attempts (Gentry, 1982; Henderson & Templeton, 1986; Wilde, 1992). As indicated in Chapter 8, these early spelling attempts have been called *invented spelling.* Through invented spelling, children experiment with written language and attempt to negotiate the relationships between sounds heard in words and the written/alphabetic symbol system.

Primary children may vary in their approaches to spelling, from those who are just beginning to figure out the orthographic system to children who are more sophisticated in their representations of phonemes. Thus, it is important for primary teachers to be aware of the developmental progression of orthographic/phonetic knowledge in young children. Children's very early writing attempts may use letters of the alphabet without any consistent phonetic representations (prephonemic spelling). Prior to acquiring conventional spelling, children may go through one or more stages of phonemic spelling, as representations of phonemes become more consistent and complete. Examples of this developmental progression are offered in Chapter 8.

Detailed study of children's invented spellings has been documented by Bissex (1980), Sulzby, Barnhart, and Hieshima (1989), Teale and Martinez (1989), Temple, Nathan, and Burris (1982), and Temple, Nathan, Burris, and

Temple (1988). Each of these studies describe in more detail children's growing phonemic awareness and their transition to conventional orthography. In classrooms where children are encouraged to write using invented spellings, teachers can use these writings to examine children's growing phonetic knowledge.

In the following example we see one child's attempts to communicate through invented spelling as he described a story he had just read. Craig (age 8) had just read Sharmat's (1978) book, *Nate the Great and the Sticky Case.* When asked to write his response to the book, he wrote (punctuation and spelling are Craig's):

> I think that the Sticky case was funny. Also it was mistrais. In the biginy I did not know Where to start to find a cool. But as the case went on I thowt and thowt. But I still cood not crack the cace. Then all the cols started to come together. Then I know it was that fang *(the dog)* had it."

Several of Craig's invented spellings showed highly developed phonemic awareness. For example:

mistrais	for	*mysterious*
biginy	for	*beginning*
cace	for	*case*
thowt	for	*thought*
cood	for	*could*
cols, cool	for	*clues, clue*

In each of Craig's invented spellings, he dealt with sounds that are represented in English in several ways (Temple, Nathan, Burris, & Temple, 1988). For example, in the word *case,* the /s/ sound can also be represented by *c,* as in *face.* Similarly, in *cood* for *could,* Craig used the same letter representations of sound used in *wood.*

Children's experiences that contribute to their oral and written vocabularies and the ways in which they are encouraged to use and examine those words influence their acquisition of orthographic knowledge (Henderson & Templeton, 1986). A key factor in this process appears to be opportunities children have to apply what they are learning about word spelling patterns to their reading and writing activities. Specific activities that enhance this knowledge will be described in Chapter 11. Since English is a language with a wide variety of orthographic patterns for phoneme representation, the acquisition of conventional spelling also involves a visual sense (Does the word "look right"?) and the internalization of a large number of spellings (Wilde, 1992).

DEVELOPMENT OF SEMANTIC KNOWLEDGE

Vocabulary

During primary school years, elaboration and differentiation of concepts occur along with the acquisition of labels attached to concepts. Primary children's expressive vocabularies range from 800 to 20,000 words (Berko Gleason, 1989; Crystal, 1987). Semantic development continues to occur informally as children interact with their environment in conversations with family and friends, exposure to various media, and family trips or vacations. Semantic development also occurs more formally in literacy-related instruction in which children are introduced to specific words and encouraged to participate in discussing what those words mean. Such discussions of word meaning are metalinguistic in the sense that children are asked to focus consciously on meaning as an aspect of words.

Although children and adults share many of the same concept labels at this time, children's concepts in many instances are not as complete or elaborated as adults' concepts. This difference becomes evident in discussions where the concepts and their labels are topics of conversation, as in when discussing a storybook or nonfiction book. During the primary years children develop deeper, more complete concepts and become aware of synonyms and antonyms. Children also develop an awareness of implied meanings of words and their emotional content as they begin to differentiate between denotative and connotative word meanings. The **denotative meaning** is the word's objective definition or its simple referent. The **connotative meaning** is the word's subjective definition, reflecting social/affective/emotional meaning. For example, an *attaché case* and a *book bag* have similar denotative meanings: a case or bag for carrying books and papers. Yet, their connotative meanings are quite different. The *attaché case* carries the higher social status and is assumed to be more related to business matters than does the *book bag*. If you were reading a story in which a "man walked down the street carrying an attaché case," you would make different assumptions about the character than you would if "the man walked down the street carrying a book bag."

Figurative Language

Children's use and understanding of figurative language continues to increase during the primary years (Owens, 2001). They begin to realize that figures of speech are not always meant to be taken literally, and if they are taken literally an amusing situation develops. Children this age are often fond of *Amelia Bedelia* books, which focus on literal interpretation of figurative language, creating hilarious situations (e.g., "stealing home base" and "turkey dressing").

Figurative language is a special aspect of semantic knowledge that begins to become evident during the primary school years. It requires a special understanding of semantic knowledge since the meaning of a word is used to create a comparison between two objects or settings. Similes ("she dances like a fairy") are more explicit in their comparison than metaphors, which create an implied comparison ("she was a fairy, dancing across the stage"). In creating a metaphor, a child must be able to see the ways in which two objects or settings are similar on a more abstract or symbolic level (Hulit & Howard, 1993). In earlier years, children's thinking is more concrete and focuses on immediate contexts rather than the more abstract characteristics that form the basis for figurative language found in similes and metaphors.

The riddles created by first and second graders tend to be completely nonsensical or too realistic and thus are not really riddles, but "pre-riddles" (Sutton-Smith, 1975). During third grade, most children are able to grasp the double meanings of riddles simultaneously (McGhee, 1979). Throughout the primary years, children become more aware of possible double meanings and incorporate puns and riddles into their linguistic play.

Semantic development is also evident in primary-age children's appreciation of puns and riddles. This appreciation comes from children's ability to realize that words may have double meanings or may have a similar phonological sequence to other words (Pepicello & Weisberg, 1983). Primary-age children appear to be using their morphemic, phonetic, and semantic knowledge in comprehending and creating riddles. Mahoney & Mann (1991) devised phoneme/morpheme riddles that were used in a riddle completion task. Children were directed to choose the answer that answered the riddle's question in a "funny way" (p. 33). For example: "What goes 'oom oom'? a) a cow walking backwards or b) an old vacuum cleaner" (p. 33). In selecting *a* as the answer, children used their phonetic knowledge of sounds to figure out what the word would be if the sounds of a cow ("moo") were reversed ("oom"). Additionally, children would need to use their semantic knowledge in selecting the funniest answer. In the following example, further use of phonemic and semantic knowledge in appreciating the humor of a riddle is evident: "Q: Why did the cookie cry? A: Because its mother had been a wafer so long" (Schultz, 1974, p. 100). In this riddle, "wafer" is phonetically similar to "away for," and cookie and wafer have similar denotative meanings, creating a surprise answer that is entertaining.

A parent described the following instance in which her 7-year-old son used figurative language. He had accidentally discovered his birthday present hidden in a closet. When he saw his mother nearby and became fully aware of his discovery, the child said, "Uh-oh, looks like I just cooked my goose!" In their family, the phrase "cooked his goose" described people who had gotten themselves in predicaments. Realizing his similar situation, the boy used the figure of speech to express his awareness of his situation.

As with earlier ages, semantic knowledge, including the use of metaphors, reflected in primary children's written stories is based on their conceptual knowledge and schemata.

In Danny's (age 8) illustrated story, "A Trip to North Carolina," he wrote:

> . . . me and my friend went to the beach. We dived into the waves. The water was cold, but the sun kept us warm. We gathered seashells and brought them

home. . . . The next morning we went to the U.S.S. North Carolina Battleship. The cannons were longer than four Michael Jordans. It was 8000 feet long.

Danny's story indicates that as a part of his conceptual schema for beaches, he has the related concepts of warm weather, seashells, cold water, and waves. As a part of his conceptual schema for battleships, he includes big cannons and a length of 8,000 feet. His use of metaphor in describing the length of the cannons as "longer than four Michael Jordans" creates a meaningful metaphor that would be understood by his classmates. During the term when Danny wrote his story, Michael Jordan played for the Chicago Bulls basketball team. Jordan's height was well known among Danny and his friends.

DEVELOPMENT OF SYNTACTIC KNOWLEDGE

Sentence Complexity

In the primary grades, children's use of sentence structure becomes more elaborate and complex in both their oral and written language. Story texts created by children mirror that complexity. Children's stories provide a way of examining children's monologues for syntactic structures. Syntactic development during the primary years is influenced by language use in home, school, and community settings and by children's semantic language knowledge. Children who have been exposed to more complex language in a variety of settings in poetry, drama, nonfiction, and narrative stories and who have many opportunities to create their own extended texts will develop more detailed syntactic knowledge. Classrooms where most of the instruction occurs in teacher-directed large groups and in individualized activities in which children work alone offer little opportunity to develop language skills needed for complex literacy tasks (Raphael & Hiebert, 1996). Primary-age children's knowledge of syntax is evident in their creation of both narrative and informational writing (Scott, 1995). Development of children's ability to produce both narrative and informational genres increases during elementary school and extends through the secondary school years.

In her written story about losing a tooth, Maribel (age 8) incorporated narrative structures ("one day. . ."), sequencing clauses (e.g., "after that," "then," "when," "the next day"), and a cause-and-effect relationship:

One day me and my friend Sophia are riding our bikes outside. We got bored riding our bikes so we got a drink. After that we went in my room. I said, "So what should we do?" She said, "Let's play a game." I said, "Maybe we can play Sweet Valley High." "O.K." she said. Sophia won the game. She kept on saying, "I won!" Then we jumped on the bed. We were laughing so hard because we were making funny jokes. I jumped so high I hit my head on the ceiling and dropped on the floor. I started to cry. Sophia called my mom and told her what happened. My mom said, "No more jumping on the bed!" My tooth was loose. I told my mom my tooth was loose. My mom asked if my tooth is bleeding. I said only a little bit. When Sophia went home it was night time so I went to sleep. The next day my mom took me to the dentist. When he took my tooth out it did not hurt. because he gave me medicine. Before I went home he gave me a little cace to put my tooth in. I said thank you, and the dentist said your welcome. Now whenerer I smile my mom and dad laugh. That's what I don't like! My sister makes fun of me she says, old lady! It's hard to eat food like an apple. But I can eat bananas, that's good! Now my tooth is back and I'm never going to jump on the bed any more. I wonder what is going to happen when Sophia comes tomorrow! And I hope my tooth doesn't come out again, or els I have to go to the dentist again.

Children's dictated stories may further show their acquisition of more complex syntactic knowledge. As they dictate a story, their awareness of the literate register is evident. Since the story is dictated, the child is free of the challenge of putting the story on paper. Earlier in this chapter we examined Craig's (age 8) written response to a storybook. In this section we will look at his story, "The All-Star Game," which was dictated. This dictated story is longer and involves more complex syntactic structures than did his earlier book response. (Line numbers have been added for discussion purposes.)

[1]One day I was playing in the All-Star game.
[2]It was my turn up to bat. I swung at the first
[3]pitch and missed it.
[4]And then I hit a triple! Then I ran very fast to
[5]first, then second, and then third. Then my
[6]friend, Tony, was up to bat.
[7]He got a single and drove me in. And then
[8]another person on the team struck out. And then
[9]another person on my team hit a pop-up,
[10]and then Tony tagged up and got to second. Then
[11]another person on my team got a hit, and Tony
[12]ran to third and then home.
[13]The other person was tagged out at the plate.
[14]Then the other team was up to bat. I was at
[15]first base. The person on the other team hit a
[16]grounder to first, and I picked up the ball and
[17]tagged him! Then another person on that team hit
[18]a line-drive out. And the inning was over. The
[19]next person on our team up to bat was Chris. He
[20]swung at the first pitch and hit a foul ball.
[21]He swung the second time and broke the
[22]scoreboard!! And that was an automatic home
[23]run! We continued the game on Monday night and
[24]the final score was 35 to 10!

Craig's personal interest in the story he told, and the opportunity to create the story during dictation, contributed to his use of more complex language and to a more detailed story. Although Craig's story contained a variety of sentence structures, he frequently used *and, and then,* and *then* to begin new thoughts or events. Use of these conjunctions in this manner is typical of primary-age children.

Pronoun Reference

Primary-age children continue to develop a clearer understanding of how pronouns are used in oral and written language (Menyuk, 1988). When pronouns are used in oral language, their referents are often indicated by the context/ setting in which the speech occurs; however, in written language pronoun referents need to be identified through specific syntactic features. **Anaphora** is a term used to refer to the "linking of a pronoun or an article back to its prior referent or mention in the linguistic context" (Warren & McCloskey, 1990, p. 215).

In Craig's story about "The All-Star Game," he was able to use pronouns effectively to refer to his friend, Tony, in line 7, and to Chris in lines 19 and 21. Although Craig's effective use of pronoun reference was limited, it is interesting to note that when he referred to Tony again in lines 10 and 11, he used Tony's name rather than a pronoun. To use the pronoun *he* to refer to Tony in those two instances would not have been effective because Craig had referred to "another person" in between the two references to Tony. Appropriate use of pronouns involves not only knowing which pronoun to use but also knowing when pronouns can be used effectively in text to refer to a previous noun without confusing the reader or listener. Craig demonstrated his awareness that in certain situations, the initial reference to "Tony" should be reintroduced (Menyuk, 1988).

Passive Sentences

During primary grades, children are more accurate in understanding and producing passive sentences. As we noted in Chapter 8, passive sentences require a different type of linguistic processing because passive sentences do not follow the expected subject-verb-object sequence. Children appear to use a variety of clues in understanding passive sentences: contextual support, the presence of action verbs, and the presence of a preposition such as *from* or *by* (Owens, 1988), as in "The window was broken by the ball." Teachers can informally observe primary children's syntactic knowledge by providing opportunities for children to participate in creating their own written stories and participating in story dictation. Through careful observation, teachers can become better acquainted with children's current and developing syntactic knowledge of oral and written language. Children's conscious/metalinguistic awareness of syntax becomes increasingly important as they are expected to manipulate syntactic features in such language arts tasks as identifying complete (or incomplete) sentences, using spelling words in sentences (Scott, 1995), or placing punctuation in paragraphs. Children's metalinguistic awareness of syntax appears to be enhanced during the process of learning to write when children begin to consciously manipulate language at the phrase, clause, and sentence levels (Scott, 1995).

DEVELOPMENT OF MORPHEMIC KNOWLEDGE

Primary age children have acquired most of the inflectional morphemes for marking plural, possession, and past tense; however, their knowledge of how to comprehend and use derivational morphemes is still developing. *Derivational morphemes* are bound morphemes used with word stems that change the way in which the word functions in the sentence (Owens, 2001). For example, adding *-ly* to an adjective makes the word an adverb, as in *quick-quickly*. Adding *-ness* to an adjective makes it a noun, as in *mad-madness*. Derivational morphemes include both prefixes and suffixes. Examples of word stems with specific derivational morphemes are listed in Figure 10.3.

During primary grades, children begin to form adverbs using the suffix *-ly* and may use other derivational morphemes as well depending upon the presence of such morphemes in their oral and written language environments.

Jenny's story demonstrates two instances of adverb use:

> I was riding my bike with the kids, and then sudden*ly* a car came, and I stopped as quick*ly* as I can.

In some instances, the use of derivational morphemes also changes the last vowel in the word. In the primary years, children begin to learn this "vowel-shifting" (Owens, 2001). For example, *divine* becomes *divinity,* and *explain* becomes *explanation.* This knowledge is acquired gradually through opportunities to hear and use more semantically complex language.

As children enter and progress through the primary grades, they may encounter more formal morphemic instruction in reading and language arts classes, as decoding and comprehension are emphasized. Teachers may emphasize the morphemic knowledge present in Standard American English when children participate orally in class discussions and conversations. Children also develop morphemic knowledge when decoding and comprehending

FIGURE 10.3
Examples of Free Morphemes and Derivational Bound Morphemes

Free Morpheme	Bound Morpheme	Changed Word
happy	un-	unhappy
happy	-ness	happiness
respect	dis-	disrespect
respect	-ful	respectful
quick	-ly	quickly
quick	-er	quicker

written text and workbook exercises, such as studying prefixes, suffixes, and root words. Anglin's research (1993) indicates that primary-age children use their knowledge of morphemes (bound and free) to figure out word meanings. This research examined children's receptive vocabulary and found that children were using their knowledge of morphemes to develop clues about the meaning of a specific word.

Around the age of 7, children begin to create gerund forms (Hulit & Howard, 1993). A **gerund** is a verbal noun formed by adding -*ing* to a verb; for example, *walk* becomes *walking*. Gerunds are used in any way that nouns are used. Kiki's story indicates knowledge of gerund formation in her use of *spanking* as a noun and *spanked* as a verb:

> Once upon a time there was a bad giraffe and she thought there was house nearby, and then she went in it, and she sort of got a *spanking,* and then they saw there was a box of candy nearby, and they *spanked* her some more, and then they went in the garbage, and then it was the end.

Primary-age children's morphemic knowledge may be observed in their early attempts at encoding their thoughts into words on paper. While this knowledge is related to children's phonemic knowledge, as discussed in an earlier section, their invented spellings also indicate their understandings of word formation and morphemes.

In Johnny's (age 8) story, "The Boy and the Bird," he used a variety of inflectional endings and derivational morphemes in communicating his story. An excerpt from his story follows, with some of the inflectional endings and derivational morphemes in italics.

> One morning Tom went out to play. He saw a big bird. The bird was red and brown. It was the bigg*est* bird Tom had ever seen. The bird flew down, Tom gave him some bread. Tom went clos*er* and the bird didn't fly away. He went even clos*er*. Then he pet the bird, the bird was not scared. After a few years he nam*ed* the bird Luke. One day Tom got on the bird, he started to run, he flapp*ed* his wings and flew over Tom*'s* house. The big bird land*ed*. Tom got off. Tom went in his back yard. The bird follow*ed* him. Tom got on Luke and said, bring me to my friend Joe*'s* house.

In Johnny's story he used inflectional endings for past tense with regular verbs and to show possession. Comparative suffixes, a form of derivational morphemes, were also used (e.g., clos*er*, bigg*est*). Past tense was appropriately used, except in one instance (see pet*). In the last line of the story, present tense was more appropriate since it was a part of a dialogue.

Children's oral language may not contain the same use of morphemic knowledge as their written language. When using more casual language orally, such as slang and dialect, children may not observe the same use of inflectional endings as they do when using written language.

DEVELOPMENT OF PRAGMATIC KNOWLEDGE

During the primary years children begin to make specific requests for clarification and become increasingly more competent in conversations (Owens, 2001). They are better able to take into account what their listeners know when engaged in conversation. In reference to Anderson's (1992) study discussed in Chapters 6 and 8, primary-age children indicated a wider range of registers and more complex modifications in their speech to fit in the various contexts of communication. Primary-age children are also better able to maintain a conversational topic, produce polite direct and indirect requests, and make adjustments in their speech in response to requests for clarification from others (Warren & McCloskey, 1997). Children now give more complete descriptions and comparisons when referring to specific objects (Menyuk, 1988).

Indirect Requests

Primary-age children become more aware of the intent of indirect requests and the appropriate response to such requests (Menyuk, 1988; Owens, 2001). The indirect request is meant to be interpreted as a request, even though it appears to be a yes-no question. This indirectness is considered a more polite way of requesting a particular action from another person. Requests can be direct, as in "Open the door," or indirect, as in "Can you open the door?" Six-year-olds are likely to respond to an indirect request literally, responding with a "yes," while 8-year-olds generally respond with the requested action (Owens, 2001).

Pragmatic Knowledge of Written Language

Children's awareness of the pragmatic aspects of written language is influenced by the contexts surrounding them. During the primary years a good part of each day is spent in a school setting. The ways in which written language is used and the opportunities for children to participate in a wide range of contexts influences the development of their pragmatic knowledge. Children will show this awareness when they are given opportunities at home and at school to use writing in a variety of ways (Taylor & Vawter, 1978). Teachers who carefully observe the ways children engage in reading and writing can use these observations and new understandings to better develop and implement curriculum (Dixon-Kraus, 1996).

In her detailed study, Bissex (1980) identified various forms or purposes of writing in her son's spontaneous (not elicited) writing during his kindergarten and primary years (ages 5–9). During that time seven forms were used consistently: (1) signs, labels, and captions; (2) stories; (3) little books; (4) directions; (5) lists or catalogues; (6) newspapers; and (7) cards, notes, letters. Three forms appeared early, but were discontinued by age 8: (1) statements; (2) school-type exercises; and (3) riddles. Late-appearing (after age 6) forms included: (1) rhymes;

(2) charts, organizers, and planners; (3) diary; (4) quizzes (questions and answers); (5) information and observation notebooks; and (6) codes.

In Heath's (1983) ethnographic study (described in Chapter 3), she noted the uses of literacy activities within the two communities of Trackton and Roadville. In each community reading and writing served a variety of purposes and functions. Preschool children in these environments learned the value of literacy from the interactions of those around them, and later when attending formal schooling, they learned the ways in which language is used to form written messages. Gradually children began to incorporate features of stories they had read in their reading books into their own written stories, features such as character introduction, story parts, and chronological order. In a second grade class observed by Heath, children were encouraged to note, categorize, and analyze the ways people spoke and the way those people used reading and writing. The teacher also encouraged children to become aware of five different ways of talking: dialect, casual, formal, conversational, and standard. In this classroom children's acquisition of pragmatic knowledge provided a framework for language learning in general. They became aware of how they were using language and why.

Dahl, Freppon, and McIntyre's (1992) research emphasized the importance of opportunities for primary-age children to engage in the writing process. Their study observed children's writing in classrooms that offered varied opportunities for writing. In classrooms with opportunities to write frequently and more social and instructional support for beginning writing, children showed more gains in being able to compose more complex writing.

Children's beginning writing and reading also appears to be enhanced in classrooms that offer varied and frequent opportunities for children to talk with each other and with the teacher during literacy-related activities, such as talking, collaborating, and conferencing during story writing (Dahl, Freppon, & McIntyre, 1992; Galda, Pellegrini, Shockley, & Stahl, 1994–95).

The variety of written text genres used in primary classrooms may also influence the ways in which children construct their own texts (Chapman, 1995; Duke, 2000). While it is not known how much experience with a genre is needed to comprehend and produce that genre, there is widespread agreement that substantial experience with a genre is needed. Chapman (1995) studied the types of texts (genres) created by first graders along with the range of genres embedded in their classroom curriculum. Children used a variety of genre, including simple and more complex narratives (i.e., recounting events or "news"), notes, written dialogues, and verse/poetry. Chapman emphasizes the need for primary teachers to examine the range of genres included in the classroom curriculum since children may be learning about genre through this immersion even though explicit instruction in the genre does not occur.

Duke's research (2000) documented the relative scarcity of informational texts used in first grade, with an average of only 3.6 minutes per day for activities involving written informational texts and a lack of informational text in the classroom environment on walls, bulletin boards, and shelves. This scarcity was even more pronounced in low SES school districts, where the average time spent on informational texts was only 1.9 minutes; half of the low SES class-rooms experienced no informational texts.

Throughout the primary years, language acquisition and development in each of the five areas of language knowledge (phonetic, morphemic, syntactic, semantic, and pragmatic) is influenced by the home and school environments in which the children interact. In Chapter 11, specific strategies and activities for enhancing primary children's language acquisition and development are described.

SUMMARY

In the primary years, children's language continues to develop and increase in amount and complexity with respect to phonetic, semantic, syntactic, morphemic, and pragmatic knowledge. With increased time spent at school and with an increased emphasis on formal instruction, children's language environment changes dramatically from the preschool and kindergarten settings. Classroom interactions increasingly incorporate the academic/literate register, and children are expected to begin to manipulate language units consciously. Thus, primary age children's metalinguistic language knowledge becomes important to their success at school.

✳ ✳ ✳ CHAPTER REVIEW

1. Terms to review:

   onset   connotative meaning
   rime   anaphora
   denotative meaning   gerund

2. How is the primary linguistic environment different from a preschool language environment?

3. What two phonemes are children typically acquiring during the primary years?

4. Give several examples of onset and rime.

5. Describe the central concerns of the current controversy regarding phonics instruction.

6. In what ways does invented spelling indicate a child's phonetic knowledge?

7. Distinguish between *denotative* and *connotative* meanings.

8. What is the range of expressive vocabulary (word count) for primary children?

9. In what ways does a child's comprehension of figurative language indicate more complex semantic knowledge?

10. Describe the increasing complexity of primary children's syntactic knowledge.

11. List the three inflectional morphemes acquired by most primary children.

12. Define *derivational morpheme.* What derivational morphemes are primary children acquiring?

13. Summarize the pragmatic language competencies of primary-age children.

✳ ✳ ✳ CHAPTER EXTENSION ACTIVITIES

1. Observe in a first-grade classroom writing center for 30 to 40 minutes. Describe children's use of phonetic knowledge in their writing. Give specific examples.

2. Collect several children's original stories from a second- or third-grade classroom. Look for instances of invented spelling. Determine whether the spelling is letter-name or phonemic. Are there consistencies in the way phonemes or sounds are represented? Give examples.

3. Read a book that features figurative language, such as an *Amelia Bedelia* book, to a group of primary-age children. Discuss with the children the figurative language. Record your observations about children's comprehension of the specific figurative language.

4. Ask a primary-age child to dictate a story to you. Analyze the story for the child's use of anaphora, passive sentences, and sentence complexity.

5. Collect the written stories of three primary-age children. Analyze their stories for morphemic endings (inflectional and derivational).

6. Observe a primary writing center for 30 minutes on three different occasions. Examine the children's written stories/texts to determine the genre of the text. Compare your observations with the purpose of writing documented by Bissex (1980).

✳ ✳ ✳ REFERENCES

Adams, M. (1990). *Beginning to read: Thinking and learning about print.* Urbana, IL: Center for the Study of Reading, University of Illinois at Urbana-Champaign.

Anderson, E. (1992). *Speaking with style: The sociolinguistic skills of children.* London: Routledge.

Anglin, J. (1993). *Vocabulary development: A morphological analysis.* Monograph of the Society for Research in Child Development. Serial No. 238, Vol. 58(10).

Berko Gleason, J. (1989). Studying language development. In J. Berko Gleason (Ed.), *The development of language* (2nd ed., pp. 1–34). Columbus, OH: Merrill.

Bissex, G. (1980). *GNYS AT WRK: A child learns to write and read.* Cambridge, MA: Harvard University Press.

Chall, J. (1967). *Learning to read: The great debate.* New York: McGraw-Hill.

Chall, J. (1983). *Learning to read: The great debate* (Rev. ed.). New York: McGraw-Hill.

Chapman, M. (1995). The sociocognitive construction of written genres in first grade. *Research in the Teaching of English, 29*(2), 164–192.

Chomsky, C. (1972). Stages in language development and reading exposure. *Harvard Educational Review, 42,* 1–33.

Crystal, D. (1987). *The Cambridge encyclopedia of language.* New York: Cambridge University Press.

Dahl, K., Freppon, P., & McIntyre, E. (1992, April). A comparison of knowledge construction in writing by low-SES urban children in skills-based and whole language classrooms in the early grades. Paper presented at the annual meeting of the American Educational Research Association, San Francisco.

Dixon-Kraus, L. (1996). *Vygotsky in the classroom: Mediated literacy instruction and assessment.* White Plains, NY: Longman.

Duke, N. (2000). 3.6 minutes per day: The scarcity of informational texts in first grade. *The Reading Teacher, 35*(2), 202–224.

Fields, M., Spangler, K., & Lee, D. (1991). *Let's begin reading right: Developmentally appropriate beginning literacy.* New York: Merrill.

Foorman, B., Francis, D., Novy, D., & Liberman, D. (1991). How letter-sound instruction mediates progress in first-grade reading and spelling. *Journal of Educational Psychology, 83*(4), 456–469.

Galda, L., Pellegrini, A., Shockley, B., & Stahl, S. (December 1994–January 1995). Talking to read and write. *Reading Today,* 32.

Gentry, J. R. (1982). An analysis of developmental spelling in GNYS AT WRK. *The Reading Teacher, 36*(2), 192–200.

Goswami, U. (1986). Children's use of analogy in learning to read: A developmental study. *Journal of Experimental Child Psychology, 42,* 73–83.

Goswami, U. (1990). A special link between rhyming skill and the use of orthographic analogies by beginning readers. *Journal of Child Psychology and Psychiatry, 31*(2), 301–311.

Goswami, U., & Mead, F. (1992). Onset and rime awareness and analogies in reading. *Reading Research Quarterly, 27*(2), 153–162.

Harris, T., & Hodges, R. (Eds.). (1995). *The literacy dictionary: The vocabulary of reading and writing.* Newark, DE: International Reading Association.

Heath, S. (1983). *Ways with words.* Cambridge, MA: Cambridge University Press.

Henderson, E., & Templeton, S. (1986). A developmental perspective of formal spelling instruction through alphabet, pattern, and meaning. *The Elementary School Journal, 86*(3), 305–316.

Hulit, L., & Howard, M. (1993). *Born to talk: An introduction to speech and language development.* New York: Merrill.

Jewell, M., & Zintz, M. (1990). *Learning to read and write naturally* (2nd ed.). Dubuque, IA: Kendall Hunt Publishing.

Mahoney, D., & Mann, V. (1991). Using children's humor to clarify the relationship between linguistic awareness and early reading ability. Paper presented at the Biennial Meeting of the Society for Research in Child Development, Seattle, Washington. ERIC ED 341 498.

McGee, L., & Richgels, D. (2000). *Literacy's beginnings: Supporting young readers and writers* (3rd ed.). Boston: Allyn & Bacon.

McGhee, P. (1979). *Humor: Its origin and development.* San Francisco: W.H. Freeman & Company.

Menyuk, P. (1984). Language development and reading. In J. Flood (Ed.), *Understanding reading comprehension* (pp. 101–121). Newark, DE: International Reading Association.

Menyuk, P. (1988). *Language development: Knowledge and use.* Glenview, IL: Scott Foresman.

Owens, R. (1988). *Language development: An introduction* (2nd ed.). Columbus, OH: Merrill.

Owens, R. (2001). *Language development: An introduction* (5th ed.). Boston: Allyn & Bacon.

Pepicello, W., & Weisberg, R. (1983). Linguistic and humor. In P. McGhee & J. Goldstein (Eds.), *Handbook of humor research: Volume I. Basic issues* (pp. 59–83). New York: Springer-Verlag.

Raphael, T., & Hiebert, E. (1996). *Creating an integrated approach to literacy instruction.* Fort Worth, TX: Harcourt Brace College Publishers.

Sander, E. (1972). When are speech sounds learned? *Journal of Speech and Hearing Disorders, 37,* 55–63.

Schwartz, J. (1988). *Encouraging early literacy: An integrated approach to reading and writing in N-3.* Portsmouth, NH: Heinemann.

Schultz, T. (1974). Development of the appreciation of riddles. *Child Development, 45,* 100–105.

Scott, C. (1995). Syntax for school-age children: A discourse perspective. In M. Fey, J. Windsor, & S. Warren (Eds.), *Language intervention: Preschool through the elementary years* (pp. 107–144). Baltimore, MD: Paul H. Brooks.

Sharmat, M. (1978) *Nate the Great and the sticky case.* New York: Coward, McCann & Geoghegan.

Sulzby, E., Barnhart, J., & Hieshima, J. (1989). Forms of wiring and rereading from writing. In J. Mason (Ed.), *Reading and writing connections* (pp. 31–64). Boston, MA: Allyn & Bacon.

Sutton-Smith, B. (1975). A developmental structural account of riddles. In B. Hirschenblatt-Gimblett (Ed.), *Speech, play and display.* The Hague, Netherlands: Mouton.

Taylor, N., & Vawter, J. (1978). Helping children discover the functions of written language. *Language Arts, 55*(8), 941–945.

Teale, W., & Martinez, M. (1989). Connecting writing: Fostering emergent literacy in kindergarten children. In J. Mason (Ed.), *Reading and writing connections* (pp. 177-198). Boston, MA: Allyn & Bacon.

Teale, W., & Sulzby, E. (1987). *Emergent literacy: Writing and reading.* Norwood, NJ: Ablex Publishing.

Temple, C., Nathan, R., & Burris, N. (1982). *The beginnings of writing.* Boston: Allyn & Bacon.

Temple, C., Nathan, R., Burris, N., & Temple, F. (1988). *The beginnings of writing* (2nd ed.). Boston, MA: Allyn & Bacon.

Warren, A., & McCloskey, L. (1997). Pragmatics: Language in social contexts. In J. Berko Gleason (Ed.), *The development of language* (4th ed.). Boston, MA: Allyn & Bacon.

Wilde, S. (1992). *You kan red this!* Portsmouth, NH: Heinemann.

11

ENHANCING LANGUAGE DEVELOPMENT IN THE PRIMARY YEARS

By first grade most children have developed a basic level of communicative competence. They can participate in conversations and use language to communicate their needs and wishes. It is important, however, that primary grade teachers continue to enhance children's language development in each of the five areas of language knowledge: phonetic, semantic, syntactic, morphemic, and pragmatic.

In the primary years, curricula are more formal and more firmly established. Many school districts adopt commercially developed curricula that all teachers are expected to follow. While classroom teachers may not have control over the specific commercial curriculum that is selected for implementation, they do control the way in which the implementation occurs through the manner in which children are engaged in the curricular activities and experiences. The way in which a curriculum is implemented has a strong influence on the presence of "talk" in the classroom and the ways in which children become engaged in learning activities.

Curricula are often implemented in either of two ways: (1) task-centered or (2) learner-centered. In task-centered implementation, the focus is on adhering to the sequence and scope of learning tasks provided in the curricular materials. Learning activities strictly follow the predetermined sequence and duration. In contrast, learner-centered implementation focuses on children's individual needs, learning styles, and responses to instruction. Learner-centered implementation strives to fit the curriculum to the needs of the student. Thus, the sequence or duration of activities may vary, depending upon a teacher's perception of children's needs and learning styles. This approach recognizes that planning should always reflect an awareness of students' needs rather than simply following a presequenced curriculum (Strickland, 1998).

Lindfors (1990) challenges teachers to create "classroom communities" where children's talk is invited and sustained, allowing children "to connect with others, to understand their world, and to reveal themselves within it" (p. 38). A key component of classroom communities is talk—talk about what is being learned and about responses to the learning process. This awareness of the important role of classroom talk is a relatively recent development. In the past, a quiet classroom was considered the ideal, with students silently working independently on learning tasks. Talk was restricted to formal recitation exercises or oral reading. Researchers and classroom teachers have begun to question whether a quiet, ordered classroom is the best learning environment (Kasten, 1997; Raphael & Hiebert, 1996; Wells & Chang-Wells, 1996). When classroom talk is overly limited or restricted, children lose the opportunity to engage in focused conversations and do not learn how to express their thinking, clarify their misunderstandings, or question other's perceptions.

Teachers who understand the critical role of talk in the process of learning create classroom environments with a strong foundation for children's cognitive growth and the development of "high mental processes that constitute reading and writing" (Raphael & Hiebert, 1996, p. 90).

TEACHING/INTERACTION STRATEGIES

At the primary level, the main interaction patterns include linguistic scaffolding, mediation, and questioning. Teachers' active listening is an integral part of each of these strategies. Only through active listening can teachers develop awareness of students' needs and learning styles.

Linguistic scaffolding provides a supportive verbal framework that sustains and encourages children's participation in both social and instructional conversations. Questioning, expansion, and repetition are specific ways in which linguistic scaffolding is created (see Chapter 2). At the primary level, teachers use linguistic scaffolding to support children's participation in a whole class discussion and with small groups and individual children. Through active listening, teachers become aware of children's thinking and then can maintain and extend their verbal participation.

Mediation is an interaction pattern used by teachers to simplify a learning stimulus or task to facilitate student learning and participation (see Chapter 2). For example, when reading a book, the teacher may substitute more familiar vocabulary as a way to begin to create connections to the more precise or technical vocabulary of the text.

Mediation also occurs when teachers engage in "thinking aloud" or "reflecting aloud" (Matthews, 1999, p. 36). Through thinking/reflecting aloud, teachers verbalize to their students their own thought processes. They make explicit what is happening and why, what worked in the past, and what options may exist. In this way, teachers are showing children how language is used as a tool for learning. This type of verbal mediation is an inherent part of successful instructional interactions.

At the primary level, questioning most frequently takes place in instances where children are expected to recite what they have learned. Questioning is used as a way to evaluate or monitor children's comprehension or learning. In many instances, questions found in commercial curricula are used as the format for the expected recitation. While this recitational questioning serves a purpose in monitoring learning, questioning should also be used at the primary level to encourage children to expand their thinking through inquiry and discovery. Through active listening, teachers can develop follow-up questions that will stimulate higher levels of cognitive processing such as compare-contrast, inference making, problem solving, generalization, and synthesis.

The amount of wait time after a question is asked is critical to the type of interaction that occurs and to the content of that interaction. Rowe's research (1986; cited in Raphael & Hiebert, 1996) concluded that increasing the wait time from 1 to 3 seconds had significant beneficial effects. With 3 seconds of wait time, the development of ideas showed more continuity. While the volume of questions asked decreased, the cognitive complexity of the questions increased. The increased wait time was also characterized by teachers incorporating students' responses into the instructional dialogue, which would provide for more contingent questioning at higher levels of cognitive processing.

OVERVIEW OF LANGUAGE-RELATED PRIMARY CURRICULAR GOALS

At the primary level, the main emphasis of the curriculum is often on the acquisition of reading, with little attention paid to the other language arts, such as listening, speaking, and writing. When the acquisition of reading is emphasized to the exclusion of other language forms, children's total language competencies are limited in their continued development. Primary curricula need to address all of the language arts and recognize the differing roles of receptive and expressive language. A balanced language development program addresses each of the five aspects of language knowledge and both receptive and expressive modes (listening, speaking, reading, and writing).

Children's long-term success in school is influenced by their ability to use language for many different purposes and in different settings. This functional or pragmatic knowledge of language is represented in Halliday's (1973, 1975; Pinnell, 1996) seven categories of language function: instrumental language, regulatory language, interactional language, personal language, imaginative language, heuristic language, and informative language (see also Chapter 4). Pinnell (1996) encourages teachers to engage in strategies and activities that promote children's awareness of, and experiences with, the whole range of language functions. The primary years are a time in which children's language competencies can be developed in ways that foster effective, lifelong communication.

KEY ROLE OF LISTENING COMPETENCIES

Children's listening competencies provide access to learning, particularly at the primary level, where more of students' time during the school day is spent listening. Ineffective listening strategies make learning tasks harder and often result in frustration. Effective listening involves several components that require active cognitive processing. Lundsteen (1990) has identified seven components: receiving the message, focusing on the language used, discriminating what has been said, assigning meaning to what has been said, monitoring the ongoing communication, remembering what has been said, and responding to what has been said.

Listening competencies are critical in facilitating the other language arts (speaking, writing, and reading). At the primary level children need opportunities to further develop their listening competencies to be able to respond effectively in each of the following settings:

1. listening to and comprehending oral instructions/ directions in a large group setting;
2. listening to and comprehending explanations of concepts from teachers or guest speakers;

3. listening to peers in collaborative group work;

4. listening to class discussion; and

5. listening when engaged in conversations with one or more others.

At the primary level, listening skills are essential because within this setting, children may be expected to listen for over half of their classroom activity time, and over half of that time is spent listening to their teacher (Wilt, 1950, cited in Wolvin & Coakley, 1985). Primary teachers can enhance children's listening comprehension by modeling effective listening strategies, such as active listening and sending feedback (Wolvin & Coakley, 1985). Teachers can also explicitly encourage children to be active listeners who consciously focus on the message being spoken and then to give feedback to the speaker as to whether they have comprehended the message. Primary students should have opportunities to continue to develop their listening skills because as they progress through elementary and secondary school, the amount of time they are expected to listen is likely to increase, depending upon the specific class involved.

Teachers who constantly repeat oral directions for their students may be doing their students a disservice by this repetition since it may not encourage careful listening. It may be better for a teacher to have another listener/student repeat the directions for other students rather than the teacher repeating the directions. That way, another child provides a summary of the directions (Lundsteen, 1990).

PLANNING ACTIVITIES TO ENHANCE PRIMARY-AGE STUDENTS' LANGUAGE DEVELOPMENT

Language-enhancing activities at the primary level include both exploratory-discovery center activities and teacher-directed activities. Throughout exploratory and teacher-directed activities, children need to be encouraged to use language to learn, to reflect, and to inquire. Teachers facilitate this language use by linguistic scaffolding, mediation, and questioning.

EXPLORATORY-DISCOVERY CENTER ACTIVITIES

A main focus within developmentally appropriate practice for primary classrooms is the provision of open-ended, hands-on learning activities (Bredekamp & Copple, 1997). While these activities resemble the exploratory activities recommended for preschool and kindergarten classrooms, primary-level exploratory activities present opportunities for more focused engagement and more complex interactions with the materials provided.

Exploratory learning activities at the primary level have been described as involving "investigative play" (Wassermann, 1990). Such learning activities are characterized as being open-ended, generating ideas, enhancing the development of cross-curricular concepts, encouraging children to be active learners, and involving cooperative grouping. Classrooms with this focus are also described as having a "can-do" perspective, in which children develop self-confidence in their abilities to interact effectively in their environment through successful risk taking and problem solving (Wassermann, 1990).

Three general areas of exploratory activities appropriate for primary classrooms include a classroom library center, a writing center, and content/concept learning centers, which focus on math-science, social studies-math, or science-social studies content. All children in a classroom should have ran equal opportunity to engage in each center. Center activities should not be restricted to students who have finished their "seatwork." Procedures for using each center should also be well explained as the teacher introduces the center to the class. Implementation of each center should be consistent and simple enough for children to be independent of teacher assistance. In the description of possible center areas that follows, the emphasis is on clarifying the potential of the activity to enhance one or more aspects of language knowledge.

Classroom Library Center

The classroom library is the focal point of the primary classroom. The materials provided in the library will provide a foundation for the learning that occurs. A wide range of genre should be provided: various types of fiction (realistic fiction, fables, fairy tales, mysteries), nonfiction (alphabet books, concept books), and poetry. At the primary level it is still important for books to have frequent illustrations to provide contextual information about the concepts presented in the books. Books should also be rotated through the classroom library to keep student interest and motivation high. First graders will use the classroom library more successfully if the teacher has featured some of the books in the center in class read-alouds. As children develop more independent decoding skills, they will enjoy new books without first having them read aloud by the teacher.

Writing Center

The major goal of the writing center at the primary level is to facilitate the development of children's competencies in using written language to communicate for a variety of purposes. Children are encouraged to incorporate what they have learned throughout the classroom in their writing. Ideas generated during group shared storytime or read-alouds or concept development activities can become the focus of their writing. First-grade children may use more illustrations in their stories since illustrations can support their efforts in communicating a particular idea or action. Gradually as they are able to use print more conventionally, illustrations carry less of a role.

Big books and a comfortable place to read make a classroom library a favorite place to be.

The setup of a writing center at the primary level is similar to writing centers in kindergarten, but a few differences should be noted. Primary-level writing centers are more likely to have lined paper available, along with plain paper. Additional materials are included for primary children to use in bookmaking, such as glue, scissors, a stapler, and a hole punch. In addition, a computer or a typewriter may be included for children to use in creating their stories.

Through creative writing center activities, children's language knowledge is enhanced in the following ways during the primary years:

1. Pragmatic knowledge is increased as children have the opportunity to see how written language is used to communicate for different purposes: invitations, thank-you notes, lists, personal narratives/stories, signs, and nonfiction texts on a particular concept or related concepts.

2. Syntactic knowledge is increased from children's experiences in putting into print their experiences and thoughts. As they share their ideas through print, they gradually use more complex sentence and text structure to communicate.

3. Children's productive semantic knowledge is enhanced as they have an opportunity to use their own vocabulary in composing their written stories and other texts.

4. Pragmatic knowledge of how written language is used for different purposes is enhanced through children's writing center activities.

5. Morphemic knowledge is enhanced through writing center activities as children use inflectional morphemes to indicate past tense, possession, and plurality.

Content/Concept Learning Centers

This type of learning center focuses on a concept or set of related concepts and is designed to encourage children to explore materials independently or to solve problems. For example, a math-science center might focus on measuring the length of different common objects. A social studies-science center might focus on matching pictures of animals with separate pictures of their habitats.

To enhance children's conceptual development and their vocabulary, teachers should label the materials in each center with the appropriate vocabulary. Students should have opportunities to discuss their learning center experiences in either a large group or small group setting.

Word Walls

A word wall is a visual display of words that have been written on cards and mounted on a classroom wall. Words placed on the word wall represent children's high-frequency words and/or major content/concept words used in the learning centers. Words displayed can be added and deleted as students' needs for specific words change and develop. Once word cards are removed from the wall, they can be kept for individual student use in the writing center, perhaps on a ring or in a file box. Word walls are often placed in the area of a writing center so that children can refer to the words during the writing process (Casbergue, 1998).

Take-Home Exploratory Activities

Children may not have sufficient time at school to engage in exploratory reading and writing activities, or they may have limited literacy materials at home. One way to increase language-enhancing opportunities for children is to provide take-home suitcases or book bags that are equipped for reading or writing activities.

A reading suitcase is equipped with one or more storybooks to be either read alone or with a parent (depending upon the child's reading competencies). A spiral sketchbook along with drawing or writing implements are also included. After the child has read (or listened to the story read), he can draw or write his response to the story. When the reading suitcase is returned to the classroom after a day or two, the child may have the opportunity to share his written response with the class. As several children use the reading suitcase, a collection of responses is developed. The response book can be placed in the

Opportunities to take storybooks home allow children to explore and refine their interactions with written language.

classroom library after all children have had a chance to use the reading suitcase. Children will enjoy looking at and reading/rereading their own responses and other children's responses.

A writing suitcase is similar to a reading suitcase except that no storybook is included. Instead the suitcase contains a greater assortment of writing and drawing implements (markers, chalk, pens, and pencils) and a greater variety of materials for making different book formats: blank books, assorted papers in different sizes, scissors, transparent tape, a stapler, paper clips, construction paper for book covers, and a handheld hole punch. At the first-grade level, an alphabet card can be included to assist children in letter formation if they have questions. At the third-grade level, the letter card would be written in cursive lettering. In using the writing suitcase, children might need to have the suitcase for several days. Teachers might provide a theme or suggested story stems for children to use in their writing. When the writing suitcase is returned to the classroom, each child should have an opportunity to share her writing with the class.

Through these two take-home activities, primary-age children have extended opportunities to explore and refine their language knowledge through reading and writing.

TEACHER-DIRECTED ACTIVITIES

At the primary level, teacher-directed activities occur in both large group and whole class settings and small group settings. Whole class teacher-directed activities involve experiences in which the entire class can participate. Large group teacher-directed activities can be used to enhance children's acquisition of important aspects of language knowledge. In the large group setting, the activities provide opportunity to develop a shared knowledge base and frame of reference for the entire class. This can facilitate children's sharing of ideas and also focus their communication on shared events. Examples of large group language activities for primary grades described in this chapter include teacher read-alouds, oral discussions, dramatic improvisation, share-and-tell, language experience stories, author's chair, and media presentations on video or audio tapes.

Small group language activities are more focused on the specific needs of a subgroup of children or may focus on encouraging a higher level of involvement and group interaction between a few children. Suggested small group activities described in this chapter include word study activities, shared reading, literature circles, and collaborative/cooperative projects.

Teacher Read-Alouds

When a primary teacher reads to a class, children are encouraged to develop a shared knowledge base of the concepts in the text, the sequence of the events, and the specific language used in the text. This shared knowledge provides children a common frame of reference on which they can focus their discussions and interactions.

Books selected to share during read-alouds should have a language level appropriate to the listening comprehension of children in the classroom. By selecting and using texts with different levels of complexity, teachers can develop their awareness of the text appropriate for their students. The introduction of chapter books during teacher read-alouds is an effective way of enhancing children's ability to understand more complex story lines and characters. It is also important to include books that have dialect speech and other varied language styles, such as humor, figurative language, alliteration, and rhyme (Glazer, 2000).

Teacher read-alouds can enhance language development in many ways:

1. Receptive phonetic knowledge is increased as children hear their teacher's pronunciation of the words (and sounds) in the text. When big books are used, children can better see the relationship between speech and print, which enhances their receptive phonetic knowledge of written language.

2. Receptive semantic knowledge is enhanced as new words are encountered in the texts and explained by the teacher. Illustrations accompanying the texts may enhance comprehension of the text.

3. Receptive syntactic knowledge is increased as children hear the complex sentence and text structures contained in the shared books. A teacher's fluent and expressive reading enhances children's processing of text that may be at a higher level of complexity than their current expressive syntactic knowledge.

4. In a similar way, receptive morphemic knowledge is enhanced through hearing the teacher read the story text. Through a teacher's clear enunciation, children can become more aware of word structure and its relationship to meaning.

5. Receptive pragmatic knowledge is developed when a variety of genre are used during teacher read-alouds. Through the use of a variety of genre, children can develop different expectations for different texts (fairy tales, fables, narratives, poetry, mysteries, and nonfiction).

Oral Discussions

Teacher read-alouds are usually accompanied by an oral discussion related to the book just read. Often these discussions focus on determining children's comprehension of the text. It is important for teachers to use a variety of questions, both literal and higher level inferential. Teachers should also use linguistic scaffolding to support and extend children's responses.

In these discussions, teachers are enhancing children's productive/expressive language competencies. As children develop answers to specific questions, they are using their phonetic, syntactic, semantic, morphemic, and pragmatic language knowledge. Based upon class needs, teachers may also decide to focus the oral discussion on a particular aspect of language knowledge, such as letter-sound relationships, vocabulary, word endings, or story genre/structure. This is more easily done when oversized or big books are used. Unison or choral reading may also be used to encourage children's expressive knowledge of written language.

Dramatic Improvisation

Another way of enhancing primary-age children's language development is to use dramatic improvisation of storybooks or theme-oriented contexts. Dramatic improvisation increases children's use of language to fit different contexts, their use of specialized vocabulary, and their experiences with different speech registers (Wagner, 1990). Dramatic improvisation is familiar to primary-age children because it resembles the spontaneous pretend play in which they may have engaged during preschool or kindergarten settings. In this strategy there is no script, so children are using their knowledge of all aspects of oral communication to take on and experience the role of the character(s) involved.

Story drama can be conducted in these three ways:

1. While a teacher or student reads a text aloud, the whole class can simultaneously pantomime the story actions/events.

2. The teacher reads the text aloud first, followed by a class discussion of how the text can be acted out. Then individual students assume specific character roles.

3. Based on the context of the story/text, a teacher may direct students to dramatize a scene not actually in the story, something that might have happened based upon the context or major events in the story.

Another type of dramatic improvisation begins with a teacher describing a specific context or event to the class. Then the class discusses how such an event might be dramatized, and individual students assume specific roles. Examples are ordering food at a restaurant or imagining what might have happened at a point in history, such as riding on a wagon train, using the first telephone, or walking on the moon.

Through improvisation all five aspects of children's oral language knowledge are enhanced: receptive and expressive knowledge of phonetic, semantic, syntactic, morphemic, and pragmatic aspects of language.

Share-and-Tell

When this strategy was used at the preschool and kindergarten level, children typically brought an object to share, which became the focus of the shared conversations with the class. At the primary level, children may decide to talk about an event that they experienced in the past, relying only on their verbal description to communicate the event. As children develop their oral sharing skills, their primary teachers may need to provide less linguistic scaffolding in the form of questions to sustain the interaction. As a result, children's talks take on more of a monologic quality rather than a dialogue. A recent version of oral sharing is called "Y'all Know What?" (Galda, Bisplinghoff, Pellegrini, & Stahl, 1995). In this version, the catch phrase "Y'all know what?" is used by the child (speaker) to get the class' attention before proceeding with his oral story. During the course of a year in a first-grade classroom, this strategy evolved from an initial way for children to share their home experiences to a time in which children retold familiar stories. As children began to retell familiar stories, they also began to adopt the specific register of the original story, indicating children's awareness of pragmatic knowledge of both oral and written language.

Language Experience Stories

This technique is also used in preschool and kindergarten classrooms; however, at the primary level, the stories that children dictate will be more complex. In addition, at the primary level, a teacher can focus more specifically on language concepts such as letters, words, *or* sounds and can also focus on specific vocabulary or sentence structure.

It is important that the class' language experience stories be written in enlarged book form and placed in the classroom library. This allows individual student use during independent activity time.

At the primary level, language experience strategies can be used to create a wider variety of texts than in preschool or kindergarten classrooms. While preschool and kindergarten language experience stories may focus only on a shared class event, primary children may be able to jointly dictate/create a fictional take-off on a favorite storybook, a nonfiction account of their knowledge about a set of related concepts (e.g., the weather), a list of words with similar characteristics, or a list of questions about a particular topic.

A central aspect of the language experience strategy is children's dictation of a text. The teacher, acting as a scribe, writes on chart paper, a chalkboard, or overhead projector, exactly what children say. During the preschool and kindergarten years, children's dictation will typically be their oral language or speech register, which may contain aspects of their home dialects. At the primary level, children may now dictate text that more closely represents literate register, reflecting their knowledge of written language structure and decontextualization.

Teachers can encourage children's contributions during dictation by asking questions and providing comments to encourage further thought or response, such as:

- "Tell me more about. . . ."
- "What did it remind you of . . . ?"
- "How did you feel about that?" (Mooney, 1990, p. 42)

The language experience strategy is used when teachers want to provide an opportunity for children to create a shared text and then share the reading of that text. Since the teacher assumes the writing of the text, children are not constrained by their lack of orthographic (spelling) knowledge. This strategy is a good way for teachers to observe the expressive language knowledge children have in the areas of semantic, syntactic, morphemic, and pragmatic knowledge. Based on this observation of students' language knowledge during language experience dictation, a teacher may develop and implement specific activities designed to enhance further growth of language knowledge in one or more of the five aspects of language knowledge.

Author's Chair

In this activity, individual children share their creative writing with the whole class. Usually only two or three children share their writing each day or on the designated day of the week. The role of the teacher is to direct the children's sharing and engage the class in responding to the shared writing. In responding to a child's writing, a teacher encourages class members to focus on specific aspects of the writing they liked, questions they have about the story or text that they want to ask the author, and comments they have about the content of the writing.

Because author's chair activities involve all of the four language arts (listening, speaking, writing, and reading), such activities enhance the development of receptive and expressive language knowledge of all five aspects: phonetic, syntactic, morphemic, semantic, and pragmatic. Author's chair activities are only effective if the audience (the rest of the class) can be attentive, active listeners for the author. Thus, it is important that a teacher be aware of the attention span limits and avoid pushing the limit for the class. For this reason, author's chair activities may only involve one or two children at a time.

Media Presentations

Occasional videotapes can provide children with an opportunity to expand their listening vocabulary and receptive knowledge of syntax, particularly when the video focuses on a familiar story. Since there is no opportunity for children to have their questions answered or comments shared during the showing of the videotape, it is important that teachers take time just after the showing for children's questions and comments and to ask children questions to determine whether they comprehended the important ideas or concepts.

Audiotapes may also be used to enhance listening vocabulary, but only if the story is familiar to the children or if the story incorporates schemata already established. In order to comprehend an audiotaped story, children must be able to visualize the story characters and the events that occur. When children are inattentive during an audiotaped story, it may indicate that their listening comprehension is not sufficient to foster comprehension of the oral story.

SMALL GROUP TEACHER-DIRECTED ACTIVITIES

When teachers want to focus on the needs of a smaller grouping of students or when they want to provide an opportunity for children to become more actively engaged in verbal interaction with several children, small group activities are planned. Four example activities will be described in this section: word study activities, shared reading, literature circles, and collaborative/cooperative projects.

Teachers group students for these activities based on children's specific needs or the purpose of the activity. For word study activities children need to be able to focus on the selected concept. For literature circles children need to have read the same story/text to effectively discuss it.

Word Study Activities

Activities in this category may focus on phonetic, morphemic, or semantic knowledge related to specific words. In conducting a word study activity, the teacher first determines which children have a specific need for a focused activity and then selects an appropriate word study activity. Word study concepts are introduced in the format of a mini-lesson: an introduction to the concept, examples of the desired word analysis, and then an opportunity for children to practice the task cooperatively or independently, depending on their level of understanding.

For example, word family activities focus on onset and rime (Johnston, 1999). In these activities, children sort words (written on cards) from two or more word families, such as *hop, stop, mop, map, tap, cap.* Initially, the teacher guides the sorting process. Later on, children can work in pairs or alone. After sorting, words are written down in categories, and children are encouraged to add more words to each category on their own. Once children can quickly and

FIGURE 11.1
Resources for Word Study Activities

Bear, D., Invernizzi, M., Templeton, S., & Johnston, F. (2000). *Words their way: Word study for phonics, vocabulary, and spelling instruction.* Upper Saddle River, NJ: Merrill/Prentice Hall.

Cecil, N. (2001). *Activities for striking a balance in early literacy.* Scottsdale, AZ: Holcomb Hathaway, Publishers.

Ericson, L., & Juliebo, M. (1998). *The phonological awareness handbook for kindergarten and primary teachers.* Newark, DE: International Reading Association.

Johnston, F. (1999). The timing and teaching of word families. *The Reading Teacher, 53*(1), 64–75.

Yopp, H., & Yopp, R. (2000). Supporting phonemic awareness development in the classroom. *The Reading Teacher, 54*(2), 130–144.

correctly read and spell the selected word families, the focus can change to new word families. Word family activities enhance language knowledge by encouraging children to identify and manipulate words, which enhances their phonetic knowledge of oral and written language.

Word banks are another type of word study activity. In this activity, children make a collection of the words they can read or vocabulary words they know. Usually the words are placed on 3x5 cards and then used in word sort activities. Other types of word collections include word posters and word clusters (see Tompkins & Hoskisson, 1995). Additional word study activities are found in the resource books listed in Figure 11.1.

Shared Reading

In shared reading, children take turns reading to each other from individual copies of either basal readers or trade books. At the first-grade level, reading pairs are more effective than larger groupings. In second or third grade, children may be able to have shared reading in groups of three or four. The purpose of shared reading is to provide opportunities for children to read orally in an informal setting. Through repeated opportunities to read texts at their level of reading, children develop reading fluency.

Shared reading typically involves the entire class divided into reading pairs or threesomes for a period of 10 to 15 minutes. The classroom teacher initially determines the composition of each reading group and then monitors children's participation. In this way, children have an opportunity to practice their oral reading with a peer prior to participating in the more formal reading group with the classroom teacher. Children can be encouraged to share with each other their "detective strategies" in using their word knowledge as clues to decode and comprehend texts.

Cross-age shared reading enhances children's reading fluency and conversation skills.

Primary children will also benefit from cross-age shared reading. In this type of shared reading, students from upper grades visit a primary grade to read storybooks to 2-3 children. This activity gives children an opportunity to increase their receptive language and conversational skills.

Literature Circles

In this strategy, a small group of students meets to discuss a piece of literature (Galda, Cullinan, & Strickland, 1993). For first grade, these discussion groups may follow a teacher read-aloud; in second and third grades, students may read their selections silently, prior to their discussions. This activity enhances children's oral language communication skills in each of the five areas of language knowledge. Children's comprehension is enhanced through peer discussions (Kasten, 1997). Their knowledge of the conventions of written language may also be enhanced as they refer back to the text to support and clarify their discussion responses.

Literature circles require specific communication skills that children may not have developed before (Galda, Cullinan, & Strickland, 1993). Teachers should discuss with students which kinds of questions are appropriate for literature circles and specific texts. When initiating this activity, teachers may decide to provide specific questions for the groups to use and then gradually encourage students to develop their own questions. Encouraging children to develop and use their own questions enhances their conversation skills (Newkirk & McLure, 1996). Teachers must clearly communicate their expectations for the processes to be used in literature circles (thinking, reading, and sharing meanings) and the ways in which students are to interact, in terms of turn taking or specific roles to be assumed (e.g. questioner, scribe/recorder). Students can also be encouraged to reflect upon the success of their group in the discussion. Effective literature circles develop over an extended period of time with students gradually assuming more responsibilities in planning and conducting their discussions. When teachers of successive grade levels use this technique (e.g. first-, second- and third grade teachers), students have repeated opportunities to continue to develop their oral discussion competencies and their ability to interact effectively.

Collaborative/Cooperative Projects

In the primary grades where themed cross-curricular instructional units are used, children may work in small groups, exploring specific topics through a variety of library resources or in constructing a group project, such as a model, mural, or diorama. Student-generated dramatic scripts are also a type of collaborative/cooperative project.

A wide variety of language skills are enhanced through collaborative/cooperative projects. In these projects students use listening, speaking, reading, and writing to explore, to create, and to solve problems (Morrow & Gambrell, 1998). By working together on a project, children are encouraged to reflect on their thinking. The development of this "critical reflectiveness" contributes to literate thinking (Wells & Chang-Wells, 1996, p. 165).

Like literature circles, collaborative projects require social and interactional skills that students may need to acquire over an extended period. Teachers may need to introduce collaborative projects one step at a time, providing a supportive environment in which students can gradually assume more responsibility for planning and conducting their own projects.

SUMMARY

During the primary years, children continue to develop knowledge of oral and written language in each of the five aspects of language knowledge. Classrooms that encourage children's active explorations of language through hands-on, collaborative activities increase the breadth of children's language competencies. At the primary level, linguistic scaffolding, mediation, and questioning are used by teachers to encourage children's expressive language. Children's listening competencies are critical to their language development and success at school. Language enhancing activities include both exploratory-discovery center activities and teacher-directed activities.

✻ ✻ ✻ CHAPTER REVIEW

1. List the components of effective listening.
2. What listening competencies are needed by primary-age children?
3. What two main factors influence curricular decisions?
4. Select two of the recommended large group teacher-directed activities. Identify the aspects of language knowledge that are enhanced by those activities.
5. Describe the three ways in which story drama can be conducted.
6. Explain the ways in which language experience activities at the primary level may differ from language experience activities in preschool and kindergarten classrooms.
7. What is the value of small group teacher-directed activities to language development? Give an example and explain its value.
8. Develop three guidelines for teachers to follow when conducting literature circle activities.
9. What is the rationale for including exploratory-discovery center activities in primary classrooms?
10. What is the major goal of the writing center?
11. How do content/concept learning centers enhance language development?
12. Describe the writing suitcase strategy. State your rationale for using it in a primary classroom.

✻ ✻ ✻ CHAPTER EXTENSION ACTIVITIES

1. Observe in a primary classroom for a morning. Which activities were teacher-directed? Which activities were exploratory/independent?
2. Observe in a writing center in a primary classroom. Describe the way in which the writing center is organized. Identify the types of writing in which children engage.
3. Observe children engaged in a literature circle. Describe the ways in which they are using language.
4. Select a storybook for a teacher read-aloud for a first-grade class. State your rationale for selecting the storybook. Identify five vocabulary words you will explain to students.
5. Observe in a classroom where learning centers are used. Describe the learning center and the expectations for student participation. In what ways does the learning center enhance language development?

6. Develop your own writing suitcase. Explain your rationale in selecting the materials for the writing suitcase. Also explain the way in which you would introduce it to a second-grade classroom.

✳ ✳ ✳ REFERENCES

Bredekamp, S., & Copple, C. (1997). *Developmentally appropriate practice in early childhood programs serving children from birth through age 8.* Washington, DC: National Association for the Education of Young Children.

Casbergue, R. (1998). How do we foster young children's writing development? In S. Neuman & K. Roskos (Eds.), *Children achieving: Best practices in early literacy* (pp. 198–222). Newark, DE: International Reading Association.

Galda, L., Bisplinghoff, B., Pellegrini, A., & Stahl, S. (1995). Sharing lives: Reading, writing, talking and living in a first-grade classroom. *Language Arts, 72*(5), 334–339.

Galda, L., Cullinan, B., & Strickland, D. (1993). *Language, literacy and the child.* Fort Worth, TX: Harcourt Brace Jovanovich.

Glazer, J. (2000). *Literature for young children* (4th ed.). Upper Saddle River, NJ: Merrill/Prentice Hall.

Halliday, M. (1973). The functional basis of language. In B. Bernstein (Ed.), *Class, codes, and control: Vol. 2. Applied studies toward a sociology of language.* Boston: Routledge & Kegan Paul.

Halliday, M. (1975). *Learning how to mean: Explorations in the development of language.* London: Edward Arnold Ltd.

Johnston, F. (1999). The timing and teaching of word families. *The Reading Teacher, 53*(1), 64–75.

Kasten, W. (1997). Learning is noisy: The myth of silence in the reading-writing classroom. In J. Paratore & R. McCormack (Eds.), *Peer talk in the classroom: Learning from research* (pp. 88–101). Newark, DE: International Reading Association.

Lindfors, J. (1990). Speaking creatures in the classroom. In S. Hynds & D. Rubin (Eds.), *Perspectives on talk and learning* (pp. 21–40). Urbana, IL: National Council of Teachers of English.

Lundsteen, S. (1990). Learning to listen and learning to read. In S. Hynds & D. Rubin. (Eds.), *Perspectives on talk and learning* (pp. 213–225). Urbana, IL: National Council of Teachers of English.

Matthews, L. (1999). Not just onions! Exploring layers of meaning in texts. In J. Hancock (Ed.), *The explicit teaching of reading* (pp. 29–38). Newark, DE: International Reading Association.

Mooney, M. (1990). *Reading to, with, and by children.* Katonah, NY: Richard C. Owen Publishers.

Morrow, L., & Gambrell, L. (1998). How do we motivate children toward independent reading and writing? In S. Neuman & K. Roskos (Eds.), *Children achieving: Best practices in early literacy* (pp. 144–161). Newark, DE: International Reading Association.

Newkirk, T., & McLure, P. (1996). Telling stories. In B. Power & R. Hubbard (Eds.), *Language development: A reader for teachers* (pp. 132–138). Upper Saddle River, NJ: Merrill/Prentice Hall.

Pinnell, G. (1996). Ways to look at the functions of children's language. In B. Power & R. Hubbard (Eds.), *Language development: A reader for teachers* (pp. 146–154). Upper Saddle River, NJ: Merrill/Prentice Hall.

Raphael, T., & Hiebert, E. (1996). *Creating an integrated approach to literacy instruction.* Fort Worth, TX: Harcourt Brace College Publishers.

Strickland, D. (1998). *Teaching phonics today: A primer for educators.* Newark, DE: International Reading Association.

Tompkins, G. & Hoskisson, K. (1995). *Language arts: Content and teaching strategies.* (3rd ed.). Upper Saddle River, NJ: Merrill/Prentice Hall.

Wagner, B. (1990). Dramatic improvisation in the classroom. In S. Hynds & D. Rubin (Eds.), *Perspectives on talk and learning* (pp. 195–211). Urbana, IL: National Council of Teachers of English.

Wassermann, S. (1990). *Serious players in the primary classroom: Empowering children through active learning experience.* New York: Teachers College Press.

Wells, G., & Chang-Wells, G. (1996). The literate potential of collaborative talk. In B. Power & R. Hubbard (Eds.), *Language development: A reader for teachers* (pp. 155–168). Upper Saddle River, NJ: Merrill/Prentice Hall.

Wolvin, A., & Coakley, C. (1985). *Listening.* Dubuque, IA: Wm. C. Brown.

12

EXPLORING CHILDREN'S USE OF LANGUAGE: ASSESSMENT

The first step in creating a developmentally appropriate language environment in early childhood settings is to explore the ways in which children use language. Teachers who are aware of their children's language competencies can better develop and implement learning activities that further stimulate language acquisition. The ways in which children use language can be explored through two main approaches: informally through naturalistic observation and more formally through the use of standardized tests. This chapter provides an overview of informal and formal assessment techniques with an emphasis on examining children's developing language competencies within all five components of language knowledge: phonetic, syntactic, semantic, morphemic, and pragmatic. The focus of this chapter will be limited to the use of assessment measures in the classroom for these three purposes: (1) determining children's instructional needs, (2) evaluating curriculum effectiveness, and (3) screening children for further diagnostic testing. Procedures and issues involved in evaluating children for placement in special education programs are beyond the scope of this text.

RELATIONSHIP BETWEEN ASSESSMENT AND CURRICULUM

Evaluation of students' characteristics and achievement is an inherent part of the process of teaching. Some form of assessment accompanies many aspects of teaching, whether it might be deciding if a student answered a question completely or if directions were completely understood (Lindfors, 1987). To be effective, teachers need to become familiar with the characteristics and competencies of children in their classroom. Teachers also need to have a way of determining the effectiveness of their curriculum in fostering growth and development. Formal and informal assessment techniques can provide teachers with important insights into the needs and accomplishments of their students.

The relationship between assessment and curriculum is a controversial one. In some settings, assessment procedures and timetables have such a dominant influence on curricula that teachers and administrators have voiced concerns that the curriculum is test-mandated and test-driven (NAEYC, 1988). These concerns focus mainly on formal, standardized testing procedures that may have been implemented in response to administrative and community concerns for accountability. When standardized test content drives the curriculum, important aspects of learning are ignored or trivialized. Instead of challenging students' thinking, standardized testing encourages only "right" answers (NAEYC, 1988). Assessment should be embedded within curriculum planning and implementation. Knowledge of specific ways in which children's language can be observed and documented assists teachers in determining the direction and scope of the curriculum and the success of classroom curriculum in enhancing children's language acquisition.

An outline of steps in embedding assessment in an early childhood curriculum is presented in Figure 12.1.

DETERMINING THE PURPOSE OF ASSESSMENT: FORMATIVE AND SUMMATIVE

Within early childhood settings, informal, observational assessments and formal, standardized tests can be used to serve two distinct purposes: formative and summative. **Formative assessment** focuses on tracking children's growth and development on an ongoing basis throughout the year. **Summative assessment** determines the final outcomes of learning and development at the end of the school term. Summative assessment is often considered a "high stakes" assessment since far-reaching decisions relative to future educational placement may be made based on summative assessment.

Formative assessment involves looking at children's language use on an ongoing, periodic basis throughout the school year. Awareness of children's

FIGURE 12.1

Steps in Exploring and Documenting Children's Language

1. Determine the purposes of assessment: formative and/or summative.
2. Determine the impact of the assessments on curriculum and the classroom environment.
3. Review the types of assessments available, focusing on general features and constraints: What type of information will this measure/technique provide? How is the information collected?
4. Select assessment measures/techniques that correspond to the types of information needed and to the resources (time and staff) available to collect the information.
5. Develop a language acquisition portfolio for each child, composed of a variety of assessment measures that provide information on language acquisition.
6. Use the assessment information to continue to develop and refine classroom curriculum and to enhance children's language acquisition.

current language knowledge can be used to adjust classroom curricula to meet their needs. For example, if formative assessment indicates children's vocabulary development is an area of concern, the curriculum can be modified to incorporate more concept-rich and vocabulary-focused activities.

A majority of the assessment procedures conducted by classroom teachers will probably be of the formative type; however, teachers need to be aware of summative evaluation since such evaluations may be required for administrative and accountability purposes. Summative assessment occurs when assessment measures are used to establish year-end performance levels or achievement. Results obtained in summative assessment may be used to determine the effectiveness of curricular approaches. For example, did a specific curriculum appear to enhance children's learning and development? This assessment may also indicate areas of strength or potential growth areas for individual children. Sometimes summative assessment measures are used to make placement decisions for the upcoming year. Due to the long-term nature of these types of decisions, it is critical that any summative assessment process incorporate a variety of measures that provide a comprehensive sample of children's language behaviors. Some specific assessment measures can be used for both formative and summative assessment.

Formative assessment is emphasized in the National Association for the Education of Young Children's position statement on Developmentally Appropriate Practices in Early Childhood (Bredekamp & Copple, 1997). It specifies that assessments should: (1) be "ongoing, strategic and purposeful" (p. 21), (2) primarily involve observation and description of children's development and sample work, and (3) reflect children's progress in attaining developmental goals.

DETERMINING THE IMPACT OF ASSESSMENTS ON CURRICULUM AND CLASSROOM ENVIRONMENT

Informal and formal assessments influence the early childhood curriculum in several ways. One of the most noticeable ways is in the time needed to complete the assessment. Assessments that require individual administration and an extended length of time interfere with regular classroom activities and require additional staff. It may also be necessary to have a separate area in which the assessment can be conducted. In varying degrees, each assessment requires that it be administered by someone trained in the specific procedures. This is an additional consideration in determining the impact of testing on the classroom.

Another way in which assessments impact the classroom is in the focus of the assessment. What is the scope of the language knowledge measured by the specific assessment? Is the focus on receptive language and/or expressive language? If a measure examines only receptive language, its value is limited if information is needed on children's expressive competencies. Assessments also vary in the aspects of language knowledge measured. All components or aspects of language may be addressed in assessing language (Wyatt & Seymour, 1999). Knowing the scope of the assessments helps teachers assess the value of the proposed assessments.

Additional considerations focus on the effect the assessment will have on the children. Will children be expected to perform in a testing situation for periods of time that exceed their attention spans and disregard their need for physical activity? Do children have sufficient small muscle coordination to respond to assessments requiring a form of written response?

A teacher's/administrator's conclusion regarding the impact of an assessment procedure upon a classroom needs to balance the amount and usefulness of the information provided by the assessment and the cost of assessment in terms of time, staff resources, and the impact on children. When the assessment procedures are so time-consuming that they have a negative impact on the classroom curriculum or when the assessments result in a pressure on staff resources, teachers and administrators need to rethink the purpose and value of such assessment procedures.

REVIEWING THE TYPES OF ASSESSMENTS AVAILABLE

Assessment measures can be grouped into two categories: informal and formal. These types vary in the specific information obtained through the assessment and the manner in which the information is collected. Both types of assessments have strengths and weaknesses that influence teachers' selection of assessment measures. The inclusion of both types of assessments in the evaluation of children's learning and development contribute to a more complete understanding of each child. Of the two types, teachers will more often administer informal measures; however, knowledge of the characteristics and utility value of formal assessments is also necessary for teachers to make appropriate judgments in using information available from formal, standardized measures.

INFORMAL ASSESSMENTS

Informal measures of assessment involve observing children in their daily environments in familiar surroundings. The process of observation requires that the observer know what to look for, how to record the behavior, and how the behavior should be interpreted or explained (Bentzen, 1985). A teacher's educational philosophy and professional knowledge form the basis upon which observations of children's language behaviors are made. This process involving focused, yet naturalistic, observation has been termed "kid-watching" (Goodman, 1985).

A necessary part of observation or kid-watching is developing ways to document what was observed. This can be done in several ways: (1) checklists or observation scales, (2) anecdotal records, or (3) audio/video tapings. The particular way a teacher decides to document observations will be based on the time involved and the ease in carrying out the documentation. Any type of documentation used to represent observations should contain certain identifying information: children's first and last name, date of observation, name of observer, and length of time observed.

Individual types of informal assessments are characterized by specific strengths and weaknesses. As a group, informal measures have several strengths and weaknesses.

Strengths

Informal assessments occur in real language settings where naturalistic use of language occurs. Children's verbal and nonverbal communicative interactions in pragmatic contexts can be sampled. Informal measures can be used frequently since practice effects are unlikely as there are no specific items to answer. Thus, informal measures facilitate comparing development over shorter time periods than do formal measures. Informal assessment measures are flexible and can be adapted to specific situations in the classroom. Many informal measures involve observation that can be conducted unobtrusively when children are engaged in independent activities. Thus, a teacher can conduct observations of several children during an independent activity time.

Weaknesses

Most informal assessments are unstructured and open-ended, requiring teachers to make interpretations of student performance or response. This subjectivity may cause the assessment to become susceptible to teacher bias (Smith, 1990). To overcome this weakness, more than one teacher should participate in administering and interpreting informal measures of language assessment.

Informal measures also require extensive preparation on the part of teachers to ensure appropriate administration and interpretation. The old adage, "A little knowledge is a dangerous thing," applies here. If teachers do not know what specific behaviors or benchmarks to look for when conducting informal assessments and how to interpret the behaviors observed, conclusions based on such assessments will be invalid and may result in inappropriate decisions.

The necessity of keeping extensive written records is another weakness of informal assessment. Data collected during informal assessment must be organized and maintained over a period of time. It must also be interpreted and synthesized rather than simply filed away.

In addition, informal measures may not be well understood by administrators and parents since the outcomes of informal assessment are more descriptive than quantitative and normative. Teachers may need to explain carefully to parents and administrators the nature of the informal measure and interpretations or conclusions arising from this assessment.

EXAMPLES OF INFORMAL ASSESSMENT MEASURES

Four frequently used forms of informal assessment include checklists, observation scales, anecdotal records, and audio/video recording. These forms of assessment take longer to administer and interpret than do some formal measures; however, these informal measures frequently provide valuable information not elicited through formal measures.

Checklists and Observation Scales

Checklists or observation scales are composed of lists of characteristics that are the focus of the observation. The difference between a checklist and an observation scale is in the type of observation made. In a checklist, the presence or absence of a characteristic is noted, whereas in an observation scale, the amount of a characteristic is determined (see Figures 12.2 and 12.3).

The strength of a checklist or observation scale is that it systematizes the observation to focus on specific behaviors. When two or more teachers are observing several children or conducting repeated observations of one child, a

FIGURE 12.2
Checklist

Child's Name: Sarah T.	Date Observed: 2/15/02	
Oral Language Characteristic	Characteristic Present	Characteristic Not Present
Speaks confidently in group settings	✓	
Speaks distinctly enough for adults to understand	✓	
Speaks in expanded sentences		✓

FIGURE 12.3
Observation Scale for Oral Language

Child's Name: Steven C.	Date Observed: 3/4/02		
Oral Language Characteristic	Frequently	Occasionally	Not Observed
Speaks confidently in classroom	✓		
Speaks distinctly enough for adults to understand		✓	
Speaks in expanded sentences		✓	

checklist or observation scale provides for more uniformity for the focus of the observations.

Teachers may develop their own checklists/observation scales or may use checklists previously developed. When teachers develop their own checklists, it is important that the behaviors or criteria they include are representative of developmental competencies that have been identified in early childhood research and assessment literature. Before using a checklist, the teacher should review the checklist/observation scale to determine whether the characteristics listed are those relevant to the information the teacher needs. Checklists and observation scales may also contain space for additional comments or for noting behaviors related to the target characteristics. Checklists and observation scales may be designed to document observation of several children. The checklist shown in Figure 12.4 focuses on children's pragmatic language behaviors and may be used over a period of time with dates recorded in the columns to document when a particular characteristic was observed. It is called an *annotated checklist* because it contains comments about the behavior observed. These

FIGURE 12.4
Annotated Checklist of Pragmatic Language Behaviors

Observer/Teacher:	J. Smith	
Child's Name	Responds to Routine Greetings/ Farewells	Expresses Needs or Wants
1. Heather	9/7 *Good morning, Miss Smith.*	9/15 *Can I have more milk?*
2. Teddy	10/2 *When asked how he was, Teddy replied, "I am fine". Then he asked me, "How are you?"*	11/30 *Asked teacher how to spell 'happy' for him at the writing table.*
3. David	9/7 *"Good-bye Miss Smith."*	*"Teacher, please tie my shoe."*
4. Marco	9/15 *"Hi, teacher."*	*"Teacher, I need help."*

FIGURE 12.5
Longitudinal Checklist of an Individual Child's Pragmatic Language Behaviors

Child: _____		Observer/Teacher: _____		
Language Behavior		Date #1:	Date #2:	Date #3:
1. Responds to verbal greeting and departure routines Appropriate facial expression Appropriate verbal response				
2. Responds to story questions Detailed or inferential responses				
3. Expresses needs/wants				

comments document the context (setting) in which the language behavior occurred. The value of an annotated checklist is that it documents more completely the behavior and provides the teacher with more specific assessment information to use in making curricular decisions and to share with parents regarding children's language acquisition.

Another version of a checklist is shown in Figure 12.5. This type of checklist focuses only on one child, providing a longitudinal record of pragmatic language behaviors.

Goodman (1992) describes an evolutionary process that many checklists go through in which teachers who create their own checklists report that checklists are initially developed to evaluate various language behaviors in detail. As the checklists are used, they may undergo frequent revision and modification. As a result of this developmental process in using a specific checklist or observation scale, teachers often report they no longer need to use the written format to assess children's language behaviors. Goodman concludes that checklists initially help teachers identify and distinguish important behaviors. With use, knowledge of what to look for and what it means becomes internalized by the teacher. Subsequently, teachers find themselves using these refined kid-watching techniques throughout the day and not just when the checklist is on hand.

Anecdotal Records

This form of documentation provides more detail than observation checklists. Anecdotal records may provide a running account of behaviors during a specified time or may focus on certain behaviors throughout a day or class. Anecdotal records are an effective way to describe children's language behavior within a classroom setting and can provide a record of detailed observations over time. In preparing to develop an anecdotal record, a teacher should identify the purpose of the observation. Is it to record a child's conversational interactions with peers or to document vocabulary growth? It is also important that a teacher's interpretations of a specific behavior be separated from the description of the behavior itself. An example of an anecdotal record is represented in Figure 12.6.

The value of anecdotal records is limited by the inherent lack of structure and open-ended format. The actual content, wording, and nature of the anecdotal record is determined by the person writing/composing the narrative. Anecdotal records may be highly subjective, influenced easily by the attitudes and value systems of the observers. One way of addressing this weakness is to distinguish between what was observed and how the observer interprets the child's behavior.

There may be little reliability or agreement between multiple observers. When this occurs, teachers need to discuss their observations and attempt to reconcile their different interpretations before any conclusions can be drawn or decisions made.

Anecdotal records are time-consuming to develop and maintain. To acquire an awareness of children's language development, a large body of anecdotal records must be collected, reviewed, and summarized. This may involve more time than is available to the classroom teacher. For these reasons, teachers in most classrooms use anecdotal records only on a limited basis.

Audio and Videotape

Samples of children's communicative interactions can be captured on audio and videotape. Videotaping provides a more complete language sample since nonverbal communication and the setting can also be recorded. While this method of documenting language behaviors provides a full and rich sampling, this strat-

FIGURE 12.6
Example of an Anecdotal Record on Vocabulary and Conceptual Development

Child: ___Teddy_____   Observer Teacher: ___Sue_____

Date: 10/2   Comments/Interpretations:
Behaviors: *Teddy is able to see the similarity of*
Teddy had the three larger plastic   *the three barrels and a caterpillar. It*
  barrels at the table. After he had   *also shows his developing*
  stacked them according to size, with   *conceptual and symbolic knowledge.*
  the largest at the bottom, he said, "This
  is a caterpillar."

Date: 11/20   Comments/Interpretations:
Behaviors: *Teddy is continuing to develop his*
Teddy glued several pieces of white   *awareness of the similarities of*
  paper end to end. Then he added a   *certain shapes to objects in the real*
  triangular piece of green construction   *world. We just read a story about*
  paper and said, "This is a kite."   *kites this week. I wonder if the story*
                                              helped Teddy to see the similarity
                                              between his creation and the kite
                                              pictured in the story. It was white and
                                              green, too.

egy for assessment has several limitations. First, it is essential that children's language behaviors not be influenced by the presence of the audio or videotape equipment or equipment operators. Second, some early childhood classrooms cannot afford to purchase the necessary recording and viewing equipment. A third limitation is the time involved in reviewing the tapes and agreeing on what the behaviors on the tape indicate. If detailed written transcriptions are to be made, extensive additional time will be required. Fourth, written parental/guardian permission is needed to audiotape or videotape children.

Checklists, observation scales, anecdotal records, and audio/videotaping provide ways in which children's use of language can be documented during informal classroom observations. In the section that follows, three specific informal assessment measures will be described. These measures focus on children as they begin to acquire knowledge of written language. In addition, these informal measures are structured in their administration and focus on a comprehensive range of language behaviors. Since these assessments involve considerable amounts of time, most classroom teachers will not find that they use them frequently. These measures are described here as examples of more comprehensive informal assessments. Teachers who have had the opportunity to use these assessments will find that they employ aspects of the assessments in their day-to-day informal observations of children in their classrooms.

Primary Language Record

This observation measure incorporates several types of assessment: checklists, anecdotal records, interviews, and samples of the child's reading and writing. It was developed by the Center for Language in Primary Education in London, England (Barrs, Ellis, Hester, & Thomas, 1989). Designed for children ages 5–7, the Primary Language Record collects information on the child's use of oral and written language during the early years of schooling. This measure also incorporates information on children's bilingual development. It distinguishes between languages understood (oral receptive), languages spoken (oral productive), languages read (receptive written), and languages written (productive written). Procedures for making multiple observations throughout the school year are described. As with other informal measures, teachers must have knowledge of which information/behaviors to record, how to interpret, and how to use the data collected. It is a comprehensive measure that has been extensively field-tested. (For further information on this measure, contact Heinemann Educational Books, Inc., Portsmouth, NH.)

Storybook-Based Language Observation

Storybook-based Language Observation (Otto, 1992) provides a method to observe, record, and analyze children's expressive language. This measure was developed for preservice and inservice teachers to provide an overview of children's developing language knowledge. To use and interpret this informal measure appropriately, teachers should have background knowledge of the five aspects of language knowledge described in earlier chapters: phonetic, semantic, syntactic, morphemic, and pragmatic.

The Storybook-Based Language Observation elicits young children's expressive language during their attempts to recreate the story from a familiar storybook. This task provides a setting for children to engage in a monologue that can then be examined for evidence of specific language development knowledge. When children's oral storybook interactions are audiotaped, compared with the original text, and analyzed, a comprehensive picture of children's language development emerges.

In Figure 12.7, a segment of a kindergartner's (Andrew) re-creation of *Harry, the Dirty Dog* (Zion, 1956) is provided, along with the original text and examiner-teacher analysis.

Andrew's interaction with the book provided numerous examples of his use of phonetic, semantic, syntactic, morphemic, and pragmatic knowledge. In the segment featured in Figure 12.7, Andrew's language showed he used past tense consistently (morphemic, lines 2–7), was able to summarize story content (semantic, lines 2–7), sometimes did not clarify pronoun referents (syntactic, line 4), could use comparative forms of adjectives (i.e., dirtier, morphemic, line 6), simplified sentence structure (syntactic, line 7), provided a title and setting

FIGURE 12.7
Andrew's Storybook-Based Language Observation

CHILD	TEXT (Zion, 1956, p. 1–5)	ANALYSIS
1. The Harry Dog.	HARRY, THE DIRTY DOG.	*Child provides own title for story.*
2. Once Harry heard the bathwater running.	HARRY WAS A WHITE DOG WITH BLACK SPOTS WHO LIKED EVERYTHING EXCEPT . . . GETTING A BATH. SO ONE DAY WHEN HE	*Child gives setting statement; uses past tense and* ing *form of verb.*
3. So he hid, he hid, he hid the, he ran down the stairs.	HEARD THE WATER RUNNING IN THE TUB, HE TOOK THE SCRUBBING BRUSH . . .	*Child uses repetition, perhaps as a placeholder. Child uses past tense, summarizes story content. Content refers to illustrated action.*
4. He dug up it He put it He buried it in the ground.	AND BURIED IT IN THE BACKYARD.	*Pronoun reference is vague for* it, *since two different referents (it = ground and it = scrub brush) are indicated.*
5. He went out.	THEN HE RAN AWAY FROM HOME.	*Vague use of "out."*
6. He got dirtier.	HE PLAYED WHERE THEY WERE FIXING THE STREET	*Comparative use of* dirty; *anticipates upcoming text.*
7. He got dirty from the street.	AND GOT VERY DIRTY.	*Semantically similar content but syntactically more simple than text.*

Harry the Dirty Dog, text copyright © 1956 by Eugene Zion. Pictures copyright © 1956 by Margaret Bloy Graham. Used by permission of HarperCollins Publishers.

statement (pragmatic, lines 1 & 2), and used semantically equivalent words (semantic, line 4) when he said *ground* in place of *backyard.*

Specific directions for completing the Storybook-Based Language Observation are found in the appendix to this chapter, along with an example of a pre-service teacher's completed observation (Kempfer, 1993). While classroom teachers will not have the time to engage in storybook-based language observations with each child, an awareness of the types of information provided by such observations and knowledge of the techniques in conducting an observation will provide insights into the value of taking a close look at children's early storybook interactions as they occur informally in the classroom.

Clay's Observation Survey

Clay (1993) developed a series of informal assessments that focus on children's early reading and writing behaviors. These assessments are jointly referred to as "An Observation Survey" and involve the following tasks:

Part I:

- Running record—evaluation of reading accuracy, error analysis, and self-corrections

Part II:

- Letter identification—letter names
- Concepts about print—word units, letters, word spacing, and punctuation marks
- Word tests—lists of high frequency/beginning reader words
- Writing—evaluation of writing samples for "language level, message quality, and directional features" (p. 57)
- Hearing and recording sounds in words—a dictation task; evaluated for the number of sounds recorded in writing and relationship to correct orthography

Clay cautions teachers that using multiple tasks is critical in providing a more complete and reliable understanding of a child's early reading and writing knowledge.

FORMAL ASSESSMENTS

Formal assessments are standardized measures or tests. They typically involve a series of stimuli, such as pictured items, used to elicit specific language responses. Scores are then derived by determining the amount or proportion of correct responses. Specific items composing formal tests have been carefully developed to elicit certain types of language or behavior. Exact procedures must be followed for administering and scoring these assessments.

All formal tests have been **normed.** This means that during the development of the test, scores from a large number of subjects (children) have been collected to provide a basis for comparison between this initial, norming sample and future test takers (Wortham, 2001). The normative sample must represent an extensive range of diversity, including gender, age, geographic location, socioeconomic background, and ethnicity. If the normative sample is not representative of the students being assessed, the normed scores should not be rigidly applied when interpreting individual children's scores. For example, when a test contains items that focus only on knowledge or development specific to one culture and thus are inherently more difficult for children from other cultures, the test is said to be culturally biased. Most formal measures have been thoroughly developed with norms derived from field testing with a diverse, nationally representative sample. Teachers should determine the similarity between the norming sample and their students prior to interpreting individual scores. Information on the composition of the norming sample (and other features of the test measure) can be found in either the examiner's manual or the technical manual available from each test publisher/developer.

Formal assessment measures differ according to the following three characteristics:

1. Scope of development assessed

2. Degree of formal training required of examiner

3. Purpose served by measure (diagnosis or screening)

Reviewing these characteristics helps teachers understand the function and usefulness of specific assessment measures.

Scope of Development Measured

Some formal measures are comprehensive in thoroughly assessing several developmental areas. Comprehensive measures may include subtests on cognitive functioning, language, quantitative concepts, physical motor development, and social development.

Examples of early childhood comprehensive measures include the McCarthy Scales of Children's Abilities (McCarthy, 1972) and the Gesell Preschool Test (Haines, Ames, & Gillespie, 1980). The McCarthy Scales of Children's Abilities is targeted for children ages 2 years-4 months to 8 years-7 months and includes subtests in these areas: verbal, perceptual-performance, quantitative, general cognitive, memory, and motor. The Gesell Preschool Test is for children ages 2 years-6 months to 6 years-0 months and includes subtests in the areas of motor, adaptive, language, and personal-social. Other formal measures focus only on language development, such as the Peabody Picture Vocabulary Test-R (Dunn & Dunn, 1997) and the Clinical Evaluation of Language Fundamentals-Preschool (CELF-PRESCHOOL) (Wiig, Secord, & Semel, 1992). See Figure 12.8 later in this chapter for a listing of respective subtests. When selecting a formal assessment measure, it is also important to determine which of the five aspects of language knowledge are assessed and whether receptive and productive language are assessed.

Examiner Training

Some assessment measures require that those who use them have formal specialized training in test administration and scoring while others can be administered and scored by classroom teachers. Test manufacturers may require evidence of specific training at the time assessment measures are purchased. This professional policy is designed to ensure appropriate use of assessment measures. It was developed in response to situations in which assessment measures were used inappropriately, resulting in invalid assessments.

Purpose Served by Measure: Diagnosis or Screening

Formal measures function either to diagnose specific areas of weakness or strength or to provide a general screening of one or more areas of development. For example, the Revised Brigance Diagnostic Inventory of Early Development (Brigance, 1991; Cohen & Spenciner, 1994) provides detailed information of development from birth to age 7 via specific subtests involving language: speech and language, general knowledge and comprehension; social and emotional development, basic reading; and manuscript writing. This specific language information can then be used in prescribing specific follow-up learning opportunities. Other subtests assess preambulatory, gross, and fine motor skills, self-help skills, and basic math.

In contrast, the Denver II (Frankenburg, Dodds, Archer, Bresnick, Maschka, Edelman & Shapiro, 1990) provides a general assessment of language development that can be used with children from infancy to age 6 to identify those in need of further assessment. The language items elicit expressive and receptive language in the areas of semantic, syntactic, and morphemic knowledge. In addition to language development, other Denver II subtest areas include personal-social, fine motor, and gross motor.

Strengths of Formal Measures

One of the main strengths of formal measures comes from their thorough development. Formal measures are designed to be used on a large-scale basis in many classrooms and by numerous test administrators/examiners. To ensure similar use, test developers specify exact procedures for giving the test, scoring it, and interpreting the results. This uniformity gives confidence to the test results across a classroom of students and between classrooms. Established procedures for administration and scoring also reduce the possibility of bias due to examiner subjectivity or error. Since formal measures have been normed, students' scores can be compared with those of the norming sample to see how the development of specific children compares with a larger, nationwide population.

Another strength of formal measures comes from the established validity and reliability of each measure. Both of these properties are established through the use of statistical procedures. **Validity** refers to the notion that the test actually measures what it is intended to measure. There are several kinds of validity. For example, predictive validity exists when test scores can be used to predict children's performance on another measure. If a reading readiness measure has predictive validity, scores obtained by children on it will indicate which children will be more successful in reading. Content validity indicates that test items measure what the test purports to measure.

Reliability indicates that a measure is designed to produce consistent, dependable, or repeatable scores (Meisels, 1989; Wortham, 2001). Reliability must be established to ensure teachers that they can be confident in test scores. Otherwise, the score differences between children could be due to errors in test construction or administration. During the process of test development and standardization, test developers establish several kinds of reliability. *Test-retest reliability* is established during text construction. A high level of test-retest reliability indicates that students' scores will be consistent over several administrations of the test. *Inter-rater reliability* refers to the level of scoring agreement among two or more scorers administering and scoring the same assessment measure with the same children. Information on a specific test's reliability and validity is usually located in the Examiner's Manual for that specific test or is available from the test publisher. Validity and reliability information is also published in test review reference books, such as the *Mental Measurements Yearbooks* (Buros, 1938–) and *Tests in Print IV: An Index to Tests, Test Reviews, and the Literature on Specific Tests* (Murphy, Condey, & Impara, 1994).

Teachers also need to evaluate test results with respect to the relationship of the standardized scores to a child's day-to-day behavior/responses in the classroom. When distinct differences between observed classroom behaviors and formal test scores occur, additional assessments (both formal and informal) are warranted.

Weaknesses of Formal Measures

Many formal measures involve individual testing in which the examiner and child are secluded in a separate room apart from the classroom, requiring additional staff and room space. Language elicited in this isolated setting is in response to specific test items and has a stimulus-response quality rather than a communicative quality. In many formal measures, language information obtained is in isolated segments rather than the natural dialogue or monologue that occurs in classroom interactions. Other formal measures require group administration; however, this approach is limited since all children must follow the same directions. No exception can be made to accommodate individual students' needs. During group administration a teacher cannot stop to provide individualized instructions or to clarify test items for children who appear confused or lost.

Another weakness of formal measures involves the need for specialized training in test administration. Many formal measures cannot be administered by classroom teachers. This necessitates additional personnel who have received specialized training in test administration, scoring, and analysis.

Formal measures cannot be used frequently since to do so would result in "practice effects." This means that because the child is familiar with the test items, the resulting score would be higher due to that familiarity. When it is necessary to use a formal measure more than once a year, alternative equivalent forms of the measure should be used.

Teachers who are considering the use of formal assessments should also observe the following guidelines developed by the National Association for the Education of Young Children (NAEYC, 1988):

1. **Standardized tests used with young children need to meet professional technical standards for reliability and validity.** When a test does not meet high technical standards for reliability and validity, the scores obtained from the test will have little merit and may be sources of misinformation about the children tested.

2. **Multiple sources of information rather than a single test score should be used when decisions are made about enrollment, retention, or special class assignment.** Decisions regarding placement of children in certain classes or grade levels must involve comprehensive information about a child's total development in a variety of educational contexts over an extended period, rather than just the child's performance on a test on one particular day involving only one specific aspect of development.

3. **Teachers and administrators should exercise professional responsibility to ensure that the selected tests are used only for the purposes the tests were designed to serve.** For example, the Peabody Picture Vocabulary Test is designed to assess a child's receptive vocabulary. The child responds to a verbal request to "point to _____ (concept pictured)." No verbal response is elicited from the child. Thus, it would be inappropriate to conclude that a child's total language development is delayed based only on results from this measure of receptive vocabulary.

4. **Test results and interpretations should be accurately and carefully explained to parents, other school staff, and the media.** This requires that teachers and administrators acquire knowledge of testing standards, procedures, and appropriate interpretations. Misinformation regarding children's test performance and how it should be interpreted can create negative effects for the children, their parents, and the school.

5. **When standardized tests are used to measure program outcomes, careful consideration should be given to determining whether or not the measure represents the curriculum and its underlying theory, philosophy, and goals.** If the test focuses on knowledge or skills that are not explicitly or implicitly part of the classroom curriculum, the test is an inappropriate assessment.

6. **Personnel administering the tests must be properly qualified and have an understanding of young children's developmental needs during the assessment process.** Test scores can be influenced by the way in which the test is administered. If improperly administered, the test scores are not accurate representations of children's knowledge and competencies.

7. **The testing procedures and content of the tests should acknowledge linguistic and cultural diversity. Children's home or first language should be used during the testing process.** Tests that are culturally biased are not appropriate assessments of children from linguistically and/or culturally diverse backgrounds. Using a child's home language during test administration ensures that

the child understands better what is expected and how to respond to specific test items. When the purpose of the testing is to assess children's knowledge of a second language, the person who administers the test should speak the children's home language in case they need to have test procedures clarified in their home language.

The classroom teacher is often a part of a team approach to assessment. A teacher's understanding of these guidelines contributes to developmentally appropriate use of formal assessment measures with young children.

OVERVIEW OF SPECIFIC FORMAL ASSESSMENT INSTRUMENTS

Although early childhood teachers are unlikely to administer many formal tests due to the requirement of specialized training, results from these measures (administered by a school psychologist or other trained professionals) may be made available to the classroom teacher. Thus, it is important that classroom teachers be aware of the scope of information provided by test scores. In examining such scores, teachers should look at the types of subtests composing the measure along with the nature of specific items in the subtests. In Figure 12.8, characteristics of the nine formal measures are presented. Each measure requires individual administration by a trained examiner.

Several of the formal measures reviewed in Figure 12.8, the PLS-3, TELD-3, CELF-PRESCHOOL, and the ITPA-3 are comprehensive in assessing language development since they elicit responses that involve four or more of the aspects of language knowledge. Assessments such as these eliciting a more comprehensive range of language areas provide a more complete evaluation of a child's language development than assessments that focus only on one area of language development.

DEVELOPING A PORTFOLIO ON LANGUAGE ACQUISITION

Portfolio assessment involves the collection of a variety of assessment measures for each child (Martin, 1994). The term *portfolio* implies that the collection will be gathered in a type of portfolio or file folder. This approach to assessment has been implemented at all levels of education from early childhood through college. At each level, portfolio assessment is implemented somewhat differently based upon the particular learning contexts in which it is used.

At the early childhood level, language acquisition portfolios are usually composed of both formal and informal measures and are predominately formative in nature. However, at the end of the school term, information or scores

FIGURE 12.8
Overview of Selected Formal Assessments

Name of Test	Age Level	Focus	Subtests	Aspects of Language	Time Needed
McCarthy Scales of Children's Abilities (McCarthy, 1972) (Note: Use discouraged due to outdated norms. Salvia & Ysseldyke, 1998)	2 1/2 to 8 1/2 years	General intellectual ability	Verbal, perceptual-performance, quantitative, memory, motor	Verbal scale: syntax, pragmatics, semantics, phonetics	45 minutes
Test of Early Language Development (TELD-3) (Hresko, Reid, & Hammill, 1999)	2 to 7 years	Oral language development	None	Semantic, syntactic, morphemic, pragmatic, phonetic* (*receptive only)	Untimed
Test of Language Development-Primary 3 (TOLD-P3) (Newcomer & Hammill, 1997)	4 through 8 years	Expressive and receptive language	Picture vocabulary, oral vocabulary, grammatical understanding, sentence imitation, grammatical completion, phonology	Semantic, syntactic, phonetic	One hour
Clinical Evaluation of Language Fundamentals-Preschool (CELF-Preschool) (Wiig, Secord, & Semel, 1992)	Preschool–kindergarten	Receptive and expressive language	Receptive: linguistic concepts, sentence structure, basic concepts Expressive: recalling sentences, formulating labels, word structure	Semantic, syntactic	30–44 minutes
				Semantic, syntactic, morphemic	
Preschool Language Scale-3 (PLS-3) (Zimmerman, Steiner, & Pond, 1992)	Birth–6 years	Oral language—receptive and expressive	Articulation screener, language sample checklist, family interview	Semantic, morphology, syntax, phonetic-articulation, pragmatic	20–30 minutes

Name of Test	Age Level	Focus	Subtests	Aspects of Language	Time Needed
Peabody Picture Vocabulary Test III A & B (PPVT) (Dunn & Dunn, 1997)	2–0 to 18 years	Receptive oral language (Standard English)	None	Semantic, syntactic	10–20 minutes
Expressive One-Word Picture Vocabulary Test-Revised (EOWPVT-R) (Gardner, 1990)	2–0 to 11 years–11 months	English and Spanish expressive vocabulary	None	Semantic	20–30 minutes
Early Learning Milestone Scale, 2nd Edition (ELM-2) (Coplan, 1993)	Birth to 36 months	General language development and speech intelligibility	Auditory Expressive Auditory Receptive Visual Language (nonverbal)	Prelinguistic expressive and receptive, semantic syntactic, phonetic	1–4 minutes
Illinois Test of Psycholinguistic Abilities-3rd Edition (ITPA-3) (Hammill, Mather, & Roberts, 2001)	5 yrs–0 months through 12 yrs–11 months	Spoken and written language	Spoken Language Analogies Vocabulary Morphological closure Syntactic sentences Sound deletion Rhyming sequences Written Language Sentence sequencing Written vocabulary Sight decoding Sound decoding Sight spelling Sound spelling	Semantic, morphemic, syntactic, phonetic, pragmatic	45–60 minutes

(continued)

from summative instruments are often added. All of the instruments mentioned in this chapter could be included in a language acquisition portfolio.

The purpose of portfolio assessment is to provide a broader understanding of a child's development than that provided only by standardized, formal measures. The accompanying table lists the language assessment measures used in two preschool classrooms. Classroom A uses only one standardized measure, while Classroom B has a portfolio of both formal and informal measures.

Classroom A	Classroom B
Peabody Picture Vocabulary III	Peabody Picture Vocabulary III
	Storybook language observation
	Pragmatic language checklist
	CELF-Preschool
	Samples of child's writing
	Audiotape of story retelling

When teachers summarize the growth of the children in these respective classrooms, Classroom B will have richer, more comprehensive information on language development than will Classroom A.

A major challenge in using a portfolio assessment approach is managing the volume of information collected and using the information contained in the portfolio. The volume of materials to be included in the portfolio should be determined at the beginning of the school year. The classroom teacher needs to first identify which language goals the early childhood curriculum will have for the upcoming school year. Then assessment measures (formal and informal) can be selected to address specific language goals. Assessments conducted in the first part of the school year can be used as baseline information for planning specific curricular activities. Provisions should be made for conducting formative assessments periodically throughout the year, typically every 4 to 6 weeks. These periodic assessments are usually informal in nature and may take the form of observation checklists, anecdotal records, or, for kindergarten-primary children, work samples. The inclusion of student work samples, such as invented spelling/writing or dictated stories, should be carefully selected as examples of significant work and evidence of change over time.

USING THE ASSESSMENT INFORMATION

Recommendations for instruction or further referral following assessment are limited to the type of language behavior sampled by that instrument or collection of instruments. To conclude that a child's productive semantic knowledge (oral vocabulary) is delayed is more valuable than just the general conclusion that the child is "language delayed."

When a classroom teacher receives a child's scores from a standardized test, it is valuable for the teacher to take a closer look at items that were missed along with those that were correct. In doing this analysis, the teacher considers the type of language or information assessed by specific test items. For example, on the TELD test (Hresko, Reid, & Hammill, 1981) item 19 requires children to imitate or repeat target sentences: (a) "The grass was eaten by the goat," and (b) "Tell everyone what you want to do." These two sentences represent more complex sentence structures than simple subject-verb sentences. Look to see how closely children's imitated responses mirror the stimulus sentence. What is missing? The subject? The verb? The subordinate clause? The prepositional phrase? The missing part of the target sentence indicates which syntactic structure has not yet been acquired.

Item analysis may also reveal instances where regional variations in semantics may be responsible for errors. For example, if the stimulus word is "rig" and the items pictured include an oil well structure and a semi-trailer truck, children in locales where oil is not produced might select the semi-trailer as a "rig" since they are not as familiar with oil wells. Thus, the resulting error may actually reflect cultural differences rather than linguistic deficits. Some specific measures, such as the early version of the Peabody Picture Vocabulary Test, have been criticized as lacking cultural fairness (Datta, 1975).

As a way of reviewing language assessment measures prior to using them, the grid in Figure 12.9 provides a structure for categorizing the content of specific measures. Categorization of test items on the Preschool Language Scale-3 (Zimmerman, Steiner, & Pond, 1992) is provided as an example.

Referral of specific children for further assessment and evaluation should only occur after the classroom teacher thoroughly assesses a child's receptive and productive language knowledge through a variety of measures. It is inappropriate to refer a child for further assessment based upon the conclusions reached from a single assessment measure. Assessments must be conducted over a period of time and be conducted by more than one teacher to allow for a more objective and reliable evaluation.

WORKING WITH PARENTS

Teachers need to work closely with parents in communicating the specific assessments used in their classrooms. While parental consent is required for all formal assessments, parents should also be aware of informal measures used to assess student progress. Parents' observations of their child's language at home can make valuable contributions to the overall understanding and assessment of a child's language development. When sharing the results of formal or informal assessments with parents, it is important for the teacher to avoid overly technical language or premature diagnostic labels and to listen actively to parents' comments and questions. Teachers should thoroughly explain the testing or assessment procedures so

FIGURE 12.9
Example Categorization Chart for Reviewing and Using Assessment Measures

Preschool Language Scale-3*   Name of Measure Reviewed
(Zimmerman, Steiner & Pond, 1992, pp. 5–7 Test Booklet)

Aspects of Language Knowledge	Receptive Language	Expressive Language
Phonetic	embedded in comprehension of test items	embedded in child's verbal responses tells how an object is used
Semantic	descriptive concepts distinguishes colors	identifies categories
Syntactic	comprehends passive sentences	repeats sentences uses auxiliaries
Morphemic	responds to comparative question: "Which one is heavier?"	uses prepositions uses present and past tense for both
Pragmatic	no specific items; range of responses elicited indicates knowledge of language intentions	regular and irregular verbs describes several step procedure

*Examples present in test items for developmental ages 3-0 to 5-0 years.

that parents understand the assessment process. In many instances it is valuable to make an audiotape or videotape of the actual assessment so parents can observe and hear the child's spontaneous language and/or elicited responses. (Parental consent is necessary prior to audiotaping or videotaping.) Through the review of the audio or videotape, parents have an opportunity to ask more specific questions and clarify other concerns they may have. Teachers also can clarify the nature of any concerns they have for the child's language development.

ASSESSMENT-BASED CURRICULAR CHANGES

Information obtained through the use of various assessment measures is valuable in determining the effectiveness of specific curricula. For example, if assessment measures indicate children's vocabulary acquisition should be enhanced, then the curriculum should be reexamined to determine what changes could be made to increase the introduction and elaboration of vocabulary-related experiences. When children's syntactic knowledge needs to be enhanced, increasing their exposure to storybooks (during teacher read-alouds) with varied syntactic structures would be beneficial, as would opportunities to engage in story retellings and story dictation.

SUMMARY

Assessment of young children's language development is an important part of early childhood education. Teachers who are aware of the strengths and limitations of formal and informal measures are better able to develop an assessment program that provides direction for curriculum development and implementation. Knowledge of assessment also assists teachers in identifying children who may need further referral in determining their language development needs.

✳ ✳ ✳ CHAPTER REVIEW

1. Terms to review:
   formative assessment
   summative assessment
   normed
   validity
   reliability
2. What is the relationship between assessment and curriculum?
3. Distinguish between formative and summative assessment.
4. What are two strengths and two weaknesses of informal assessment?
5. List frequently used forms of informal assessment.
6. Identify the value of using a checklist over using anecdotal records.
7. What is the goal of the storybook-based language observation?
8. What are two strengths and two weaknesses of formal assessment?
9. Name two formal language measures and indicate which aspects of language knowledge are measured.

✳ ✳ ✳ CHAPTER EXTENSION ACTIVITIES

1. Conduct a storybook-based language observation following the guidelines and format presented in this chapter.
2. Interview a speech clinician or educational psychologist. Find out what type of assessment measures they have found useful in assessing language development.
3. Interview a classroom teacher. Ask the teacher how children's language development is assessed formally and/or informally in his or her classroom.

4. Examine a copy of a standardized test for assessing language development. Write a brief summary of the scope of language development measured by the test.

5. Observe and record the speech of young children interacting in a dramatic play corner for 20 minutes. Transcribe the audiotape. Analyze the children's language for examples of language development in each of the five aspects of language knowledge.

✳ ✳ ✳ REFERENCES

Barrs, M., Ellis, S., Hester, H., & Thomas, A. (1989). *The primary language record: Handbook for teachers.* Portsmouth, NH: Heinemann.

Bentzen, W. (1985). *Seeing young children: A guide to observing and recording behavior.* Albany, NY: Delmar.

Bredekamp, S., & Copple, C. (Eds.). (1997). *Developmentally appropriate practice in early childhood programs* (Rev. ed.). Washington, DC: National Association for the Education of Young Children.

Brigance, A. (1991). *Revised-Brigance Diagnostic Inventory of Early Development.* Woburn, MA: Curriculum Associates.

Brown, R. (1973). *A first language: The early stages.* Cambridge, MA: Harvard University Press.

Buros, O. (1938-) *Mental measurements yearbooks.* Highland Park, NJ: Gryphon Press.

Clay, M. (1993). *An observation survey of early literacy achievement.* Portsmouth, NH: Heinemann.

Cohen, L., & Spenciner, L. (1994). *Assessment of young children.* New York: Longman.

Coplan, J. (1993). *Early language milestone scale* (2nd ed.). Austin, TX: Pro-Ed.

Datta, L. (1975). Review of the Peabody picture vocabulary test-R. In W. Frankenburg & B. Camp (Eds.), *Pediatric screening tests.* Springfield, IL: Thomas.

Dunn, L. M., & Dunn, L. (1981). *Peabody picture vocabulary test-revised.* Circle Pines, MN: American Guidance Service.

Dunn, L. M., & Dunn, L. (1997). *Peabody picture vocabulary test IIIA and IIIB.* Circle Pines, MN: American Guidance Service.

Frankenburg, W., Dodds, J., Archer, P., Bresnick, B., Maschka, P., Edelman, N., & Shapiro, H. (1990). *Denver II Technical manual.* Denver: Denver Developmental Materials, Inc.

Gardner, M. (1990). *Expressive one-word picture vocabulary test-revised.* Novato, CA: Academic Therapy Publications.

Goodman, K. (1992). Myths, metaphors, and misuses: The case of the vanishing checklists. In K. Goodman, L. Bird, and Y. Goodman (Eds.), *The whole language catalog: Supplement on authentic assessment* (p. 110). New York: SRA, Macmillan/McGraw-Hill.

Goodman, Y. (1985). Kidwatching: Observing children in the classroom. In A. Jagger & M. T. Smith-Burke (Eds.), *Observing the language learner.* Newark, DE: International Reading Association.

Haines, J., Ames, L., & Gillespie, C. (1980). *The Gesell preschool test.* Lumberville, PA: Modern Learning Press.

Hammill, D., Mather, N., & Roberts, R. (2001). *Illinois test of psycholinguistic abilities* (3rd ed.). Austin, TX: Pro-Ed.

Hresko, W., Reid, D., & Hammill, D. (1981). *Test of early language development (TELD).* Austin, TX: Pro-Ed.

Kempfer, G. (1993). *Rebecca's storybook-based language observation.* Unpublished manuscript, Northeastern Illinois University, Chicago.

Lindfors, J. (1987). *Children's language and learning* (2nd ed.). Upper Saddle River, NJ: Prentice Hall.

Martin, S. (1994). *Take a look: Observation and portfolio assessment in early childhood.* New York: Addison-Wesley.

McCarthy, D. (1972). *Manual for the McCarthy scales of children's abilities.* New York: Psychological Corporation, Harcourt Brace Jovanovich.

Meisels, S. (1989). *Developmental screening in early childhood: A guide* (3rd ed.). Washington, DC: National Association for the Education of Young Children.

Murphy, L., Condey, J. C., & Impara, J. (1994). *Tests in print IV: An index to tests, test reviews, and the literature on specific tests.* Lincoln, NE: University of Nebraska Press.

National Association for the Education of Young Children (NAEYC). (1988). Position statement on standardized testing of young children 3 through 8 years of age. *Young Children, 43,* 42–47.

Newcomer, P., & Hammill, D. (1988). *Test of language development-primary* (2nd ed.). Austin, TX: Pro-Ed.

Otto, B. (1992). Storybook-based language observations. Unpublished manuscript. Northeastern Illinois University, Chicago, IL.

Reich, P. (1986). *Language development.* Upper Saddle River, NJ: Prentice Hall.

Salvia, J., & Ysseldyke, J. (1998). *Assessment* (7th ed.). Boston: Houghton Mifflin.

Smith, J. (1990). Measurement issues in early literacy assessment. In L. Morrow & J. Smith (Eds.), *Assessment for instruction in early literacy* (pp. 62–74). Englewood Cliffs, NJ: Prentice Hall.

Wiener, R., & Cohen, J. (1997). *Literacy portfolios: Using assessment to guide instruction.* Upper Saddle River, NJ: Merrill.

Wiig, E., Secord, W., & Semel, E. (1992). *CELF-PRESCHOOL.* San Antonio, TX: Psychological Corporation, Harcourt Brace Jovanovich.

Wortham, S. (2001). *Assessment in early childhood education.* Upper Saddle River, NJ: Merrill/Prentice Hall.

Wyatt, T., & Seymour, H. (1999). Assessing the speech and language skills of preschool children. In E. Nuttall, I. Romero, & J. Kalesnik (Eds.), *Assessing and screening preschoolers: Psychological and educational dimensions* (2nd ed., pp. 218–239). Boston: Allyn & Bacon.

Zimmerman, I., Steiner, V., & Pond, R. (1992). *Preschool language scale-3.* San Antonio, TX: Psychological Corporation, Harcourt Brace Jovanovich.

Zion, G. (1956). *Harry the dirty dog.* New York: Harper & Row.

APPENDIX

✳ ✳ ✳

STORYBOOK-BASED LANGUAGE OBSERVATION GUIDELINES

GOAL FOR OBSERVATION

Observe and describe a child's language development with respect to the five aspects of language knowledge.

SECTION I: DIRECTIONS FOR LANGUAGE ANALYSIS ASSIGNMENT

1. Select a child you know between the ages of 2½ and 5 years.
2. Select two storybooks that are moderately familiar to the child.
3. Have a tape recorder and blank audiotape ready. (Videotape is also acceptable.)
4. Ask the child to read the book to you or if the child refuses, tell the child you will read it together. Or, you may tape the parent reading to/with the child. Ask general questions and make comments only to sustain the storybook interaction. Do not supply information not found in the story. Avoid asking questions that the child can answer with only one or two words as this limits the syntactic complexity shown by the child. Encourage the child to go ahead on his or her own (i.e., "Read to me any way you want to." "Just pretend." "Tell me about the pictures.").
5. Make no notes during the storybook interaction.
6. Transcribe the storybook interaction, using the form provided. Duplicate the form as needed. (See format at end of guidelines.)
7. Photocopy the books used by the child.
8. Prepare a written analysis following the guidelines/format given in Section II. Additionally, attach the transcript and the audiotape.

SECTION II: LANGUAGE ANALYSIS

In answering each question, provide examples to clarify your responses.

Phonetic Knowledge

1. What sounds did the child produce clearly?
2. Which words appeared more difficult for the child? Were the difficult sounds at the beginning of the word? in the middle? at the end?
3. Were words (syllables and sounds) articulated clearly?
4. Did the child indicate an awareness that specific letters or words have specific sounds? Did the child focus on print?

Semantic Knowledge

1. Did the child use synonyms when referring to ideas, objects, or people in the book?
2. Did the child refer to real-life objects or events related to the book's content?
3. Did the child appear to use story illustrations to cue memory for vocabulary?

Syntactic Knowledge

1. Describe the range of sentence/phrase structure represented in the child's utterances.
2. To what extent does the child's syntax mirror the structure of the story text?
3. Did the child use questions?
4. Did the child use dialogue carriers?

Morphemic Knowledge

1. Describe the child's use of derivational and inflectional morphemes.
2. Were any overgeneralizations applied to comparatives or verb tense markers?

Pragmatic Knowledge

1. Did the child hold the book correctly?
2. Were pages turned at appropriate times?
3. Did the child show an awareness of any of these concepts: title, author, page, words, beginning, end?

4. Did the child show direction when reading? Did the child read from front to back of book? from left to right? from top to bottom?

5. Did the child use formal beginnings and endings, such as "Once upon a time," "One day . . .," or "The End"?

6. Did the child use reading intonation?

7. Did the child check to see if you/the listener were comprehending the story?

8. Did the child pause or encourage turn taking or your comments about the story?

9. Did the child show awareness that books have stable texts, such as self-corrections or memory for text?

Additional Notes

Record other information based on additional interaction with the child, siblings, teacher, or parent, related to the child's development of the five aspects of language knowledge (oral or written).

Conclusions/Summary

Summarize your observations and analysis of the child's language development.

Transcription Format for Storybook-Based Language Observation Assignment

Child's Name: _____   Age: _____

Book Title(s): _____

Observer: _____

Line No.	Speaker	What was said

EXAMPLE OF A STORYBOOK-BASED LANGUAGE OBSERVATION

From Kempfer, G. (1993). Rebecca's storybook, based language observation. Unpublished manuscript. Northeastern Illinois University, Chicago. Printed by permission of author.
(See transcription of audiotape, which follows.)

PHONETIC KNOWLEDGE

Rebecca had no problems producing any sounds in the storytelling. Her enunciation was clear, and to my ears, of adult competence. Not all phonological combinations were represented, however, so it's possible that she could have difficulty with the "z" sound or the "th" sound as in "thigh" or others that were not included.

Rebecca slurred short words a number of times and mispronounced four words. All errors were within the bounds of normal oral English and the sentences were all able to be understood. In her first sentence, she left the "w" off "was"—"that 'as covered with vines." She left the "d" off of "and" three times, the first time—"a man an' a horse"—line 21. On line 51, Rebecca again left the "d" off "and"—"when they walked in an' saw the toys and candy," and again in line 78, "that's Bruno, an' there's the wicked step-mother." On line 33, Rebecca slurred "her," leaving off the "h"—"Madeline was in 'er arms." She used the common slur, on line 75, "gonna" for "going to"—"Her name is gonna be Cinderella." Rebecca stumbled once on the word "Miss," line 44—"One day M-Miss Clavel." She did not stumble on it again anywhere else, though. She mispronounced "pumpkin" in line 123, saying "punkin" instead, also a common error in oral speech—"There's the little mice, there's the punkin." On line 27, Rebecca mispronounced "skating," saying "shkating" instead—"now they're shkating." This might give me pause except that she had no problem with the pronunciation of "S" elsewhere and said "shkating" so fluently that I wonder if it's not a favorite "pet" or "cool" way of saying the word for her. Likewise, on line 81, Rebecca says "cindies" for "cinders"—"she got so covered with cindies from cleaning the fireplace." Again, I suspect Rebecca has no trouble recognizing the word when spoken but has "cutened" it up to her taste, since she can enunciate "Cinderella" very well. Finally, Rebecca mispronounced "dialed" as "deealed" but immediately corrected herself with no hesitation. There were some parts of her speech that were unintelligible on the tape. I was later able to distinguish some with headphones on during the transcription process. The rest I still wasn't sure about. These were times when Rebecca rushed a bit and spoke softly. Both these times she seemed to be distracted by trying to remember something about the story.

It appears that Rebecca knows the Madeline book very well. She recited a good deal of it from memory (as did her just two-year-old sister). She identified what was on the illustrations by saying "There's the horse," etc. She did not focus on the print by, for instance, following the text line with her finger; instead, she pointed at items in the pictures. She turned all pages individually and looked at all the pictures but did not always comment on the picture or correlate her recitation with the picture. For example, she recited, "She was not afraid of mice" from page 13, looked at page 14, recited what she remembered (so it seemed to me) from page 15, then commented on page 14. She ignored page 16 ("and nobody knew so well how to frighten Miss Clavel") altogether and continued her recitation on page 17, "in the middle of the night . . ." The result was a fluent telling of the story of Madeline's adventure, although she did leave off the actual ending of the book. She did not recite from the Cinderella story; mostly she identified the pictures by saying "There's the horse," "There's the prince," etc.

SEMANTIC KNOWLEDGE

I found one example of Rebecca defining "footman" when she couldn't remember the word itself, in line 107. She also uses the word "step-witch" instead of "stepmother" on line 88 and 98, clearly a synonym in her mind! Not so clear is her usage of the words mom and mother for Miss Clavel, lines 28 and 50. She may be using them as a synonym for "mother superior" (her father is Catholic, her mother is Jewish) or she may simply be seeing Miss Clavel as an adult mother-figure. I would guess the latter myself. Otherwise, Rebecca used the exact words from the page when she recited what she remembered or she named objects. Rebecca made no references to anything outside the actual story lines and pictures.

SYNTACTIC KNOWLEDGE

Rebecca used complete sentences most of the time. Her recitations were complete sentences. She did not use a complete sentence to indicate the end of the story, instead she said, "All done," both times (lines 73 and 133). Also, she did not always use complete sentence structure when she was adding comments to the story. For example, in lines 26–28, Rebecca says about the skating party, "Now they're shkating. Even the mother." On line 52, she repeats a phrase from what she'd just recited, "From the toys and candies from Papa." (She's aware that she's repeating that portion of the story and seems a little bemused by it, indicating that she's probably skilled at observing her own speech fluency.) In answer to my question, line 104, of how Cinderella got a prettier gown, Rebecca answered with an incomplete sentence, "From the fairy." On lines 35, 98, and 126, she left out the conjunction "and" to join her two clauses.

When Rebecca was reciting from the Madeline story, her language mirrored the text very closely. Other times, she mirrored it less closely. A more developed example though is on line 48, when she says, "There's the kids in a straight line," which was not in the text for that illustration but had been used in the text previously. The parallel was not close in the Cinderella story. This story line is not rhymed and has more text. Rebecca mostly identified the pictures or characters in the pictures in present tense. The story was in past tense. There were no phrases taken from the text and paraphrased in her oral storytelling, although Rebecca clearly knew the story well. Since she saw the film before getting the book, it may be that she's remembering scenes from the film when she "reads" the Cinderella storybook rather than relating directly to the book. If so, it makes me pause to think about the relative place of movies and books for young children.

MORPHEMIC KNOWLEDGE

Rebecca used the progressive ending "ing" in "going," line 11, "brushing," line 13, "standing," line 18, "saying," line 53, "crying," line 64, "sweeping," line 80, "tearing," line 101, "running," line 115, and "getting," line 127. She used the irregular past tense of "do," "done," twice in "all done," at the end of the stories, and the past of "get," "got," in line 104. She used the "er" suffix for comparing in "bigger," line 80. She expressed possession by saying her father, her horse (line 78), her gown (line 105), her slipper (line 113), and their coach (line 133). She used no inflectional possessives. She did use regular plurals and plural pronouns: they, line 22; houses, line 35; kids, line 46; birds, line 70; and witches, line 101. Rebecca used no derivational morphemes.

Rebecca overgeneralized once in creating past tense, on line 104, when she said, "And there she is [with] her teared (torn) dress."

PRAGMATIC KNOWLEDGE

Rebecca held the book correctly and turned the pages well, indicating much practice. She turned each page and looked at each picture, but in the telling of the Madeline story, as previously described in the phonetic knowledge section, her narrative did not always coincide exactly with the page sequences. Sometimes she swept both pages with her eyes first before making her story line. Usually, the story line, that is her identifying of the characters and pictures, was sequential with the pictures but not always. For instance, she identifies the step-witch (sister) on page 5 (left page), then describes page 6 (right page, lines 86–88), then goes back to page 5 (left page) to identify Lucifer. Again, on page 14 (right page, lines 112–113) she identifies the prince first and Cinderella, then goes back to page 13 (left page) to point out the fairy.

Rebecca clearly understood the concept of front to back of the book, reading from left page to right page and beginning to end. It's possible that she understands or recognizes top to bottom, but, even though Madeline has some pages with two pictures, one above the other, on them, I couldn't discern that she was looking at them top to bottom, since she was reciting during this portion of the storytelling.

ADDITIONAL NOTES

Rebecca is the older of two sisters. She is just five years old and her sister is just two years old. Both her parents are professionals involved with education. Her mother produces films for medical education and her father teaches college history. They both speak excellent standard English. Stephanie, the two-year-old, has excellent enunciation and a large vocabulary. (She also loves Madeline.) This is a child-centered family. The parents share equally in childcare. Rebecca has been in daycare part-time for three years and is starting kindergarten the fall of 1993. Stephanie will also be starting part-time daycare in the fall. The girls are generally affectionate and cooperative, as evidenced by the portion of the audiotape 0–33. I observe that they play well with the other children on the block outside (their parents supervise). Rebecca did her storytelling in the evening. An energetic child, she nevertheless appeared to become fatigued by this task. The storybook she had selected was a long one. She sighed between pages toward the end and gave scantier attention to each page but dutifully fulfilled her commitment without asking to stop early. She enjoyed hearing the tape played back, as did her sister.

CONCLUSION

Looking at the table of Ages for English Consonants Acquisition in Reich's text (Reich, 1986, page 57), Rebecca articulated well all the consonants listed: p, m, n, h, w, b, k, g, d, t, f, j, l, s, the *ch* as in chip, the *sh* as in ship, the *y*, the *r* as in roar, the *ng* as in king and the *th* as in this. There was no example of the ng sound as in kong, z, j as in gyp, th as in thigh, sh as in vision. Her enunciation is as good as most adults'.

On the whole, given this small sample, Rebecca's syntax seemed typical for her age. Rebecca's mean length of utterance was about 6 and this is to be expected for her age according to Reich. Rebecca phrased two questions, a *why* question and a *what* question. At five years old, she would have been doing this for a good two and one-half years. I suspect that had I prodded, as I did toward the end of the Cinderella story (lines 114–116), Rebecca could have given more complex responses, as she did then, to the illustrations instead of simply labeling them. Her reaction to Cinderella's new ball gown was appropriately typical for a five-year-old girl and described in greater detail.

Rebecca's development in morphology also appears typical for her age, although again, the sample is not the best for this analysis, due to her recitation for portions of it. She used no possessives in this example. She consistently used the pronouns showing distance—there, that, those. This seems like appropriate usage to me, since it was in the context of reading a story which she was not verbally relating in any way to her own life or to anything outside of the books.

Most difficult to determine from this audiotape alone is Rebecca's understanding of the words and ideas she was saying since she recited parts and used simpler construction than her capability for most of her own comments. However, being in her physical presence confirmed that she connected specific words with referents on the page and ideas, that is parts of the story line, to specific pages. She also made comments on how bad Lucifer the cat was (line 96) and how pretty the flowers were (line 108).

This format works well, I think, as a simple screening. There may be more subtle problems that are not picked up. On the other hand, if a five-year-old can't succeed in following along a simple story with his/her own words some informal remedial work is probably in order, such as intensive exposure to books. We can conclude that Rebecca, as made evident by her memorization of the Madeline story line, clearly uses well-written, easily remembered text as models for her own speech, since she carries it in her head. This points out the significance of appropriate reading material for children (and adults). In any case, it is my beginner's evaluation that Rebecca's language is well-developed for her age.

Transcription of Storybook-Based Language Observation

Child's Name: Rebecca   Age: 5 (June)

Book Titles: *Madeline; Cinderella*   Examiner: Gail Kempfer

Line #	Speaker	(What was said)
1	Adult	OK, we're ready.
2	Child	In a little house in Paris that'as covered with vines lived
3		twelve little girls in two straight lines. They left their
4		house at half past nine in rain or shine. In two
5		straight lines they broke their bread, brushed their
6		teeth, and went to bed. The smallest one was
7		Madeline. Umm . . . I forget this page.
8	Adult	That's OK. You just talk. You know, you don't
9		have to really read it. Just tell me the story that's
10		happening. Just talk the story.
11	Child	Umm . . . The kids are going to bed.
12	Adult	Uh huh.
13	Child	Now they're brushing their teeth.
14	Adult	That's right.
15	Child	Umm . . . They smiled at the good and frowned at the

(continued)

Transcription of Storybook-Based Language Observation *(continued)*

16		bad.
17	Adult	Um hmm.
18	Child	And sometimes . . . [hm] they're standing in their
19		line . . .
20	Adult	Um hmm.
21	Child	And there's a man an' a horse. And there's a building.
22		I think they live in [it]. And sometimes they were
23		very sad. They left the house at half past nine, in
24		rain or shine. The smallest one was Madeline. She
25		was not afraid of mice, to the tiger in the zoo,
26		Madeline just said pooh pooh. Now they're shkating.
27	Adult	Right.
28	Child	Even the mother. In the middle of the night, Miss Clavel turned
29		on the light . . . And said, "Something is not right!" Madeline sat
30		in bed, cried and cried, her eyes were red. When Dr. Cohen
31		came, he rushed out to the phone. He deealed-he dialed
32		Danton-ten-six. "Nurse," he said, "it's an appendix." Everybody
33		had to cry, not a single eye was dry. Madeline was in 'er arms
34		in a blanket safe and
35	Child	warm. There's a car, there's some houses.
36	Adult	Uh huh.
37	Child	Madeline woke up in a room with flowers. Soon
38		she ate and drank. On her bed there was a crack.
39		There's a rabbit!
40	Adult	Right.
41	Child	That's a crack.
42	Adult	Right.
43	Child	There's a chair [place] and I don't know what that is.
44		One day M-Miss Clavel said, "Isn't this a fine day to
45		visit Madeline?" Oh, there's a bus, and there's the
46		flowers and there's all the kids.
47	Adult	Right.
48	Child	Umm . . . There's the kids in a straight line, there's the
49		Mommy and there's a sign. I don't know what that says.
50		There's the kids and the Mom. When they
51		walked in an' saw the toys and candy from Papa,
52		they looked in and said, "Ahhh." From the toys and
53		candies from Papa. I keep saying it.
54	Adult	Umm.
55	Child	But the biggest surprise by far, on her stomach was a
56		scar. "Bye," they said, "we'll come again," and the
57		little girls left out in the rain. In the rain, they
58		went home, broke their bread and brushed their teeth
59		and went to bed. "Goodnight, Little girls, I hope you

60		sleep well, goodnight, goodnight." said Miss Clavel.
61		In the middle of the night, Miss Clavel turned on the
62		light, and said, "Something is not right." She went
63		fast and even faster. Umm . . . There's the little girls
64		and they're crying. I wonder why they're crying. Why?
65		I don't know. Oh no, [maybe] they're
66		[unintelligible]-stakes. [Thinking]-there's Miss
67		Clavel!
68	Adult	Yeah.
69	Child	Yeah.
70		Are those birds?
71	Adult	Ah, well, I think those are the angels, guardian
72		angels, and stars.
73	Child	All done. (Child closes first book and sets it down)
74	Adult	OK. (child begins second book)
75	Child	Her name is gonna be Cinderella, but her name—I
76		don't know her name.
77	Adult	'Kay.
78	Child	That's her father, that's her horse, that's Bruno, an'
79		there's the wicked step-mother. Whoa. Now she's
80		bigger. And she-umm-is sweeping the
81		floor and she got so covered with cindies from
82		cleaning the fireplace.
83	Adult	Um hmm.
84	Child	And, then they named her Cinderella. And, there's
85		the horse, there's Bruno, there's the little mice and
86		there's bad Lucifer.
87	Adult	Uh huh.
88	Child	There's the wicked step-witch. There's the king
89		and who's he?
90	Adult	Who is that?
91	Child	That's the King, that's the -
92	Adult	Is that the Prince?
93	Child	No. That isn't the Prince.
94	Adult	Ahh. Is that like a Duke?
95	Child	Yeah, that's the Duke. There's the Duke. And
96		there's umm, Lucifer, he's of course the bad cat.
97	Adult	[Laughs in response]
98	Child	There's the step-witch, there's Cinderella, there's
99		Cinderella at her door.
100	Adult	Uh huh.
101	Child	There she's in a party dress, the witches are tearing
102		it, and there she is [with] her teared dress. But
103		now she got a prettier gown.
104	Adult	How did she get that?

(continued)

Transcription of Storybook-Based Language Observation *(continued)*

105	Child	From the fairy. There's her gown, too. She looks
106	Child	. . . . beautiful! There's her coach, there's some
107		horses, there's . . . who open the door for her. And
108		there's the flowers-those are pretty. Water fountain!
109		There's - that's the Prince.
110	Adult	Oh.
111	Child	There's the Prince, there's Cinderella, there's the
112		fairy. There's Cinderella. There's Cinderella,
113		there's her slipper.
114	Adult	What's happening?
115	Child	She's running down the stairs.
116	Adult	What happened that he's running after her?
117	Child	Because it's midnight and the fairy said she had to
118		leave . . .
119	Adult	Ahh.
120	Child	. . . at midnight. But there's the other glass slipper.
121		[There's] a heart that says love. And there's Bruno,
122		there's the horse. And there's the step-mother.
123		There's the little [mice], there's the punkin, and
124		it broke into pieces right here and right here.
125		[Cinderella-unintelligible]. There's the little
126		mice, there's the key. There's the Duke, and there
127		they're getting married. Whoa. Umm . . . there's the Prince
128		and the Duke and the horse and Bruno and the little
129		mice. And now they're in their coach going to the
130		wedding! All done.
131	Adult	Thank you.

13

ENHANCING LANGUAGE DEVELOPMENT AMONG CHILDREN WITH COMMUNICATIVE DISORDERS

Not all children acquire language easily. An estimated 10 percent of elementary school children have some type of communication disorder (Owens, 2001). Difficulties in acquiring language may stem from problems in reception and/or production of language. For example, children with hearing impairments experience difficulty with language reception. Children who have problems producing specific sounds have difficulties with language expression. This chapter will focus on the special needs of children who have hearing impairment, cognitive impairment, language delay, articulation disorders, and fluency disorders.

Teachers must develop a clear understanding of the distinction between *communicative disorders* and *communicative differences* (Piper, 1993). Different styles of speaking and communicating that are culturally based are not communicative disorders but simply different ways of communicating. Children with communicative disorders use language in a way that significantly interferes with their ability to communicate with others who speak the same language and dialect, or they cannot use language at all. Children who are becoming bilingual may not be able to communicate clearly in their second language; however, that is not a communicative disorder but only a developmental stage in the process of becoming fluent in two languages.

Because early childhood teachers interact with children who are in the process of developing communication skills, they need to be aware of the characteristics of specific communication disorders so they can alert other teachers, administrators, and parents to potential difficulties. Children who are at risk for speech and language disorders include those who (1) have had numerous ear infections, (2) do not talk or have limited speech, and/or (3) experience problems interacting (Patterson & Wright, 1990). In some instances, intervention programs may be appropriate. At the elementary level, most school districts have a speech-language pathologist who works with students who have been referred and identified as having mild to severe communication disorders. In some states, school districts have screening programs for children from birth to age 5.

A TEAM APPROACH TO HELPING CHILDREN WITH COMMUNICATIVE DISORDERS

During all levels of early childhood education, it is important that the classroom teacher and the speech-language pathologist work as a team to address the needs of children with communication disorders. In the past, children who were diagnosed as having mild speech or communication problems were placed in a "pull-out" program. They would see a speech-language pathologist, commonly referred to in elementary schools as the "speech teacher" or "speech therapist," for a specific time period during the day or week, depending upon the severity of the speech problem. A more current approach is for the speech teacher to come to the regular classroom and work with the child within the classroom setting (Owens, 1991). Sometimes this involves the classroom teacher and the speech teacher team teaching; the classroom teacher works with most of the class while the speech teacher works with a smaller group of children needing special teaching techniques. Both groups work on similar learning activities.

In addition, the speech-language teacher serves as a consultant to the regular classroom teacher, assisting in identifying children with language impairments and describing specific ways children's impairments can be addressed in the regular classroom. The classroom teacher also can share her observations of the classroom behaviors and language interactions of a child with special needs with the speech-language teacher. By clarifying the classroom expectations for participation and communication and the ways in which specific children are having difficulty in meeting these expectations, the classroom teacher provides valuable insights to the speech teacher as to the needed intervention and language activities. Together they work to create a classroom environment that can foster growth in communication skills.

The following section describes communication disorders that classroom teachers commonly face: hearing impairment, cognitive impairment, language delay, articulation disorders, and fluency disorders. Identifying characteristics are described along with strategies for enhancing language acquisition in the classroom.

HEARING IMPAIRMENT

Characteristics

When children cannot hear the full range of speech sounds, language development is impaired. The loudness of sounds is measured in decibels. Children who are unable to perceive sounds lower than 60 decibels (i.e., a baby's cry) usually do not develop spontaneous oral language (Ratner, 1997). The amount of hearing loss is formally determined by an audiologist who administers a hearing test and documents the range of sound frequencies heard by each ear.

About one half of all hearing loss is inherited (Reich, 1986). Other causes of hearing impairment include chronic inner ear infections (see Appendix to Chapter 4) and brain damage due to injury or prenatal conditions. Through careful observation of a child's responses to oral speech and environmental sounds, a teacher can determine whether a hearing impairment might exist (Cohen & Spenciner, 1994). Specifically, a teacher should explore whether the child turns her head when a sound occurs or startles at a loud noise. In addition, the teacher should ask himself the following questions:

- Does the child only respond when being spoken to in close proximity and in face-to-face situations?
- When her name is called, does the child respond?

- Can the child follow one- or two-step directions without having multiple repetitions?
- Does the child ignore or misunderstand what others say?
- Does the child nod her head to a question or direction and then behave as if she did not hear? (Patterson & Wright, 1990)

Additionally, if the child has a history of ear infections, colds, or allergies, either temporary or permanent hearing loss may have occurred. Even a minor, temporary hearing loss can have an effect on a child's interactions in the classroom (Harris, 1990). Whatever the reason for the hearing loss, the classroom teacher needs to be aware of the loss and make appropriate adjustments in implementing the classroom curriculum.

Techniques for Enhancing Language Development

When a child has a mild hearing impairment due to an ear infection or a slight hearing loss, a teacher should:

1. Always speak to the child in close proximity and face-to-face.
2. In large group settings, such as story time or circle activities, place the child nearby so that he can see the pictures and hear more clearly.
3. Use gestures to accompany any directions or conceptual explanations.
4. Encourage the child to use the listening center where ear phones are used and the volume on the tape player can be adjusted to meet the child's needs.
5. Speak distinctly, using a moderate volume.
6. Encourage other children in the classroom to speak to the child in close proximity and in face-to-face orientation.

Teachers should also provide visual and tactile aids through the use of illustrations, concrete objects, and hands-on activities and continually check to be sure that the child understands what has been said (Harris, 1990; Russell-Fox, 1999).

COGNITIVE IMPAIRMENT

Characteristics

Children who have a cognitive impairment may not process language effectively and may not be developing conceptual knowledge necessary for further language acquisition. They have difficulty paying attention to others' speech, processing it, and remembering what was said (Harris, 1990). They may be unable to sustain attention long enough to enjoy listening to a story and may have difficulty participating in conversations.

Techniques for Enhancing Language Development

In planning curriculum for children with cognitive impairment, teachers should focus on children's linguistic level rather than their chronological ages (Cook, Tessier, & Armbruster, 1987). It is particularly important to provide children who have cognitive impairments with opportunities to develop pragmatic language competencies for using language in their everyday settings to communicate their needs and wants to others in their home, school, and community environments (Ratner, 1997). Since cognitively impaired children may need more repetition, teachers should provide opportunities for children to have multiple interactions with the same storybook, song, action poem, or concept-building activity. Teachers should also monitor children's interactions and encourage them to ask questions or to seek assistance.

LANGUAGE DELAY

Characteristics

Children with language delay are lagging behind only in their language development (Rice, 1989). They are at age-appropriate levels in their sensory, cognitive, and emotional development. When measured on nonverbal assessments, children with language delay perform in the normal range. The causes of language delay are unknown; however, environmental deficiencies are not thought to be a cause. Current hypotheses as to the cause of language delay focus on difficulties in mental representation or linguistic processing (Rice, 1989).

Specific characteristics of children with language delay involve limitations in semantic, syntactic, and pragmatic knowledge (Dumtschin, 1988). Compared to normally developing children's speech, the vocabularies of children with language delay are smaller (semantic), and their sentences are less complex, contain frequent grammatical errors, and show less variation (syntactic). A difficulty with the pragmatic aspect of language is also evident among children with language delay, who are likely to have difficulty in maintaining a conversation and may have problems understanding others or being understood. They are less likely to engage in dramatic play. In addition, children with language delay are likely to focus talk on the here and now rather than the past or future, which may indicate a limitation of symbolic representation.

The limited vocabulary of children with language delay may manifest itself in a difficulty in classifying objects or distinguishing similarities and differences. In addition, their difficulties in conversation may show up in general problems in interacting with other children in the classroom.

Techniques for Enhancing Language Development

As with other forms of communicative disorders, the classroom must be a positive language environment where the focus is on interactive communication. The classroom teacher should be an active listener, truly listening to what each child is saying and responding to what is said. In this way, the conversations become child-centered as the teacher incorporates the child's topic into her speech (Dumtschin, 1988). Verbal mapping and linguistic scaffolding are techniques that teachers will find effective in encouraging interactive communication (see Chapter 2). Rather than directly trying to "teach" language or "correct usage," a teacher should focus on the communicative intent of the child and follow up with verbal mapping or linguistic scaffolding, which clarifies the child's message.

Storybook sharing is another way to encourage children with language delay to become more involved in using language to communicate their thoughts, questions, and ideas (McNeill & Fowler, 1996). During storybook sharing a teacher (or parent) closely interacts with the child in communicating the story to the child and in eliciting the child's responses to what is read. Praise is given for children's appropriate comments about the content or about their interest in what was read or illustrated. Expansion can also be used to elaborate upon a child's comment or response (see Chapter 2).

Open-ended questions can also be used to elicit linguistic participation from a child, although the teacher must be sensitive to the level of questioning that is appropriate for each child. Children with language delay may initially need to have lower levels of literal questioning to build up their self-confidence and also to build up their competencies in responding to questions (McNeill & Fowler, 1996). By using linguistic scaffolding techniques that involve a series of questions, children are encouraged to participate in longer conversations.

ARTICULATION DISORDERS

Characteristics

Speech production requires that the components of the physical speech mechanism (vocal cords, tongue, lips, teeth, soft and hard palate, and lungs) work together in specific ways to produce the needed sounds. Articulation disorders result from impairments in this coordination.

Articulation disorders are indicated when a child's speech at age 3 cannot be understood by an unfamiliar adult, and additionally, at age 8, when errors in articulation are still evident (Patterson & Wright, 1990). In some instances articulation problems may simply represent a delay in muscle development or coordination needed for articulating specific sounds. Articulation problems can also result from a child's chronic ear infections. Because the child could not clearly hear the speech sounds during the time in which the specific sounds were acquired, the child may have not learned how to produce the specific sounds correctly.

In other instances, articulation problems may reflect specific physical impairment, such as cleft lip, cleft palate, or tongue-tie, which is known as *restrictive lingual frenum*. Each of these physical impairments come from abnormalities that occurred during prenatal development. Cleft lip is a separation or split in the upper lip. A split that extends to the roof of the mouth is a cleft palate. Although the exact causes of cleft lips and cleft palates are not known, both genetic and prenatal environmental factors may be involved (Moller, Starr, & Johnson, 1990).

Tongue-tie occurs when the piece of skin under the tongue (*lingual frenum*) is too short or is "totally adhered to the floor of the mouth" (Boshart, 1999, p. 31). When the tongue is "tied" or restricted in its movement due to the shortened piece of skin, articulation is limited. Eating problems may also be evident.

Physical impairments such as cleft lip, cleft palate, and tongue-tie indicate long-term problems if no intervention occurs. In each of these instances, surgery can correct the problem; however, depending upon the age of the child and the severity of the original physical impairment, extensive speech therapy may be needed.

When a teacher notices a child who may have long-term articulation problems, it is important for the teacher to share those observations with a speech-language pathologist so that a more focused assessment can be made. Because of their physical appearance, cleft lip and cleft palate conditions are usually recognized at birth and surgery is performed during the first few months. Children with tongue-tie may not be identified until later when problems with eating or articulation are noticed. Children with long-term articulation problems need a specialized program implemented by both the classroom teacher and the speech-language therapist.

Techniques for Enhancing Language Development

The most important factor in enhancing language development among children who have articulation disorders is to create and maintain a positive classroom environment where children are encouraged to communicate and where any problems in communication are dealt with in a sensitive, caring manner. The classroom teacher should not embarrass the child who is having difficulty with a particular sound or draw the attention of the rest of the class to this child's difficulty.

Children who do not have articulation difficulties will often notice when their peers' speech exhibits articulation irregularities. Under no circumstances should children in the classroom be allowed to tease or make fun of a child who has articulation difficulties. Instead, other children in the classroom should be encouraged to accept the sound approximations from the child with articulation problems. A teacher can also explain to the class that some children are learning how to make specific sounds or explain that the child does not hear all of the sounds that others may hear. In addition, the focus of the classroom language should be on the meaning of what is communicated instead of on a rigid standard for phoneme production/articulation. As mentioned earlier, it is also important for the classroom teacher and the speech-language pathologist to work closely in developing and implementing specific techniques or activities for children with articulation disorders.

Children with articulation problems may not participate in group discussions as readily as other children and may be more comfortable participating in small group activities where they are interacting in a conversational setting. In large groups, activities with unison responses (e.g., reciting an action poem, song, or refrain from a predictable book) provide children with articulation problems an opportunity to participate verbally in a nonthreatening setting. Regardless of the activity, it is important for the classroom teacher and all of the children in the classroom to respond positively to the child's attempts to communicate and to focus on the meaning of the communication rather than on the difficulties the child is having.

FLUENCY DISORDERS: STUTTERING

Characteristics

The most common speech disfluency is stuttering (Culatta & Leeper, 1987). Stuttering involves difficulty in producing a smooth stream of speech, particularly the beginnings of words. Although stuttering usually involves oral speech, it may show up in young children's oral reading as well. Stuttering involves an involuntary repetition of isolated sounds or syllables, prolonged speech sounds, or a complete halt in the flow of speech (Cook, Tessier, & Armbruster, 1987). No specific factors have been identified as the cause of stuttering, either from hereditary, environmental, or organic factors (Ratner, 1997).

Most children experience speech disfluencies during their preschool and early school years as their language knowledge expands in each of the five aspects of language. Preschool and kindergarten children's language normally contains frequent disfluencies as they explore and experiment with language production using their phonetic, syntactic, semantic, morphemic, and pragmatic knowledges. Typically children's disfluencies show day-to-day variations and month-to-month variations and may vary with the communicative setting. Normal disfluencies involve whole word repetition (*that . . . that ball*), phrase repetition (*I want. . . . I want the truck*), sentence revisions (*I went . . . We went to the store*), hesitations or grammatical pauses (*Mommy, I want . . . some cookies*) or interjections (*I saw, . . . uh . . . the fire truck*) (Gottwald, Goldbach, & Isack, 1985; Swan, 1993). These disfluencies may simply reflect a heightened emotional state or the child's hurried speech.

Disfluencies that may indicate the onset of stuttering include multiple part word repetitions (*g . . . g . . . g . . . g . . . go*) and sound prolongations of more than one second (*hhhhhhhat*) (Swan, 1993). Stuttering may be accompanied by facial grimaces or gestures, reflecting the speaker's emotional tenseness, and by a rise in pitch and loudness. Some children may withdraw from verbally participating in the conversation or discussion. Approximately 70 percent of the children who develop stuttering recover; the remaining children may need specific speech therapy (Swan, 1993).

When a child's speech disfluencies are frequent and have the characteristics of stuttering, it is important for the teacher to consult with a speech-language pathologist to determine further appropriate intervention or remediation. In addition to receiving speech therapy, a child who stutters can benefit from specific techniques implemented by the classroom teacher.

Techniques for Enhancing Language Development

In the preschool or kindergarten classroom, the teacher should avoid paying any direct attention to children's speech disfluencies or stuttering (Stuttering Foundation of America, 1993). Instead, interact with the child in a patient, calm, and relaxed manner, focusing on the meaning of the communication. It is beneficial if the language and communicative environment of the classroom is characterized by slow, relaxed speech with frequent pauses to keep the pace of verbal interaction unhurried. Children who are upset about their disfluencies need reassurance that they are accepted and respected by the teacher and by others in the class. Teachers need to discourage children from interrupting others and from trying to finish an utterance for someone who is having difficulty talking (Gottwald, Goldbach, & Isack, 1985). Teachers should also avoid telling the child to slow down, to start over, to think, or to take a deep breath since these requests indicate to the child that his speech is unacceptable and may increase his anxiety and disfluencies (Gottwald, Goldbach, & Isack, 1985). When talking with a child who is having fluency problems, the teacher should maintain eye contact with the child and a pleasant facial expression so the child does not feel he is being rejected or avoided.

Primary children's stuttering and other disfluencies may interfere more with their classroom performance because learning activities may require more group participation and more focused oral responses and oral reading. The Stuttering Foundation of America (1993) offers several guidelines for elementary teachers who are interacting with children who stutter or have frequent disfluencies.

1. Ask the child questions she can answer with only a few words.
2. Call on the child early in a discussion since tension and anxiety may increase as the child anticipates her turn.
3. Communicate to all students that they do not have to answer the question(s) in a hurry, and that you want them to take their time and think about their answers.
4. Encourage children (not just the stutterers) to practice reading in pairs, taking turns or in unison.
5. Encourage children to practice reading their stories at home before they are expected to read individually in the classroom.
6. Encourage children to practice reading along with a taped version of the story at home or in the library corner of the classroom before they are expected to read individually in the classroom.
7. Monitor the social interactions in your classroom so that peers do not tease or embarrass a child who stutters.

SUMMARY

Early childhood teachers have an important role in enhancing language acquisition among children who may have special communication needs. Children who are hearing impaired, language delayed, or cognitively impaired, or who have articulation difficulties or speech disfluences need to have classroom environments in which they can feel comfortable and are encouraged to communicate in a relaxed manner. Early childhood teachers who notice children with communication difficulties should first observe the child's behavior in a variety of classroom interactions to determine the nature and extent of the difficulty. Referral to a specialist (a pediatrician or speech-language pathologist) should be made only after the teacher has documented the difficulties over a period of time and only after the teacher has talked over her concerns with the child's parents.

✳ ✳ ✳ CHAPTER REVIEW

1. Distinguish between *communicative disorders* and *communicative differences.*
2. What are the known causes of hearing impairment?
3. List behaviors that might indicate a hearing impairment.
4. Describe three ways a teacher might enhance the language acquisition of a child with a hearing impairment.
5. Identify several characteristics of children with language delay.
6. Describe the ways in which storybook sharing can encourage conversations with children with language delay. Why is this important?
7. Define *articulation disorders.*
8. State three guidelines for teachers to follow when interacting with children who have articulation difficulties.
9. List the characteristics of stuttering.
10. State three guidelines for interacting with primary age children who stutter.
11. Describe the team approach to helping children with communicative disorders.

✳ ✳ ✳ CHAPTER EXTENSION ACTIVITIES

1. Observe in a preschool or kindergarten classroom for a half day. Document several examples of children's oral disfluencies. Also describe the communicative context of the speech (e.g., during discussion time, during independent/exploratory time).

2. Talk with a speech-language pathologist. Discuss the types of speech difficulties present in the school or school district (however, do not inquire about specific children, or identify children by name). Ask the speech-language pathologist to describe the techniques she recommends to teachers when interacting with children having specific speech difficulties.

3. Read a professional journal article about a specific type of speech difficulty. Summarize the article and then describe how the article relates to the information presented in this chapter.

✳ ✳ ✳ REFERENCES

Boshart, C. (1999). *Treatise on the tongue: Analysis and treatment of tongue abnormalities* (Available online: www.speechdynamics.com). Speech Dynamics Incorporated.

Cohen, L., & Spenciner, L. (1994). *Assessment of young children.* White Plains, NY: Longman.

Cook, R., Tessier, A., & Armbruster, V. (1987). *Adapting early childhood curricula for children with special needs* (2nd ed.). Columbus, OH: Merrill.

Culatta, R., & Leeper, L. (1987). Disfluency in childhood: It's not always stuttering. *Journal of Childhood Communication Disorders, 10*(2), 95–106.

Dumtschin, J. (1988, March). Recognize language development and delay in early childhood. *Young Children,* 16–24.

Gottwald, S., Goldbach, P., & Isack, A. (1985). Stuttering: Prevention and detection. *Young Children, 41*(1), 9–16.

Harris, J. (1990). *Early language development: Implications for clinical and educational practice.* New York: Routledge.

McNeill, J., & Fowler, S. (1996, Summer). Using story reading to encourage children's conversations. *Teaching Exceptional Children,* 43–47.

Moller, K., Starr, C., & Johnson, S. (1990). *A parent's guide to cleft lip and palate.* Minneapolis, MN: University of Minnesota Press.

Owens, R. (1991). *Language disorders: A functional approach to assessment and intervention.* Merrill/Macmillan.

Owens, R. (2001). *Language development: An introduction* (5th ed.). Boston: Allyn & Bacon.

Patterson, K., & Wright, A. (1990). The speech, language or hearing-impaired child: At-risk academically. *Childhood Education, 67*(2), 91–95.

Piper, T. (1993). *Language for all our children.* Upper Saddle River, NJ: Prentice Hall.

Ratner, N. (1997). Atypical language development. In J. Berko Gleason (Ed.), *The development of language* (pp. 348–397). Needham Heights, MA: Allyn & Bacon.

Reich, P. (1986). *Language development.* Upper Saddle River, NJ: Prentice Hall.

Rice, M. (1989). Overview of language acquisition. *American Psychologist, 44*(2), 149–156.

Russell-Fox, J. (1999). Together is better: Specific tips on how to include children with various types of disabilities. In K. Paciorek & J. Munro (Eds.), *Annual editions in early childhood education* (20th ed., pp. 100–102). Sluice, Dock, Guilford, CN: Dushkin/McGraw-Hill.

Stuttering Foundation of America. (1993). *The child who stutters at school: Notes to the teacher.* [Brochure] Memphis, TN: Author.

Swan, A. (1993, Spring). Helping children who stutter: What teachers need to know. *Childhood Education,* 138–141.

14

Fostering Language Development Through School-Home Connections

Children's families play a critical role in their language development and literacy acquisition. For some children, the family unit is composed of their birth parents and siblings. Other children's family units may be composed of one parent and/or one or more extended family members. Other children may live in foster care or with their grandparents or adoptive families. It is important for early childhood teachers to establish connections with each child's family unit and parental figures so that the lines of communication and mutual respect are strong. The "teacher provides the bridge from school to home" (McCaleb, 1997, p. 191).

The ways in which teachers invite and engage parents in communicating with them and the school are critical to establishing positive connections. When teachers want to develop connections with children's homes, they must acknowledge and anticipate the diversity of the family units that may be involved rather than assuming that all children come from families that are nuclear and traditional in membership. For the purpose of this chapter, the term *parent* will refer to a primary caregiver of a child, with the understanding that this primary caregiver may be a birth parent, step-parent, foster parent, adoptive parent, or an aunt, uncle, or grandparent who has assumed the parental role for that child. The primary caregiver role may also be shared between two parents or other family unit adults.

GOALS FOR ESTABLISHING SCHOOL-HOME CONNECTIONS

Establishing positive school-home connections has the potential to significantly facilitate children's language development and other areas of development. Teachers should keep three general goals in mind when establishing home-school connections:

1. Increasing parents' awareness of their role in their child's language and literacy development
2. Increasing parents' awareness of the classroom's curriculum
3. Increasing the teacher's/school's awareness and understanding of the child's home/family environment.

Each of these goals contributes to the strength of home-school connections.

Increasing Parents' Awareness of Their Role

While most parents understand their role in supporting and caring for their children's physical and emotional development and well-being, they may not be fully aware of their potential role in their children's intellectual and linguistic development.

Research studies have found a strong relationship between the language and literacy activities engaged in at home and children's subsequent emergent literacy behaviors (Baghban, 1984; Bergin, Lancy, & Draper, 1994; Heath, 1983; Jordan, Snow, & Porche, 2000; Nord, Lennon, Liu, & Chandler, 1999; Taylor, 1983; Teale, 1986). There is evidence that parents should begin reading to their children in early infancy. Allison and Watson (1994) report that "the earlier a parent began reading to their child, the higher the child's emergent reading level was at the end of kindergarten" (p. 68). In their research, Allison and Watson noted that some parents began reading to their children at birth.

Teachers facilitate increasing parents' awareness by sharing with parents the importance of talking with their children, listening to them, reading to them, and reading with them. They should encourage parents to stimulate conceptual development through activities at home and in the community. Additional suggestions for supporting parent-child activities will be introduced in a later section of this chapter.

Increasing Parents' Awareness of Classroom Curriculum

According to Piper (1993), "Parents who understand what the teacher is doing and why are more likely to be supportive of what happens in the classroom" (p. 298). Teachers can enhance this awareness by communicating regularly with parents through informal conversations, open houses, and newsletters. Specific suggestions for these activities are included in a later section of this chapter.

Increasing Teacher's/School's Awareness and Understanding of Home Environment

Children benefit from being able to make smooth transitions each day between home and school. The key to strong school-home relations, according to Vandergrift and Green (1992), is to know the parents well and to have a wide variety of options for parental involvement. When there are distinct cultural and linguistic differences between the home and the school or when a family experiences specific stresses (e.g., poverty, unemployment, or divorce), children's ability to transition between home and school smoothly may be impaired. By becoming more familiar with the issues faced by children's families, teachers can more effectively address the needs of children in transitioning from home to school each day.

Children must see their school and teacher as valuing and respecting their home and family culture. Children's self-concepts are influenced by their perceptions that the larger society values and respects their home cultures. When there are significant differences in language and literacy between home and school, the school needs to concentrate more on bringing families into a closer relationship with the school (Diamond & Moore, 1995). Benefits of this closer relationship with parents include children's stronger sense of self-identity and worth (Allen & Marotz, 1999).

Teachers' understanding of children's home/family cultural environment may be reflected in their implicit judgments of parents' levels of competence as parents (Elicker, Noppe, Noppe, & Fortner-Wood, 1997). Teachers need to avoid making culturally or economically biased snap judgments of parental competence based on a lack of understanding of the child's cultural/social home environment. They need to keep the avenue of communication open and avoid quick judgments. Teachers need to be respectful of the values and traditions of the families in which their students live and "guard against cultural and class arrogance" (Salinger, 1996, p. 71). Teachers should also avoid assuming that homogeneity exists among families of similar cultural/linguistic backgrounds since variations among families are likely to exist (Piper, 1993).

When effective school-home communication is fostered, parents and teachers become partners in meeting the educational needs of children. In order to develop a partnership with parents, teachers must create effective ways of communicating with the family from the first day of attendance. School systems must develop ways to continually involve families in the life of the school in a wide variety of activities of varying participation.

ESTABLISHING A LEARNING COMMUNITY

One way for schools to involve families is to focus on developing a learning community. A learning community is fostered through the establishment of school-home connections that increase parents' awareness of their roles and of classroom curricula. Conversely, schools and teachers must be aware of children's home/family environments. This learning community is manifested in the early childhood classroom and in the nature of the relationships established with children's parents and homes. Learning communities are characterized by mutual respect, cooperation, collaboration, and frequent, effective communication.

Mutual Respect

One aspect of a learning community is mutual respect. Parents need to be assured that teachers and child caregivers are knowledgeable and compassionate. Teachers need to see parents as competent as well and need to understand their cultural perspectives. When there is frequent communication with parents in a respectful manner and when communication serves to inform parents of activities in their children's classrooms, parents are more likely to see their children's teachers as competent and welcoming. In learning community classrooms, children are treated with respect and are encouraged to treat each other with respect.

Two important aspects of showing mutual respect involve observing confidentiality regarding family information and active listening. Confidentiality should be observed with respect to personal information about family relationships and other family matters (Cataldo, 1983). Such information should not be communicated to other staff or to other parents unless there are justifiable professional reasons for sharing the information.

Actively listening to parents involves listening closely to what they are saying and observing their nonverbal cues for additional meaning. According to Wilson, Douville-Watson, and Watson (1995), "Active listening involves objectively listening, in a non-defensive way, for the deeper message [of the parent]" and responding by giving feedback to the parent that clarifies the parent's message rather than judging or criticizing what the parent just communicated (p. 46). Through a teacher's active listening, parents feel their opinions, ideas, and values are respected.

Cooperation and Collaboration

Learning community classrooms emphasize learning activities that occur in small groups (McCaleb, 1997). In these groups, students learn how to share, how to focus on common goals, and how to contribute to the learning task. This type of activity is not developmentally appropriate (or manageable) in infant-toddler classrooms or to a certain extent even in preschool classrooms. However, early childhood teachers who view cooperation and collaboration as a long-term goal for students' development can begin to encourage cooperation and collaboration through encouraging young children to share and to show empathy and concern for each other.

When a partnership is created between the school/teacher and parents, one result is often a mutual sharing of educational goals for the children. Teachers become aware of specific learning goals parents might have for their children and vice versa. This partnership between school and home does not develop overnight or even after a few months. It is the result of long-term efforts in establishing and maintaining communication between school and home. The school-home relationships established when children are first enrolled in day care, preschool, or kindergarten programs may set the tone and expectations of the parents involved for years to come. Parents who feel welcomed into their children's first schools, and who experience positive communicative relationships with their children's first teachers, are more likely to continue to be more involved in their children's education than are parents who do not experience positive school-home connections.

Frequent Communication

In a learning community, frequent and effective communication takes place. In the classroom, this means that the teacher and the students engage in frequent informal conversations and the more structured dialogue found in the planned learning activities. The learning community that encompasses school-home connections also has regular, frequent communication with parents. It is important that the communication be both ways, not just teacher to parent, but reciprocal (teacher to parent and parent to teacher). Parent-to-parent communication is also encouraged since the learning community approach recognizes the roles and worth of all members in the learning community.

FACTORS INFLUENCING FAMILY/PARENTAL INVOLVEMENT

In addition to being aware of the characteristics of effective school-home relationships, teachers need to understand specific factors that may influence whether or not a family or parent decides to become involved in school-home connections.

Parents' Own Experiences in School

Parents' memories of their experiences in school often have an impact on their level of comfort in attending school events and teacher conferences and in participating in their child's classroom. If their past experiences as a student were positive, they are more likely to feel comfortable at their children's school and in monitoring their child's schoolwork at home. Parents who did not experience success when they were in school may avoid contact with their child's teacher and school administrators since they associate school with negative feelings of failure, inadequacy, or low self-esteem. They may feel unable to help their children with their homework. When required to come to school for a conference, these parents may be defensive and uncommunicative. Particularly if the parents lack literacy or language competencies, it may be difficult for them to facilitate their children's acquisition of the necessary language and literacy competencies. In these instances, the classroom teacher needs to focus on welcoming these parents so that they feel comfortable in the school.

It may be necessary to provide for someone to act as a translator for the parent conference; however, the translator should not be an older child in the family or an older student since that places both parents and student-translator in a difficult situation. The teacher needs to help parents understand in what ways they can help their children at home, even if they are limited in their own language and literacy competencies.

While parents who have been successful in school usually have a positive orientation to school-home connections, they may also have unrealistically high expectations for their children's achievement, placing pressure on their children to perform, be "above average," and even become "gifted." In these instances, the classroom teacher needs to share with parents developmentally appropriate expectations and emphasize the importance of facilitating children's enthusiasm for learning and their curiosity rather than simply their performance of rote information or attainment of high achievement.

Cultural Diversity

As cultural diversity increases in classrooms, teachers become more aware of the different cultural orientations that influence parents' involvement in their children's education and interactions with teachers. In some cultures the school and its teachers are highly regarded as the experts; this orientation may discourage parents from "interfering" with teachers since education is the sole responsibility of the school. Parents with this orientation may also feel that all learning, or "school work, " should be done at school under the supervision of the teacher. In these situations, teachers need to work more closely with parents so they understand the school curriculum and their role in enhancing their child's learning at home. Teachers should clearly establish the learning community partnership with parents in this regard rather than sending parents the message that they must be "instructed" by the school and teacher as to what they need to do as parents.

Participation by parents of different cultures in school-home relationships is also influenced by the parents' perception of the school's and teacher's attitude toward their home language or dialect. Specifically, is the home language or dialect viewed as a "deficit" or as an "asset"? Will the school and their children's teachers pressure their children to assimilate mainstream American (i.e., white, middle class) culture (Piper, 1993)? Parents' participation is also influenced by their perception of how the school and teacher respond to instances of racism that may occur in the form of name calling, bullying, or social rejection.

Parents' Work Obligations

The work schedule of parents and family obligations may make it impossible for parents to be available for daytime classroom visits and conferences. Thus, teachers should not assume that the parents' absence at a conference or classroom visit means that the parents are not interested in the educational progress of their children. It may mean that they are just unable to leave work at the scheduled time or have responsibilities for caring for other family members. The classroom teacher should provide parents with alternative times or ways to conference about their children's progress or to visit the classroom.

Parents' Perceptions of Available Opportunities for Involvement

Parents' decisions to be involved in their children's school are also related to their own perception of the available opportunities to become involved (Hoover-Dempsey & Sandler, 1997). If the only opportunities for involvement conflict with their work schedule or if the opportunities require a substantial time commitment, parents may decide that such involvement is not possible. Parents' perceptions of their own capabilities and talents are also a factor. For example, if their child's teacher is asking for parents to come to class to read stories to the whole class, some parents may not see themselves as having the literacy and speaking skills needed to feel comfortable in this role. For these reasons, teachers must offer a wide range of opportunities for parents to participate in school-home connections.

OPPORTUNITIES FOR PARTICIPATION AND INVOLVEMENT

All opportunities for participation and involvement contribute toward strong school-home connections. The wider the range of opportunities, the more likely a greater number of parents will be able to fit some school involvement into their busy schedules.

Types of Interaction in School-Home Connections

School-home connections involve three types of interactions. The first type involves parents socially participating at the school through informal conversations with teachers, visiting the classroom, and/or attending school events. The second type of interaction occurs when parents engage in at-home learning activities that support the school curriculum. The third type of interaction occurs when parents participate in classroom activities, assisting the teacher in conducting specific learning experiences.

These types of interaction represent a continuum of involving parents from minimal involvement in social events, to at-home activities supporting the curriculum and their child's learning, to direct and active involvement in classroom learning activities. While this is a continuum, teachers should avoid expecting or assuming that involvement of parents in the classroom learning activities is the ultimate goal of establishing school-home connections. Instead, the main goal of establishing positive school-home connections is the enhanced learning and development of children. Furthermore, longitudinal research suggests that individualized connections—one-on-one relationships between the teacher and parent—may be more beneficial than focusing only on establishing parent involvement in group activities of parents (Seitz & Apfel, 1994; Seitz, Rosenbaum, & Apfel, 1985; cited in Powell, 1998).

ENCOURAGING PARENTS TO COME TO SCHOOL

When parents are encouraged to visit the school/classroom, they become more familiar with their children's teachers and the classroom curriculum.

Informal Conversations and Social Events

The initial step in creating a partnership with parents is to encourage parents to come to the school and to attend school events. At early childhood centers and most kindergarten classrooms, teachers and parents are in daily contact as parents bring their children into the school and pick them up at the end of the day. In these daily contacts, teachers can communicate in an informal way with parents, sharing information with parents about their children, the curriculum, or other important news.

Teachers' greetings to parents should be enthusiastic and friendly, but brief, since it is usually a busy time when the teacher must greet many arrivals. If it is necessary to discuss problematic behavior or personal issues, a private conference should be arranged. These brief conversations with parents are a good time to mention classroom projects or other events. When time permits, a teacher can also mention the purpose of such activities so that the parents are aware of the educational value or focus in the activities and can continue the focus at home. For example, "Today, we're taking the children on a walk to the park. We're going to be talking about color words." Parents might then talk with their children at home (or on the way home) about different colors.

Parent-teacher rapport is also enhanced when teachers can provide the opportunity for parents to visit the classroom for a longer time. This may take the form of a Parent's Day/Night where parents participate in learning activities with their children. Such participation is critical to parents' understanding of the process of learning and their child's active involvement in classroom learning activities. During these classroom visits, there are no "conferences" regarding student performance or development since the purpose of the classroom visit is simply to become more familiar with the curriculum of the classroom, the children's daily activities, and their child's teachers. Some early childhood classrooms call these events, "Bring your Mom/Dad/Aunt/Uncle/Grandparent to School," with the children serving as "tour guides" for their guests.

Other school events, such as student performances in music or drama, are ways in which parents can be encouraged to come to school and be part of the school community. To encourage parent attendance, it is important that these events be held when parents are not working and that all members of the family and extended family are welcome.

When teachers greet parents from families in which English is not the primary language, they must keep in mind that face-to-face communication may be the most difficult form of communication for these parents. Face-to-face communication requires that a response be formulated quickly. This requires a high level of language fluency (Tabors, 1997). Thus, teachers should carefully word their questions and comments to parents to facilitate comprehension and encourage conversation. Teachers who take the time to learn the social greetings of another language such as "Hello. How are you?" and "I'm glad to see you" enhance their rapport with parents. Parents who speak a different language see the teacher's willingness to learn some of their language as an indication that their language and culture are accepted and valued.

Open House

The purpose of a school's open house is for all classrooms to share with parents the activities and content of the curriculum. Some open houses involve only classroom displays; others include a short, formal presentation by the classroom teacher on the rationale or purpose of various aspects of the curriculum. Teachers should focus on explaining the process of learning as well as the products that come from the processes. At this time teachers can also emphasize the role that language contributes to lifelong learning and the role of oral language in the development of literacy competencies. Open houses are not a time to focus on the specific difficulties of individual children. The focus of teacher-parent conversations should be on the positive aspects of children's participation in the classroom. Any children's work that is displayed should not have grades or evaluative comments or marks. Many teachers have found that parents enjoy having a guest book to sign, or to be given the opportunity to leave a note for their child in the child's cubby or desk. Children are delighted to find a note from their parents the following day.

Some schools encourage children to attend the open house with their parents and serve as guides to their parents, explaining the displayed school work and activity centers. To facilitate this experience, open houses may be scheduled to give each family time and space to see all aspects of the learning environment.

Conferences

Several times a year, teachers set up specific times to meet with parents to discuss their children's progress. If parents do not understand English sufficiently, a translator must be present. If possible, the translator should be another educator and not an older student or older sibling in the family since confidentiality is an issue in conducting individual conferences (Swiniarski, Breitborde, & Murphy, 1999). During this time teachers share with parents descriptions of students' performance or examples of their work, explaining how they have evaluated or assessed what was done. The focus is on children's strengths and achievements, along with mentioning areas in which growth and development are needed. Parents should be asked for their interpretations of what teachers shared with them and how it corresponds with their children's behavior and performance at home. Teachers then need to describe to parents what they can do at home to enhance their children's learning, keeping in mind that parents may have time constraints or may be limited in their own literacy and language skills. Teachers should not overwhelm parents with extensive lists of what "should be" done at home, but instead focus on a few possible activities that parents and their children can engage in, such as those listed later in this chapter in the section on: "At-Home Learning Activities" and in Figure 14.1. If a parent requests additional information, the

FIGURE 14.1
Tips for Parents in Supporting Children's Learning at Home

1. Arrange for your child to visit the public library regularly.
2. Share age-appropriate books with your child for 10 to 15 minutes a day.
3. Take time to visit with your child about the day's events.
4. Encourage interactive viewing of television and computer use as a starting point for language-related activities.
5. Provide opportunities to engage in creative activities at home with art/manipulative media, cooking, drama, and music, for example.
6. Provide opportunities to participate in community outings and social gatherings.

teacher should conscientiously follow up the conference by contacting the parent with the requested information.

When a teacher is concerned about the learning difficulties a child may have, an important first step is to document those situations through the use of anecdotal records and work samples, or other informal, performance-based measures (refer to Chapter 12 on Assessment). Before approaching parents with a request for further testing or referral, the teacher should also ask other teachers in similar classrooms or support professionals to unobtrusively observe the child's learning interactions in the classroom. The classroom teacher should also consider possible curricular or program modifications to determine if that alone might address the learning difficulty.

If it is necessary to make a referral for further testing or evaluation, teachers need to avoid alarming parents needlessly. When the teacher recommends a referral, the emphasis should be on the need for more information that can be obtained through additional evaluation/testing. It is also important to share the belief that further evaluation will help the school and teacher better meet the child's needs. Since parental permission is needed for the referral, parents should feel comfortable with the referral and the potential benefits for their child. Avoid prematurely labeling any child's difficulty since that may unnecessarily alarm parents. The purpose of the referral is to more thoroughly evaluate the child's development. Abbott & Gold (1991) describe specific steps teachers should take in setting up, planning, and conducting a prereferral conference:

1. Contact the parents in person to set up a meeting, keeping in mind their availability. Tell the parents that you need to talk with them about their child, but do not indicate their child is "failing."

2. Plan the meeting, choosing a private setting that has comfortable, informal seating. Be sure sufficient time is allowed. Assemble the documentation related to the child's learning achievements and challenges. This documentation may include work samples and/or anecdotal records. List the modifications you have made in your

program and curriculum in an attempt to better meet the child's needs and the outcome of those modifications. List the other professionals with whom you have consulted regarding this situation. Prepare a listing of appropriate referral agencies or the school's referral professionals.

3. Conduct the meeting. Begin by welcoming the parents and telling them that you appreciate their coming. Have all materials ready. Describe the child's overall progress, specifically mentioning areas in which the child is meeting expectations. Encourage parents to share their observations of their child's learning at home. Begin to address the specific learning behavior that is of concern at school. Share the documentation you have regarding the situation and any concerns you have about the child's progress. Ask parents if they have noticed any similar behaviors at home. Be an active listener, allowing parents to express their concerns and feelings. Emphasize the need to find out more information so that the child will have the best possible learning environment. Communicate to parents what legal rights they have with respect to future testing and referral. Throughout the meeting, it is important for the teacher to focus on the shared concern with the parents for the best education for their child.

Newsletters

The purpose of sending home a biweekly or bimonthly newsletter is to share with parents news from the classroom or school. A newsletter may contain information about school policies and upcoming events and an overview of curriculum and general child development (Bundy, 1991). Newsletters should be kept short, only one or two pages, and be reader-friendly. DeMelendez & Ostertag (1997) offer these four guidelines: (1) use simple, clear language, (2) avoid using figurative language when parents represent different linguistic or cultural backgrounds, (3) use attractive, colorful paper, and (4) organize the newsletter with clear headlines and sections. In linguistically diverse classrooms, newsletters should also be made available in other languages for homes where English is not read. The tone of the newsletter should be conversational rather than academic. Professional jargon should be avoided since many parents will not understand it. Form letters from commercially prepared curricula or books should also be avoided since such letters are impersonal and will not enhance school-home communication.

Newsletters should be shared with children in the classroom prior to sending the newsletter home (Salinger, 1996). This sharing offers several benefits. Children become aware of the basic information in the newsletter so they know why it is being sent home. It encourages the older children to read or "emergent read" the newsletter. Children are also more likely to encourage their parents to read the newsletter if they know what information it contains.

When newsletters focus on upcoming curriculum or related events, parents are encouraged to reinforce the curriculum through their family's visits to the local library, area museums, or other family activities, such as picking apples, traveling, and home projects.

Home Visits

Some early childhood programs have found home visits a beneficial way to establish school-home connections (Bundy, 1991; Wolfgang & Wolfgang, 1992). Others have experienced resistance from families who considered such visits an invasion of privacy (Maxim, 1993). Successful home visits focus on the opportunity for the teacher to introduce herself to the child and parent in the familiar surroundings of the family home. The visit should last only 15 to 20 minutes and, if possible, should be scheduled within the two-week period prior to the child's first attendance in the school/classroom. The visit should clearly focus on becoming socially acquainted with the child and parent. No personal questions should be asked of the parent about the family or the child. Instead, the teacher should share with the child and parent information about herself or her classroom and planned learning activities, such as "We're going to read stories about animals and then plan our trip to the zoo."

Telephone Calls

Teachers need to let parents know how to contact them at the school. Many school systems have phone-message systems that allow parents to leave messages for their teachers, indicating when is the best time to reach them. It is important for teachers, then, to return the parents' calls as promptly as possible.

When teachers contact parents who may not be fluent in English, they need to realize that phone conversations may be a difficult form of communication for the parent. This is because the entire communication takes place auditorily. It lacks the comprehension-enhancing nonverbal communication that takes place face-to-face, involving gestures, facial expression, body language, and other aspects of the conversational context. Telephone conversations also involve an instant response, which requires a higher level of language fluency. For this reason, teachers may find face-to-face conversations or written communication more effective with parents whose primary language is not English.

AT-HOME LEARNING ACTIVITIES

Parents' conversations with their children from birth on significantly impact children's acquisition of language, as do their literacy-related interactions with their children at home and in their community. While teachers may encourage parents to engage in specific at-home learning activities with their children, it is important that parents not be overwhelmed with a long list of "should do" activities. Much of the success of at-home activities depends upon the parent's appropriate selection and implementation of the activities. If a given activity is not developmentally appropriate for the child, it will not benefit the child and may even negatively impact future learning or development. A relaxed, playful atmosphere is critical for at-home activities. Teachers also need to recognize the importance of including extended family members in the opportunities for at-home activities (Au, 1993).

While many books have been written describing specific at-home learning activities that can potentially facilitate language acquisition and development (see the Appendix at the end of this chapter for a list of recommended books), the focus of this section will be on the general ways in which parents can be encouraged to facilitate language acquisition and development throughout the early childhood years. These general ways involve three basic communicative processes: conversations, modeling, and collaborative sharing. In each of these processes, parents are focusing on their children's individual "zone of proximal development," providing the supportive scaffolding needed for development (see earlier discussion in Chapter 2). Embedded in these processes are the patterns of interaction described in Chapter 2.

Conversations about books and shared reading enhance children's developing language competencies.

Conversations

Parents of young children, regardless of age, can facilitate their children's language development through the informal conversations that occur each day at the dinner table, while doing errands, or riding in the car or on a bus (Nardi, 1992-93). Through the patterns of interaction described in Chapter 1 (eye contact and shared reference, verbal mapping, questioning, linguistic scaffolding, mediation, and adult-to-child speech), children's language development is facilitated and encouraged.

Modeling

Parents show children how language is used every day as children accompany them on their errands and around their homes (Hannon, 1992). For example, children may see their parents using oral language to ask for information, to tell stories, to make appointments, or to find and purchase a particular product. Similarly, children see their parents using print in the environment as they engage in reading to locate information in the telephone book, place an order at a restaurant, worship in religious ceremonies, locate a particular store in a shopping mall, follow a recipe, or assemble a bookshelf. When parents use writing, they are showing their children the way to produce written messages. Children may see their parents paying a bill by writing a check, writing a message in a

When parents include their young children in literacy-related events, they are modeling ways of interacting with written language.

greeting card, filling out a job application, using a word processing program on a computer, or making a shopping list.

Collaborative Sharing

When parents and children collaborate in a particular activity, a supportive scaffold is often created that provides further facilitation of language development. For example, when parents share storybooks with their children, children can be encouraged to participate in the story reading at their own level, perhaps through echo reading or pretend reading. Sharing cooking tasks by following a recipe demonstrates the value of written language. Shared tasks also provide an opportunity for parent and child to engage in focused conversations on the task at hand, whether it be planting a garden, cleaning out a cupboard, washing the family car, or making the list for weekly grocery shopping. While the shared task needs to be developmentally appropriate for the child, the critical aspect is the sharing and joint focus of the conversation between parent and child.

Shared tasks, such as carving a pumpkin, provide rich opportunities for conversation and vocabulary development.

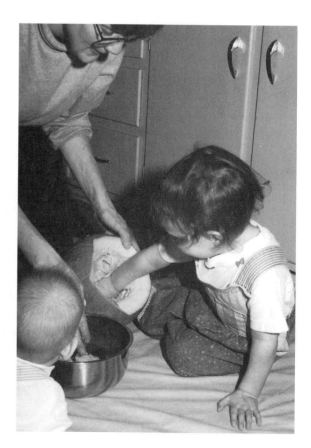

In two areas of family life, the collaborative sharing process may not always occur: watching television and using a computer. Both activities can be engaged in individually and inherently foster verbal passivity. Without parental monitoring, these activities can come to dominate home life. Some parents find that television is an easy way to occupy young children's attention. That is the danger. Television is not interactive. Similarly, in some homes, using the computer may be an individual activity. This is especially true in homes where parents have provided a computer for their child's room. However, parents can facilitate language development at home through encouraging a more interactive approach to television watching and computer use.

Parents can use the many informative and entertaining programs on television as the focus of extended conversations and related activities. A particular television program might be followed up with a trip to the library or a museum along with reading or writing activities. By monitoring what children are watching and even watching television with them, parents can use television as a starting point for a wide range of language facilitating activities.

Parents can encourage a more interactive approach to using a computer by purchasing software that encourages joint participation of two or more people and by locating the computer in the family/rec room or living room, where family members gather for shared activities. Similarly to the use of television, parents can facilitate language development by engaging their children in conversations based upon information obtained through the software or Internet sites. Related reading and writing activities can focus on a topic initially explored via the computer.

Not all parents can respond to teachers' encouragements to engage in at-home learning activities. Although computer use at home is increasing, many families do not have access to computers at home due to financial limitations or personal choice. Likewise, in some homes, few literacy-related materials are present. Allington & Cunningham (1996) remind teachers that "all parents cannot read to their children" (p. 5) and may struggle daily to physically care for their children in providing sufficient food, clothing, and housing. Allington & Cunningham also contend that the school curriculum needs to be developed and implemented in a way so that when parental education and resources are lacking, children will not be placed further at risk. Thus, while at-home learning activities can facilitate language development, teachers need to acknowledge the realities some parents face and take that into consideration when developing the classroom curriculum and establishing school-home connections.

IN-CLASS PARTICIPATION

Benefits from parents' in-class participation include the parents' learning about classroom activities and the teacher receiving some assistance in conducting activities. In some instances, the presence of their parents increases children's feelings of social confidence and comfort in the classroom (Tabors, 1997).

In some respects, in-class participation by parents is the highest level of parent involvement since it may involve a significant commitment in terms of time and talent. That said, teachers should avoid selectively paying more attention to parents who participate in the classroom than to those parents who are not able to become involved in classroom activities. Parents are quick to pick up on verbal and nonverbal cues that reflect a sense of respect, favoritism, or lack of respect from the teacher. With the increasing demands of work and other commitments, teachers may find few parents who are able to become involved in classroom activities. For those parents who can make the commitment to participate in their child's classroom learning activities, a wide variety of potential ways to become involved are available.

When encouraging parents to become involved, teachers need to share with parents the following types of information regarding their involvement: frequency of participation, opportunity for orientation and specialized training, special talents needed, and specific responsibilities. Some teachers have found it valuable to prepare brief descriptions of the specific volunteer assignments and to plan for volunteer orientations and training (Pryor, 1995).

Parents who make a commitment to participate in classroom activities on a regular basis, such as one or more times a week, might be invited to assist students in one of the classroom learning centers, work with individual students at the classroom computer, assist the librarian in helping students locate storybooks, or even read books to children as they visit the library area.

Parents who are limited to participating in the classroom activities on an occasional basis might be invited to assist with a holiday party, chaperon a class field trip, assist with class plays or puppet shows, give a book talk, demonstrate a particular craft or skill, or read stories to children on an individual or group basis.

CHARACTERISTICS OF SUCCESSFUL PARENT PROGRAMS

Parent involvement refers to the wide range of possible avenues for participation in the school classroom, from parents attending social events and informal parent-teacher conversations, to facilitating learning at home, to parents becoming involved in classroom learning activities. In contrast, *parent programs* involve more specific arrangements and detailed organization. In many instances specific parent programs have a strong "parental education" component and may even be mandated by the particular early childhood program such as federal, state, or grant-funded programs (e.g., Head Start, Child-Parent Centers, or EvenStart/at-risk early childhood programs). Enrollment of children in these programs may require a specific level of involvement from their parents.

Successful programs have several characteristics in common.

1. *A range of clearly communicated and organized opportunities
   encourages parent participation and involvement.* Early in the year,

parents are given information on the ways in which they can become involved in their child's classroom and the opportunities they will have to participate in social events and interactions with their child's teacher and school.

2. *All levels of parent participation and involvement are valued.* Parents are welcomed warmly and respectfully to the school whether it be to attend an open house, parent conference, or potluck supper.

3. *Teachers are sensitive to parents' needs and life situations.* Special events for parents and families are scheduled to accommodate as much as possible their individual time constraints and life situations. Translators are arranged for parents lacking fluency in English. Younger children are welcomed or babysitting services are provided to facilitate parental participation or attendance at scheduled parent meetings or conferences.

4. *Teachers foster an atmosphere of mutual respect* (Morrow & Young, 1995). Parents are treated with respect for their cultural background and individually as partners in the classroom's learning community.

5. *Parents are part of the planning and decision-making process* (Galen, 1991; Rasinski, 1995). When possible, parents are included in the planning and decision-making process regarding parent involvement activities through the involvement of the school's parent-teacher organization, local school council, or other parent-based group.

EXAMPLES OF SUCCESSFUL HOME-SCHOOL CONNECTIONS

One successful parent program that was implemented in an inner-city child-parent center involved inviting parents to visit their child's preschool classroom once a month for an hour-long group "read-in" (Otto & Johnson, 1996). Parents who came selected a book from the classroom library, sat down in a child-sized chair, and were quickly joined by one or more children ready for the book sharing. The classroom had a large collection of big books, which facilitated enjoyment of the parents' reading by a group of several children. The classroom teachers also participated in the read-in. This program incorporated a classroom lending library and recognition for children who took books home to share with their families. Parents took turns in the classroom, helping to check books in and out. Some of the parents decided that it would be good to have special book bags for children to use and made arrangements to make a book bag for each child. Most parents went on to personalize their child's book bag with additional decorations or their child's name. The classroom teachers noted an increased interest in taking books home to read and also observed children's excitement and pride when their parents came to participate in the read-in.

Another example of successful school-home connections involves a first-grade classroom. Manning, Manning, and Morrison (1995) describe a letter-writing activity that fostered school-home connections and facilitated children's writing competencies as well. Each child was given a three-ring notebook, called the "newsbook." The teacher then wrote and inserted a letter to parents describing how the notebook would be used throughout the year. Each week on Friday, the classroom teacher added a letter describing the week's learning activities, and each child wrote a letter or drew a picture focusing on what they remembered of the past week's activities. Parents were asked to engage their children in conversation about their letters and then write a short letter back to their children to take back to school on Monday. The parents' letters were then shared throughout the following week as the children met in small sharing sessions. While not all parents participated to the same extent, there was generally a high level of response, with members of children's extended families becoming involved (aunts, siblings, and grandmothers). Benefits from this program included parents' increased awareness of classroom curriculum, parents' awareness of children's development of written language and conceptual knowledge, and teachers' new insights about children's home environment and culture.

SUMMARY

The classroom teacher plays a critical role in establishing and maintaining positive school-home connections. While parent involvement and communication may be encouraged in many ways, each teacher needs to find out what works best for the families represented in his classroom. Throughout these efforts, it is important for the classroom teacher to focus on establishing mutual respect with parents and providing an opportunity for a wide range of activities that facilitate school-home communication. When this is done, everyone benefits—the children, their parents, their teachers, and the school.

✳ ✳ ✳ CHAPTER REVIEW

1. List three goals for establishing home-school connections.

2. What are the defining characteristics of a *learning community*?

3. List and describe four factors that influence family/parental involvement at school.

4. State five guidelines for teachers to follow when interacting with parents at school.

5. Describe four ways parents can encourage language acquisition at home.

6. List and explain the characteristics of successful parent programs.

1. Visit an early childhood classroom for one day. Prepare a draft of a newsletter to parents that would explain to them the day's learning activities.

2. Attend a parent-teacher organization meeting at an early childhood school or elementary school. Write a summary of the types of activities planned and carried out by that organization.

3. Visit the children's section of the local public library. Review the size and range of materials in the children's section on parenting. Write a summary of your findings.

4. Attend an open house in a early childhood center or elementary school. Describe the ways in which parents are able to learn more about the school's curriculum and learning environment.

❋ ❋ ❋ REFERENCES

Abbott, C., & Gold, S. (1991). Conferring with parents when you're concerned that their child needs special services. *Young Children, 46* (4), 10–14.

Allen, K., & Marotz, L. (1999). *Developmental profiles: Pre-birth through eight.* Albany, NY: Delmar Publishers.

Allington, R., & Cunningham, P. (1996). *Schools that work: Where all children read and write.* New York: Harper Collins.

Allison, D., & Watson, J. (1994). The significance of adult storybook reading styles on the development of young children's emergent reading. *Reading Research and Instruction, 34* (1), 57–72.

Au, K. (1993). *Literacy instruction in multicultural settings.* Fort Worth, TX: Harcourt Brace Jovanovich.

Baghban, M. (1984). *Our daughter learns to read and write: A case study from birth to three.* Newark, NJ: International Reading Association.

Bergin, C., Lancy, D., & Draper, K. (1994). Parents' interactions with beginning readers. In D. Lancy (Ed.), *Children's emergent literacy: From research to practice* (pp. 53–78). Westport, CN: Prager.

Bundy, B. F. (1991). Fostering communication between parents and preschools. *Young Children, 46* (2), 12–17.

Cataldo, C. (1983). *Infant & toddler programs: A guide to very early childhood education.* Reading, MA: Addison-Wesley.

DeMelendez, W., & Ostertag, V. (1997). *Teaching young children in multicultural classrooms: Issues, concepts, and strategies.* Albany, NY: Delmar.

Diamond, B., & Moore, M. (1995). *Multicultural literacy: Mirroring the reality of the classroom.* White Plains, NY: Longman Publishers USA.

Elicker, J., Noppe, I., Noppe, L., & Fortner-Wood, C. (1997). The parent-caregiver relationship scale: Rounding out the relationship system in infant child care. *Early Education and Development, 8,* 83–100.

Galen, H. (1991). Increasing parental involvement in elementary school: The nitty-gritty of one successful program. *Young Children, 46* (2), 18–22.

Hannon, P. (1992, August). *Intergeneration literacy intervention: Possibilities and problems.* Paper presented at Adult Literacy: An International Urban Perspective, United Nations headquarters, New York.

Heath, S. (1983). *Ways with words: Language, life, and work in communities and classrooms.* Cambridge, MA: Cambridge University Press.

Hoover-Dempsey, K., & Sandler, H. (1997). Why do parents become involved in their children's education? *Review of Educational Research, 67,* 3–42.

Jordan, G., Snow, C., & Porche, M. (2000). Project EASE: The effect of a family literacy project on kindergarten students' early literacy skills. *Reading Research Quarterly, 35* (4), 524–546.

Manning, M., Manning, G., & Morrison, G. (1995). Letter-writing connections: A teacher, first-graders, and their parents. *Young Children, 50* (6), 34–38.

Maxim, G. (1993). *The very young: Guiding children from infancy through the early years.* New York: Macmillan.

McCaleb, S. P. (1997). *Building communities of learners: A collaboration among teachers, students, families and community.* Mahwah, NJ: Lawrence Erlbaum Associates.

Morrow, L., & Young, J. (1995). *Parent, teacher, and child participation in a collaborative family literacy program: The effects on attitude, motivation, and literacy achievement. Reading Research Report,* No. 64. Washington, DC: Office of Educational Research and Improvement. ED398551.

Nardi, W. (1992–93). Nurturing our youngest learners: What American families can do at home to help their children succeed in school. *ETS Developments, 38* (2), 5–7.

Nord, C., Lennon, J., Liu, D., & Chandler, K. (1999). *Home literacy activities and signs of children's emergent literacy, 1993–1999.* U.S. Department of Education, Office of Educational Research and Improvement, NCES 2000–026.

Otto, B., & Johnson, L. (1996). Parents in your classroom: A valuable literacy link. *Teaching K–8,* 56–57.

Piper, R. (1993). *Language for all our children.* Upper Saddle River, NJ: Prentice Hall.

Piper, T. (1998). *Language and learning: The home and school years.* Upper Saddle River, NJ: Merrill/Prentice Hall.

Powell, D. (1998). Reweaving parents into the fabric of early childhood programs. *Young Children, 53* (5), 60–67.

Pryor, E. (1995). Parent volunteers: Partners in literacy. In T. Rasinski (Ed.), *Parents and teachers: Helping children learn to read and write* (pp. 179–184). Fort Worth, TX: Harcourt Brace & Company.

Rasinski, T. (Ed.). (1995). *Parents and teachers: Helping children learn to read and write.* Fort Worth, TX: Harcourt Brace & Company.

Salinger, T. (1996). *Literacy for young children.* Upper Saddle River, NJ: Merrill.

Seitz, V., & Apfel, H. (1994). Parent-focused intervention: Diffusion effects on siblings. *Child Development, 65,* 666–676.

Seitz, V., Rosenbaum, L., & Apfel, H. (1985). Effects of family support intervention: A ten-year follow-up. *Child Development, 56,* 376–391.

Snow, C. (1998, August-September). Catherine Snow on helping your child develop language. *Scholastic Parent & Child.*

Swiniarski, L., Breitborde, M., & Murphy, J. (1999). *Educating the global village: Including the young child in the world.* Upper Saddle River, NJ: Merrill/Prentice Hall.

Tabors, P. (1997). *One child, two languages: A guide for preschool educators of children learning English as a second language.* Baltimore, MD: Paul H. Brookes.

Taylor, D. (1983). *Family literacy: Young children learning to read and write.* Portsmouth, NH: Heinemann.

Teale, W. (1986). Home background and literacy development. In W. Teale & E. Sulzby (Eds.), *Emergent literacy: Writing and reading* (pp. 173–206). Norwood, NJ: Ablex.

Vandergrift, J., & Green, A. (1992). Rethinking parent involvement. *Educational Leadership, 50*(1), 57–59.

Wilson, L., Douville-Watson, L., & Watson, M. (1995). *Infants & toddlers: Curriculum and teaching.* Albany, NY: Delmar.

Wolfgang, C., & Wolfgang, M. (1992) *School for young children: Developmentally appropriate practices.* Needham Heights, MA: Allyn & Bacon.

APPENDIX

✣ ✣ ✣

RECOMMENDED REFERENCES FOR AT-HOME LANGUAGE/LITERACY ACTIVITIES

Clay, M. (1982). *Reading begins at home: Preparing children for reading before they go to school.* Portsmouth, NH: Heinemann.

Clay, M. (1987). *Writing begins at home: Preparing children for writing before they go to school.* Portsmouth, NH: Heinemann.

Cullinan, B. (1992). *Read to me: Raising kids who love to read.* New York: Scholastic.

Honig, A. (1982). *Playtime learning games for young children.* Syracuse, NY: Syracuse University.

Lawrence, L. (1998). *Montessori read and write: A parent's guide to literacy for children.* New York: Three Rivers Press.

Maxim, G. (1990). *The sourcebook: Activities for infants and young children* (2nd ed.). Upper Saddle River, NJ: Merrill/Prentice Hall.

Miller, S. (1991). *Learning through play: Language—A practical guide for teaching young children.* New York: Scholastic.

Rasinski, T. (Ed.). (1995). *Parents and teachers: Helping children learn to read and write.* Fort Worth, TX: Harcourt Brace & Company.

GLOSSARY

academic register   the variation of Standard American English that is used in educational and corporate settings; also known as *literate register* or *literate discourse*

activity boxes   small boxes containing high-interest manipulative items used by a caregiver to enhance vocabulary and expressive language among toddlers

adult-to-child speech   specific ways in which language is altered when communicating with young children; also known as *baby talk, motherese,* or *child-directed speech*

African American English (AAE)   a dialect used by a significant number of people of African-American descent.

anaphora   the link between a pronoun or article and its referent that was used in a prior part of a sentence or paragraph

babbling   production of consonant-vowel sounds of varying intonation, usually involves reduplicated sounds, such as ba-ba-ba-ba, developing when a child is between 4 to 6 months old

bilingualism   the ability to use two languages when communicating orally or in writing

blend   when two or more phonemes (represented by consonant letters at the beginning of a word) are blended so that elements of each separate phoneme are still heard, such as in *cl*ear, *br*ing, *sk*ate, and *gr*eat

bound morphemes   morphemes that must be attached to a free morpheme (e.g., house*s*, slow*ly*)

clarifying questions   questions used to explain or elucidate something previously said

code switching   instances where a person appears to be mixing two languages when communicating

communication loop   a circular or cycle-like exchanging of the roles of speaker and listener

conflict resolution   the use of language dialogue to resolve disagreements

connotative meaning   the meaning of a word reflecting a value judgment, attitude, or emotion

conversational skills   specific ways communication is enhanced between two or more people; for example, turn-taking, shared reference, establishing and maintaining eye contact, giving feedback

cooing   extended vowel sounds, such as *ooo, ahh, eee, aaa,* often made in relative isolation of each other, usually beginning when an infant is 6 to 8 weeks old

creole   a pidgin language that has been learned by a second generation of speakers

derivational morphemes   bound morphemes that may change the way a word is used in a utterance/sentence (e.g., happy-happi*ness;* construct-construc*tion*)

developmental level   a child's independent competencies

diacritic markings   marks added to written letters to aid in pronunciation

dialects   variations of a language that are characteristic of a particular social or geographical group (i.e., Southern dialect, adolescent dialect, Bronx dialect)

digraph   two consonant letters used together to encode a single phoneme not associated with either letter (e.g., *ch*icken, *ph*onics, *sh*are)

discovery centers   learning centers that encourage open-ended exploration of manipulatives, artifacts, or other concept-rich materials

distancing   the gradual process in which a concept label becomes comprehended without the actual referent being present

echolalic babbling   a type of babbling that appears to echo the rhythm and phonation of adult speech in a child's environment, developing when an infant is around 8 to 10 months old; also referred to as *jargon* or *intonated babble*

emergent literacy   the gradual acquisition of knowledge about reading and writing through informal interactions with written language

eustachian tubes   tubes that connect the middle ear and upper throat area, which allows equalization of pressure on both sides of the eardrum

expansion   an interaction pattern used by an adult to "fill out" what a child says; modeling of more complex syntax, morphology, semantics, and correct pronunciation

expressive language   the language that a person is able to produce, as in speaking or writing

fast mapping   when a child learns the label for a concept or entity quickly with only a few exposures and without specific reinforcement

formative assessment   periodic assessment that tracks children's growth and development on an ongoing basis throughout the year

free morphemes   morphemes that are used alone as a word

gerund   verbal noun formed from adding *-ing* to a verb (e.g. *walk* becomes *walking)*

grammar   a rule-governed system of sequencing linguistic units into oral speech and written sentences

hypothesis testing   the process of learning language in which children try out different ways of manipulating language

idiomorphs   see *protowords*

inflectional morphemes   bound morphemes that changes a word to correspond to syntactic rules (e.g., cat-cat*s*; Mary-Mary*'s* hat; walk walk*ed)*

informational questioning   questions used to elicit information that the questioner does not know

International Phonetic Alphabet   a specific written symbol system, composed of Roman letters, letter-like symbols, and diacritic markings, used to encode oral speech

intonated babble   babbling that is expressed with marked variations in intonation; also termed echolalic babbling or jargon

intonation   the variations of pitch and accent used when speaking

invented spelling   individualized ways of spelling that reflect a child's knowledge of phonemes and letter-sound relationships

jargon   see echolalic babbling and intonated babble

language   system of oral or written symbols used for communication

language acquisition   unconscious learning of language in natural settings with a focus on meaning

language acquisition device (LAD)   an inborn mechanism described by Chomsky as aiding language development

language acquisition support system   ways in which an environment supports children's language explorations

language competencies   specific skills in using language to achieve success in communication

language learning   conscious rule learning in formal instructional settings with an emphasis on the form of language

linguistic level   unconscious knowledge of how language is used

linguistic scaffolding   language used to support a child's attempts to communicate; may involve questioning, expansion, and/or repetition

mapping   using language to represent an entity, action, or event

mediation   an interaction pattern in which an adult focuses on simplifying the learning stimulus or task to facilitate the language interaction with, and comprehension by, a child

metalinguistic knowledge   conscious knowledge of how language can be manipulated

metalinguistic verbalization   the highest level of language knowledge that involves verbally reflecting upon one's language concepts

modes of language   the medium in which language is used, such as oral or written

monologues   extended speech to a listener without conversational turn-taking

morpheme   smallest unit of meaning in language

morphemic language knowledge   knowledge of word structure or how words are composed of one or more meaningful linguistic unit(s)

normed   an average score or level determined by sampling a large, representative population

object permanence   an awareness that an object continues to exist even when it is out of sight

onset   refers to the initial consonant or consonant cluster of a syllable, which precedes the first vowel of that syllable (e.g., the *c* in *cat;* the *sp* in *speed*)

oral language modes   comprehension of oral language through listening, production of oral language through speaking

otitis media   inflammation of the middle ear

overextensions   when a label or word is used inaccurately for referents that resemble the appropriate referent in some way; for example, labelling all vehicles trucks

overgeneralizations   instances where speaker assumes that a word follows a specific regular pattern or rule when it does not (e.g., go-*goed,* good-*goodest*)

phoneme   smallest linguistic unit of sound, which is combined with other phonemes to form words

phonetic knowledge   knowledge of sound-symbol relationships and sound patterns represented in a language

pidgin   language that developed in response to the interaction of two groups of people who did not initially share a language

pragmatic knowledge   knowledge of the different ways in which language is used in different settings and for different purposes

productive language   language a person is able to express, as in speaking or writing; synonymous with expressive language

prosodic features   way in which a language is spoken during communication involving intonation, loudness, tempo, and rhythm

protowords   early invented or individualized "words," also known as *idiomorphs*

recasting   see *expansion*

receptive language   the language a person is able to comprehend, as in listening or reading

recitational questioning   questions used to determine a child's knowledge or awareness of a concept or action

registers   different ways of speaking in different settings reflecting different social roles

reliability   an assessment measure's consistency in producing dependable or repeatable results

rime   refers to the vowel and any remaining consonants of a syllable (e.g., the *at* in the word *cat*)

schemata   abstract cognitive structures stored in human memory to represent events, concepts, or relationships (schema is the singular form)

selective reinforcement   when a child is encouraged to produce and repeat sounds that are appropriate and necessary for the language of people in his or her environment

semantic knowledge   the aspect of language knowledge that involves word meanings/vocabulary

shared reference   when two people (e.g., adult and child) attend to the same stimulus (event or object)

social registers   a specific way in which language is used in a particular social setting or context

Standard American English   a dialect of English used by the majority of Americans which is often modified by regional variations

strategic scaffolding   linguistic scaffolding that is used by an adult in a conscious way for encouraging a child's language development

successive bilingualism   when children acquire their second language after age 3

summative assessment   end-of-the-term or end-of-year assessment that determines the final outcome of learning and/or development; is often used for future educational placement

suprasegmental elements   the use of pitch and stress to separate a stream of speech in order to communicate a specific meaning

symbol formation   the process by which a specific oral or written symbol becomes associated with a referent through interaction between the addressor, addressee, referent, and symbolic medium

syntactic language knowledge   knowledge of how words can be combined in meaningful sentences, phrases, or utterances

syntax   the grammar of a language

telegraphic speech   child's use of two or three content words in an utterance with no functor words

underextension   when a label or word is inappropriately restricted or limited in referring to objects/events

universal grammar   the rule system that underlies all human languages

unreferenced pronouns   pronouns whose noun referent is not clearly indicated by the pronoun and sentence structure

validity   the notion that a test or assessment actually measures what it is intended to measure

verbal mapping   the interaction pattern in which an adult verbally describes the object or action in a level of detail appropriate to the developmental level of the child

vicarious experiences   experiences where the concept or action is experienced or communicated through visual representations or through verbal description alone without the actual referent being present

vocabulary counts   the volume of distinct words in a child's vocabulary

wait time   the amount of time between the end of a teacher's question and expected student responses; may also be referred to as think time

written language modes   the way written language is used expressively in writing and receptively in reading

zone of proximal development   the difference between what a child can accomplish alone and what she can accomplish with an adult's mediation or assistance

Index

Numbers in **bold** indicate figure entry